Early Childhood Language Arts

MARY RENCK JALONGO
Professor of Education
Indiana University of Pennsylvania

ALLYN AND BACON
Boston London Toronto Sydney Tokyo Singapore

Series Editor: Sean W. Wakely
Series Editorial Assistant: Carol L. Cherniak
Editorial-Production Service: Raeia Maes
Composition and Manufacturing Buyer: Louise Richardson
Cover Administrator: Linda Dickinson
Cover Designer: Suzanne Harbison
Signing Representative: Leslie Wardrop

Copyright © 1992 by Allyn and Bacon
A Division of Simon & Schuster, Inc.
160 Gould Street
Needham Heights, Massachusetts 02194

Library of Congress Cataloging-in-Publication Data

Jalongo, Mary Renck.
    Early childhood language arts / Mary Renck Jalongo.
      p.   cm.
    Includes bibliographical references (p.) and index.
    ISBN 0-205-13281-2
    1. Language Arts (Preschool)   I. Title.
LB1140.5.L3J35   1990
372.6—dc20   91-26361
                                                    CIP

Printed in the United States of America

10 9 8 7 6 5 4 3 2 1   96 95 94 93 92 91

F.A.R. and H.H.R.—Thank you for the listening and the lively conversation, the book reading and story writing, the love and encouragement.

F.S.J.—my in-house editor and support system

CONTENTS

PREFACE

Young children's language . . . what makes it so special, so distinctive from that of adults? Even with a limited vocabulary, children can communicate clearly—"No! *Me* do" or "I can't like it." Sometimes their words can express joy, like Kerri, who saw her hometown decorated with Christmas lights and bells and chanted "Kissy yights, Kissy yights, ing wong, ing wong." At other times, a child's words can be insightful:

> *Adult:* "How does daddy like the new house?"
>
> *Child:* "He yells at it sometimes."

The innocence of children's words can be striking as well, as in this conversation between Bobby and his grandmother at the shopping mall:

> *Grandmother:* "Honey, you don't want to stand in that long line, do you?"
>
> *Bobby:* "No, I just wanna see the Easter Bunny."

Sometimes, the candor of the very young can embarrass us, as, for example, when Julianna walked up to a dwarf and asked "How's your momma, Snow White?"

If examples like these intrigue you and remind you of other anecdotes about children's language, it is a fine beginning to a course on early childhood language arts. For unless you care enough about children to observe them carefully, to really listen to them, and to take pleasure in conversing with them, the study of young children's language will teach you something but it won't teach you enough. Learning the terminology, knowing the developmental milestones in language acquisition, or even understanding the recommended ways of fostering language growth are all necessary, but they are not sufficient. Professionals who choose to work with infants/toddlers, preschoolers, kindergartners, and first- or second-graders must do much more than follow a teacher's manual, must do much more than teach basic literacy skills. Early childhood educators need to go beyond knowledge and skills and display those attributes which reflect artistry in teaching: spontaneity, perceptivity, creativity, and decision-making (Rubin, 1985).[1]

For most human beings, early childhood is the most rapid period of language growth. This is why you will encounter three recurring themes in this book: the early childhood educator must be a keen observer of children, an expert in the developmental and curricular needs of the very young, and an advocate for children.

If you doubt that the responsibility of helping young children to become more effective communicators is an awesome one, just wait until a toddler is frantically trying to tell you something that you can't understand . . . or a preschooler scrawls on a page and asks, "What does this say? . . . or a first-grader asks on the first day of school, "When will I read?" As compelling as these reminders of our immediate responsibilities to young children may be, the long-term consequences of our actions are even more significant. Early childhood education in the language arts of listening, speaking, reading, and writing sets the tone for future language learning. Will the children in our classes become adults who can express ideas and emotions? Will they be good conversationalists and listeners? Will they succeed when they are given an on-the-job writing assignment? Will they read for pleasure and discuss favorite books with friends? These things are so highly valued in our society that it is very tempting to push children instead of guide them. In guiding young children's language development, we must never lose sight of their fundamental needs. What *is* basic where young children are concerned?

Over twenty-five years ago, Cornelia Goldsmith (1964)[2] identified the fundamental needs of young children. At the very least, children *need to feel secure and loved*, to be accepted and respected as individuals, and *need to be safe*, protected against physical, moral, and social hazards. Equally basic and relevant to early childhood language arts instruction are the following four needs:

1. The *need to be active in exploring and to move about freely*, using the senses in experimenting with a variety of objects and materials.
2. The *need to develop various means of communication*: language, art, music, science, and other media.
3. The *need to feel pride in their own achievements*, to gain independence, to develop self-confidence, to handle problems with increasing competence, and to deal with human relationships.
4. *The need to play*, to have adequate recreation, to pursue interests, and to enjoy spontaneous laughter, joy, and humor (Goldsmith, 1964).

Today there is a real battle in the field of early childhood education. There are those who believe that hurrying and pressuring children will make them tougher and smarter and there are those who believe that unless their fundamental needs are met, children will become insecure human beings and reluctant learners. My

---

[1]Rubin, L. (1985). *Artistry in teaching*. New York: Random House.
[2]Goldsmith, C. (1989). Statement on the child one to six in the world today. *Young Children, 44*(3), 52–53 (original publication date, 1964).

position on these issues is reflected in everything about this book. Fostering children's language learning should be a joyous process for children, parents, and teachers. I believe that children's growth in literacy blossoms in a supportive environment and withers in a harsh one. As you gain experience in facilitating young children's language learning, you too will learn to trust children, to let them lead the way on the path to communicative competence.

I extend thanks to the following reviewers whose contributions have enriched the text: Patricia Hanley, University of South Florida; Leslie Marlow, Northwestern State University of Louisiana; Margie McMahon, Cameron University; Louise Swinarski, Salem State College; and Joan Symonds, Diablo Valley College.

M.R.J.

TO THE STUDENT

As early childhood educators, we exert a tremendous positive influence on children's language growth when we:

- appreciate children as language learners and respect what children know
- function as enthusiastic role models in all of the language arts (reading, writing, speaking, and listening)
- understand language development theory and research
- master the professional vocabulary used to describe children's language behavior so that the child's language needs can be identified and communicated
- learn to observe children's speaking, listening, reading, and writing development
- converse with young children without "talking down" to them or "talking over their heads"
- recognize that children's literature is the foundation of literacy
- interact effectively with parents, the child's first teacher
- plan, teach, and evaluate a child-centered early childhood language arts curriculum
- self-assess personal and professional growth as an early childhood educator

All of these are emphasized in this textbook. Each chapter begins with "Key Concepts and Terms" to provide an overview of the content. Professional strategies that will enable you to become a more effective teacher are highlighted in the "Focus On" section of every chapter. The chapter concludes with "In the Field": assignments, observations, and interviews with young children, teachers, and parents.

Features of and Suggestions for Using this Textbook

1. Self Assessment Before beginning your reading, complete the pre-assessment that corresponds to the chapter (see Appendix A) to see how much you presently know about children's language development. Then, as you finish each chapter, return to Appendix A, "Chapter-by-Chapter Self Assessment," and chart your mastery of each chapter's content.

2. Ethical Issues   All of the examples used in this book were obtained with parental permission. Be certain to obtain parental approval before interviewing children or using any samples of their work. If you use a child's writing or drawing, make a copy (with his or her permission, of course) and give the original back to the child. Label each sample with child's sex and age (Example: Boy, 4 years, 7 months).

3. Reading Children's Dialogues   This book contains several different texts or scripts of children's conversations. In general, they can be read much like the script of a play in that

- the person speaking is identified at the left
- descriptions of children's nonverbal behavior or other events relating to that behavior are in parentheses
- the texts are verbatim records of what the children said
- if the text has been abbreviated to highlight a particular point or in the interest of conserving space, an ellipsis (. . .) is used

4. Describing Children's Behavior   When discussing children's work in your groups, do not label ("He seems sort of slow"), overgeneralize ("She couldn't sit still for one minute"), or judge ("This is a really good writing for a first-grader"). *Remember:* the focus is always on what the child knows stated in behavioral terms and supported by data, for example: "This is a sample of prealphabetic writing from a thirty-eight-month-old boy. There is evidence that he has learned something about the features of print because the marks he made are controlled rather than random. The child's writing is also placed on the paper in a linear fashion."

5. Using Professional Vocabulary   Practice using the terminology you are acquiring. In talking about a children's book, for instance, you should say *"The Post Office Book: Mail and How it Moves* is an information book by Gail Gibbons that follows a letter from the mail slot and all the way through the postal system. The illustrations are black line drawings. Three colors are used: red, white, and blue." Do not say "Isn't this a cute little book? I really like it."

6. Observational Skills   One of the best ways of learning how children develop is to observe them as you study developmental theory and research. When educators observe thoughtfully, objectively, and precisely, they gain insights from and about children. If you were asked to teach some people anything—how to register for college classes, how to ski, how to bake chocolate chip cookies—you would first need to determine what they already know about the task. It is the same with children learning language. We need *to focus on what the children already know.* In this way, the children function as informants about their own language development. Teacher observations are the key element in this process of learning about children's language. Appropriate observations of young children share the following characteristics:

- Good observations use direct observational data and rely on that data for interpretations. High inference, value-laden terminology is avoided.
- Good observations accurately record the observable behavior of the child.
- Good observations describe the context—the time, setting, circumstances, and behaviors of other children or adults related to the episode.
- Good observations of children's language development record children's nonverbal and verbal behavior precisely. All of the child's words are verbatim and are not altered in any way.
- Good observations are used by teachers to plan a developmentally appropriate language arts program.

Finally, keep in mind the words of John Ruskin (1835):

Education does not mean teaching people what they do not know. It means teaching them to behave as they do not behave. . . . It is done by kindness, by watching, by warning, by precept, and by praise, but above all—by example.

PART ONE

Language Acquisition, Literacy, and the Child-Centered Philosophy

PART ONE SETS THE stage for teaching language arts to young children. Chapter 1, "Language Acquisition," describes how children, ages infancy through eight, learn to talk, and presents major theories of language acquisition. Chapter 2, "Oral and Written Language," examines oral language and written language skills from a cross-cultural perspective. Chapter 3, "The Child-Centered Language Arts Classroom," provides a philosophical orientation to language arts instruction for young children. Together these three chapters form a theoretical and philosophical foundation for the remainder of the book.

Photo: Carol Sobczak

1

Language Acquisition

OUTLINE

Key Concepts and Terms
Introduction

I. The Communicative Process

II. Paralinguistics and Linguistics

III. A Developmental Sequence for Language
    A. Prelinguistic Speech
    B. Beginnings of Linguistic Development
    C. Telegraphic Speech
    D. Complex Sentences

IV. Language Acquisition Theories
    A. Behavioral Theory
    B. Maturational Theory
    C. Preformationist Theory
    D. Cognitive-Developmental Theory
    E. Psycho-sociolinguistic Theory

V. How Young Children Use the Components of Language
    A. Phonology
    B. Syntax
    C. Semantics
    D. Pragmatics

VI. Fostering Functional Communication in the Classroom
    A. Instrumental Language
    B. Regulatory

3

C. Interactional
D. Personal
E. Heuristic
F. Imaginative
G. Informational

Conclusion
Summary
Focus On: Guiding Group Discussions
In the Field: How Children's Language Affects Adults' Language

In or out of the classroom, language gives our thoughts substance; as we talk to ourselves, language helps us plan, understand what happens to us, and form our ideas. Language is part of the individual's uniquely human ways of knowing, feeling, and being. As we use language with others, it shapes our identities and social lives. The way our own language sounds to listeners leads them to make judgments about where we are from, what our occupation is, how friendly or clever we are.   —CECILIA GENISHI (1987)

KEY CONCEPTS AND TERMS

paralinguistics	communication
linguistics	pragmatics
language acquisition	language
prelinguistic speech	phonology
expressive jargon	stress
holophrases	juncture
telegraphic speech	syntax
Language Acquisition Device (LAD)	overregularization
assimilation	semantics
accommodation	functional

Lauren is meeting a couple who are her parents' friends for the first time. The three-year-old hides behind the curtains, then behind a visitor's chair. "She's a little shy at first," Lauren's parents explain, "and sometimes difficult to understand." The preschooler comes out from behind the chair and looks admiringly at the woman's necklace. Then Lauren says with perfect pronunciation and a tone of command in her voice: "I want to wear it."

The Communicative Process

Lauren's behavior illustrates the communicative process. It includes a *sender* (Lauren), a *message* ("I want to wear it"), a *medium* (spoken words), a *receiver* (the visitor), and a *context* (the living room). When people are communicating with one another, those who send messages also expect some response on the part of the receiver. A baby who cries expects someone to appear in the doorway, ready to comfort her. Children who are experimenting with a paper cup and string "telephone" expect the person on the other end of the line to listen and talk back. A child who sends a letter to her grandparents awaits a reply. Human communication is "a person sending a message to another individual with the conscious intent of evoking a response" (Johnson, 1972, p. 11).

Paralinguistics and Linguistics

Basically, there are two means of communication available to the young child: paralinguistics (nonverbal) and linguistics (verbal). **Paralinguistics** are those nonverbal means of communication that are related to language, such as facial expressions, gestures, body posture, and intonation (Menyuk, 1988). **Linguistics** refers to verbal (oral and written) language and its study.

Let's look at how Katie, a two-year-old, uses both nonverbal and verbal means of communication. She sees a battery-operated toy that has three plastic penguins who climb up a staircase, zoom down a sliding board, and then repeat the whole process all over again, complete with chirping noises. She points to the toy and says "Birdies! Birdies!" while beckoning toward the toy with her fingers. "See it?" she asks in a hopeful voice. When the toy is placed within reach, Katie asks, "Touch it?" The toddler deftly picks up each penguin, inspects it closely, and then puts it back in place. She is clearly delighted by this newfound ability to intervene in the penguins' rhythmic climbing and their roller-coaster descent. Finally, she pats her chest with her hands and asks, "Have it?"

Katie's behavior illustrates the strides that are made in children's language development in just two years. When she was a newborn baby, her only means of communication was crying. How did she manage to travel this far in her ability to communicate? How will she progress to the conversational ease of a five-year-old or the complex sentences of a second-grader?

A Developmental Sequence for Language

The process of learning to talk is referred to as **language acquisition**. Cultures differ somewhat in their criteria for deciding when to "officially" begin regarding a child as a speaker of the native language. The Kaluli in Papua, New Guinea, believe that a child has started to talk only after he or she can say the word for "milk" and "breast" (Schieffelin, 1979). In America, we tend to confer the status of a beginning speaker on a child who says "mama" and "dada." Thus, in American society, most children begin to use recognizable words at about the same time that they begin to take their first steps, around twelve months of age. Five young learners of language (see below) enrolled in a day-care center help to illustrate the stages through which young children progress.

Prelinguistic Speech

Angie is a five-month-old who makes sounds that are similar to syllables. She *babbles*, making consonant-vowel sounds like ma, ta, da, and *coos*, making vowel sounds like the "uuh." Kaoru, an eleven-month-old in her class, is stringing these sounds together in word-like ways. He uses the intonation and gestures of speech, but no actual words are discernible. Basically, Kaoru's vocalizations are English-*sounding*, but no real words are spoken. This flow of gibberish with speech-like characteristics is referred to as **expressive jargon**.

Beginnings of Linguistic Speech

Thirteen-month-old Eileen uses expressive jargon too but her language is interspersed with a few sounds that are identifiable as words, including: "mama," "dada," "keekot" (kitty cat), and "buh-bah" (bottle). These one-word utterances are called **holophrases**.

Telegraphic Speech

Across the hall in the same day-care center, a group of two- and three-year-olds are playing together. If we listened to their conversations, we would hear many children using holophrases. Others are using the simplest of sentences such as "Billy cry" to mean "Do something, teacher. Billy is crying," "Look book" to mean "Please read this book to me now," or "Portia sammich" to mean "I want to have my lunch now and eat my sandwich."

Notice that in each case, the children omit the auxiliary verb and verb endings ("Billy cry" instead of "Billy *is* cry*ing*"); the prepositions and articles ("book" instead of "*at the* book"); and do not use pronouns ("Portia" instead of "me" or "I" or "my"). This type of language, reduced to its most essential elements, is referred to as **telegraphic speech** because it is comparable to the way we communicate when we are trying to save words. Most of us would not write, for example, "I am desperately in need of cash. Please send money as soon as you possibly can" when we are paying for each word in the message. Instead, we write: "Help! Send money." The child's telegraphic speech does much the same thing, it distills the message into its essential elements.

Complex Sentences

As children mature, of course, their speech begins to sound more and more like that of adults. Sentences become longer and more complex, and eventually all of the things that were omitted in telegraphic speech are incorporated into children's language.

By the time that children begin kindergarten or first grade, they typically have:

- developed command of oral language (know its rules, how to use it)
- amassed experience with oral and written language and may be reading environmental print (such as fast-food signs, cereal-box labels, road signs)
- learned to associate printed materials with reading and expect reading and writing to make sense (Early Childhood and Literacy Development Committee, 1985).

Table 1.1 is intended to give a rough estimate of when various language milestones might be achieved. It should not be regarded as a set of rigid standards to which every child is expected to adhere because, as linguist Roger Brown (1973) once observed, a child's age does not tell us that much about language development. Language behavior, on the other hand, informs about *what* a child has learned, but it does not explain *why* language learning occurs. That question has intrigued people for centuries. Some contemporary theorists have emphasized the importance of heredity, some have stressed importance of environment, and still others have noted the interaction of the two. In the next section, we will examine each of these theories and the contributions they have made to our understanding of language development.

Language Acquisition Theories

Whether you realize it or not, you already have some theoretical leanings. Complete the following sentence: I think that children learn to talk primarily through _____. Now compare your ideas with these statements:

A. Children learn to talk primarily through imitation. They make certain sounds and are rewarded or reinforced for making those sounds because those particular sounds are language.
B. Children learn to talk because it is part of their normal progression of development, which is greatly influenced by heredity.
C. Children learn to talk because the human brain is "wired" for language. They seem to learn language naturally, almost like miniature language processors.
D. Children learn to talk because of the constant interaction between their emerging abilities and their experiences. They are always working at making sense out of their world through language.

TABLE 1.1   Overview of Language Development

Stage One: Prelinguistic Speech *Speech-type Sounds but No Words* *(Approximately Birth–11 Months)*	
Birth	Crying is the major way of communicating needs
2 weeks	Less crying, random gestures and vocalizations
6 weeks	Squeals, gurgles, and *coos* (makes vowel sounds such as "uhh")
3 months to 6 months	Child *babbles* (makes consonant-vowel syllable sounds like ma, de, da)
6 months to 9 months	Accidentally imitates sounds, more repetition of syllables (such as ah ba ba); utterances express emotions

9 months to
11 months
	Deliberately imitates sounds, shows definite signs of understanding some words
	  and simple commands; uses *expressive jargon*, a flow of gibberish that has the
	  intonation of real speech

Stages 2–4: Linguistic Speech
The Child Uses Language in Increasingly Complex Ways
(Approximately 1 Year and Up)

Stage Two: One-Word Utterances
(approximately 1–2 years)

At approximately 12 months	Child uses *holophrases* (one-word utterances); complex meanings can underlie one-word vocabulary of 3–6 words

12 months–
18 months
	Intonation is complex and speech-like; extensive use of nouns
	  vocabulary: 3–50 words
	  social: child does not attempt to convey additional information or show
	    frustration when not understood

Stage Three: Making Words into Phrases
(approximately 2–3 years)

Around 2 years	Great strides in receptive language; child uses *telegraphic speech*, 2- or 3-word
	  utterances
	  vocabulary: 50–200 words
	  social: definite increase in communicative efforts; beginnings of conversation

Around 3 years	Often considered to be the most rapid period of language growth
	  vocabulary: many new words acquired daily, 200–1000-word vocabulary
	  social: child strives to communicate and shows frustration if not understood; the
	    ability of unfamiliar adults to understand the child increases dramatically

    E. Children learn to talk primarily because they need to communicate. Their emotional and social drives greatly affect the process of language development.

Which of these statements was most closely aligned with your own ideas? Perhaps it was difficult to decide. Some of them may sound familiar because they include

TABLE 1.1   *Continued*

Stage Four: Using Complete Sentences
(approximately 4–6 years)

---

4 years	Pronunciation and grammar improve *vocabulary:* 1400–1600 words *social:* child seeks ways to correct misunderstandings; begins to adjust speech to listener's information needs; disputes with peers can be resolved with words and invitations to play are more common
5 to 6 years	Complex, grammatically correct sentences; uses pronouns; uses past, present, and future verb tenses; average sentence length per oral sentence increases to 6.8 words. *vocabulary:* uses approximately 2,500 words, understands about 6,000, responds to 25,000 *social:* child has good control of elements of conversation

Stage Five: Using Language Symbolically
(reading and writing)
(approximately 6–8 years)

6–7 years	Uses more complex sentences, more adjectives; uses If . . . then conditional clauses; average number of words per sentence is 7.6. *vocabulary:* speaking vocabulary of about 3,000 words
7–8 years	*social:* uses adjectival clauses with *which*, more gerunds, subordinate clauses

---

Sources: Dale, 1976; Loban, 1976; Maxim, 1989; Papalia and Olds, 1986.

theoretical orientations you have encountered in a psychology or child development course. The first statement, as you may have guessed, is a behavioral theory. Item B reflects a maturational theory, C a preformationist theory, D a cognitive-developmental theory, and E is part of a new theoretical orientation, **psycho-sociolinguistic theory**.

Behavioral Theory

A nine-month-old pats the family dog while saying "duh duh duh." Her father gets excited and says, "Yes! That's right—it's a doggie. Say *dog-gie*" Then he calls to his wife in the next room, "Hey, honey! Come here. Alyssa just said doggie!" This situation offers one possible answer to the question of language acquisition. The child makes random sounds, certain sounds are reinforced, and after thousands of such experiences, the child begins to talk. The stimulus-response dynamic is the essence of a behavioral theory of language acquisition. Behaviorists like B. F. Skinner emphasize the influence of the environment on language development.

Maturational Theory

Another group of theories notes that even though most children are saying their first words around their first birthdays, individual children may vary considerably from that timetable without having any language problems. One child might talk exceptionally "early" at eight months and another child might not begin talking until twenty months. Despite these initial differences, it may be that both children are doing well in school four years later, and it might be difficult to ascertain who had been the first to talk. The conviction that children are on their own "schedule," so to speak, is referred to as *maturational theory*. Maturationists emphasize individual biological readiness. Children's language, according to a maturational view, gradually unfolds in accordance with the child's "inner clock," just as a plant moves predictably from bulb to flower but not necessarily blooming at the same moment as other bulbs. Integral to the modern concept of maturation is brain periodization. Brain periodization has to do with the development of neural pathways in the brain. Rather than being systematic and incremental, it appears that these growth patterns are irregular. Thus, the child's language abilities might surge ahead at one point and then enter a period of relatively slow growth.

Preformationist Theory

During the 1960s, several researchers learned through cross-cultural research that the basic sequence of language acquisition is the same regardless of the specific language being learned by the child. Whether a baby was learning French, Japanese, or Balinese, the *steps* in language acquisition were basically the same: babble and coo, expressive jargon and holophrases, telegraphic speech, simple sentences, and increasingly complex sentences. They further noted that for the vast majority of children around the world, this task is accomplished during the preschool years and, if it is not accomplished during that time, the language ability of that child often suffers. Even though children do attain these language milestones at their own pace, the markers along the way remain consistent.

The cross-cultural consistencies convinced theorist Noam Chomsky (1988) that there was a particular portion of the brain that controls language acquisition. He proposed that this hypothetical area of the brain, called a **Language Acquisition Device** or **LAD**, was responsible for the remarkably similar patterns in language acquisition around the world. Preformationists believe that the brain is "wired" for language acquisition and that the preschool years are the time when this mechanism is activated.

Thus far we have seen two theories that emphasize heredity (preformationist and maturationist) and one that emphasizes environment (behaviorist). Now we will look at two theories that emphasize the *interaction* between heredity and environment.

Cognitive-Developmental Theory

The process of personal-environment interaction is the essence of cognitive-developmental theory. It assumes that the organism (in this case, the child) changes the environment and is changed by the environment. Also essential to the theory is the understanding that children go through a series of steps or stages in their language learning. The basic premise of cognitive-developmental theory is _constructivism_:

> According to this theory, children acquire knowledge by creating one level after another of being "wrong," rather than by internalizing correct, adult knowledge from the beginning. The most obvious example of the constructive process is young children learning to talk. They do not speak in complete sentences from the beginning . . . children create their own knowledge out of what they experience in the environment. These "wrong" ideas are necessary steps in the child's construction of increasingly higher levels of knowledge. (Kamii, 1988, p. 182)

The behavior of Marjorie, a twelve-month-old, helps to illustrate the dual processes that are used to construct knowledge about language, assimilation, and accommodation. Marjorie created the word "fuh fuh" which she used to describe the fox-fur collar on her mother's coat, a white dog puppet, and a faded yellow blanket. Evidently, this word described a category of objects that could be labeled as "white, furry things." In **assimilation**, existing mental structures keep expanding to include new concepts. If Marjorie indiscriminately referred to everything as a "fuh fuh" it would be pure assimilation; her mind would operate like one giant file drawer without any dividers or separate files. In **accommodation**, new mental structures are formed. If Marjorie created a new category every time she encountered something unfamiliar, it would be pure accommodation; her mind would be like a file drawer containing a new divider and a separate file for every slip of paper. In order for children to form new, useful, and meaningful mental structures, assimilation and accommodation must work together. Now Marjorie sees a toy horse with a mane and tail of white hair. Where does she "file" it—as a "fuh fuh," as a horse—or does it warrant a whole new category? She decides that the features of "horseness" in this particular item supersede its furriness and categorizes it as a horse. From a cognitive-developmental perspective, children are, just like Marjorie, actively building their understandings about language.

Psycho-sociolinguistic Theory

Of the theories discussed thus far, psycho-sociolinguistic theory is the most recent. From this perspective, language use and development is both an individual intellectual activity and a fundamentally social activity. In order to become a successful user of language, the child must learn to communicate appropriately in a wide variety of social contexts.

Psycho-sociolinguists would argue that it is social interaction that motivates children to learn language and this interaction serves as an opportunity to teach language. For an illustration of this theory, let's return to Marjorie. One morning she toddles into the kitchen, points at her face and says, "Fuh fuh, Mama." Her parents are completely mystified by this statement. What does the white and furry category have to do with her face? Marjorie is attempting to use language for social interaction, but no one can fathom her meaning. The question is answered after Marjie develops an upper respiratory problem and the pediatrician discovers a piece of frayed blanket fuzz the toddler had pushed into her nostril! So even though the toddler has mastered only a handful of words, mostly nouns, these words are being used for social interaction, not merely as labels. Marjorie is using language to **communicate**, even if adults fail to understand her.

Because psychosocial theory deals with the social dimension of language, it emphasizes pragmatics. **Pragmatics** refers to the different types of language that are socially appropriate with different people and social contexts. In order to understand how social situations affect **language**, think about how you would describe a graduation party to your best friend, to an elderly neighbor, or in a composition for English class. Your language would be least formal in the first situation with a peer and would probably be most formal in a written assignment. Young children are just learning that situations call for different types of language. They learn, for example, that although it might be acceptable to teasingly insult a sibling or peer, the same behavior will be frowned upon in an interaction with a great-aunt or a clergy member.

These five theoretical orientations—behaviorist, maturationist, preformationist, cognitive developmentalist, and psycho-sociolinguist—are all attempts to organize our thinking about the sequence of language development. Even though theorists may disagree about the predominant influence on the child's language development, most theorists would agree on the basic chronology of language learning. Perhaps the best way of balancing these theoretical orientations is to use Genishi's (1988) explanation: "Language occurs through an interaction among genes (which hold innate tendencies to communicate and be sociable), environment and the child's own thinking abilities" (p. 1).

How Young Children Use the Components of Language

The four components of language are phonology, syntax, semantics, and pragmatics. Table 1.2 is an overview of these dimensions.

Phonology

Phonology refers to the complex system of sounds that constitute a language. Listen to Mark, age four, as he explores the sounds of language in the block corner.

> *"One, Two, Three." (He counts the blocks as he picks them up). I wonder if this will fall if I put three more blocks on top? (He is stacking blocks on the roof of his garage. As he puts the second block on the stack, he bumps it and it all falls down). Oooohhh! What'd ya fall for! (He begins to build it again, but doesn't stack so many on this time). That's done. (He finishes it and grabs a toy car). Are you gonna fit? Brrrroom (He drives his cars around and makes car noises). Hi, Sandy! Hi, Bill! Let's go to the ice-cream place. O.K. Brrroooom, almost here, eerrrch. Let's get out. I want a biiggg ice-cream cone! O.K. Hey Lady, gimme a five-scoop ice-cream cone. Thanks. Here, Sandy. Now gimme a six-scoop*

TABLE 1.2   Components of Language Acquisition

Dimension of Language	Behaviors of Child
1. PHONOLOGY Mastery of sound system	*Comprehension of sounds* *Example:* Hearing the words "You can bring your bear" and responding appropriately *Production of sounds* *Example:* Learning to say the word "no"
2. SYNTAX Mastery of grammatical system	*Recognition of structure in utterances* *Example:* Realizing that plural nouns often end in s *Production of correctly structured utterances* *Example:* Learning to rearrange noun-verb order to ask a question: "Why can't he play?" instead of "Why he can't play?"
3. SEMANTICS Mastery of meaning system	*Comprehension of meanings* *Example:* Associating the words "bye-bye" with departures *Production of meaningful utterances* *Example:* Saying the word "truck" when a truck passes by
4. PRAGMATICS Mastery of the social interaction system of language	*Comprehension of social implications of utterances* *Example:* Knowing that "Help! Help!" is a way to attract attention and get assistance in an emergency *Production of utterances that are appropriate for the social situation* *Example:* Learning to say "please" and "thank you"

Source: Adapted from Levin, G. (1983). *Child psychology.* Belmont, CA: Wadsworth.

> *ice-cream cone. Thanks. Let's go. That was good! Verooom. (He drives to the garage and pretends to get gas, then changes his voice to a lower pitch). I have to get some gas, honey. (Switches to a higher pitch). O.K., Billy, buy me some gum while you're in there."*

Mark uses *onomatopoeia* or words that imitate sounds, such as the car-engine noises. He imitates the phrases he has heard. Mark also changes the *pitch* of his voice. His voice is at a higher pitch when he role-plays a woman or child, lower when he takes on the role of father. The *timbre* or amount of resonance in his voice changes as well. When he says "oohh" and "verooom," for example, the amount of vibration in his vocal chords changes. Mark's *tone*, the expression of emotion in his voice, changes when he gives a command or asks himself a question.

The sound of Mark's language is also affected by stress and juncture. **Stress** refers to the amount of emphasis placed on a word. **Juncture** refers to the slight breaks or pauses between words and sentences. When he says "O.K., Billy, buy me some gum . . . ," he stresses the word "gum" and there is a juncture (represented by the comma) after the words "O.K." and "Billy." These features of the sound system of language are one reason why a computer voice usually sounds so flat and mechanical in comparison to a human voice. Our ear for language relies on phonological features of language to increase listening comprehension and maintain attention.

Syntax

Syntax refers to the set of rules or the grammar of a language. Mickey, a kinder-gartner, knows something about the rules of language. He explains how to form plurals to a classmate like this: "Because, Vickie, when you have lots of stuff, like more than one stuff, then you put a "s" at the end." Word order is another syntac-tical aspect. In English, the noun usually precedes the verb (e.g., "The boy ran" rather than "Ran the boy."). The use of inflections or word endings is another syntactical rule. Children learn that the past tense of a regular verb is formed by adding -ed. If a child says, "We goed to Sea World," that child has learned the rule. It just happens that this is an irregular verb that deviates from the general rule by having "went" as its past tense.

The same is true for plurals. If a child says, "I need new slippers for my foots," he or she has learned some of the rules about forming plurals. Although these examples might be viewed by adults as "mistakes," they are evidence of the child's emerging ability to master the syntactical aspects of language. When children apply common grammatical rules to irregular words, such as saying, "Look at the deers," or "She teached us about animals," it is called **overregularization**.

Semantics

Semantics refers to the meaning of words. How do children come to understand word meaning? Take, for example, a common object like a potato. If you consider the dramatically different objects that are categorized as potatoes, it is easy to see why building vocabulary is such a challenge. Consider three-year-old Lee who looks at her dinner plate and sees a small white mound. It tastes bland and has a smooth texture. "Do you like your potatoes?" her father asks. The next day, her family stops at a restaurant and she eats some white circles covered with an orange, rubbery substance—potatoes *au gratin*. "You like potatoes, huh?" her mother comments. On Saturday, she goes to the grocery store and watches a woman who is handling brown, dirty objects in the produce section and she overhears the woman say, "I think I'll get a couple pounds of potatoes." Some weeks later, she visits relatives and sees her cousins playing a game they call "hot potato" with a pillow in the living room. Then her aunt says to a group of relatives who are watching television, "Time for lunch, you couch potatoes!" The variety of Lee's experience with just one word during a few weeks illustrates why word meaning can be troublesome for the beginning language learner.

Typically, children's difficulties with word meaning fall into one of three categories: (1) not knowing the correct word, (2) interpreting words or phrases literally, or (3) mistaking one word for another. Four-year-old Anna's experience illustrates the first type, not knowing the correct terminology. Anna is playing by her sandbox and calls to her teenage sister "There's a worm, a big worm. I don't want it to get me." "Anna," her sister replies, "worms don't bite. Don't worry about it." "But it's a *big* black worm with a head. I can see it looking at me." Her sister climbs down from the porch, sees an 8-foot black snake, screams, and they both run inside. Based upon this experience, Anna learns the word "snake" and the differences between snakes and worms.

Another common difficulty with language is the literal interpretation of words, especially idiomatic expressions. *Idioms* are expressions which have figurative rather than literal meanings such as "I'm all tied up," or "He let the cat out of the bag." When Nicole's father comments to his friend "I see you got a haircut," Nicole looks at the man curiously and whispers to her father, "I think you're wrong, Daddy. He got *a whole bunch* of hairs cut."

Children also mistake one word for another. Usually this happens because they are trying to make sense out of whatever they hear. Four-year-old Anita is at a family reunion picnic where coleslaw is being served. She likes it and wants more, except that she refers to it as "cold slop."

In each of the preceding examples, we see how children strive to understand word meaning. An equally challenging task is using language appropriately in a social context.

Pragmatics

As we saw in the discussion of psycho-sociolinguistic theory, *pragmatics* has to do with who can speak, to whom they can speak, what they can say, how they should say it, when and where it is said, and the medium used to communicate (Hymes, 1971). To illustrate how pragmatics affects language, think about how you would express disagreement with your boss, your parents, your classmate, or a preschooler. One of the best ways to assess children's understanding of the social side of language is by observing them during play. After children begin to understand that language is a social instrument, their language changes when they take on different roles during sociodramatic play. The amount of formality and the signs of mutual respect vary considerably when the child takes on authoritative roles (such as parent or teacher), subordinate roles (such as the obedient child) or the role of a social equal (peer group member). The following play text illustrates pragmatics at work. Two preschool girls are playing with little plastic people, two coffee cans set up like houses (beds, bath and kitchen), and a "school" with desks. Maria plays the role of teacher and mother while Luan plays the part of the three children.

Maria (teacher):   (In an authoritative voice) "O.K., children." (She switches back to normal voice, then says to her playmate, "Pretend they are talking to each other.") "No chewing gum in school!"

Luan (playing all three children) (silly voice):   "Chomp, chomp, chomp!" "But . . . that's fun!" (picking up one figure) "Teacher, I have to go home now, I don't feel good!" (moves the figure to the home) "Mom, mom!" (returns figure to school) "OK, I'm back now!" "I just have a cold, achoo!" (back home again) "Hi, mom!"

Maria (she switches role to become mother): "Take a bath!"

Luan (puts figure into tub): "I'm finished, Mom! Achoo, achoo, achoo! Now there's three absent from school."

Maria: "Stay home and stay in your beds."

Luan: "But mom! Oh, mother, oh, mother, oh, ma ma ma, moooother!!" (Clean-up time is announced by the teacher)

As Luan's and Maria's play reveals, they have learned many things about the social side of communication, including how to adjust their language to the social situation. By attending to all four components of language—phonology, syntax, semantics, and pragmatics—teachers can enhance children's language growth.

Fostering Functional Communication in the Classroom

Teachers are often advised to make the language activities of the classroom **functional**. This means that language is being used purposefully, being used to communicate. How, exactly, can this be achieved? Halliday (1975) identified seven functions of language. As Goodman (1982) points out, we can use those language functions to design appropriate language activities.

Instrumental Language

Instrumental or "I want" language is used to satisfy needs or desires. Instrumental language activities include such things as signing up for learning centers, checking out library books, playing store, reading advertising, filling out order blanks and using a picture menu to select food at a "restaurant."

One third-grade teacher presented this challenge to students: "Design your dream room, using old catalogs. Tell or write about what is in your room and why." Brian created a room with wipe-off wallpaper "So you can change it whenever you feel like it."

Regulatory

Regulatory or "Do as I tell you" language is used to control others. Language activities with a regulatory function include guidelines for the care of class pets and plants, directions on the use of classroom materials (such as the computer), and follow-the-leader type games, such as "Simon Says."

A kindergarten teacher used rhythm band instruments and Ella Jenkins' (1966) rhythm band song, "Play Your Instruments" with her students. By following the explicit instructions on the recording, children gained experience with regulatory language.

Interactional

Interactional or "me and you" language is used to establish and maintain relationships. Some examples of the interactional function of language include: correspondence from teacher to child and child to child, writing to pen pals at other grade levels or schools, and working in groups to achieve a common goal, such as a class get-well card for a classmate who is ill.

Ms. Torrez cares for infants in her home. As she works with Leticia, a three-month-old and Liang, a six-month-old, we can see how she uses language to interact even before the babies in her care have begun to talk. Ms. Torrez knows that these infants are listening and learning the rhythms of conversation. She also knows how to adjust her interaction style to the individual child. With Leticia, Ms. Torrez moves in close, then pulls away while smiling and talking. Leticia's family reports that she laughed out loud for the first time last week when her older brother was tickling her stomach, so Ms. Torrez plays this game and is successful in getting a laugh from the baby too. When the teacher sees Leticia disengaging, looking away, she senses that the baby is getting too excited and needs to calm down. The teacher slows the pace and as soon as Leticia hears her favorite lullaby, "All the Pretty Horses," she snuggles her head against Ms. Torrez's neck and starts to fall asleep. Now Ms. Torrez turns to Liang who has just started to sit with support, a "lap baby." Liang is fascinated by his ability to imitate and be imitated, so Ms. Torrez echoes his vocalizations. When Liang says "ma ma ma," and Ms. Torrez repeats it, Liang looks rather surprised and tries it again. Then the teacher maintains his interest in the game by saying the sounds with a different inflection: *ma*ma, and Liang repeats it, this time mimicking the adult's emphasis.

Personal

Personal or "here I come" language is used to express personal opinions, feelings, and individuality. The personal functions of language include such things as songs into which each child's name can be inserted, books about self and family, individually dictated stories, story characters to identify with or family photographs that are captioned by the children.

Ms. Klingensmith, a day-care teacher, used pictures of children's parents at work to help her three-year-olds adjust to starting school. Each child brought a photograph of his or her parent(s) at work and dictated a caption to go with it. The photos and captions were placed on the bulletin board to remind students where their parents were and that they would return as soon as work was over.

Heuristic

Heuristic or "tell me why" is language used to explore and find out. Language activities with an heuristic function include: keeping journal on a class pet, conducting simple science experiments, keeping a question box in the classroom where children can deposit a question and have it answered, or sharing books that explain things.

Mr. Kowalski, a second-grade teacher, invited the ambulance and its crew members to talk to the children during a unit on safety. They explained the use of a blood pressure cuff for a baby, a soft cast, and the oxygen tank. The children then toured the ambulance and asked other questions about rescue procedures.

Imaginative

Imaginative or "let's pretend" is language used to create a world of one's own. Some examples of using language imaginatively are: dress-up play, play with miniatures (farms, gas stations, etc.), puppetry, storytelling, listening to picture-story books read aloud, joining in stories, creating original stories and enacting them.

Ms. Jacobs, a kindergarten teacher, found several old pith helmets that mail carriers wear in the summer at a thrift store and this simple prop led to an imaginative play theme called "Expedition." The children used all of the jungle animal toys already in the classroom and more were brought in. Children created all sorts of themes—pursuit and capture, daring rescues, finding treasures—and then dictated stories about their play each day.

Informational

Informational or "something to tell you" is language used to convey information. Informational uses of language include: message boards, bulletin boards, notes to parents and children about upcoming events, class newspapers, weather board, community newspaper, and creating signs, posters, and flyers about events.

Ms. Thompson, a first-grade teacher, had just completed a unit on friendships and wanted to gather information about the good deeds that were occurring in the classroom. In her "Christmas Tree" activity, each child drew a large tree shape on green construction paper, but the children did not decorate their own trees. Instead, the trees were decorated with "ornaments" from classmates. These ornaments had drawings and writings that conveyed information about the kindness and helpfulness of another classmate. It was only by doing good deeds for others that the child's own tree was beautifully decorated.

Through functional language activities, teachers can create a communication environment that supports young children's language growth.

Conclusion

Contrary to popular opinion, adults do not "teach children to talk." That phrase implies that the child is a passive repository for adult language, that language is bequeathed to the child. We now know that children are far from being passive recipients of adult language. Children are the primary agents in the process of acquiring language because it is the child who is active and determined in building and achieving linguistic competence.

Summary

The communicative process involves a message, a medium, a context, a sender, and a receiver. In the process of acquiring language, young children strive to become communicators by using both paralinguistics (nonverbal communication) and linguistics (verbal communication). At first, their vocalizations are not true words; they coo, babble, and use expressive jargon—all forms of prelinguistic speech. Gradually, children begin to master words and progress from holophrases to telegraphic speech to complex sentences.

There are five major theoretical orientations that attempt to explain the complex process of language acquisition: behavioral, maturational, preformationist, cognitive-developmental, and psycho-sociolinguistic. The study of language, has identified four components of language: phonology, syntax, semantics, and pragmatics. In order to foster functional communication in classrooms, teachers should plan experiences and activities that build children's functional language abilities in seven areas: instrumental, regulatory, interactional, personal, heuristic, imaginative, and informational. Children construct their own understandings of language and they must be treated as intelligent, active partners throughout the process of learning to communicate.

Focus On: Guiding Group Discussions

In most preschool and kindergarten classrooms, there is a group time when children are asked to share an experience or bring in an object and discuss it. This practice is variously referred to as sharing, group time, discussion, or "show and tell." Why is this activity such an enduring part of the early childhood curriculum? As we have seen in this chapter, children are learning the "rules of the communication game," and experiences in talking to peers and adults can support children's development in the use of dialogue. The ability to use dialogue is essential to social interaction, not just during preschool years, but throughout life.

Despite the importance of conversational skills, many educators of young children find group discussions difficult to direct. They say that children have short attention spans, are too distractable, and have not learned to listen to one another. But this is less a reflection of children's inability to discuss than it is evidence of developmentally inappropriate practice. Katz (1988) says, "The relevant principle of practice in fostering communicative competence is that the younger the child, the more the teacher uses small group and one-to-one conversations and avoids too much one-way communication to the entire class" (p. 26).

Hendrick (1986) provides these general guidelines for group time:

- Convey enthusiasm and enjoy interacting with the children.
- Keep the group small and stable.
- Minimize tensions and distractions.
- Plan carefully and be flexible.
- Begin promptly when children start to gather.
- Adjust pace and include variety.
- Encourage discussion through supportive comments.
- Ask skillful, open-ended questions.
- Draw group to a close before it falls apart.

Some specific guidelines that apply to group discussions with young children are the following:

- Focus on children's communication rather than their material possessions.
- Model the kinds of behaviors you want to see in the children—listening attentively, making comments or asking questions.
- Recognize that young children's contributions may be wish-fulfillment rather than factual reporting.
- Allow children to take the lead and say what they want to say rather than quizzing them.

Now look at the following situations that have actually occurred during group time and decide how you would respond.

Situation 1:   Tommy, a first grader, has been an avid viewer of reruns of the cartoon series, "The Flintstones." During group time, he says, "Last night I went over to Fred's house and he and Barney were lookin' for a job. Wilma helped us look in the newspaper ads and I stayed overnight. I was almost late for school but I had a clock by my bed with an illuminated dial and I saw it was time for school and ran down Bedrock Drive and got on the school bus." Most of the children are silent, then Shaina says, "You can't really go to Fred Flintstone's house—he's just a cartoon, right, teacher?" How would you respond to Shaina's comment and Tommy's story?

Situation 2:   One of the children has just reported that her cat had seven kittens last night. Tanya, seeing the admiration this announcement engenders among her peers, gets up before the group and reports that *her* dog had puppies. "How many did she have?" another child asks. "Oh, about twenty," Tanya replies. How would you respond to Tanya's statement?

Solutions 1 and 2:   The line of demarcation between fantasy and reality in the young child's mind is not very distinct (Piaget, 1959). Some of the things that seem magical (like an escalator) are not, and some of the things that seem relatively simple from a child's point of view (like repairing a burst balloon) are virtually impossible. Understanding this enables adults to be tolerant of children's wish fulfillment being reported as fact. It is not lying because the child does not intend to deceive. Instead, the child is using language imaginatively when adults expect the child to use language informationally. A sensitive teacher might respond to Tommy with: "It *would* be nice to visit a character from TV or a book." These kinds of responses are far more appropriate than "Now you know that isn't the truth." By the way, Tanya actually *was* giving factual information—she was simply reporting the total number of puppies her dog had borne over the years!

Situation 3:   Joshua enthusiastically volunteers to participate in a group discussion, but when he gets in front of the group, he says nothing. "What was it that you wanted to tell us?" his teacher asks gently. After some hesitation, Josh says, "Frog," and cannot be coaxed into saying anything more. What would you do?

Solution 3:   Children who are unsure of themselves in front of the group need to feel at ease. It is particularly important for teachers to avoid rattling off a number of questions that will only serve to intimidate the child further. Simply posing an open-ended question ("What would you like to say about frogs?") instead of closed questions ("Tell us all about frogs." "What color is a frog?") allows children to share what they want to share rather than expecting them to display some bit of knowledge an adult has in mind. If, despite the teacher's best efforts, the child obviously feels uncomfortable or seems to have forgotten what he or she intended to say, the best approach is to graciously help them out of the limelight and move on, then come back later if the child seems interested in contributing.

Situation 4:   Jacinda watches several other children discuss the expensive toys that they received as Christmas gifts. She goes in front of the class and says, "These are my legs. They can move fast like this (she makes a running motion) or slow like this (she walks). Grandma says I have beautiful legs just like my mother." How would you react to this group discussion in general? To Jacinda's comments in particular?

Solution 4:   As you may have surmised, this use of "Show and Tell" should not have occurred in the first place. In this classroom, "Show and Tell" has deteriorated into "Bring and Brag." Jacinda may have felt excluded, but she was resourceful in figuring out something to share. When teachers make coveted toys the focus of a group discussion, it subverts the whole purpose of a sharing time. Not only does it take away from the language focus, it also tends to reinforce competition rather than cooperation. These feelings often spill over into other times and places throughout the day, usually resulting in disputes over the toy. Then the teacher is put in the difficult situation of encouraging sharing, yet protecting the owner's rights to a treasured object. Sometimes an expensive toy gets damaged and there are angry parents to contend with as well. The best approach is to make it clear to parents that sharing is not for the purpose of flaunting possessions.

In the Field: How Children's Language Affects Adults' Language

Grace Smith (1974), a nursery school teacher, used to keep an "important book," a blank notebook that she filled with examples of children's speech. If children saw her writing and asked what she was doing, she would say "Writing your words—they are important." She often asked children questions such as "What do you see?," "How does it feel?," or simply "And?"

Children's efforts to define words are often poetic and profound, such as these comments by young children:

Lost is   Hop is   Separate means
where it is.   like up.   in a cage.
(Smith, 1974, pp. 134–135)

Once, while I was working late after school, I found a kindergarten boy in the hallway who was lost and needed help. "I was walking home," he sobbed, "and all the houses started to look the same." What a perfect description of being lost and going around in circles!

The language of children is sometimes incorporated into adults' language, not as "baby talk," but out of respect for the child's ability to speak volumes with so few words. Many family stories are built around the language behavior of young children. One student told the story of her three-year-old sister who had a negative reaction to the whole concept of trick-or-treat and Halloweeners in costumes appearing at her door: "Don't wike 'weeners!" That phrase became her family's way of expressing disapproval of almost anything. Another student told about herself as a toddler who, during a brief car trip, begged to stop at every fast-food restaurant. She was completely ignored until she said, "Doesn't anybody hear this baby in the back seat cryin' for a hamburger?" and her parents burst out laughing. The phrase "Doesn't anybody hear this baby in the back seat cryin' for . . . " became her family's way of pleading for attention and assistance.

Interview

Arrange to interview a teacher or parent of young children. Explain that you are interested in collecting memorable examples of young children's words. (You may want to share some examples of your own or those described above.) Be certain to mention this goal during your initial contact with the adult so that he or she has time to think about it before you actually conduct the interview. Use the following questions and/or others of your own:

1. Could you describe any particularly memorable examples of children's language?
2. Can you recall any specific situations when

   a. you were amused or surprised by something a child said?

b. you incorporated a word or expression invented by a child into your own speech?

c. you shared the example of the child's language with other adults?

3. Why do you think that these incidents were especially memorable?

References

Brown, R. (1973). *A first language: The early stages*. Cambridge, MA: Harvard University Press.

Chomsky, N. (1988). *Language and mind*. New York, NY: Harcourt, Brace and World.

Dale, P. (1976). *Language development*. New York: Holt, Rinehart, and Winston.

DeHaven, E. P. (1983). *Teaching and learning the language arts*. Boston, MA: Little, Brown.

Early Childhood and Literacy Development Committee. (1985). *Literacy development and pre-first grade*. Newark, DE: International Reading Association.

Genishi, C. (1988). Young children's oral language development. *ERIC Digest*. Urbana, IL: ERIC Clearinghouse on Reading and Communication Skills.

Genishi, C., and Dyson, A. H. (1984). *Language assessment in the early years*. Norwood, NJ: Ablex.

Goodman, K. (1982). In F. Gollasch (Ed.). *Language and literacy: The selected writings of Kenneth S. Goodman, Volume II*. London: Routledge and Kegan Paul.

Halliday, M. A. K. (1975). *Explorations in the functions of language*. London: Edward Arnold.

Hendrick, J. (1986). *Total learning: Curriculum for the young child* (2nd ed.). Columbus, OH: Merrill.

Hymes, D. (1971). Competence and performance in linguistic theory. In R. Huxley and E. Ingram (Eds.). *Language acquisition: Models and methods*. New York: Academic Press.

Johnson, D. W. (1972). *Reaching out: Interpersonal effectiveness and self-actualization*. Englewood Cliffs, NJ: Prentice-Hall.

Kamii, C. (1988). Autonomy or heteronomy: Our choices of goals. In M. A. Johnson and G. F. Roberson (Eds.), *Leaders in education: Their views on controversial issues* (pp. 99–104). Lanham, MD: University Press of America.

Katz, L. (1988). *Early childhood education: What research tells us*. Bloomington, IN: Phi Delta Kappa.

Levin, G. (1983). *Child psychology*. Belmont, CA: Wadsworth.

Loban, W. (1976). *Language Development: Kindergarten Through Grade Twelve*. Urbana, IL: National Council of Teachers of English.

Maxim, G. (1989). *The very young: Guiding children from infancy through the early years*. (3rd ed.). Columbus, OH: Merrill.

Menyuk, P. (1988). *Language development: Knowledge and use*. Glenview, IL: Scott, Foresman.

Papalia, D. E., and Olds, S. W. (1986). *A child's world: Infancy through adolescence* (4th ed.). New York, NY: McGraw-Hill.

Piaget, J. (1959). *The language and thought of the child* (M. Gabain and R. Gabain, Trans.). London: Routledge and Kegan Paul. (Original work published in 1926.)

Piaget, J. (1963). *The origins of intelligence in children*. New York: Norton.

Schieffelin, B. B. (1979). Getting it together: An ethnographic approach to the study of communicative competence. In E. Ochs and B. B. Schieffelin (Eds.). *Developmental pragmatics*. New York: Academic Press.

Smith, G. (1974). On listening to the language of children. *Young Children, 29*, 133–140.

Nonprint Media

Jenkins, Ella. (1966). *Play your instruments*. New York: Folkways.

Photo: © 1990 Frank Siteman

2

Oracy and Literacy in Early Childhood Education

OUTLINE

Key Concepts and Terms
Introduction

I. Defining Literacy

II. Oracy and Literacy: A Comparison

III. Three Types of Literacy
   A. Visual Literacy
      1. Activities to develop visual literacy
         a. pictures
         b. film
   B. Oracy: Oral Language
      1. Activities to develop oracy
         a. fingerplays
         b. action rhymes
   C. Literacy With Print
      1. Literacy learning at home
      2. Literary learning at school
   D. Literacy and Computer Software
   E. Acquiring Literacy With Print

IV. The Literacy Event: Key to Literacy
   A. Nick's Literacy Event
   B. Rebekah's Literacy Event

Language is a keyhole peeking in on the mind and, since the human mind can formulate so many different ambitions, sentiments, and attitudes, the keyhole has to be flexible and creative if it is to let us express what is in our minds.

—E. B. BOLLES (1982)

KEY CONCEPTS AND TERMS

oracy

literacy

visual literacy

fingerplays

literacy with print

computer software

literacy events

phonological awareness

literacy process

cultural literacy

private speech

Mario is a Canadian child who lives in Montreal. He is expected to understand, speak, read, and write both English and French, just like most other members of his community.

Talat lives in the Kalahari desert with her family. No one in her family reads or writes, nor do they see much reason to. Their major goal is to survive the harsh climate and to interact with family, friends, neighbors, and visitors. This they can accomplish through speaking and listening.

Krystal lives in the city of Philadelphia. Her parents are very concerned about Krystal's reading and writing because they feel these skills are the key to a happy, productive life in America.

Defining Literacy

As these examples illustrate, our definition for literacy is affected by the culture in which we live.

What has distinguished one society from another has not been the ability to think logically, but rather the communication system used in the thinking. Art was a more important communication system in some societies, dance in others, and so on. Persons in such societies used all the forms of thinking we currently use. We have a tendency to assume otherwise because we do not value some communication systems as much as we value the one that is dominant in our society—namely language. (Harste, 1989, p. vi)

Oracy and Literacy: A Comparison

Oral language, or **oracy**, refers to speaking and listening. Written language, or **literacy**, by its most common definition, refers to reading and writing. Table 2.1 is a schematic of how these concepts relate to the language arts. Several theorists have discussed the differences between oracy and literacy (Chafe, 1985; Nickerson, 1981; Smith, 1984). The highlights of their observations are:

A Comparison of Oracy and Literacy

Oracy	*Literacy*
(Speaking and/or listening)	(Reading and/or writing)
is nearly universal in normal individuals	is far from universal and often poorly developed
is acquired without much formal training during the first few years of life	is acquired after considerable, deliberate effort and after oral/aural language
typically involves face-to-face contact	typically has sender and receiver removed from one another temporally and spatially
often violates formal grammatical rules	is expected to conform to grammatical rules
is produced at a rapid rate	is produced at a relatively slow rate
may be quickly forgotten but, paradoxically, words may endure forever due to emotional reaction from the listener	may endure longer (e.g., as a published work) but, paradoxically, can be changed in nearly limitless ways before sharing with an audience
is believed to be subject to more flaws or errors due to composing "on the fly"	is believed to reflect more accurately personal knowledge, beliefs, and attitudes
tends to change rapidly due to slang, fads, etc.	tends to remain more traditional and be somewhat resistant to fads
implies a less binding commitment to the words produced	implies a more enduring commitment to the words produced
tends to connect ideas together loosely	tends to connect ideas together in a complex structure

TABLE 2.1   Oracy, Literacy, and the Language Arts

	Receptive	*Expressive*
ORACY: Skills of effective listening and speaking	Listening	Speaking
LITERACY: Skills of effective reading and writing	Reading	Writing

Source: Wilkinson, A. (1970). The concept of oracy. *English Journal, 59,* 70–77.

Three Types of Literacy

There are at least three types of literacy that are valued in various ways by different cultures; visual literacy, oral literacy, and literacy with print. These types of literacy and language arts activities that are well suited to developing them are discussed in the next section.

Visual Literacy

When individuals "use line, shape and color to interpret actions, recognize objects, and understand the message of symbols," it is called **visual literacy** (Read and Smith 1982, p. 927). Generally speaking, visual literacy focuses on a person's interpretation of visual images. It is entirely possible to be visually literate and yet be illiterate where reading and writing are concerned. Visual literacy enables a preschooler who is not yet reading to arrange pictures in a correct story sequence. Visual literacy is the reason why a toddler can locate his favorite book or record, even though there are many others strewn around the room. Of course, skills in visual literacy develop far beyond these initial abilities. Lacy (1986) enumerates four categories of visual literacy:

1. *Comprehension of the main idea*—the ability to understand the intended message of a visual work
2. *Perception of part/whole relationships*—the ability to identify details that contribute to the whole
3. *Differentiation of fantasy/reality*—the ability to infer relationships between symbols and reality
4. *Recognition of artistic medium*—the ability to identify unique properties of the medium used

Activities to Develop Visual Literacy
Two types of pictorial images, pictures and film, are ideal media for developing the visual literacy.

Pictures   Pictures displayed in an early childhood classroom should be *varied* and should include good photographs, picture books, prints of famous artists' work, art produced by children, posters (such as those from the American Library Association), calendars (such as the Caldecott calendar of award-winning picture books), travel posters, bright pictures of food, flowers, etc., scavenged from grocery stores or card shops, collages of pictures cut from magazines, and original art by local artists. Pictures should *spark children's interest*. Avoid pictures that "add nothing to what children already know"; look for a picture "that makes the child stop and say 'Look at that!' or better still: 'What is that?' " (Hymes, 1981).

One first-grade teacher found a magazine photo essay of greatly magnified objects. Included in the collection were such things as a housefly's eye, a grain of salt—all photographed through an electron microscope. You can imagine the interest this display created when the children were told that they had seen every object thousands of times! In addition to unusual pictures like these, pictures that are full of interesting details are another good vehicle for building visual imagery. Of course, the child's developmental level should be taken into consideration when deciding how much detail is appropriate and the details themselves should be meaningful.

One third-grade teacher used information from *The Encyclopedia of How It's Made* (Clark, 1978) and *The Way Things Work* (Macaulay, 1988) to stimulate students' interest in details. These books include diagrams that illustrate how simple machines and everyday objects are made and used, such as a diagram showing how a guitar is fashioned, or a chart that explains how a photocopier works. At the close of each school day, she would pique the children's interest with a statement: "Everyone take a look at your pencil. What questions do you have about how it is made?" The children would generate a list of questions such as: How does the lead get inside? Does the metal hold the eraser on? Is it painted with a machine? How do they print the writing on? The next day, the diagram from the book would provide some answers.

Action is another feature of appealing pictures for children. A colt running alongside his mother is more interesting than a horse standing in a stall. Pictures from magazines noted for their photography, such as *Ranger Rick* or *Life*, are good sources of pictures depicting action. The advertising in business magazines often contains unusual, high-quality pictures that children are less likely to have seen already. Pictures that stimulate the child's imagination and suggest a story are appropriate. One first-grade teacher created a picture file that included a photograph of a dejected-looking child at a lemonade stand with the price marked down several times, a picture that inspired second-grader Tonya to speak from the pictured child's viewpoint: "I keep hopin' somebody will buy my lemonade, but the cars just keep going by and nobody stops. I tried making it cheaper and I still can't get any customers. Maybe I should just give up and go inside and drink the lemonade with my mom and my little brother."

How pictures are displayed is another consideration. They should be positioned not at an adult's eye level, but at the child's. The display should not be so cluttered that it is difficult to tell if anything new is up. Sometimes posting a picture in a location other than the bulletin board—on the classroom door, over a cubby, next to the sink—gets it noticed.

Film   The moving pictures of film can contribute to children's **visual literacy** as well. In studies of children's film interests, Cox (1989) found that children prefer

> films that tell a story (such as "Corduroy")
>
> live action films (with live actors rather than drawings). Such as "Harry the Dirty Dog" and "Frog Goes to Dinner," based on the children's books by the same titles (Zion, 1956; Mayer, 1974).
>
> realistic films with contemporary settings and a humorous tone with children their own age involved in solving problems and being themselves (such as

"Molly's Pilgrim," an award-winning film based on Barbara Cohen's (1983) book for primary grade children)

But no matter how well a picture or film tells a story, no matter how action-packed or well-wrought it is, the full benefit to visual literacy is lost unless teachers share and discuss print and nonprint media with students.

Oracy: Oral Language

Oral language refers to both listening and speaking. *Aural language*, the ability to hear and understand words, is found in nearly all individuals without auditory or cognitive functioning problems. Typically, our aural language operates at a higher level than our speaking. This can be illustrated by the fact that we can hear and understand an eloquent speaker of our native language without being able to speak that well ourselves. Usually, children's receptive oral language (listening) is more fully developed than their expressive oral language (speaking).

In many cultures, the major ways of communicating are speaking and listening. Reading and writing are viewed as important skills, but not as the "survival skills" they have become in the United States. This oracy perspective is often unappreciated by Americans who have had the literacy perspective so deeply impressed upon them. A useful analogy might be to think of language in the same way that we think of currency: oracy becomes the gold and silver currency, literacy is the paper currency. The analogy works well because just as paper money represents real money, written and read text represent speech. Both are "paper currencies." So it is entirely possible to be illiterate by American standards and function successfully in many different cultures around the world.

Activities to Develop Oracy

> Five little monkeys,
> swinging in a tree
> saying to Mr. Crocodile:
> "You can't catch me"
> "You can't catch me!"
> Along comes Mr. Crocodile,
> as mean as he can be and
> SNAP! goes the crocodile.
> Four little monkeys . . .
> (repeat words of the poem)
> Three little monkeys . . .
> (repeat)
> Two little monkeys . . .
> (repeat)
> One little monkey,
> swinging in a tree
> Saying to Mr. Crocodile

> "You can't catch me!"
> "You can't catch me!"
> Along comes Mr. Crocodile
> As mean as he can be and . . .
> SNAP! goes the crocodile.
> Now there's no little monkey
> Swinging in the tree
> And away swims Mr. Crocodile
> As FULL as HE CAN BE
> (rub stomach)

If you watched a group of preschoolers reciting this poem, you would see that they are doing more than saying the words. One hand represents the wriggling monkeys. The other hand is bent with four fingers on top and the thumb on the bottom to represent Mr. Crocodile's mouth. When the crocodile snaps, the children clap their hands together loudly.

Fingerplays   A rhyme that is accompanied by hand and finger actions like "Five Little Monkeys" is called a **fingerplay**. You are probably familiar with "Eency Weency Spider" or:

> Here is the church
> Here is the steeple
> Open the doors
> And here are the people

Fingerplays have been part of human life for centuries. Seefeldt and Barbour (1986) report that records of Roman times contain descriptions of fingerplays. Fingerplays were also part of Frederick Frobel's first "garden of children" or *kindergarten*. Through fingerplays, children not only practice listening and speaking, they also link language with action (see Graham, 1986; Grayson, 1962; Scott, 1983). Consider how a fingerplay helps children to understand symbols; a clap of the hand to represent a crocodile's snapping mouth, five wiggling fingers to represent the mischevious monkeys, and so forth. This connection between actions and words is an essential precursor of literacy with print.

Action Rhymes   *Action rhymes* are simple poems or chants which involve the child's entire body in the activity. Karen, a toddler, has learned "Ring Around the Rosie." As she moves in a circle with her sister, she says "Rind round . . . pocketful" and, as she drops to the floor, "BOOM!"

Literacy with Print

Literacy with print is defined as "activities and skills associated directly with the use of print—primarily reading and writing, but also such derivative activities as playing Scrabble or Boggle, doing crossword puzzles, alphabetizing files, and copying or typing" (Snow 1983, p. 165). Thus, when we speak of *literacy* in America and in most highly developed countries, we mean the ability to read and write at some level acceptable to the dominant culture. In fact, modern society is a "scribal community," a culture in which the creation and use of texts is a central activity (Purves, 1990).

Literacy Learning at Home

In 1986, Teale studied children's literacy learning in low-income homes. He found that there was considerable variation in the amount and type of literacy with print activities. He also found that in approximately 80 percent of the reading and writing activities observed and for almost 90 percent of the time spent in those activities, literacy was a means to an end rather than an activity pursued for its own sake. Children read or wrote because it helped them to organize their lives and served some useful purpose. Teale (1986) categorized the types of activities mediated by literacy as follows:

>*Daily living routines and basic needs*, such as preparing food, getting dressed, making a list of household chores
>
>*Entertainment purposes*, such as reading a TV guide, reading the words in cartoons, or reading the rules of a game
>
>*School-related*, such as playing school or doing homework
>
>*Emulations of adult work*, such as children filling out an expense report or reading a technical manual as they have observed their parents doing
>
>*Religious purposes*, such as reading the Bible, church newsletter, or Sunday School materials
>
>*Interpersonal communication*, interacting with people physically or temporally removed through cards, letters, or thank-you notes
>
>*Participation in information networks*, such as reading the sports page of the newspaper or a magazine, or reading a calendar of events
>
>*Children's literature*, such as an adult or older sibling reading a picture book to a young child
>
>*Teaching/learning*, such as learning the basic skills of letter formation

Literacy Learning at School

The following description of a second-grade classroom will describe several literacy behaviors that are occurring simultaneously. Shawana has just finished her collage. She unfastens her name tag and uses it as a model to print her name on her paper. Raphael and Levon are using magnetic alphabet letters to spell the name of their favorite dinosaur, Tyrannosaurus Rex. Kyle has learned the song "We Wish You a Merry Christmas" and now he is singing along with the words in a picture book by the same title (Pearson, 1983). Frankie and Wen-Shen have heard the book *Whose Mouse Are You?* (Kraus, 1970) so often that they memorized it and now they are reading it in unison. Each of these examples is literacy in action.

Literacy and Computer Software

When microcomputers first arrived in classrooms, most of the software that enabled children to word-process relied on their keyboarding (typing) skills. In addition, many of the programs would not accept nonconventional spellings (i.e., "hav" for "have"), something that was often frustrating for beginning writers and readers. Recent advances in technology have made computer software much more accessible to the young child. Some of the software enables children to speak their words, rather than type them, and then see their spoken words transformed into print on the screen. Computer software that connects oral language with written language in this concrete yet flexible way is a tremendous literacy-learning tool in early childhood. Appendix B contains guidelines for evaluating early childhood language arts software, some recommended programs, and resources for software reviews.

Acquiring Literacy with Print

What is involved in learning to read and write? Is it knowledge? Surely a person's knowledge influences his or her level of literacy with print. Is literacy a complex set of abilities that the child must practice in order to master? Certainly abilities such as decoding of words or spelling them correctly rely upon skill to some extent. But reading is not simply seeing words or even deciphering them. The reader must understand what is seen and deciphered. Writing is more than copying. The writer must compose his or her ideas and make them understandable to readers. "Texts consisting of only a few simple words repeated in equally simple and stilted sentence patterns are typically less predictable and thus more difficult to read than texts consisting of a greater variety of words that occur in more natural sentence patterns resembling normal speech" (Weaver, 1989, p. 7). The real skill in reading and writing is "intelligent construction by the child" (Ferreiro and Teberosky, 1982, p. 345).

The equation that literacy is basically knowledge plus skill has dominated much of our thinking and instruction in America during the last several hundred years. Increasingly, early childhood educators and experts in the field of literacy are looking at literacy in a different way.

Lilian Katz (1988) suggests that although knowledge and skill are types of learning, there are at least two other categories of learning. These she calls "dispositions" and "feelings." *Dispositions* are "habits of mind," such as being curious or persistent. Dispositions, Katz (1988) argues, are learned from other people, from role models. The fourth level of learning, *feelings*, is defined as the learner's emotional responses to the learning situation. A child might feel pressured when the teacher says impatiently, "Everyone should be finished now and ready for story-time." Or, a child might feel elated after she shares her story about leaving her puppy behind and moving into an apartment when a classmate says, "I liked your story and you know what? I have a puppy and you could come over and play with it sometimes if your Mom would let you." Of course, these examples of immediate responses to literacy activities. We also know that responses to the language arts are often deeper and more enduring, like the college student who still fondly remembers Ezra Jack Keat's (1962) book, *The Snowy Day* (Mikkelsen, 1989).

What do feelings and dispositions like these have to do with print-related activities? Quite a bit. Frank Smith (1989), one of the leading authorities on literacy, has this to say:

> *Literacy is a social phenomenon. Individuals become literate, not from the formal instruction but from what they read and write about and who they read and write with . . . . Many students leave school having learned the "basics" of reading and writing but with no inclination ever to pursue these activities voluntarily; they have no understanding of what literacy can do for them (apart from getting them through school). How literate are they? Literacy is not a set of skills or a finished state; it is an attitude toward the world. A literate attitude makes learning to read and write both possible and productive. (pp. 354–355)*

How does a literate attitude develop in children? It seems to be based on literacy events.

The Literacy Event: Key to Literacy

In order for an athlete to learn and practice a team sport, he or she must participate in sporting events. In order for children to become literate in the Western Culture sense of reading and writing, they must participate in literacy events. **Literacy events** are situations when a piece of writing is integral to the nature of the participants' interaction and their interpretive processes (Heath, 1982). Using this definition, a child who is absentmindedly copying a poem from the chalkboard onto a piece of paper is not engaged in a literacy event. There are two reasons why. First, there is no social interaction and second, the writing is being transcribed rather than interpreted. Moreover, the child may not be focused on the message. Using Heath's (1982) definition, relatively little of what occurs in an ordinary classroom might qualify as a literacy event. But before it begins to seem like literacy events are unusual or difficult to provide, let's look at three examples that meet the criteria of (a) social interaction focused on a piece of writing, and (b) involvement in interpretive process.

Nick's Literacy Event

Nick, a three-year-old, talks and sings for his cousin Maria while he builds with blocks:

Nick: "I build wif (with) me Mommy's song 'kay?"

Maria: "Sure Nick, build whatever you want!"

Nick: (begins to sing) "London Bridge is building up, building up, building up. London Bridge is building up, my fair yady (lady)." (while he is singing he is constructing a bridge) "I haf (have) to build a bridge 'cause 'cause de're (they're) hard for to build . . ." (pause) and I always singed London Bridge wif (with) me Mommy, so yook (look), I'm done pretty soon!"

Maria: "Wow! You could drive a pretend car under your bridge, Nick."

Nick: "No, you can't, 'cause it can fall down—and show ya how, Ria (Maria)." (Nick begins to tug at the big "B" block and as he pulls it out slowly the other blocks fall.)

Nick: "See, Mommy says, London Bridge is falling down, falling down, falling down. London Bridge is falling down my fair yady (lady)!" (Nick now laughs.) "See Ria, it falled down. It's not gonna have a car pretend to go under no more! It's gonna need work. It's done now (laughing)!"

Maria: "You're right, Nick, it's done now! I have an idea: let's build *another* bridge and I'll show you how to make a sign for it." (Nick nods enthusiastically)

Nick's obvious enjoyment of words and play with the sounds of language portend well for his future language development. Nick has acquired **phonological awareness**, a sensitivity to the sounds of language. There is still considerable debate about the relationship between phonological awareness and learning to read and write. As Ehri and Wilce (1985) point out, it could be that (a) phonological awareness is a prerequisite for literacy with print, (b) phonological awareness facilitates literacy with print, or (c) phonological awareness and literacy are related, but the apparent relationship is coincidental. Young children bring different strengths to the task of becoming literate. These talents may be primarily hereditary or may be the result of parental encouragement. Whatever their source, children seem to fall into four basic categories where literacy with print is concerned: (1) those who have an aptitude for meaning and an aptitude for the sounds of language, (2) those who have good comprehension but not a sensitivity to sound, (3) those who are sensitive to the sounds of language, but not meaning, and (4) those who need help with both (Pinsent, 1988).

Rebekah's Literacy Event
A second example of a literacy event involves drawing and writing about an experience. Five-year-old Rebekah drew and wrote the letter to her grandma in Figure 2.1 and this is what she said about it:

> *"This is the doll that you made me, I love her. I caught a butterfly, Grandma, but she only had one wing. Daddy said she was suffering and we couldn't fix her. He made me go inside and he made the butterfly go to sleep.*
> *I wish you would come back to your house so I could visit you. I love you.*

Rebekah's letter and interaction with her father meet the dual criteria for a literacy event: there is *social interaction* focused on a piece of writing and the five-year-old *interprets* her drawing and writings in words.

Dianesha's Literacy Event
Now let's look at another common literacy event, storybook reading. Dianesha, age six, has heard Rosemary Wells' (1981) *Timothy Goes to School* a few times and now she is reading it to her mother:

FIGURE 2.1   Rebekah's Letter to Her Grandma.

Text of the Book	*Dianesha's Retelling*
Timothy's mother made him a brand new suit.	Timothy's mother braid, (pause) made him a brand new sunsuit.
Timothy went to school in his new sunsuit with his new book and his new pencil.	Timothy went to school with his new *sunset*-suit, with his one (pause) new book and his pencil.
Claude, this is Timothy	Claude this is Timmy, Tim-o-thy

Mother: "Uh oh, here's the part where Claude makes fun of the sunsuit Timothy's mom made for him."

Dianesha: "Yeah. Claude is a real brat. Just like Matthew at my kindergarten. He always says 'You're doing that wrong,' or 'That's an ugly picture.' It ruins my whole day."

The Literacy Process

In each of three preceding examples, a piece of writing is the focal point of social interaction and interpretation. These three incidents also illustrate **literacy process**. The literacy process has four universal elements (Harste, Burke, and Woodward, 1981):

1. *Textual intent*—There is a written message which has communication as its purpose
2. *Negotiability*—The meaning of that message is interpreted by the child and the intended audience
3. *Language used to fine-tune language*—In order to clarify the message, the child uses more language
4. *Risk taking*—The child accepts new challenges in language

These features of the literacy event and the literacy process also suggest reasons why some children who have the ability to become literate do not become literate with print. Ogbu (1980) contends that illiteracy is not the cause of exclusion from the "good life," but the result. This means that when children are deprived of literacy events, however humble those events might seem, their language growth suffers.

Conclusion

As we have seen, it is entirely possible for children to do "schoolwork" and continue to be deprived of authentic experiences with print. Increasingly, our concept of literacy is moving beyond the cognitive, intellectual realm and into the affective, emotional realm. In 1987, Hirsh coined the phrase **cultural literacy**. He argued that literacy was more than a matter of learning basic skills in reading and writing. "A culturally literate person is someone who uses what he or she knows about the culture to understand the self and to enrich life" (Shuster, 1989, p. 540). As Shuster points out, the mere accumulation of knowledge is not enough. If it were, computers would be more "literate" than people. So the child who is truly literate, the culturally literate child, can *use* what he or she has learned through visual images, through oral language, and through literacy with print.

Summary

Young children's literacy skills may be conceptualized in three categories: visual literacy (ability to interpret visual images), oracy (listening and speaking) and literacy with print (reading and writing). Parents make an important contribution to the child's growth in literacy before he or she enters school. Both at home and at school, the keys to fostering children's literacy learning are an understanding of the literacy process and the provision of literacy events. Literacy is not simply what the child knows about language but how he or she uses that knowledge to communicate, to function in society, and to enrich life.

Focus On: Private Speech: Children Talking to Themselves

Adults rarely talk aloud to themselves in public, partly because others might think they are mentally unstable and partly because most of us want our thoughts to remain private. With young children, it is quite another story. They have not learned to be concerned with others listening in on their inner speech, and **private speech**, or talking aloud to themselves, is common. This "speech for oneself" (Vygotsky, 1962) is an interesting part of language development because it is a way of glimpsing the interaction between thought and language. One question that has been debated in the past was "Does thought develop through language or does language develop through thought?" Vygotsky held that language enabled people to think, while Piaget argued that thought enabled people to use language. Actually, they were both right. Most researchers now believe that thought and language are interrelated and that intellectual milestones and language growth go hand-in-hand. The study of children's private speech gives us a glimpse of thought and language interacting. Some of the questions often asked by parents about this behavior and research-based answers are presented below.

Is It Normal for a Child to Talk to Himself or Herself?

Evidently, private speech is commonplace. Berk (1985) reports that children between the ages of four and ten use private speech in about 20 percent of their language. Private speech enables the child to relate vocal speech with his or her inner thought in a more concrete way (Vygotsky, 1962).

Is There More Than One Type of Private Speech?

The young child's private speech takes on a number of different forms. Private speech usually begins as word play and repetition (Kohlberg, Yaeger, and Hjertholm, 1968). Then it becomes "self-coaching" that mirrors the kind of positive social interactions children have with the important people in their lives. Listen to Reynaldo, a kindergarten boy who is completing a math activity that he missed when he was absent from school. The lesson is on units of measure and he is using paper clips to measure pictures of fish in various sizes:

> *"Hey, fish! You are blue, blue, blue. I like the color blue. (arranges the paper clips across the fish). He is seven long. (reads the instructions and looks at the sample item) I got to write that down. Now I got to do the next fish. All done with that one and only one more. This is ugly . . . ugly-mugly fish. I stuck one of those clips right in his eye. (begins to hum*

a tune) I'm done! Where is the teacher? Oh, over there. (the teacher instructs him on how to record his findings and he resumes working) 1, 2, 3, 4, 5, 6, 7, 8, 9. Nine. 1, 2, 3, 4, 5, 6, 7. Seven paper clips. Count, count, 3, 4, 5, 6, 7, 8. Eight paper clips. I am gettin' tired of this counting, but I got to count. 1, 2, 3, 4, 5, 6, the last fish, the last fish has six. Now I gotta draw."

Why Do Children Talk to Themselves?

Reynaldo's words illustrate many of the purposes for private speech, including the following

1. To address nonhuman objects ("Hey fish . . .")
2. For word play and repetition ("ugly . . . ugly-mugly")
3. To describe their own activities ("I stuck one of these clips right in his eye.")
4. To express emotions ("I'm getting tired of counting . . .")
5. To regulate motor behavior ("count, count, 1, 2, 3")
6. To self-answer questions ("Where is the teacher? Oh, there she is.")
7. For fantasy play and relaxation (humming a tune)
8. For praise and self-reinforcement ("I'm done!")
9. To facilitate transitions ("Now I gotta draw.")
10. To focus attention on the task at hand ("the last fish has . . .")
11. When learning to read ("I got to write that down.")

When Do Children Usually Stop Using Private Speech?

By the time that most children are in first or second grade, they begin to whisper or mutter inaudibly rather than talk out loud, at least when there are other people around. Finally, it becomes silent inner speech or thought (Kohlberg, Yaeger, and Hjertholm, 1968). But even after "speech for oneself" has apparently disappeared, mature human beings will often revert to private speech if they are facing a complicated, stressful task or feel confident that no one else can overhear them.

In the Field: A Personal Profile of Literacy Development

Arrange to interview at least one person who has been a primary caregiver for a young child. You may interview a parent, grandparent, day-care teacher, etc. It is important that the adult know one particular child very well and has been responsible for the child's care over an extended period of time. You may choose to interview your parent(s) about your own or a sibling's language development. If you are a parent, you may want to answer these questions about your child or be interviewed by a classmate. Obtain responses to the following questions:

1. When did _____ begin to talk? What were _____'s first words? first sentences?
2. What fingerplays, songs, rhymes, stories, books, or activities did _____ enjoy as an infant, toddler, or preschooler?
   infant:
   toddler:
   preschooler:
3. Did _____ ask to hear the same book over and over again? Which one? (give book title if possible)
4. Did _____ ever pretend to read? (Please describe)
   Did _____ ever memorize a favorite book? Which one(s)?
5. Did _____ ever attend any special programs (such as storytime at the library)?
6. Has _____ begun to read? When and where did _____ first learn to read?
7. Does _____ scribble, draw, or write? What kinds of things does he or she write? Do you have any samples that you can share?

Summary Statement: What oral and written language skills has this child acquired? Use the information from this chapter to summarize and organize your findings.

References

Berk, L. (1985). Why children talk to themselves. *Young Children, 40*, 46–52.

Bolles, E. B. (1982). *So much to say*. New York: St. Martin's Press.

Chafe, W. L. (1985). Linguistic differences produced by differences between speaking and writing. In D. R. Olson, N. Torrance, and A. Hilyard (Eds.), *Literacy, language and learning* (pp. 105–123). London: Cambridge University.

Cox, C. (1989). Focus on film as an expressive art. In S. Hoffman and L. Lamme (Eds.), *Learning from the inside out: The expressive arts* (pp. 35–43). Wheaton, MD: Association for Childhood Education International.

Ehri, L. C., and Wilce, L. S. (1985). Movement into reading: Is the first stage of printed word learning visual or phonetic? *Reading Research Quarterly, 20*(2), 163–179.

Ferreiro, E., and Teberosky, A. (1982). *Literacy before schooling*. Exeter, NH: Heinemann, 1982.

Graham, T. L. (1986). *Fingerplays and rhymes for always and sometimes*. Atlanta, GA: Humanics.

Grayson, M. F. (1962). *Let's do fingerplays*. New York: David McKay.

Harste, J. C. (1989). In M. Siegel and R. F. Carey (Eds.) *Critical thinking: A semiotic perspective*. Bloomington, IN: ERIC Clearinghouse on Reading and Communication Skills.

Harste, J. C., Burke, C., and Woodward, V. (1981). *Children, their language and world: Initial encounters with print*. Bloomington, IN: Indiana University.

Heath, S. B. (1982). *Ways with words*. New York: Cambridge University Press.

Hirsch, E. D. (1987). *Cultural literacy: What every American needs to know*. Boston: Houghton Mifflin.

Hymes, J. (1981). *Teaching the child under six*. (3rd ed.). Columbus, OH: Merrill.

Katz, L. (1988). *Early childhood education: What research tells us*. Bloomington, IN: Phi Delta Kappa.

Kohlberg, L., Yaeger, J., and Hjertholm, E. (1968). Private speech: Four studies and a review of theories. *Child Development, 34*, 691–736.

Lacy, L. E. (1986). *Art and design in children's picture books.* Chicago: American Library Association.

Mikkelsen, N. (1989). Remembering Ezra Jack Keats and *The Snowy Day*: What makes a children's book good? *Language Arts, 66*(6), 608–624.

Nickerson, R. S. (1981). Speech understanding and reading: Some similarities and differences. In O. J. L. Tzeng and H. Singer (Eds.), *Perceptions of print: Reading research in experimental psychology* (pp. 257–289). Hillsdale, NJ: Erlbaum.

Ogbu, J. U. (1980). Literacy in subordinate cultures: The case of Black Americans. Paper delivered at Library of Congress Conference on Literacy. Washington, DC.

Pinsent, P. (1988). The implications of recent research into early reading. *Early Child Development and Care, 36*, 65–70.

Purves, A. (1990). *The scribal society: An essay on literacy and schooling in the information age.* White Plains, NY: Longman.

Read, D., and Smith, J. (1982). Teaching visual literacy through wordless picture books. *Reading Teacher, 35*, 928–933.

Scott, L. B. (1983). *Rhymes for learning times.* Minneapolis, MN: Dennison.

Seefeldt, C., and Barbour, N. (1986). *Early childhood education.* Columbus, OH: Merrill.

Shuster, E. (1989). In pursuit of cultural literacy. *Phi Delta Kappan, 70*(7), 539–542.

Smith, F. (1984). A metaphor for literacy: Creating worlds or shunting information? In D. R. Olson, N. Torrance, and A. Hildyard (Eds.), *Literacy, language and learning* (pp. 195–213). London: Cambridge University.

Smith F. (1989). Overselling literacy. *Phi Delta Kappan, 70*(5), 352–359.

Snow, C. (1983). Literacy and language: Relationships during preschool years. *Harvard Educational Review, 53*(2), 165–189.

Teale, W. H. (1986). Home background in young children's literacy development. In W. H. Teale and E. Sulzby (Eds.), *Emergent literacy: Reading and writing* (pp. 173–206). Norwood, NJ: Ablex.

Teale, W. H. (1984). Reading to young children: Its significance for literacy development. In H. Gollman, A. A. Oberg, and F. Smith (Eds.), *Awakening to literacy* (pp. 110–130). Portsmouth, NH: Heinemann.

Vygotsky, L. (1962). *Thought and language.* Cambridge, MA: M.I.T. Press.

Wilkinson, A. (1970). The concept of oracy. *English Journal, 59*, 70–77.

Children's Books

Clark, D. (1978). *The encyclopedia of how it's made.* New York: A & W.

Cohen, B. (1983). *Molly's Pilgrim.* New York: Lothrop, Lee, and Shepard.

Freeman, D. (1983). *Corduroy.* New York: Penguin.

Keats, E. J. (1962). *The snowy day.* New York: Viking.

Kraus, R. (1970). *Whose mouse are you?* New York: Scholastic.

Macauley, D. (1988). *The way things work.* Boston: Houghton Mifflin.

Mayer, M. (1974). *Frog goes to dinner.* New York: Dial.

Pearson, T. C. (1983). *We wish you a Merry Christmas.* New York: Dial.

Wells, R. (1981). *Timothy goes to school.* New York: Dial.

Zion, G. (1956). *Harry the dirty dog.* New York: Harper & Row.

Photo: Anne Peterson

3

The Child-Centered Language Arts Classroom

OUTLINE

Conclusion
Summary
Focus On: Classroom Management in a Child-Centered
Language Arts Program
In the Field: Observing Children's Learning Process

*Curriculum is often thought of as a course of study—content to be taught, skills
to be mastered . . . When the goal of the language arts curriculum is seen as the
exploration and expansion of human potential . . . then growth can be seen as
continuous and the curriculum as the mental trip that the language user takes
during a literacy event . . . what we ought to do is to establish an environment
in which the child can experience and come to value the psycholinguistic and
sociolinguistic activities we associate with successful written language use and
learning.*
—JEROME HARSTE, VIVIAN WOODWARD, AND CAROLYN BURKE (1984)

KEY CONCEPTS AND TERMS

curriculum	process-oriented
whole child	child-initiated activity
whole language	integration of language arts
developmentally appropriate practice	project method
technician	demonstrations
decision-maker	individualization
content-oriented	philosophy-reality conflicts
	classroom management

The poet William Blake once said, "I must create a system or be enslaved by another man's." As early childhood educators, we too can design instructional systems or allow someone else to make all of our decisions for us. But whether we take the path less traveled or the path of least resistance, curriculum is the result. **Curriculum** is the overall plan for promoting children's learning. It includes all of the experiences and activities in an educational program (English, 1983; Hendrick, 1986).

The Child-Centered Classroom

One of the most important questions facing early childhood educators today is: What sort of curriculum is suitable for young children? The ideal early childhood curriculum is one that provides for all areas of a child's development: physical, emotional, social, and cognitive. A quality curriculum for young children is planned with attention to the needs, interests, and developmental levels of each child (Bredekamp, 1987).

> *A developmentally based preschool must dovetail with the active, exploring mode that is natural to the child: encourage fantasy and playfulness; lay the groundwork for a vigorous style of intellectual curiosity and learning, personally motivated rather than externally dominated; and connect language concepts, and the beginning process of reading and writing to meaningful experience and communication. (Minuchin, 1987, p. 250)*

Because quality early childhood programs address every aspect of the young child's development, programs with this philosophy are also referred to as a "total curriculum," one that educates the **whole child**.

> *. . . early childhood educators recognize that the domains of development are intertwined. Consequently, the language of early childhood education is the language of the "whole child" . . . integrated experiential learning has been the constant cornerstone of early care and education. With Dewey, Froebel, Piaget and Pestalozzi as its pedagogical pioneers, early childhood education espouses the development of social competence, embracing and integrating children's physical, social, emotional and cognitive development. (Kagan, 1989, pp. 108, 109)*

In the teaching of language arts, this is referred to as a **whole language** philosophy (Graves, 1983).

Developmentally Appropriate Practice (DAP) in Language Arts

In language arts, a developmentally appropriate early childhood curriculum

- enables children to build on their existing knowledge of written and oral language
- builds positive attitudes in children toward their own emerging literacy abilities
- promote meaningful verbal interaction, not only from teacher to child, but also from child to teacher and child to child
- supports the child when confronted by linguistic challenges
- involves children in meaningful listening, speaking, reading, and writing experiences
- encourages the child to use language at the most sophisticated level possible
- uses predictable types of language to build the child's confidence as a learner of language (Early Childhood Literacy Development Committee, 1985; Snow, 1983).

As you become a professional in the field of early childhood education, what sort of language arts curriculum will you provide? To a considerable extent, this will depend upon what you believe and value.

Two Classroom Scenarios

The following descriptions of two classrooms will enable you to see two very different language arts curricula in action.

Scenario 1: Ms. Park

Ms. Park teaches 28 five-year-olds in a full-day public school kindergarten. She arrives at school early so that she can make copies of worksheets for her students. These worksheets include such tasks as matching familiar objects, identifying the initial consonant of pictured objects, cutting and pasting pictures in the correct sequence, coloring in the lines, and tracing dotted alphabet letters. Each evening, Ms. Park corrects the papers. Her grading system is a star, a sticker, or a "smiley face" for excellent work, an "OK" for satisfactory work, and a frowny face or negative comment ("Messy work," "Pay attention") for poor work. Throughout most of the morning, children are expected to work quietly at their seats so that Ms. Park can meet with each of the three reading groups for approximately twenty minutes. The reading groups are determined by ability: high, medium, or low. The children in the groups take turns identifying letters or, if they are in the top reading group, they are learning to recognize common words by sight, such as: *I, in, not, go the*. After reading groups, the children have phonics in a large group for approximately thirty minutes. They follow along in their workbooks as Ms. Park goes over each item on the page. Some of the children are obviously confused by today's lesson on the sound of *h*. When she asks for words that begin with the "huh" sound, one child suggests "umbrella" and several others agree that "umbrella" has the sound of *h*. Ms. Park has eighteen minutes to devote to handwriting. She wants the children to practice writing their names correctly so that they can put their names on their papers. Ms. Park feels satisfied that she has individualized the work by preparing a tracing page for each child with his or her first and last name. She stayed after school last night to laminate the pages so that children could wipe the crayon off and continue to practice their names. The remainder of the day is for lunch, recess, math workbooks, a science or social studies activity, and "specials" (art, music, physical education). Ms. Park usually saves a picture book for the end of the day and reads the story while she dismisses children to get their coats, one row at a time.

Scenario 2: Mrs. Sanchez

Ms. Sanchez is a kindergarten teacher in an urban area where many of the Spanish-speaking students are newly immigrated to the United States. Her instructional day begins with a chart-sized version of *You'll Soon Grow Into Them, Titch* (Hutchins, 1983). She introduces the new book by discussing the cover and title with the children, relating the story to the children's experience, and inviting them to hypothesize about the plot. Next, she reads the story aloud, pointing to the words as she says them. The story is read again. This time she pauses for comments and questions. Because the story has a catchy refrain, most of Ms. Sanchez's 30 students are able to read along with at least a portion of the book by the third reading. After the story, children have many activities from which to choose: drawing pictures, dictating original stories, enacting a scene from the story, creating a puppet play, listening to the story again on tape, or reading a familiar book with a partner.

Students are encouraged to write. Some make scribbles, squiggles, and letter-like forms, some write collections of the letters that they know, and others are beginning to match sounds with letters. In Ms. Sanchez's room, children move about freely and converse with their teacher. There are three dramatic play centers in the room; an office, a toy store, and a post office. The office contains an old typewriter, paper and envelopes, rubber stamps, a stapler, and paper clips. The toy store contains old toys (donated by the teachers and parents), play money, order blanks, a cash register, gift cards, and recycled wrapping paper. The post office has a service "window" made from a refrigerator box, a mail slot, a mail carrier's bag and cap, Christmas stickers (used as postage stamps), and a cancellation stamp that Ms. Sanchez has made from styrofoam. Later in the day, children will share the work they have done with other class members. Ms. Sanchez takes home children's stories, letters, and drawings, and writes questions or comments rather than grading them. Shelly has created a party invitation for her birthday party at the rollerskating rink (Figure 3.1). Ms. Sanchez writes her a note: "This sounds like fun! Happy birthday, Shelly."

Using the guidelines for developmentally appropriate curriculum, it is clear that Ms. Sanchez's classroom comes closer to a child-centered language arts environment than Ms. Park's.

FIGURE 3.1   Shelly's Birthday Party Invitation.

How Teachers' Assumptions Affect Curriculum

Ms. Park, like every teacher, is operating from a set of assumptions about how young children learn. She feels that it is her job to get them prepared for literacy by presenting small, digestible bits of information. She believes that pointing out children's errors is the best way to help them become literate. To some extent, Ms. Park is teaching as she was taught. Much of her day is spent supervising children as they plow through the materials she feels obligated or pressured to use. If her students are quiet and diligent, they "fit in" with the school culture in which she works. Children's literature is often neglected by Ms. Park because her curriculum is so overloaded with paperwork. Perhaps she feels as this kindergarten teacher does:

> *My concern is that as more and more companies publish kindergarten workbooks, worksheets, ditto materials, letters to parents and that sort of thing, I see a huge volume of printed materials for kindergarten becoming available . . . I find myself doing more and more . . . when I really don't feel that they [children] learn that much or learn that way.* (quoted in Hatch and Freeman, 1988, p. 22)

Ms. Sanchez is operating from a completely different set of assumptions. She thinks that children know quite a bit about language already and that it is her job to encourage them to want to know more. She is teaching as she feels young children should be taught, regardless of what she experienced as a child or what the pre-packaged teaching materials may suggest. About children's literature, she says, "I couldn't teach without it! I get most of my good ideas from picture books. My curriculum is literature-based." Ms. Sanchez also believes that a classroom should be a place where animated conversation is commonplace. She seems to trust children and have confidence in her own ability to facilitate many different activities at once. Ms. Sanchez really listens when she talks with children. In addition, she enjoys reviewing children's work because it gives her an opportunity to assess each child's growth in literacy and reaffirms her belief that children are imaginative, resourceful learners of language.

Technician or Decision-Maker?

In comparing these two teachers we could say that Ms. Park is functioning as a **technician** while Ms. Sanchez is functioning as a **decision-maker** (Barbour, 1986; Jalongo, 1986). Technicians and decision-makers differ dramatically in terms of their perceptions of the teacher's role, assumptions about the child, source of authority, and dominant mode of communication (see Table 3.1)

Content-Oriented or Process-Oriented?

How might we describe the educational philosophies of these two very different classrooms? Ms. Park's classroom could best be described as **content-oriented**. It is

TABLE 3-1   Technician or Decision-maker: Which Will You Be?

Technician	*Decision-maker*
PERCEPTIONS OF TEACHER'S ROLE	
Transmitting what textbook publishers or programs dictate; curriculum decisions are limited to procedural matters	Shaping the curriculum—changing or omitting goals, extending or adding materials, or creating a well-balanced curriculum
ASSUMPTIONS ABOUT THE CHILD	
Students should fit in to the predetermined curriculum; learn primarily by listening	Curriculum should be adapted to meet the child's needs; child is an active partner in the learning process
SOURCE OF AUTHORITY	
External mandates, administrative dictums, parental pressure	Knowledge of child development and experience with young children
DOMINANT MODE OF COMMUNICATION	
Simple, one way—(from adult to child)	Complex, interactive, (adult to child, child to child, child to adult)

Sources: Barbour, N. (1986), Teachers can make decisions, *Childhood Education*, 62(5), 322–323. Moyer, J. (1986), Child development as a base for decision making, *Childhood Education*, 62(5), 325–330.

governed by teacher-directed, prepackaged curriculum. The goal is to cover the material and get every child "on track," conforming to the content demands of the written material. Each day, many products (papers) are completed and these products are evaluated by quality control (in this case, the teacher). Those who submit to the expectations of this paper curriculum get rewarded; those who do not get negative feedback. More good products mean that everything is operating smoothly. Sounds like a factory assembly line, doesn't it? That is because this efficiency approach really *does* seems to make the assumption that we are preparing children to become adult factory workers in a highly industrialized nation (Callahan, 1962).

If this is true, then what orientation is reflected in a classroom like Ms. Sanchez's? The children in her class have more autonomy. They make choices, based upon their own needs and interests. They participate in decisions about which topics, processes, equipment, and space to use. Children also have a say in determining how much time to devote to a learning activity. Instead of being motivated by external rewards, this **process-oriented** motivation comes from within as children see that they are capable of producing high-quality work (Glasser, 1990). Ms. Sanchez's classroom makes the assumption that we are preparing children for the information age, a time when interpersonal skills, creativity, and self-directedness are at a premium.

Past, Present, or Future?

The way that we envision the future of the children in our society influences curriculum. Kagan (1989) asks, "Are preschool programs preparing youngsters for kindergarten and the demands of schooling, or are they preparing children for later life, when motivation, curiosity, and creativity are important skills? How one answers this question determines the curricular orientation that will be established" (p. 436).

We know that tomorrow's workers need to be "responsible, self-disciplined, able to learn and equipped with problem-solving skills" (Research and Policy Committee, 1985, pp. 17–18). They have to "figure out what they need to know, where to get it, and how to make meaning of it" (Task Force on Teaching as a Profession, 1986, p. 20). The best way to educate children for the future is to make our curriculum child centered.

Child-Centered Teaching Strategies

What general teaching strategies will prepare the children of today for the challenging world of tomorrow?

Direct Instruction vs. Child-Initiated Activity

The ancient philosopher Comenius once observed that it is the teacher's goal "to seek and find a method by which teachers teach less and learners learn more." Not only do people learn more when they participate in decisions about their own learning, they also enjoy it more. In 1915, John and Evelyn Dewey (1915/1962) talked about the differences between direct instruction and **child-initiated activity** by calling them "old" and "new" education, respectively:

> The old education . . . may be summed by stating that the center of gravity is outside the child. It is in the teacher, the textbook, and anywhere and everywhere you please except in the immediate instincts and activities of the child himself . . . Now the change which is coming into our education is shifting the center of gravity . . . The child becomes the sun about which the appliances of education revolve. He is the center about which they are organized. (p. 4)

Ironically, many of our "modern" programs for young children sound more like Dewey's description of the *old* education!

The assumption of the old education was that all children needed was information. Because adults have more information than children, they become founts of wisdom. Teaching a child becomes comparable to packing a suitcase—the more we can stuff in and manage to keep from falling out, the more successful we have been. Direct instruction, in which the teacher mostly talks and the child mostly listens, is the "old" education Dewey describes.

This is not to say that there are no appropriate uses for direct instruction, however. It is ideal for teaching discrete, low-level learning tasks as rapidly as possible. So if a child needs to learn how to skip or tie a shoe or use scissors, direct instruction is appropriate. For a complex task like literacy learning, however, direct instruction is of very limited value. The instructional approach that is best suited to the mastery of complex tasks is child-initiated activity.

Child-Initiated Activity

When the child is treated as an active participant in the learning process (rather than a passive recipient of someone else's information), child-initiated activity is taking place. Child-initiated activity (Schweinhart, 1988):

- *Acknowledges both the developmental limits of young children and their potential for learning.* It does not fall into "the sooner-the-better" philosophy of pressuring children, nor does it take a *laissez-faire* approach where teachers sit back and wait for children to become "ready" to read.
- *Allows the child to choose from among several alternatives.* This means that the teacher structures the environment, provides different materials, and facilitates children's learning. It does not mean that the teacher ignores the environment, preselects all the materials, and assigns children work that results in some predetermined product.
- *Emphasizes reciprocal communication.* In child-initiated activity children interact, not only with adults, but also with peers, thus extending the child's opportunities to practice functional language skills.

Developmental Language Learning

The language arts curriculum is fundamentally different from other school curricula. As Moffett and Wagner (1983) point out, language learning ". . . is now a *new* subject, and it is not even a *subject*. It permeates every part of people's lives . . ." (p. 38). Temple and Gillet (1989) go on to say:

> Language arts as a subject has always run the risk of being reduced to nonsense because it is really not a body of content, but a set of processes. Mathematics, science, social studies, and health can each lay claim to a body of facts that can be imparted during an hour a day, year after year. But when we try to create a subject of language arts in the image of these others, we condemn children to rules for punctuation. In other words, we teach the peripherals of the language arts, and miss the substance. (p. 27)

One way to avoid missing the meaning is by designing programs that have these attributes (Holdaway, 1979):

> *Emulative*—children see adults and other children using language in interesting ways

Consistently purposeful—what the learners are doing has meaning for them; what the teachers are doing is satisfying to them as well

Globally activating—the activities have consequences beyond the confines of school

Powerfully reinforced—children are motivated by the power of being able to communicate more effectively

Meaningfully related to other aspects of development—language is not seen as an object, but as a means of communication

Supported, regulated, and paced by the learner—a child does not suffer the frustration of doing work that is far too difficult, nor the boredom of doing work that is unchallenging

Integrating the Language Arts

Another important concept in which the language arts are concerned is integration. If you examined a daily schedule for a primary classroom, you might see 50 minutes allotted for reading, 20 minutes for spelling, 15 minutes for writing, 15 minutes for reading aloud or listening, and no time designated for speaking. In this sort of schedule, the language arts are fragmented rather than integrated. **Integration of the language arts** may be conceptualized in three basic ways (Wagner, 1985, p. 1):

Interdependent—An integrated approach encourages the child to learn and use reading, writing, and speaking skills together, rather than as separate subjects. The assumption is that the child's abilities in each area of the language arts are interrelated with the others.

Irreducible—An integrated approach assumes that each of the language arts cannot be reduced to small, isolated components. Instead, reading, writing, speaking, and listening are conceptualized wholistically.

Cross-curricular—In an integrated view, the language arts are not detached from the other content areas. Instead, facility with language is a fundamental ability that cuts across all the traditional subject areas, including science, social studies, mathematics, art, and music.

Instructional Strategies for an Integrated Curriculum

Some specific techniques that teachers can use to deliver an integrated early childhood language arts curriculum are **projects**, **demonstrations**, and **individualization**.

The Project Method, Demonstrations, and Individualization

Consider the following early childhood memories of three college students:

In second grade, we built a huge baby brontosaurus out of wood, chicken wire, papier maché and paint. It took weeks of searching through reference materials to plan it and even longer to construct it. I guess the classroom teacher and the art teacher decided that it would be a "grand finale" to the unit on dinosaurs. When it was finished, we put our dinosaur on display in the cafeteria. It was accompanied by an illustrated poster modeled after those we had seen in the museum. We even wrote a script and created a tour tape. Looking back on it now, I realize how much we learned about science, math, reading and just plain cooperation."

In nursery school, one child's grandfather (who had recently retired) volunteered to build some shelves. Evidently, what began as a good deed ended up being a long-term commitment because he used to visit every week. Not only did he build things for us and show us things he had built, he also helped us with our own woodworking projects. I think my conversations and cooperative planning with Mr. Stanislaski are the reason I feel at home with a hammer, saw and nails today!

Ms. L. loved Beatrix Potter, and so did we. We heard Beatrix Potter books and marveled at Ms. L's collection of toys, china, music boxes, and needlework with a Beatrix Potter motif. We enacted scenes from our favorite characters, made puppets (mine was Jemima Puddleduck) and did drawings, paintings, recipes, and a class newspaper—all with the Beatrix Potter theme. It was a pure delight.

Notice some of the things that these memorable childhood learning experiences share: they are relevant; they require active participation from children; they involve a substantial time commitment; they have atypical content; and they involve children in meaningful listening, speaking, reading, and writing experiences. The dinosaur activity could be described as a project; the woodworking, a series of demonstrations; and the Beatrix Potter theme, an individualized literature-based unit of study. Each approach is developmentally appropriate, based on child-initiated activity, and integrates the language arts. In the sections that follow, you will examine each strategy in greater detail.

The Project Method

The project method has been around for decades. In 1918, Kilpatrick described a method that involved motor, aesthetic, and intellectual activities while emphasizing real life experiences. He defined a project as a wholehearted purposeful act carried on amid social surroundings. More recently, Katz has initiated a revival of the project approach (Katz and Chard, 1989). She defines a project as "an in-depth study or investigation that a group of children undertake on a particular topic or theme" (Katz, 1988, p. 30).

A recent article by Plourde (1989) describes a first-grade project on collections. The teacher began by sharing her personal collection of teddy bears. They discussed the bears' outfits, names, facial features, construction, and history. Next, the children voted for their favorite by stating a reason for their choice. Following this introduction to the concept of being a collector, children were put in small groups of three to five children. They were instructed to arrive at a group decision about what to collect during the next two weeks. The teacher ruled out expensive items and suggested things such as rocks, leaves, stamps, stickers, stuffed animals, and cloth. Then a note was sent home to the parents and each group was given a special box in the classroom to store their collection. By the end of the second week, each group made a 5 to 10 minute presentation. Other related activities were interviews with collectors from the local community; using the collections for classification and seriation; brainstorming lists of similarities and differences; guessing games (one object in a total collection was described and other children had to guess); and the creation of imaginary collections, such as a collection of extraterrestrials.

Demonstrations

Another powerful teaching strategy is the

> *opportunity to see how something is done. I shall call such opportunities demonstrations . . . The world continually provides demonstrations through people and through their products, by acts and by artifacts. (Smith, 1982, p. 108)*

The demonstration is an important teaching tool because it can be incredibly inviting. Think about the many times when persons, their products, or an artifact prompt us to try something without the slightest bit of direct persuasion. It could be a *person*, such as an excellent storyteller, a *product*, such as beautifully arranged flowers, or an *artifact*, such as a patchwork quilt.

A demonstration may be summarized in one sentence: Can you do _____ if I show you how? A good example is the teacher who wants to encourage students to write. Which of the following in each pair would motivate your students more?

a. Telling them that there are mailboxes in the classroom for their use or
b. Writing a note to each child and delivering it to their mailbox

a. Distributing paper and telling students to begin a journal or
b. Presenting several examples of children's books written as journal entries (Williams, 1981) and sharing some of *your* journal entries with them

a. Telling children to revise their writing or
b. Showing children five revisions of former students' writings so that they can see the revision process

Of course, you recognized that the second alternative in each pair was the more motivating of the two. That is because in every case, the second choice involved a demonstration.

Individualization

Ask teachers the best way to teach and most of them will say to individualize; ask them why they do not individualize and they will say they have too many students.

But individualizing does not require one-to-one teaching. Rather, teachers individualize by providing "an optimal match between the child's cognitive level and task demands" (Kitano, 1989, p. 163). The *activities* are the units of individualization of the child. How does this work? Kitano (1989) givs the example of a backyard field trip on vegetation. The samples of vegetation obtained by the children could be

observed and collected

categorized

analyzed in terms of their usefulness (from least to most useful)

the basis for predictions about how human life might be different without vegetation.

In this way, the same activity can range from simple to complex and every child can experience success at some level. Imagine all the different ways that each child might develop listening, speaking, reading, and writing skills through the backyard field trip. The linguistically gifted child who is already reading and writing might consult a book such as McMillan's (1988) *Counting Wildflowers* and create a wildflower display, complete with labels. Another child could participate in the discussion and collect many examples of the basic parts of a plant (leaf, stem, seed, root) and compare and contrast them within and across categories. A newly immigrated child who has not learned English could get a vocabulary lesson from listening and observing as each plant is discussed. So individualization does not mean preparing a different ditto sheet for each child. It means designing activities that provide many different alternatives and will meet young children's needs.

Philosophy-Reality Conflicts

There is tremendous pressure on early childhood educators to go against the "whole language" philosophy. A kindergarten teacher may believe that play is essential but finds he is expected to complete many pre-reading workbook pages every day. A first-grade teacher might recognize that many of her students need to listen to stories but do test-like activities instead because her performance evaluation is based on the children's test scores. A second-grade teacher could believe in the project approach, but use direct instruction and drill because she finds her day parceled into thirty-minute segments. This discrepancy between teacher beliefs and required instructional practice is called a **philosophy-reality conflict** (Hatch and Freeman, 1988) and the conflict is perhaps nowhere more intense than in the area of literacy.

Under these circumstances, it is essential that teachers keep their goals for children uppermost in mind. Three educators succinctly stated what goals for a language arts program ought to be when they said:

We wanted the children to develop a love of books, an enthusiasm for reading and writing, and a realization that there are many ways to communicate one's ideas. We wanted them to develop thinking and problem-solving strategies so they could face academic challenges confidently and constructively. (Crowell, Kawakami, and Wong, 1986, p. 145)

Conclusion

As we work with young children, we must keep in mind that:

Early childhood education is not an exercise or a schedule or a machine. It is young children exploring their world with sensory thoroughness, experimenting with people and places and materials, encouraged by a teacher who respects and uses their ideas and ways of learning to help them discover what has meaning for them in our society. (Law et al., 1966, p. 12)

This, then, is what a child-centered language arts curriculum is all about. It builds on what children already know. It makes becoming literate seem inviting. It capitalizes on the child's natural curiosity and playfulness. And it does all of these things in a warm, supportive environment so that children feel free to take the risks associated with real learning and become self-directed learners both now and in the future.

Summary

Early childhood educators have long recognized the value of curriculum which is child-centered and wholistic. In language arts, a child-centered curriculum emphasizes process over content, provides authentic learning experiences, educates the "whole child" (cognitive, social, physical, emotional) and casts teachers in the role of decision-makers. In a developmentally appropriate early childhood language arts classroom, three important teaching strategies are individualization, the project approach, and demonstrations. When teachers' commitment to child-initiated activity is at odds with the school curriculum, they are caught in a philosophy-reality conflict. Educators of young children must draw upon the field of early childhood education's long and distinguished tradition of educating the "whole child" and base their arguments for sound teaching practices on their knowledge of child development.

Focus On: Classroom Management in a Child-Centered Language Arts Program

As every teacher knows, children cannot benefit from a curriculum, even a developmentally appropriate curriculum, if the classroom is chaotic. Dealing with children's inappropriate behavior is a major concern of educators, especially beginning teachers. Student teachers often worry about how to manage a child-centered language arts classroom. The first important piece of advice is to project self-confidence and have high expectations for students. Consider, for a moment, the behavior of this student teacher. Ms. Dylan is doing a lesson on environmental print. She has decided to have children work in groups to locate the words that they know. Unfortunately, she forgot to gather plenty of newspapers and magazines beforehand. As a result, she spent the half hour before the children arrived trying to borrow materials from other teachers. When class begins, Ms. Dylan puts materials at each table and then begins giving instructions. The second-graders quickly perceive that there are not enough newspapers to go around and some children begin to lay claim to them. An argument breaks out at one table. Ms. Dylan tries to divert attention from the argument and says, "Okay. Would you like to get into groups or something?" The children begin negotiating noisily about who will be in which group. Meanwhile, she has forgotten to give children large pieces of paper on which to glue their words and several children come up and ask her what to do with the words they have cut out. Other children ask her how many people are allowed to be in a group. "Everyone sit down and be quiet, please!" she tells the children. Later, when speaking with her supervisor about the lesson, she says, "You came at a really bad time. It's Friday and the kids are so wound up. I know my lesson was a disaster. I just couldn't control the class. My teacher said this is a difficult group—especially those two boys who started to argue. If they were just absent once in a while, maybe I'd have a good lesson."

It is clear that Ms. Dylan is finding fault with everyone and everything except herself. She is disorganized, gives confusing directions, and is nonassertive. What are the best ways to avoid a "disaster" like this? In a review of the research on effective early childhood teaching, ten basic principles of **classroom management** were identified (Lay-Dopyera and Dopyera, 1987). These principles and examples are detailed below.

1. *Plan ahead*. In order for children to have a clear idea of what they are to do, teachers also must have a clear idea. Planning ahead also means "troubleshooting," anticipating those things that are likely to be unfamiliar or difficult for the students.

2. *Communicate expectations to children*. Children need explicit instructions. In teaching young children, very few assumptions can be made about children's prior understanding of classroom procedures. The teacher who announces "Time to clean up" without demonstrating the behaviors associated with "cleaning up" is expecting too much. Young children are just learning what such phrases mean. Take, for example, "Let's get ready to hear a story." What does this mean to a child? To find a book, to stop and listen, to put things away, to go to the carpeted area of the room, or all of the above?

3. *Use modeling, rehearsal, and incentives*. If you were in an unfamiliar setting with a complicated set of directions to a destination, which would you rather do— follow a map or have a "copilot" in your car? Most of us would prefer to have someone show us the way. The same holds true for children who are learning proper classroom procedures. If we want to have individual conferences with young children about their favorite books or their writing, we need to explain the purpose of a conference and teach children how to conduct themselves, both during their own conferences and during the conferences of others.

4. *Practice the necessary procedures and establish routines and smooth transitions*. Young children are familiar with many routines when they come to school: getting dressed, having meals, taking a bath, getting ready for bed. Such routines are learned through daily practice. Establishing classroom routines requires the same basic ingredient—practice. Let's suppose that a teacher wants children to return books, records, and toys to the shelf. She can model that behavior herself, set up demonstrations, and give children an opportunity to practice until it becomes a routine.

Breakdowns often occur when children are stopping one activity and starting another. These times, called *transitions*, can be smoothed with a concrete stimulus. Singing a work song while putting things away, lighting a candle to signal the beginning of a story session, or doing a fingerplay while waiting for the bus to arrive are all examples of managing transitions.

5. *Give specific, individualized reinforcement.* If a professor hands back a group of papers and nearly everyone, including you, has the word "good" written on his or her paper, how do you feel? Somehow, the word "good" means less when it is used so indiscriminately. A similar situation occurs when teachers of young children use stock phrases to praise children's efforts. Teachers who use "Good job" or "Right" or "Yes, very good" to punctuate sentences diminish the power of positive reinforcement. It is preferable to use the child's name and say something specific.

We need to be judicious in our use of praise too. If we shower children with praise ("Now, that's really special. I just love it. You're a great author!"), it can make children think that they need to repeat the same performance again in order to please an adult. It is better to leave the "creative control" for a piece of writing in the child's hands and simply ask: "How's the writing going, Carl?"

6. *Be aware of the total classroom.* Teachers can become so absorbed with the activity at hand that they disregard other classroom activities. One way of avoiding this problem is to be alert and keep moving about the room to monitor what is going on.

7. *Gain children's attention before speaking.* If a teacher gets into the habit of "talking over" children's talk or of repeating instructions several times, children soon learn that there is little to be gained by listening. A classroom mascot/puppet is a good device for capturing children's attention. Using the puppet does not require that the teacher become an amateur ventriloquist. Instead, the mascot "whispers" to the teacher, and the teacher conveys the message to the children. Ms. Lingenfelter, a first-grade teacher, had a homemade sock puppet with large dangly earrings named Miss Letters. The children did not play with this particular puppet nor could they look inside her tin-can house. This would have destroyed the puppet's mystique. Instead, children imagined what the puppet might have in her home and what she might be saying to the teacher. When the children were exceptionally noisy, the puppet would become very shy and hesitate to come out and see them. This device for getting children's attention was far more effective than admonishing them to be quiet and more creative than turning off the lights for a moment.

8. *Use voice, movement, and pacing to get and maintain attention.* When an expert teacher senses that attention is waning, he or she will change something to regain children's interest. One of the things that can be changed is the voice. If a person speaks softly while telling a good story, listeners will strain to hear every word. Another strategy is to use movement. The teacher can become more animated, or invite the children to move. A third way of attracting and maintaining attention is pacing. Teachers can quicken the pace if things are bogging down. They can slow the pace of a lesson or even start over if children are failing to understand.

9. *Limit the amount of information given.* When a teacher overwhelms young children with information it is difficult for them to decide what is important and where to begin. A good example is teaching to use the tape recorder. If they are told every operating procedure at once, they may get the steps out of sequence. But if they follow a step-by-step demonstration and have a chance to rehearse and practice, then they are more likely to be able to operate equipment themselves. A teacher could further limit the information by teaching children how to play a tape at one session and how to record on the machine at a subsequent session.

10. *Give instructions on a one-to-one basis.* Young children's reactions to instructions are sometimes like their reactions to the rules of a game—they know that these things exist, but are not very clear on whether or how they apply to them. Children are far less experienced in seeing themselves as members of a group and being addressed in a general way. Young children may easily misinterpret statements like: "Some of you need to put your things away"; "Does everyone have crayons?"; or "I hope you remembered to put your names on your papers." Probably, more often than not, the child's reaction is "I wonder if the teacher means me?" Teachers should give instructions on a one-to-one basis whenever possible. If a child is reading to a partner, the teacher might say "Christina, you will be reading this big book together with Amahl. Remember to use the pointer to slide under the words as you say them, just like I do. And Amahl, you say 'okay' when you are ready to go on to the next page. Then it will be *your* turn to read, and Christina gets to listen and tell *you* when she's finished looking at the pace. Do you have any questions?" Notice that these instructions have a personalized "coaching" tone, rather than sounding like a vague pronouncement from above. In general, this type of instruction is more likely to have the desired effect.

In the Field: Observing Children's Learning

When we are teaching, it is very easy to delude ourselves, to take credit for teaching children something they have already learned. A student teacher might plan a unit on colors, numbers, and shapes and mistakenly assume that he or she is responsible for learning that took place long ago. Or, a teacher might look back on the school year and take credit for all of the progress that children have made when the explanation for those strides is maturation rather than great teaching. How *can* we tell if authentic learning is taking place?

In a review of the research literature, Langer and Applebee (1986) identified five elements of effective learning:

1. *Ownership*—When learning is taking place, children are initiating learning activities and pursuing them with enthusiasm. If children have retained

ownership of the learning experience, they are not pressured, on a timetable, or responding to narrowly focused tasks directed entirely by the teacher.

2. *Appropriateness*—In order for learning to take place, children must be presented with a task that is neither too easy nor too difficult. Appropriateness also means that children do not waste their time with trivial, mindless "busy work" such as cutting and pasting patterns from one piece of paper to another or tracing around their own hand to help them draw a turkey, octopus, etc.

3. *Structure*—Even though authentic learning activities are child-initiated and appropriate, they are also well organized. Maria Montessori contributed a concept to early childhood education that we should cherish forever: the prepared environment. This means that the planning is implicit in how we organize the room and the materials in it. We fashion an environment that suits the child rather than forcing the child to fit the setting.

4. *Collaboration*—Most of our richest learning experiences are social and collaborative. Authentic learning experiences encourage us to learn from one another.

5. *Internalization*—The most memorable learning experiences are not superimposed on a child from outside. Instead, real learning comes "from the inside out" (Hoffman and Lamme, 1989).

Now that you are familiar with these five basic elements, arrange to visit a preschool or primary grades classroom. Review the guidelines for observation at the beginning of this book (To the Student). Look for evidence of each component and record at least ten anecdotes (brief episodes of behavior stated in behavioral terms). Here is an example of an anectode:

Time: 9:00 a.m.   *Grade level: First grade*
Date: October 16   *Description of Setting: Small Group*
While the teacher is reading aloud to the children using a big book, a child asks, "What's that?" and points to the period at the end of the sentence. Another child comments, "It looks like a dot," and the teacher explains that it is a dot, a very special kind of dot that "tells you to take a little rest when you are reading." She demonstrates how the story would sound by reading a few sentences without punctuation, then tells them that the mark is called a period. Later, when the children are doing their own writing, I observe several children using periods at the end of their sentences; some seem to be getting carried away and putting a period after each word, rather than at the end of a sentence. One child reads his paper out loud to try and figure out where the "little rest" belongs: "Cleo . . . yeah, I should put one there. I have a Calico cat named Cleo who sleeps in my bed with me at night one time she . . . Wait! I need to rest back there" (he puts a period between "night" and "one").

After you have collected at least ten anecdotes, summarize your observations into the five categories identified by Langer and Applebee (1986): 1) ownership of learning, 2) appropriateness, 3) structure, 4) opportunities for collaboration, 5) evidence of internalization. Be prepared to discuss your observations with the class.

References

Barbour, N. (1986). Teachers can make decisions. *Childhood Education, 62*, 322–323.

Bredekamp, S. (1987). *Developmentally appropriate practice in early childhood programs serving children from birth through age 8*. Washington, DC: National Association for the Education of Young Children.

Callahan, R.E. (1962). *Education and the cult of efficiency*. Chicago, IL: University of Chicago.

Crowell, D.C., Kawakami, A.J., and Wong, J.L. (1986). Emergent literacy: Reading-writing experiences in a kindergarten classroom. *The Reading Teacher, 40*(2), 144–149.

Dewey, J., and Dewey, E. (1915). *Schools of tomorrow*. New York: Dutton. (2nd ed. 1962).

Early Childhood Literacy Development Committee (1985). *Literacy development in pre-first grade*. Newark, DE: International Reading Association.

English, F.W. (Ed.) (1983). Contemporary curriculum circumstances. In F.W. English (Ed.). *Fundamental curriculum decisions*. New Alexandria, VA: Association for Supervision and Curriculum Development (pp. 1–17).

Glasser, W.H. (1990). The quality school. *Phi Delta Kappan, 71*, 425–435.

Graves, D. (1983). *Writing: Teachers and children at work*. Exeter, NH: Heinemann.

Harste, J.C., Woodward, V.A., and Burke, C.L. (1984). *Language stories and literacy lessons*. Portsmouth, NH: Heineman.

Hatch, J.A., and Freeman, E. (1988). Kindergarten philosophies and practices: Perspectives of teachers, principals and supervisors. *Early Childhood Research Quarterly, 32*(2), 151–166.

Hendrick, J. (1986). *Total learning: Curriculum for the young child* (2nd ed.). Columbus, OH: Merrill.

Hoffman, S., and Lamme, L.L. (1989). *Learning from the inside out: The expressive arts*. Wheaton, MD: Association for Childhood Education International.

Holdaway, D. (1979). *The foundations of literacy*. Sydney, Australia: Ashton/Scholastic.

Jalongo, M.R. (1986). Decisions that affect teachers' professional development. *Childhood Education, 62*(5), 351–356.

Kagan, S.L. (1989). Early care and education: Tackling the tough issues. Phi Delta Kappan, *70*(6), 433–439.

Katz, L.G. (1988). *Early childhood education: What research tells us*. Bloomington, IN: Phi Delta Kappan.

Katz, L.G., and Chard, S.C. (1989). *Engaging children's minds: The project approach*. Norwood, NJ: Ablex.

Kilpatrick, W.H. (1918). The project method. *Teachers College Record, 19*, 319–335.

Kitano, M.K. (1989). The kindergarten through grade three teacher's role in recognizing and supporting young gifted children. *Young Children, 44*(3), 57–63.

Langer, J.A., and Applebee, A.N. (1986). Reading and writing instruction: Toward a theory of teaching and learning. *Review of Research in Education, 13*, 171–194.

Law, N., Moffit, M., Moore, E., Overfield, R., and Starks, E. (1966). *Basic propositions for Early Childhood Education*. Washington, DC: Association for Childhood Education International.

Lay-Dopyera, M., and Dopyera, J.E. (1987). Strategies for teaching. In C. Seefeldt (Ed.) *Early Childhood Curriculum: A review of research* (pp. 13–33). New York: Teachers College Press.

Minuchin, P. (1987). Schools, families, and the development of young children. *Early Childhood Research Quarterly, 2*, 245–259.

Moffett, J., and Wagner, B.J. (1983). *Student-centered language arts and reading, K-3* (3rd ed.). Boston: Houghton Mifflin.

Moyer, J. (1986). Child development as a base for decision-making. *Childhood Education, 62*, 325–330.

Plourde, L. (1989). Teaching with collections. *Young Children, 44*(3), 78–80.

Research and Policy Committee. (1985). *Investing in children*. Washington, DC: Committee for Economic Development.

Schweinhart, L.J. (1988). How important is child-initiated activity? *Principal*, 6–10.

Smith, F. (1982). *Writing and the writer*. New York: Holt, Rinehart and Winston.

Snow, C.E. (1983). Literacy and language: Relationships during preschool years. *Harvard Educational Review, 53*(2), 165–189.

Task Force on Teaching as a Profession (1986): *A nation prepared*: *Teachers for the 21st century*. Washington, DC: Carnegie Forum on Education and the Economy.

Temple, C., and Gillet, J.W. (1989). *Language arts*: *Learning processes and teaching practices*. (2nd ed.). Glenview, IL: Scott, Foresman.

Wagner, B.J. (1985). *Integrating the language arts*. Urbana, IL: ERIC Clearinghouse on Reading and Communication Skills.

Children's Books

Carle, E. (1969). *The very hungry caterpillar*. Cleveland, OH: Collins-World.

Hutchins, P. (1983). *You'll soon grow into them, Titch*. New York: Greenwillow.

McMillan, B. (1988). *Counting wildflowers*. New York: Lothrop, Lee, and Shepard.

Wells, R. (1975). *Morris's disappearing bag*. New York: Dial (Pied Piper Giant edition).

Williams, V. (1981). *Three days on a river in a red canoe*. New York: Greenwillow.

PART TWO

Receptive and Expressive Oral Language

PART TWO BEGINS THE same way that children begin as they try to make sense out of language: first with receptive and then with expressive oral language. Chapter 4, "Listening and the Young Child," describes how children acquire both basic and higher-level listening skills and suggests strategies that teachers can use to build upon and to extend children's listening skills. Chapter 5, "Speaking Abilities of Young Children" describes the developmental sequence for children's speech and recommends ways of fostering children's expressive oral language growth.

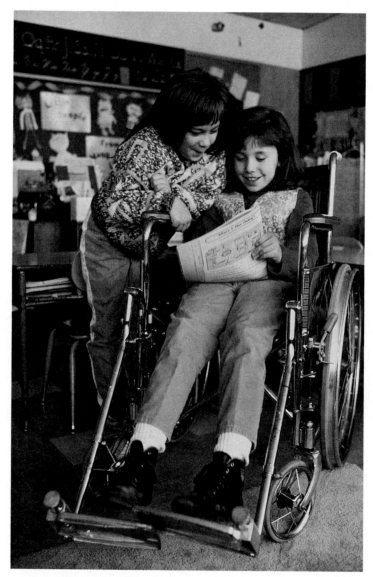

Photo: © 1990 Frank Siteman

4

Listening and the Young Child

OUTLINE

Key Concepts and Terms
Introduction

I.   Definitions for Listening

II.   Influences on the Listening Process

III.   The Importance of Listening
       A. Listening: The Child's First Language Ability
       B. Listening: The Most Frequently Used Language Art
       C. Listening: A Neglected Language Art

IV.   Characteristics of Listeners
       A. Capacity
       B. Willingness
       C. Habits

V.   Listening Abilities of Young Children
       A. Using Listening Cues
       B. Connecting Aural and Visual Input
       C. Relating Sensory Input to Experience

VI.   Guidelines for Developing Listening Skills

VII.   Listening Activities

Human beings live to express themselves ... You only become conscious of your own value when people listen to you.   —BISHOP JAMES MAHONEY (1981)

KEY CONCEPTS AND TERMS

hearing, listening, and auding
influences on listening (listener
   characteristics, situational
   factors, speaker characteristics)
capacity, willingness, and habits of
   listeners
listening and literacy

using poetry and music to build listening
   skills
critical listening skills (discriminative,
   purposeful, critical, appreciative,
   creative, active, and therapeutic
   listening)
communication skills of adults

Katya and Shirelle are two nursery-school students who are playing with clay. Their conversation illustrates several types of listening behavior:

Shirelle: I'm making pot pies.

Katya: Need some more? (offers first girl a chunk of modeling material)

Shirelle: Okay, this is hard. (each girl reaches inside the clay bucket and takes out a mound of clay, then drops it onto her own pile) mine, plop, plop. (both girls giggle loudly)

Katya: I'm making a pie instead

Shirelle: Me too. I'll ripple wopple it off (she says this while trimming off the excess with a plastic knife) and put it in the bowl. Now I'm gonna make pies.

Katya: Anyway, how *do* you make pies?

Shirelle: First you take it, and you roll it out. This is how you make it, and you roll it out. Then you cut, cut, cut, and cut. Then you go rut, rut, rut, rut, and there's some pot pie!

As Shirelle's obvious delight in the sounds of language suggests, listening is more than hearing sounds. It also involves understanding what we hear, and, at its highest level, appreciating what we hear.

Definitions for Listening

In everyday conversation, the word "listen" is often used as a synonym for compliance—not just hearing words, but heeding them. A teacher might announce to the children: "Time to go outside. Everyone get your coats on." When the teacher tells them to listen, she means that the child will hear, understand, *and* respond appropriately. Both in common parlance and in educational settings, the word "listen" means more than interpreting the vibrations that are transmitted through the ear.

Lundsteen (1979) defines listening as "the process by which spoken language is converted to meaning in the mind." Defined in this way, listening involves three things:

1. **Hearing**—a physiological process that includes auditory acuity (the ability to hear) and auditory perception (the ability to discriminate among sounds, to blend sounds together, and to hold sequences of sound in memory)
2. **Listening**—an act of perception which includes focusing, becoming aware, and selecting cues from the environment
3. **Auding**—an act of comprehension that begins with hearing and listening. It includes getting meaning from what is heard, associating sounds to something already known, organizing, imagining, and appreciating what is heard (De Stefano, Dole and Marzano, 1989, p. 184; Froese and Straw, 1981).

Influences on the Listening Process

The listening process is affected by three clusters of characteristics (Bromley, 1988):

> **Listener characteristics**—the listener's motivation, conceptual level, experience, listening strategies, and ability to use self-monitoring strategies (such as associating new information with prior knowledge or seeking clarification), and opportunities for active participation

Situational factors—the quality and appeal of the message, the amount of distraction, and the use of concrete objects

Speaker characteristics—pronunciation, eye contact, nonverbal communication consistent with the message, and the absence of distracting habits

The Importance of Listening

Most people believe that *listening*, the aural component of language, is a passive activity that requires minimal effort on the part of the listener. But listening comprehension is much more demanding and complex than previously assumed (Benson and Hjelt, 1978). As evidence of this, Wilkes (1981) points to the fact that when someone is learning a second language, listening is largely responsible for growth in speaking. Language learners often do not speak the new language at all for a period of time, then they surge ahead in speaking abilities. Evidently, meaningful aural input (listening) is the explanation for this phenomenon.

Listening: The Child's First Language Ability

Listening is the earliest language ability to emerge. As soon as the hearing organs of a fetus are fully formed, he or she is able to listen. We also know that newborns respond differently to different types of sounds; that they are usually calmed by sounds that are similar to those heard inside the womb, and distressed by the sounds of infants crying. Bayless and Ramsey (1991) describe how infants on respirators breathed more rhythmically when dance music, rather than a lullaby, was played softly in the background.

But listening affects more than the infant's mood or physical behavior. Because listening precedes the other language arts, it is the foundation for speaking, reading, and writing (Devine, 1978; Jalongo, 1991). When children are silent but attentive, it is common to speak of them "taking it all in." Linguists would put it somewhat differently, saying that young children need "meaningful aural input" in order to master language. A child may remain silent during songs or stories or fingerplays, for example, then suddenly begin to participate with great enthusiasm (Jalongo and Collins, 1985). To further illustrate the connections between listening and the language arts, consider the listening–reading relationship. Both are receptive language arts and based on the same set of cognitive structures. Both listening and reading require a repertoire of skills in phonology, syntax, semantics, and knowledge of text structure (Pearson and Fielding, 1983).

Listening: The Most Frequently Used Language Art

A second major reason that listening is important is because *listening is the most frequent language behavior*. It has been said that we listen to the equivalent of a book in a day, we talk a book's worth in a week, we read a book's worth in a month, and we write the equivalent of a book in a year (Lundsteen, 1979). When children are outside of school, listening is the most frequently practiced language art. Norton (1985) estimates that 45 percent of children's out-of-school time is spent listening. The listening demands of the classroom environment are even greater. Researchers report that elementary school children spend 60 percent of their in-school time listening, and 30 percent of that time is spent listening to one person: the teacher (Strother, 1987; Wilt, 1950).

> *To me it is especially curious that in the classroom we spend more time teaching writing than reading, more time teaching reading than speaking, and the least time, if any at all, teaching listening. Meanwhile, not only outside of school but right in the classroom we do more listening than speaking, more speaking than reading, more reading than writing. A perfect negative correlation between education and life. (Johnson, 1972, p. 4)*

Listening: A Neglected Language Art

This leads to a third reason why listening is so important. Even though listening is a frequent activity it is *seldom taught and poorly taught*. Jacobs (1986) says that listening has been virtually ignored in the preschool/primary curriculum. Why? Perhaps it is because teachers' preparation for teaching listening skills to children is inadequate. Swanson (1984) surveyed 15 textbooks used in teacher education and found that out of 3,704 pages of text, only 82 pages mentioned listening! So even though teachers may recognize the value of listening, they may not know how to develop children's listening abilities. Before planning any listening activity, teachers need to consider the young child's characteristics as a listener.

Characteristics of Listeners

Young listeners are affected by three things in a listening situation: capacity, willingness, and habits (Weaver, 1972).

Capacity

Capacity refers to young children's hearing abilities, including acuity and comprehension. There may be hearing-impaired children who would be helped by sitting closer to the speaker or seeing the speaker's lips, for example. A teacher could learn to enunciate more clearly and to use some basic American Sign Language signs to supplement the receptive language of these students. There may be children whose experiential background makes it difficult for them to understand the language of the classroom, such as the newly immigrated child. A teacher could use more gestures, pictures, and real objects in lessons to help these students better understand the messages that they hear. Listening activities must be adjusted to meet the needs of all children.

Willingness

The second aspect of listening, **willingness**, has to do with motivation. Is there a real reason for children to listen? When the words that are spoken have some purpose, when there is a real reason to listen, then children's motivation will tend to increase. The teacher who makes an audiotape of instructions for making modeling clay and allows each child to create something with the modeling material is much more likely to teach children to be good listeners than the teacher who tells everyone to be quiet while she explains how to do a packet of worksheets. If children sense tangible, immediate benefits from careful listening, they will pay closer attention.

Habits

The third aspect of listening is **habits**. Habits refer to the child's behavioral response to listening situations. Good listening habits are formed when children become *interested*, get *clear messages*, and *act upon* what they have heard. Consider this situation in a kindergarten classroom where children are involved in a writing program. Elise has just shared her writing and drawing with a small group of classmates. (See Fig. 4.1). She is seated in a place of honor, the "writer's chair," and she listens carefully to her classmates' comments. They have one recommendation for improvement: they are *interested* in hearing more about her babysitter and some of the things she and Elise do together. Elise has *a clear message*, and during the next writing class she *acts upon her experience* by revising her story about her babysitter.

Listening Abilities of Young Children

By the time young children enter kindergarten they have already acquired many listening skills such as learning to use and respond to the signals speakers give to listeners, connecting what they hear with what they see, and relating what they hear to their own experience.

Using Listening Cues

Children are usually *sensitive to cues or signals for listeners*. They have learned ways of getting someone to listen to them and initiate a conversation ("You know what?" "I'll bet you can't guess what I did yesterday.") They have learned to ask questions and seek clarification when whatever they hear is difficult to understand ("Mom,

FIGURE 4.1   Elise's Writing and Drawing

what's a Ghostbuster?" "Is a hospital a sad or a happy place?"). They have also learned to use *prestarts*, "words or phrases that have little substance but that indicate to listeners that the speaker is about to take a conversational turn" (Siefert and Hoffnung, 1987, p. 360). Prestarts can help a speaker signal to listeners that he or she wants to continue talking ("and," "uh," "I mean"), acknowledge or affirm ("Yeah," "Um-hmm," "Me too"), or move the conversation forward by commenting on a previous statement ("Yes, but," "You say _____?" "Well, *I* think . . .").

Connecting Aural and Visual Input

Another listening ability of children deals with *relating what they hear to what they see*. Listening activities can be related to real objects, to pictures and to words. A listening activity with *The Opposite Song* (Collins, 1982) is a good example. After Collins shared her song several times with a group of kindergarten children at the United Cerebral Palsy Association, she asked them to suggest pairs of opposites. Lisa, a girl whose poker-straight hair had just been transformed by a curly permanent, suggested: "I can say curly, I can say straight." When the musician asked for another pair of opposites that would rhyme, Keiko said, "I can say early, I can say late." In this way, Lisa related her listening to a personal experience and a real object—her hair. One first-grade teacher made cue cards to accompany the song at the beginning of the year (Figure 4.2). When they sang the song, she paused and had

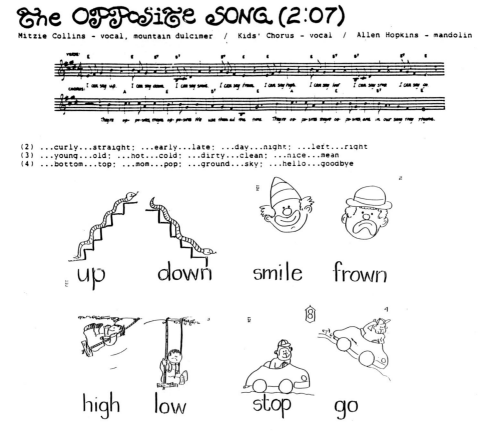

FIGURE 4.2   The Opposite Song. (Words and music from Mitzie Collins, *Sounds Like Fun*, 1982. Used with permission.) *Continued on facing page*

children fill in the opposite words. Then as a special challenge at the end of the year, the children worked with a partner and quickly wrote down the pairs of opposite words as they sang the song. As this example illustrates, listening activities need not be dull routines that lack intellectual challenge.

Relating Sensory Input to Experience

Another basic type of listening skill is the child's ability *to connect what he or she hears with his or her own experience.* This skill is learned primarily through listening to stories and discussing them with an adult. Nelson (1989) gives the example of telling a story called "The Tailor" (Schimmel, 1978). When Nelson (1989) shared the story with children, she used a puppet that changes its clothes to go along with the plot. In this tale, a tailor who is too busy and too poor to make himself a fine coat finally decides to make one. He wears the coat proudly all over town. When the coat becomes worn, he makes it into a jacket. When the jacket sleeves become frayed, he

curly   straight   early   late

day   night   left   right

young   old   hot   cold

dirty   clean   nice   mean

bottom   top   mom   pop

ground   sky   hello   goodbye

makes it into a vest. Time passes and the vest gets old and worn. But the tailor cannot bear to part with the fabric that reminds him of his coat, jacket, and vest so he creates a hat. Eventually, the hat gets old and worn, too. At the conclusion of the story, the resourceful tailor goes back to his shop and emerges holding a fabric-covered button. Whenever he holds that button, he is reminded of that lovely fabric and the coat, jacket, vest, and hat he made for himself long ago. When children listened to "The Tailor," they connected their own experiences with the main character's. They grasped the theme of treasured objects and began to talk about their own prized possessions and personal mementos.

Guidelines for Developing Listening Skills

As De Haven (1983) observes, children do not merely need to listen more, they need to listen better (p. 134). Instruction in listening skills should help children learn *what* to listen to and *how* to listen. This can be accomplished if teachers do the following six things:

1. *Analyze the amount of listening required in your classroom.* Teachers need to determine whether they are placing unreasonable demands on the developing listening skills of the young children in their classes. You may want to enlist the help of a colleague or simply leave a tape recorder running during the day to get an idea of how much time students are expected to listen. In the "average" classroom, teacher talk dominates about 75 percent of the time. One way to cut down on the time that children are expected to listen to teacher talk is to let children do more of the talking. Rather than repeating instructions, questions or directions yourself, ask children to do this. Another way to cut down on the amount of time children spend listening to the teacher is to encourage children to respond to classmates' comments or questions, rather than the teacher being the focus.

2. *Model good listening habits.* Teachers need to emulate good listening habits. The "Focus On" for this chapter suggests strategies teachers can use to become better listeners and more effective communicators.

3. *Create a listening environment.* The teacher who wants children to be good listeners considers possible sources of distraction and strives to eliminate or at least minimize them. When teachers make it clear that one activity is over and another is about to begin, introduce activities in an interesting way, and use flexible seating arrangements, they are helping to set the stage for good listening (Funk and Funk, 1989).

4. *Incorporate listening activities into subject areas.* It is important to regard listening as an integral part of the total curriculum, rather than as a separate subject, otherwise it will continue to be neglected in the schools (Winn, 1988).

5. *Focus the children's listening powers.* What is good listening? Surely it is not listening to everything—young children are barraged by sounds, and good listeners actually ignore much of what they hear (Smith, 1967). Children are frequently admonished to listen, but that request can be too vague and too demanding. Instead of asking children to listen *to* something, they should be directed to listen *for* something (Funk and Funk, 1989). This is a very useful distinction because in the first case, listening is unfocused while in the second, it has a clearly focused purpose.

6. *Make listening activities participatory*. Few adults give their undivided attention to anyone for an extended period of time. We nod off during a lecture, our minds wander as we listen to an audiotape, we daydream while watching a film. Even when we *are* listening, we may get distracted. We might be relating what we have heard to our own experience or formulating a question we intend to ask and temporarily lose concentration. But if we are called upon frequently to *participate*, then our listening improves.

7. *Plan follow-up and extension activities*. If children know that they will be asked to use what they have heard in an activity, they will listen more carefully. Listening activities enable teachers to check on children's listening comprehension, to clarify concepts, and to extend ideas. Children's responses should be varied and include opportunities to listen for information, to critically analyze material, to appreciate what they hear, and to express themselves creatively (Funk and Funk, 1989).

Listening Activities

Let's look at how several different teachers fulfilled these requirements in planning listening activities for their students.

1. *Explain how something functions*—In Ms. Ness's nursery school, making your own snack was a daily activity. During these cooking experiences, Ms. Ness noticed that her students were absolutely fascinated by some common kitchen gadgets, such as a hardboiled egg slicer, a garlic press, a melon baller, an egg beater, a wire whisk, an egg separator, a cheese slicer, and an orange juicer, to name a few. Her challenge: "Find out everything you can about this object. Think about how it works. I will explain how it works and you will listen. Then you will explain how it works to someone else."

2. *Tell stories*—Usually we think of children listening to adults tell the stories. But after children have heard stories many times, they can demonstrate their listening skills by retelling a story in their own words. In Mrs. Ramirez's first grade, the children wore a special storyteller's cap and cape adorned with miniature toys that represented various folktales. There was a tiny stuffed bear for The Three Bears, a pom-pom chick to represent Chicken Little and a plastic pig for The Three Little Pigs. When a child donned the hat and cape, he or she would go into a "recording booth" (a refrigerator box set up with a chair and a cassette recorder) and make an audiotape of the story. As the year progressed, more stories and objects to represent them adorned the cape. The teacher listened to the children's stories every day on her drive home as a check on the children's listening comprehension. Then the tapes became part of a listening library for children as they listened to one another.

3. *Sound effects*—The challenge of using readily available items to create sound effects encourages children to listen carefully. Mr. Antonucci demonstrated several old-fashioned radio sound effects to his third-graders. He rustled a piece of cellophane to mimic a crackling fire and then wiggled and old cookie sheet to imitate a roll of thunder in the distance. Afterward, the children listened to Tom Paxton's (1984) song, "The Marvellous Toy," and recorded their own version, complete with appropriate sound effects. For preschool children, creating the realistic animal noises of "Down on Grandpa's Farm" (Raffi and Whitely, 1985) is a good listening activity.

4. *Relate information accurately*—Ms. Stephens played a game with three- and four-year-olds called Police Officer. The game required two toy telephones, a tricycle, and a police officer's cap. It began with the police officer circling the group on the tricycle and then going where he or she could not see the other children. Next, two children were selected: one to play the parent's role and one to be the child. The parent would describe, over the phone, the person she selected to be the child. The police officer would listen to the description and try to locate the "lost" child. Then the "lost" child would hop on the back of the tricycle for a happy reunion with the "parent."

5. *Form mental images*—When children listen to a traditional song like "The Kitty Cats' Party" (Carfa, 1982), they form vivid pictures from the words they hear.

At the kitty cats' party all the kittens will be there.
They'll be dressed up in their Sunday best with flowers in their hair.
Wearing red and yellow ribbons and a tiny tinkle-bell,
There'll be kittens from the city and the countryside as well.

Chorus:

Come on little, little, little, little, little kitty cat.
Get yourself a partner—let's dance!

Mr. Tommy Cat's invited just to play his violin.
When the kittens choose their partners then the dancing will begin:
But perhaps I ought to tell you why they're such a happy crowd.
There's a sign upon the wall that says "No doggies are allowed!"

Chorus:

When it's time to eat, meow, meow.
Cans of salmon piled up to the sky!
Each one has his little bowl of milk.
For dessert there is catnip pie!

With their little bellies full and a smile upon their face.
They will curl up in a corner near a cozy fireplace.
Just a-purrin' and a-purrin' and no one makes a peep.
And before you know it all the kitty cats are fast asleep.

The teacher can extend children's thinking with questions about other types of animal parties: "What would they wear? What foods would be served? Whom would they want to keep out? What would they do to have fun?"

I Tell, You Do   In this listening activity, children work with a partner. One person has clay, the other person tells that person what to do with the clay in order to create an item he or she has in mind.

Story Line   This activity enables children to practice their listening comprehension of a story by arranging story events in the correct sequence on a clothesline. Good choices for this activity are *Bye, Bye Baby: A Sad Story With a Happy Ending* (Ahlberg and Ahlberg, 1990), in which a baby who is all alone goes on a quest to assemble an entire family. Other good story line choices are *Claude the Dog*, (Gackenbach, 1974) and *I Went Walking* (Williams, 1990).

Translate What Is Heard into Written, Graphic, Musical, or Dramatic Form   Ms. Crawford, a first-grade teacher and Ms. Cribbs, a sixth-grade teacher, collaborated on a cross-age tutoring project. Their goal was to make favorite books come alive by creating a "story land," complete with a guided tour. Each station highlighted a particular book and presented it in a different way: puppet show, storytelling apron, flannel board, and big book. The tour was cooperatively designed and presented by the children and the entire school went on the listening guided tour.

Compare Two Stories or Sources of Information   Children can listen to a recording of the song, "The Wheels on the Bus" (Sharon, Lois and Bram, 1980) and then listen to a picture-book version of the same song, one that is a book with movable parts (Zelinsky, 1990). Then they can compare and contrast the two in terms of the words, melody, number of verses, and visual imagery.

Summarize Information   Information books, books that tell all about something real in a factual way, are good resources for summarizing information. *Ant Cities* (Dorros, 1987), for instance, gives instructions on how to create an ant farm. After listening to the story, children can summarize the procedure.

Draw a . . .   Partners of primary-grades children can do this listening activity. One child listens to a description of something very familiar to another child, such as his or her house, pet, teddy bear, etc. The first child has to draw the item to the specifications of the second child by listening carefully. Then the picture can be revised based on additional information.

Story Maps   After listening to a story, children can make a large chart or map on the floor that shows the character's travels. Planning the map begins with a question about the setting, then questions about the main character that focus on his goals, and, finally, the steps the character takes to achieve those goals. Three good book titles for this activity are *The Crack-of-Dawn Walkers* (Hest, 1984), *Hazel's Amazing Mother* (Wells, 1985); and *Coco Can't Wait* (Gomi, 1979).

Recognize Implications   Stories which present the consequences of a character's actions such as *Lucky's Choice* (Jesche, 1987) or *Feathers for Lunch* (Ehlert, 1990) can be used to help children recognize causes and effects.

Listen for a Specific Purpose   An audiotape of recipes such as the ones in Figure 4.3 is a highly motivating listening activity. Children can also create their own rebus recipe after listening to taped instructions.

Separate Reality from Fantasy   De Paola's (1975) *Strega Nona*, an old Italian folk-tale, is a good story for discussing the distinction between fantasy and reality. Strega Nona or "grandma witch" has a magic pasta pot. Like the sorcerer's apprentice, her apprentice, Big Anthony, tries to use her magic with disastrous results. Some of the details in the story are realistic—the characters of the village and the

FIGURE 4.3   Rebus Recipes.

countryside, the attire of the people. Other aspects are purely fanciful, like the magic pasta pot. Listening to the story and watching the Weston Woods animated film version can lead to a lively discussion about what is realistic and imaginary in the story and in the two sequels, *Big Anthony and the Magic Ring* (de Paola, 1979) and *Merry Christmas, Strega Nona* (de Paola, 1986).

The preceding section has highlighted some challenging listening activities for young children. How do listening abilities contribute to the child's growth in literacy?

The Listening/Literacy Connection

Educators have been advised for decades to build upon what children already know. **Listening** is one language skill that children have acquired before they learn to read and write, even before they speak. Knowing this, it is not surprising that authorities in the field of reading have begun to recommend ways of basing literacy lessons on listening (Stauffer, 1975, 1980)

The Structured Listening Activity

Choate and Rakes (1987) offer the following general sequence for a structured listening activity:

1. *Concept building*—relate the listening activity to the children's previous experience
2. *Purpose setting*—evoke mental images in the listeners' minds and focus on a specific purpose for listening
3. *Reading aloud*—ask children to make predictions, listen for cues
4. *Questioning*—pose challenging questions
5. *Recitation*—ask children to summarize their responses

Listening to Poetry

One of the most pleasurable listening activities is listening to **poetry**. Young children usually enjoy poetry if it

tells a story
suggests action
has strong rhythm and rhyme
uses humor and nonsense
uses hyperbole (deliberate exaggeration)
explores the resources of language (sound patterns, imagery, repetition)
focuses on familiar experiences (Norton, 1985)

Recently, many poets and artists have collaborated to create illustrated poetry collections especially for young children. See Appendix C for a selective listing of these books.

The Directed Listening-Thinking Activity

Strickland and Morrow (1989) suggest the *Directed Listening-Thinking Activity (DLTA)* as a listening-based literacy strategy. The DLTA has three basic parts:

1. *Prepare* for listening with questions and discussion
2. *Read* the story
3. *Discuss* the story after reading

Figure 4.4 is an example of a DLTA using a humorous book suitable for the primary grades, *Two Bad Ants* by Chris Van Allsburg (1988). In this story, two ants leave the group and go through some terrifying ant's-eye-view adventures during someone's breakfast. They fall from a waterfall (the kitchen faucet and disposal), into a terrible oven (the toaster), and are tossed about on a hot, stormy sea that leads into a cave (a man sipping coffee).

The Listening-Reading Transfer Lesson

Cunningham (1982) applies a similar strategy in the *Listening-Reading Transfer Lesson*. In this approach, the purpose is to enhance children's listening *and* reading comprehension. The lesson is divided into two parts. First, the teacher sets a purpose for listening and the students listen to a short story aloud by the teacher, an audiotape, or a film. If the purpose is to develop children's understanding of sequence, for example, they can arrange pictures of story events in order. This activity serves as practice for the second part of the lesson when the children *read* a new selection that has the same comprehension goal. In the Listening-Reading Transfer Lesson, children see the connection between what they need to do when listening and when reading: to focus on comprehension.

Music and Critical Listening

Critical listening skills are higher-level listening skills such as visualizing what is heard, comprehending meaning, and responding to a message both intellectually and emotionally (Jacobs, 1990; Norton, 1985). Listening to music is a good vehicle for developing these higher-order listening skills because "listening is the most fundamental and probably the earliest musical skill to develop in young children. Listening to music does not require language (as does singing), nor does listening require motor skills or physical coordination (as does moving to music or playing musical instruments)" (Barr and Johnston, 1989, p. 14).

DLTA Using *Two Bad Ants*

A. *Prepare for listening with questions and discussion.*

Introduce the story with background information: "Today I'm going to read a story called *Two Bad Ants* (Van Allsburg, 1988). I wonder what ants could do that would be 'bad.' Any ideas? This book has puzzles in it because it shows how ants would see and talk about things, instead of the way that people would see or talk about things. Let's look at the pictures to see if you can tell what this story is about." Encourage children to respond as you turn the pages.

Focus the children on the objective for the reading with a statement such as: "This story's about two ants who leave the group and go exploring on their own. While I'm reading it, try to decide whether the ants will want to go on another adventure soon."

B. *Read the story.*

Practice reading the book ahead of time for ease of expression. Show illustrations from the story as you read and ask children how a person would describe what the ants are describing. Pause at natural breaks for children's reactions, comments, or questions.

Tie your questions in with your objective: "Do you think that the ants are enjoying their adventure? How will they decide whether they want to do this again?" Ask children to look at the pictures and predict what will happen next.

C. *Discuss after reading.*

Guide discussion by the objective for your reading—in this example, inference and judgment: "Why do you think that this story was called 'Two Bad Ants'? What decision did the ants make? What would you have decided if you were one of the ants?"

FIGURE 4.4   A Directed Listening-Thinking Activity

Russell, Ousky, and Haynes (1967) have summarized some of the ways that music listening can develop literacy skills, namely, focusing attention, listening without interrupting, associating words with actions, predicting outcomes, grasping the central idea, remembering details, interpreting what is heard, and enjoying the listening selection.

Levels of Listening

Through music, teachers can design activities that are discriminative, purposeful, critical, appreciative, creative, therapeutic, and active. These levels and teachers who designed activities to develop them are as follows:

In **discriminative listening**, the primary purpose is to differentiate among various sounds. Mrs. Yeagley has planned a unit around several distinctive examples of classical music and their picture book counterparts, including, *Peter and the Wolf* (Voight, 1980), *Swan Lake* (Fonteyn, 1989), and *The Nutcracker* (Hoffman, 1984). Children listen for the ways that music is used to create a mood that complements each story.

In **purposeful listening**, children are given a specific reason to pay attention. Mr. Callahan tells the familiar folktale "Sody Salyratus" with guitar accompaniment. In the story, a series of characters go in search of some sody salyratus (baking powder) to make biscuits. Each character is devoured by a bear until a little squirrel outwits the bear. Mr. Callahan sets the purpose for listening by telling the children that they will be singing a little song throughout the story:

> So-dy So-dy
> So-dy Salyratus

He instructs them to listen to their cue because each character sings the song as he or she walks to the store and the listeners are expected to join in at the appropriate moment.

Critical listening involves such things as comparing two sources of information, differentiating between fact and fiction. Ms. Sherrill, a teacher in a church-affiliated nursery school, used two distinctively different treatments of a song by the same title to build children's critical listening skills. "He's Got the Whole World in His Hands," was compared with The Tickle Tune Typhoon's (1987) rendition. The lyrics in their version make it an ecology song:

> We've got the great blue whale in our hands
> The little nightingale in our hands
> We've got the great blue whale in our hands
> We've got the whole world in our hands
>
> We've got the rivers and the oceans in our hands
> We've got the mountains and the meadows in our hands
> We've got the forest and the farmland in our hands
> We've got the whole world in our hands

Another difference between this song and the more traditional version is that it is a very spirited performance by a full gospel choir. Comparing and contrasting these two songs was a challenging critical listening activity for Ms. Sherrill's five-year-olds.

In **appreciative listening**, the goal is listening pleasure, and the elements that contribute to overall enjoyment. Ms. Martin's brother plays the flute in the high-school band and she invites him to perform for the children. First he plays a square-dance tune, "Turkey in the Straw." It sounds, in one child's words, "pretty, but different" from the fiddle version the children have heard on record. "What words could we use to describe it?" the teacher asks. The third-graders generate a list of words and phrases, including: "birdlike," "high," "bright," and "peppy." Then the flutist plays "Theme from MASH" and a current top-ten hit that the children recognize immediately. Once again, they generate lists of descriptive words. Finally, they select their favorite and give reasons why they enjoyed it the most.

In **creative listening**, the goal is to recombine what was heard into an original and satisfying combination. Ms. Williams' class has just seen and heard two picture-book versions of *Mary Had a Little Lamb* (Hale, 1984; Hale, 1990). The first is a traditional retelling with illustrations by Tomie de Paola; the second features a contemporary black child and has photographs by Bruce McMillan. After discussing them both, Ms. Williams asks, "What pets do you have?" "How would the story change if it were about you and your pet?" They decide to do a practice version with their classroom pet, a rabbit. It soon becomes apparent that some of the words don't fit ("lamb," "fleece," "white as snow"), and children suggest alternatives. Then children create their own illustrated versions of the poem, using their names and their pet's name.

In **active listening**, the listener goes beyond comprehension and has empathy for the speaker (Thomlison, 1984). Active listening is characterized by concern for the speaker's welfare and interests rather than the listener's personal concerns. A group of preschool children are watching a musical puppet play of Little Red Riding Hood performed by two children's librarians. The wolf turns to the audience after meeting Little Red Riding Hood and says "I think I'll take a shortcut over to Granny's and wait for that *sweet* little girl to arrive. Now *don't* tell her. *Promise?* "Yes," the children dutifully reply. The moment that the wolf disappears from the stage and Little Red Riding Hood comes on singing her song, the children begin to shout "Don't do it," "Run!" and "The wolf's gonna get you!" This is an example of active listening because the children have identified with the story character and express their concern for her welfare, even though they are breaking their promise to the big bad wolf!

In **therapeutic listening**, the message that the listener has heard contributes to mental health. If that message is music, the music affects emotions and creates a mood, such as a tape of lullabies softly playing while children are settling down for a nap.

Conclusion

Based upon listening research, we know that good listening does not occur automatically; listening skills can be taught; there is a direct relationship between listening and learning; and listening needs to be part of the total curriculum. Young children do not need to put on their "listening ears"; they need to *participate* in challenging, meaningful listening activities to develop their listening abilities. The best way to teach children how to become better listeners is to stop thinking of listening as a synonym for hearing or even for understanding what is heard. Instead, think of listening as the foundation for language development. Otherwise it will continue to be a neglected language art.

Summary

Listening is the first language ability to emerge and the dominant mode of communication for a lifetime thereafter. The three dimensions of listening are hearing, listening, and auding. Each of these three dimensions is affected by listener characteristics, situational factors, and speaker characteristics. In order to improve children's listening skills, teachers must be aware of basic guidelines and strive to promote critical listening skills. Poetry, music, and literacy-based listening activities are excellent ways of developing higher-level listening abilities in young children.

Focus On: Teachers Communicating So That Children Will Listen

Faber and Mazlish (1987) suggest eight practical ways for educators to improve their communication skills with students.

1. *Acknowledge children's feelings.* If a child says, "Teacher, I hate Ricardo!" we might be inclined to respond with "That's not a very nice thing to say." But a better strategy is to accept the child's feelings and help the child put them into words: "Are you angry because Ricardo knocked over your blocks?"

2. *Describe the problem.* If teachers use an accusing or commanding tone ("All right! Who made this mess?"), children will tend to deny their involvement in order to avoid punishment. If teachers state the problem instead, it encourages children to engage in problem-solving (i.e., "Oh, there is water all over the floor near the sink. It needs to be mopped up so that nobody slips and falls.") Usually, one child will volunteer and several others will follow. If not, the teacher should begin mopping up and say, "If somebody would help me mop, then we could have our snack." In this way, children are helped to see how their helping behavior can result in a positive outcome for everyone.

3. *Give information instead of scolding.* Imagine that you are the student. Think about your reaction to these two statements.

Scolding: "Lisette, how many times do I have to tell you to be gentle with the gerbil? If you don't learn how to be more careful, you won't get to hold him any more."

Giving information: "Lisette, gerbils are very small animals, and they can be hurt if they are held too tightly. She is tame and will stay in your hand if you make it into a little cup shape, like this."

Clearly, the second strategy is more helpful and is more likely to promote good listening habits in the child.

4. *Offer a choice*. "After we read this book together, you may do one of three things: go to the listening center and hear the story again; go to the art center and make something that you thought about during the story; or go to the library and read a book with a partner." This teacher does not overwhelm children with alternatives ("Find something to do."), nor does she completely restrict their options. ("Copy the new vocabulary words from the chalkboard and write a sentence for each word.")

5. *Say it briefly*. Instead of lecturing everyone, keep it simple and place the responsibility with the child. Instead of "Come and get this puzzle and put it on the puzzle rack right this minute. You know that it belongs there when you are finished with it. Remember, children, you are all supposed to put the toys away after you play with them. I *always* have to remind some of you," simply say: "Melanie, the puzzle belongs on the shelf." This approach gets Melanie thinking. She has to reassemble the puzzle again and slide it into the puzzle rack before she can sit down and have her lunch.

6. *Describe children's successes*. Instead of saying, "Gunther can't spell his last name yet," try "Gunther, I see that you printed your first name on your painting." This second statement encourages Gunther to keep on writing, while the first makes him feel inadequate.

Another example of being descriptive of children's successes is saying, for instance, "Cherisse, you made your puppet's voice sound like a witch's voice and your puppet *looks* wicked too!" rather than "That's a nice puppet."

7. *Describe what you feel*. Suppose that a group of children pull nearly every book off the shelf in the classroom library and leave it that way. In this situation, a teacher can simply comment on his or her feelings: "It makes me sad to see all of our favorite books thrown on the floor. They need to be put back in our library very neatly so that we can find them and read them."

8. *Put it in writing*. Kindergarten and primary-grades classrooms should have mailboxes so that teachers and children can communicate with one another. The "mailboxes" can be made out of recyclables such as milk cartons or soft-drink bottles with the tops cut off and laid on their sides, snack-food cans, or cardboard boxes with dividers inside. Children can communicate through drawing, writing, or any combination thereof with peers and with the teachers. Teachers can send positive messages to the children.

9. *Solve the problem together*. Listen to this class discussion about a toy that is the subject of frequent disputes.

Teacher: What's good about the new tricycle?

Some of the children's answers are:

"It's red."

"You can hook the wagon on to it and pull stuff around."

"I don't have one at home."

"It's bigger than the old one."

Teacher: What's bad about the new tricycle?

Some of the children's responses are:

"Kids fight about it and try to push you off sometimes."

"You want to play with it for a long time but you can't."

"Some people won't share unless you tell the teacher."

Teacher: What can we do?

"Get more tricycles."

"Make everybody share."

"Tell the teacher if somebody doesn't take turns."

Using this strategy allows everyone to participate in the solution.

In the Field: Really Listening to Children

Over the next several days, listen to adults and children interact wherever you are (e.g., in a classroom, in a store, in the laundromat, at a restaurant, at the bank) and collect at least fifteen verbatim verbal exchanges between an adult and child. Be certain to preserve the adult's and child's anonymity (just label them as "teacher," "parent," or "child," rather than using any proper names).

Now review Faber's and Mazlish's (1987) guidelines for effective listening (Focus On, this chapter). Sort your examples into two groups: adult *was* practicing good listening or adult *was not* practicing good listening skills. For those anecdotes that fall into the first group (those who were really listening to children), write one or two sentences supporting your decision to place them in that group. For those in the second group (the adults who did not really listen to the children), write one or two sentences to suggest how they should have responded to the child. Be prepared to discuss your findings with the class.

References

Barr, K.W., and Johnston, J.M. (1989). Listening: The key to early childhood music. *Day Care and Early Education*, *16*(3), 13–17.

Bayless, K.M., and Ramsey, M.E. (1991). *Music: A way of life for the young child*. New York: Macmillan.

Benson, B.C., and Hjelt, C. (1978). Listening competence: A prerequisite to communication. *Modern Language Journal*, *62*, 85–87.

Bromley, K. (1988). *Language arts: Exploring connections*. Boston: Allyn and Bacon.

Choate, J.S., and Rakes, T.A. (1987). The structured listening activity: A model for improving listening comprehension. *The Reading Teacher*, *41*, 194–200.

Chukovsky, K. (1971). *From two to five*. (M. Morton, trans.). Berkeley, CA: University of California (original work published 1963).

Cunningham, P. (1982). Improving listening and reading comprehension. *The Reading Teacher*, *35*, 486–488.

De Haven, E. P. (1983). *Teaching and learning the language arts*. Boston: Little, Brown.

De Stefano, P., Dole, J. A., and Marzano, R. J. (1989). *Elementary language arts*. New York: Wiley.

Devine, T. G. (1978). Listening: What do we know after fifty years of research and theorizing? *Journal of Reading*, *21*, 296–303.

Faber, A., and Mazlish, E. (1987). How to talk so students will listen and listen so students will talk. *American Educator*, summer, 37–42.

Froese, V. (1981). In V. Froese and S. D. Straw (Eds.). *Research in the language arts*: *Language and schooling* (pp. 12–143). Baltimore, MD: University Park.

Funk, H., and Funk, G.D. (1989). Guidelines for developing listening skills. *The Reading Teacher*, *42*(9), 660–663.

Jacobs, L. (1990). Listening to literature. *Teaching K-8, 20*(4), 34–37.

Jacobs, L. (1986). Listening: A skill we can teach. *Early Years*, *17*, 109–110.

Jacobs, L. B. (1986). Listening—A skill we can teach. *Early Years*, *17*, 109–110.

Jalongo, M. R. (1991). *Developing children's listening skills*. Bloomington, IN: Phi Delta Kappa.

Jalongo, M. R., and Collins, M. (1985). Singing with young children! Folk music for nonmusicians. *Young Children*, *40*, 17–22.

Johnson, W. (1972). *Living with change: The semantics of coping*. New York: Harper & Row.

Leverentz, F., and Garman, D. (1987). What was that you said? *Instructor*, *96*, 66–70.

Lundsteen, S. W. (1985). Listening and story structure in books for young children. Paper presented at the 6th Annual Meeting of the International Listening Association [ED 264 587].

Lundsteen, S. W. (1979). *Listening: Its impact on reading and the other language arts*, 2nd ed. Urbana IL: National Council of Teachers of English.

Mahoney, J., quoted in Butler, S. (1981). The bridge to real writing: Teaching editing skills. ERIC Document Reproduction Service No. 228 639.

Nelson, O. (1989). Storytelling: Language experience for meaning making. *The Reading Teacher*, *42*(6), 386–390.

Norton, D. E. (1985). *The effective teaching of language arts*. (2nd ed.). Columbus, OH: Merrill.

Pearson, P. D., and Fielding, L. (1983). Instructional implications of listening comprehension research. Urbana, IL: Center for the Study of Reading and Communication Skills.

Russell, D. H., Ousky, O., and Haynes, G. B. (1967). *Manual for teaching the reading readiness program*. (rev. ed.) Boston: Ginn.

Schimmel, N. (1978). *Just enough to make a story: A sourcebook for storytelling*. Berkeley, CA: Sisters' Choice Press.

Siefert, K. L., and Hoffnung, R. J. (1987). *Child and adolescent development*. Boston: Houghton Mifflin.

Smith, J. A. (1967). *Creative teaching of the language arts in the elementary school*. Boston: Allyn & Bacon.

Stauffer, R. G. (1980). *The language experience approach to the teaching of reading*. New York: Harper & Row.

Stauffer, R. G. (1975). *Directing the reading-thinking process*. New York: Harper & Row.

Strickland, D. S., and Morrow, L. M. (1989). Interactive experiences with storybook reading. *The Reading Teacher, 42*(41), 322–323.

Strother, D. B. (1987). Practical applications of research on listening. *Phi Delta Kappan, 68*, 625–628.

Swanson, C. H. (1984). Their success is your success: Teach them to listen. Paper presented at the Annual Conference of the West Virginia Community College Association, 1984.

Thomlison, T. D. (1984). Relational listening: Theoretical and practical considerations. Paper presented at the 5th Annual Meeting of the International Listening Association. [ED 257 165].

Weaver, C.H. (1972). *Human listening*. Indianapolis, IN: Bobbs-Merrill.

Wilkes, H. (1981). The aural component: What the teacher needs to know. *Canadian Modern Language Review, 38*, 68–80.

Wilt, M. E. (1950). A study of teacher awareness of listening as a factor in elementary education. *Journal of Educational Research, 43*(8), 626–636.

Winn, D. (1988). Developing listening skills as part of the curriculum. *The Reading Teacher, 42*(2), 144–146.

Children's Books

Ahlberg, J., and Ahlberg, J. (1990). *Bye bye baby: A sad story with a happy ending*. Boston: Little, Brown.

de Paola, T. (1986). *Merry Christmas, Strega Nona*. San Diego: Harcourt Brace Jovanovich.

de Paola, T. (1979). *Big Anthony and the magic ring*. San Diego: Harcourt Brace Jovanovich.

de Paola, T. (1975). *Strega Nona*. Englewood Cliffs, NJ: Prentice Hall.

Dorros, A. (1987). *Ant cities*. New York: Harper & Row.

Ehlert, L. (1990). *Feathers for lunch*. San Diego: Harcourt Brace Jovanovich.

Fonteyn, M. (1989). *Swan lake*. New York: Harcourt Brace Jovanovich.

Gackenbach, D. (1974). *Claude the dog: A Christmas story*. New York: Scholastic.

Gomi, T. (1979). *Coco can't wait*. New York: Puffin.

Hale, S. J. (1990). *Mary had a little lamb*. New York: Scholastic (photos by Bruce McMillan).

Hale, S. J. (1984). *Mary had a little lamb*. New York: Holiday (illus. by Tomie de Paola).

Hest, A. (1984). *The crack-of-dawn walkers*. New York: Macmillan.

Hoffman, E.T.A. (1984). *The nutcracker*. New York: Crown. (original publication date, 1820).

Jesche, S. (1987). *Lucky's choice*. New York: Scholastic.

Van Allsburg, C. (1988). *Two bad ants*. Boston: Houghton Mifflin.

Voight, E. (1980). *Peter and the Wolf*. Boston: Godine.

Wells, R. (1985). *Hazel's amazing mother*. New York: Dial.

Williams, S. (1990). *I went walking*. San Diego: Harcourt Brace Jovanovich.

Zelinsky, P. O. (1990). *The wheels on the bus*. New York: Dutton.

Nonprint Media

Carfra, P. (1982). "The kitty cats' party," *Lullabies and laughter*. Toronto, CA: A & M Records.

Collins, M. (1982). "The opposite song," *Sounds like fun*. Rochester, NY: Sampler Records.

Paxton, T. (1984). *The marvelous toy and other gallimaufry*. Cherry Lane Records.

Raffi and Whitely, K. (1985). "Down on grandpa's farm," *One light, One sun*. Hollywood, CA: A & M Records.

Sharon, Lois and Bram (1980). "The wheels on the bus," *Singin' and swingin'*. Toronto, CA: Elephant Records.

Tickle Tune Typhoon (1987). "We've got the whole world in our hands," *All of Us Will Shine*. Tickle Tune Typhoon, P.O. Box 15153, Seattle, WA, 98115.

Photo: Susan Batcheler

5

Speaking Abilities of Young Children

OUTLINE

VII. Designing a Talk Environment
    A. Characteristics of Positive Talk Environments
    B. Example: Ms. Jamie's Classroom
    C. Developing Children's Speaking Abilities
    D. From Speech to Print: The Language Experience Approach

VIII. Using Drama to Enhance Children's Speaking
    A. Benefits of Spontaneous Drama
    B. Seven Types of Drama
        1. Re-enactment of imaginary and everyday events
        2. Role-playing solutions
        3. Presenting a puppet show
        4. Dramatizing a portion of a story
        5. Narrated theater
        6. Choral speaking and story songs
        7. Scripted drama

Conclusion
Summary
Focus On: Choral Speaking
In the Field: Conducting Semantically Contingent Conversations With Children

Children learn oral language without formal instruction but are bombarded with assistance in learning to read. Ironically, oral language is actually the greater intellectual feat of the two. . . . In acquiring oral language, children must first discover the existence and purpose of language, then master its sounds and structure, and finally learn the multitude of oral symbols which constitute vocabulary. In learning to read, children can build on their previous knowledge of their language as they figure out the written symbol system used to represent it. —MARJORIE FIELDS AND DORRIS LEE (1987)

KEY CONCEPTS AND TERMS

oral language
noncommunicative speech
repetition
monologue
dual or collective monologue
communicative or socialized
  speech
communicative competence
speech immaturities
invented forms

language delay or disorder
bilingual or multilingual
limited English proficiency
gifted and talented
positive talk environment
language experience approach
creative dramatics
choral speaking
semantically contingent

Ms. Praisner teachers three- and four-year-olds. Here are some of their questions and comments that she recorded in her journal:

Dusty (age 3):   (puts a top on the desk and gives it a spin, then twirls around himself) "I can move like a tornado. I saw 'em on TV. I like 'em. (*Teacher:* "But didn't it show on TV how tornadoes hurt people and wreck buildings?") "Yes, but they don't know that people are in the houses when they knock 'em down, do they?"

Rene (age 3):   "Why do they always put water under bridges?"

Teddy (age 3):   "It rains, and the sun comes out and there is a rainbow."

Whitney (age 4):   "See this nail polish? My mom put it on because I have a three o'clock appointment."

Bradley (age 4):   "I saw a man who made horses today. When we got there, he was nailing on the feet."

As these examples illustrate, even very young children arrive at school ready, willing, and able to talk. For this reason, speaking and its receptive counterpart, listening, are the foundation of literacy (Holdaway, 1979).

The Importance of Oral Language

Oral language is a basic starting point of language instruction because (1) it is the most commonly used mode of expression, (2) it is the first form that a child usually learns and (3) it is the most prevalent type of language. Of the approximately 2,796 languages in the world, all have an oral form, but only about 153 have developed a written form (Stewig, 1983).

The Child's Oral Language Development

In 1968, Lovel proposed this simple formula to describe the direction of children's oral language development:

$$I > P > C$$

The way to interpret this formula is to say that at any given point in children's language development, their ability to *imitate* what they hear is greater than their ability to *produce* language independently and their ability to produce language is ahead of their ability to *comprehend* it. The behavior of three children helps to illustrate this point.

Lizbeth overhears her family talking about an ice hockey game at the Civic Arena. She hears the sounds and tries to *imitate* them, even though she cannot produce the words independently and does not comprehend their meaning. To Lizbeth, it is the "Civvie Carrena."

Three-year-old Darlene lives in Pennsylvania. Her aunt lives in California, and she knows it is far away. When her family decides to move from an apartment to a house about fifteen miles away, a neighbor asked where they are going. Darlene said, "Oh, a *long* way. Clear to Calipania! You're not gonna see me any more." Darlene is not just imitating sounds she has heard; instead she is able to *produce* a word that sounds like the names for states she already knows.

Five-year-old Stephen is going for a ride in his grandfather's new "talking car." His grandfather demonstrates how the computerized voice announces that the lights are on, the keys were left in the ignition, etc. When the car announces "Door ajar," Stephan looks disgusted and says, "Grandpa, this car is silly. A *door* is not a *jar*!" Stephan's comments show that he can imitate, produce, and *comprehend* words, even though the single word "ajar" is interpreted as two.

Young children often overestimate the clarity of their communication and assume that their understandings about language are shared by everyone else, so it is particularly important for adults to ask questions to find out what the *child* means by the words he or she uses.

Speaking Abilities of Young Children

Young children's speaking abilities may be clustered into two categories: noncommunicative and communicative.

Noncommunicative Speech

Most preschoolers exhibit three different types of **noncommunicative speech**. In Piaget's (1959) work, noncommunicative speech is also referred to as egocentric speech. "Egocentric" differs from the more common meaning of being selfish and self-centered. Instead, it means preschoolers' limited experience makes it difficult for them to incorporate another person's viewpoint in their thinking. Preschoolers are, in the words of Stone and Church (1984), "embedded in their own perspective."

The three types of egocentric speech commonly observed in children under the age of six or seven are repetition, monologue, and dual or collective monologue. Definitions and examples for each of these three terms are shown in the following paragraphs.

Repetition
Repetition occurs when the child plays with the sounds for the sensual pleasure of talking, including words that make no sense. A three-year-old girl is rocking back and forth in a wooden boat-shaped toy. As she moves, she chants in rhythm with the motion, "Row the boat, row row row the boat. Row, row, row. Rock the boat row. Rock, rock, rock the boat. Row row row."

Monologue

Monologue occurs when the child talks as though thinking aloud, yet makes no attempt to address anyone. This is also referred to as private speech (see Focus On, Chapter 2). The period between wakefulness and sleep is often a time for exploring new vocalizations or speech. Infants often babble and coo, toddlers engage in *spontaneous rehearsal*, self-initiated and directed monologues. Gardner (1980) recorded this nighttime monologue from Anthony, his 18-month-old son: ". . . See the doggie. See the doggie. I see the doggie (said two times in a falsetto voice) Kitty likes doggie. . . ."

Older children continue to use monologues in their speech as well. In a kindergarten class that had just returned from a hospital field trip, one boy talked to himself the whole time as he painted a picture saying, for example:

"There's the elevator we rode on."

"I need green for the old lady in the wheelchair."

"I liked those cookies they gave us. Mommy's aren't that big."

"I'm not going to be there but it would be fun to play with all those toys."

Notice that the monologue contains many different uses of language. The first sentence is a statement based upon observations, the second is *self-guiding speech*, where the child is using language to plan an activity, and the other comments relate the hospital experience to the child's own experience and emotional responses.

Dual or Collective Monologue

Dual or collective monologue occurs when the child talks aloud in the presence of others and takes turns talking. This behavior differs from a conversation, however, because the children's talk is not a dialogue. In a dual or collective monologue, children do not respond to other speakers or interact with them. Instead, they each speak aloud about separate topics. In the following example, which takes place in the housekeeping corner, there are two different play themes in progress among these four-year-olds. Melissa is playing the role of queen while the other children are playing house. If you read Melissa's words separately, you can see that her speech has a completely different topic and focus from that of her peers.

Melissa: "I'm the queen."

Leesha: "Are you gonna eat?" (referring to Carolyn)

Carolyn: "There's an egg stuck in here."

Leesha: "Well, you're just gonna have to leave it there!"

Carolyn: "If anyone would like the salt and pepper, this is the salt and pepper." (she holds up the shakers)

Melissa: "Uh, oh. I better get this stapled again." (referring to her crown)

Leesha: "I think it's time to go to bed. This baby is sleepy. Will you put my baby to bed?" (speaking to Carolyn)

Carolyn: "Do you have a blanket? Let's tuck her in."

Leesha: (Picks up a plastic carrot and offers it to the baby) "Do you need a carrot?"

Carolyn: "Babies drink milk. They don't eat carrots!"

Melissa: "This kingdom has lots of queens."

In this example, Melissa does not adjust her words to a listener's needs. She is using noncommunicative speech.

Communicative or Socialized Speech

As young children begin to acquire a sense of audience and grasp the social interaction aspect of conversation, their speech becomes communicative. The major types of **communicative or socialized speech** are:

1. *Adapted information*, in which the child actually exchanges thoughts with others
2. *Criticism*, including all remarks made about the work or behavior of others
3. *Commands, requests, and threats*, in which one child expects another child to alter his or her behavior immediately
4. *Questions*, including most asked among peers, which require an answer (Smith, 1974).

Each of these forms of socialized speech is evident in the following play text recorded in a kindergarten classroom near the end of the academic year. The text is labeled, using the four categories explained above.

Heather: Let's play policeman. (request) I'll be the cop and you be the bad guy. (adapted information)

Michael: Can I be real bad? (question) I know, I'll have a gun and kill people. (adapted information)

Heather: No, that's *too* mean. Just rob a bank or something. (criticism)

Michael: I want to be a killer. If I can't I won't play cops with you. (threat)

Heather: Well, OK, let's start now! (request) I'll come to your hideout to get you. (adapted information)

Michael: Who is it? (question)

Heather: It's the cops. (adapted information)

Michael: What do you want? (question)

Heather: I'm here to 'rest you, come out with your hands up. I'm going to throw you in jail. (adapted information)

Michael: Oh no you're not, I'll get away, cause you're a girl. (threat)

Heather: Wait, you don't play fair. I'm the cops. You can't get away. (criticism)

Michael: You don't play fair. I don't wanna play with you any more. (criticism)

Communicative Competence in Young Children

In order to communicate effectively, speakers have to do four things simultaneously: (1) identify, process, and interpret a message; (2) integrate and elaborate their thinking and reactions to the message; (3) understand and respond to the message; and (4) produce messages that are understandable to others (Cicourel, 1972). This is known as **communicative competence**; more specific indicators of interactional competence are as follows:

1. *Ability to adapt to changes in the setting*—adjusting to changes in the conversational topic such as using speech to keep a play theme going.

2. *Ability to use nonverbal behavior*—gestures, facial expressions, body movements, vocal intonation, and breaks or pauses in language.

3. *Familiarity with normal constraints and conditions of conversation*—children learn to take turns; to *repair* (starting all over or repeating some portion of a message to be understood); to stick to relevant topics, to use interrogatives (questions); and how to initiate or terminate a conversation.

4. *Ability to sequence*—thinking back or reflecting upon previous experience and linking it with past and possible future events, objects, and resources (Black, 1979, p. 57).

The particular way in which these abilities are used is determined by the child's culture. In a culture that values serenity and quiet, the person who says few words, chooses them carefully, and speaks them calmly is a valued conversational partner. Members of that culture may react unfavorably to a person who talks frequently, engages in small talk, and speaks in an animated way. This is not to say that any of these practices is *better* than the other, only that they are *different*. Cross-cultural research suggests that cultures differ in their expectations for conversation in several ways (Scollon and Scollon, 1981):

Proximity to the listener—When do we feel that the physical distance between conversational partners is appropriate? When do we feel that a person is invading our private space?

Amount of talk—Does silence make us uncomfortable? How much talk is too much?

Beliefs about the reasons for talking—Is the primary purpose of talking to get to know someone or must you know someone before you feel comfortable talking?

Ways in which superiors and subordinates interact—Is it the dominant person's role to talk or is it the subordinate's role to talk and try to impress his or her superior?

How speakers present themselves—Do you "put your best foot forward" or expect others to uncover your strengths?

Who controls the topic—Does the person who initiates contact have control over the topic? In American culture, for example, the person who initiates a telephone call is expected to take the lead in the conversation.

Amount of explicitness—Do we paint a vivid, detailed picture or do we expect listeners to "fill in the blanks?"

Concepts of politeness—Is it always impolite to interrupt or is it a sign of a lively conversation?

Ways of expressing ideas—Should we reveal ourselves to the listener or try to keep our feelings confidential?

Time lapses between speaking turns—Is there a critical point at which the listener feels that the conversation is moving too slowly?

Departure rituals—Are there ways of signaling that the conversation is over? If these ways are violated, is the listener offended?

Example: Children Communicating Through Play

Listen to these first- and second-grade girls who are involved in their favorite sociodramatic play theme, beauty shop. Notice how they adapt to shifts in the conversation, make their comments relevant to the previous speaker's, and use language to talk about past, present, and future. Even though their nonverbal behavior cannot be adequately represented by their words alone, you can imagine how they use their voices and bodies to make their verbal messages clearer. Kelly and Heather are the hairdressers, Tangi and Jennifer are the customers, and Justine is the cashier.

Kelly: "Have a seat, ladies."

Heather: "What will it be today?" (speaking to Tangi and Jennifer)

Tangi: "Oh! Our usual cut and perm."

Heather: "Well, you ladies came at a good time. Today is our special on perms."

Kelly: "What size curlers would you ladies like?"

Heather: "Do you want the full perm or the partial perm?"

Tangi: "I would like the pink curlers and I want the full perm. I want to look like Shirley Temple when she was young."

Jennifer: "I would like the yellow curlers and I want the partial perm; just the top of my head is to be curly."

Kelly: "Please cover your eyes with this towel while I put the solution on your hair."

Tangi: "How much does a style cost?"

Jennifer: "Is it extra or is it part of the sale price?"

Heather: "It's not extra, the styling cost is included in the sale price of perms."

Kelly: "It's time for you ladies to have your hair rinsed and curlers taken out."

Heather: "How much do you want cut off?"

Tangi: "I want just the end tips cut off."

Jennifer: "Leave enough for me to curl my hair with a curling iron. Cut off as much as you can."

Kelly: "How would you like your hair styled?"

Tangi: "Style my hair the way you think best so that it looks good with my face."

Kelly: "How do you ladies like your hair? Is it to your satisfaction?"

Tangi: "I like mine."

Kelly: "How about you, Jennifer?"

Jennifer: "I like mine too."

Justine: "Tangi, your perm comes to $19.95. Jennifer, your perm comes to $16.95. Here's your change, ladies. Have a nice day."

Tangi: "Thank you. Jennifer, let's go out for lunch. What do you say?"

Jennifer: All right, Tangi, that sounds like fun—let's go!"

As this episode illustrates, children can be amazingly adept conversational partners. In the next section we will examine some of the challenges children face as they learn to become effective speakers.

Unique Features of Children's Speech

How would you respond to these situations:

- A three-year-old named "Robbie" pronounces his name as "Wobbie."
- Alaina tells you that she saw cows standing in a "grassture" during her trip to Kentucky.

- Carin, a kindergartner, says, "You teached us how to do that already."
- Stan, a first-grader, shares a joke with the elementary principal. When the principal laughs and teases him a bit, Stan says, "Shut up."

Would you refer Robbie to a speech therapist? Tell Alaina that there's no such thing as a "grassture"? Insist that Carin say "taught" instead of "teached"? Inform Stan that he has been very rude? Would you assume that any of these children had deficient language backgrounds? Actually, all of the behaviors described above are common in young children. Each of these behaviors relates to the components of language discussed in Chapter 1: phonology, semantics, syntax, and pragmatics.

Speech Immaturities

Young children typically have many **speech immaturities**, speech difficulties that gradually disappear without intervention. Table 5.1 highlights some of the most common pronunciation problems in young children's speech, like Robbie's difficulty in pronouncing his *r*'s. Speech immaturities like these center on the sounds of language or *phonology*. In Alaina's case, she is trying to match an unfamiliar word with what she knows about horses. She has never heard of a pasture, but experience tells her that horses eat grass, so she makes the meaning or *semantics* of the word correspond to her understanding. Children often make creative errors like these, called **invented forms**. The words that children invent are efforts to make sense out of what they hear. A child who says, for instance, "I'm barefoot all over" shows that she has grasped the concept of being naked. The child who says, "We're not big shots, we're little shots" knows something about opposites. Sometimes children change a phrase into an invented compound word because that is the way it sounds to them. Several interesting examples of children's invented forms are in Table 5.2

TABLE 5.1   Common Articulation Difficulties of Young Children

Articulation Difficulty	*Example*
th for *s* or *z*	Kerri (age 4) is offered candy and says "No, thanth. I had thum candy yetherday."
d for *g*	Neesha (age 2) says: "Me doe now" for "Me go now."
w for *l* *d* for *th*	Crystal (age 4), shopping for toys: "I could wike one of dem."
b for *v*	Maria (age 3) asks for "beaumbilla" (vanilla) ice cream.
w for *wh* *d* for *th*	Paco (age 2) asks "Was dat?" for "What's that?"
w for *r*	Jennifer (age 3) asks if they can go to the Italian restaurant: "I wanna go to the Woma Woom." (Roma Room).
th or *ch* for *sh*; *sh* for *ch*	Mei (age 3), commenting on his new puppy's misbehavior. "Doggie thoo my chew."

TABLE 5.2   Examples of Children's Invented Words

Standard Form of Speech	*Child's Invented Form*
"long ago" plus "once upon a time"	"onceago"
"because" plus "except"	"becept"
"two of them"	"toodum"
"Pledge of Allegiance"	"Plegiance"
twins, Becky and Brenda	"Beckyenda"
"nice and clean"	"nickaneen"
"upset" plus "excited"	"upsited"
"a couple of minutes"	"comitz"

The third example has to do with *syntax*—the structure of language. It includes such things as inflections (word endings), word order, forming plurals and possessives, making comparisons, and conjugating verbs. Once again, children's knowledge of the rules is evident. A child who says "Mine is more better" or "This is the bestest present I ever got" knows that *-er* and *-est* are usually used to compare things. It just happens that good-better-best is an exception.

The fourth example (in which the child seemed to have insulted his principal) is an example of *pragmatics*—the social appropriateness of language. A child who playfully tells family and friends to "shut up" may generalize that behavior to other social situations. This does not mean that he or she is deliberately being rude or defiant, it is just a use of language that is not acceptable in a more formal context.

Mild to Moderate Delays and Disorders

Even though language behaviors such as these are commonly observed, there are times when young children experience language delays or disorders. A **language delay** means that the child's rate of language development is proceeding much more slowly than that of his or her peers. A **language disorder** is an expressive or receptive language problem that interferes with comprehension and communication. Table 5.3 is an overview of mild to moderate language delays or disorders.

Why do these problems occur? The difficulty can be primarily physical, environmental, social, or any combination thereof. One of the most common sources of language delays and disorders in young children is an undetected hearing problem. If the child has fluid in the ears, a very common ailment, it interferes with the flow of comprehensible input. When the input is garbled, the child's output (language) can be difficult to understand. Sometimes the delay or disorder seems to be related to an understimulating environment where a child has few opportunities to talk or is encouraged to use "baby talk." Another example of an expressive language disorder is stuttering. For some children, stuttering is a speech immaturity. It tends to occur when preschool children are excited and their thoughts are moving faster than their language can express. Usually, if the child is supported rather than

TABLE 5.3   Mild to Moderate Language Delays and Disorders

Delays/Disorders	The Linguistic System	Problem Areas
Reception	*Phonology* Sounds of language	Decoding and comprehension
Processing	*Semantics* Meaning of words	Cognition and integration
Production	*Syntax* Grammatical system of language	Encoding and expression

Source: Bromley, K., and Jalongo, M. R. (1984). Song picture books and the language disabled child. *Teaching Exceptional Children, 16,* 115–119.

criticized, taught to slow down, and gains greater mastery over language, the stuttering disappears. For other children, stuttering is a more persistent and serious difficulty, one that requires professional help. How can teachers know the difference?

Guidelines for Making Referrals

Any child who is suspected of having a speech disorder or language delay should be referred to the appropriate specialists for assessment. Criteria for making referrals include the following:

- If a child appears to have difficulty hearing.
- If family members and those closest to the child cannot understand the child after he or she has begun to talk.
- If the child is noticeably different in communicative abilities from those of his or her peers (Genishi, 1988).

The Linguistically Different Child

These are four major categories of **linguistically different children** (Menyuk, 1988):

Limited English proficiency, such as a newly immigrated child who is acquiring the language of the community as a second language

Dialectical differences, such as a black child who speaks a nonmajority dialect of the language community

Bilingual or multilingual, a child who acquires two or more languages from birth or acquires another language at school

Gifted and talented, children who use language in ways that are more advanced and more creative than the vast majority of their peers

The Teacher's Role

Teachers ought to concern themselves with children's linguistic differences for several reasons. First of all, the number of linguistic and cultural minorities is increasing steadily. Heath and McLaughlin (1987) predict that by the year 2000, more than 50 percent of the nation's school-age children will be members of what we now consider to be linguistic minorities.

A second reason to be concerned about language differences is because mastery of language is a life skill, a social instrument, and a major way of assessing intellectual functioning. Unless teachers strive to meet each child's individual needs, children's educational opportunities will be restricted.

A third reason to be aware of language differences is that every teacher confronts them daily. Sometimes these linguistic differences are dramatic, as in the case of Korean brothers ages five and seven, who were adopted by an American family and attended school without understanding more than ten words of English. At other times, the linguistic differences may be a familiar part of the regional culture, such as the **dialectical differences** of children living in rural Appalachia. In still other situations a teacher might realize that some children are exceptionally gifted users of language, like Jadran, a bilingual first-grader who read *The Story of Jumping Mouse* (Steptoe, 1984) to his classmates on the first day of school.

Responses to Linguistic Differences

There are three basic orientations to languages different from that of the majority population: to eradicate, to keep, or to add (Hennings, 1986).

To Eradicate
Eradication of language differences is a deliberate effort to make children conform and abandon their language differences. Eradication occurs when a child who is gifted and talented in language is forced to go through all the curriculum of that grade level, even when he or she is far beyond that point.

As teachers, we must be aware of our language biases. Why is it that the same adult who cringes to hear an African American child say "We be fine," or a Hispanic child pronounce "chocolate" as "shoclate" is thoroughly charmed to hear a British child pronounce "schedule" as "shedule" or finds the New England pronunciation of "idea" as "idear" charming? Perhaps some pronunciations are better tolerated than others because they are typically associated with speakers of higher social status.

To Preserve
In the 1960s, a movement to preserve and reinforce the child's vernacular emerged. In the bilingual programs of the day, most of the instruction was in the child's first language rather than English. In the wave of criticism that followed these programs,

it was pointed out that denying minorities access to the majority language was itself a subtle form of oppression because those who could not speak the majority dialect had fewer career opportunities. This perspective leads to the current thinking on appropriate responses to the linguistically different child.

To Add

The prevailing attitude in the 1980s and 1990s is a middle ground between eradication and preservation. The most widely accepted position today is to respect the child's nonmajority language or dialect, but to emphasize instruction in the majority language's dialect. As you might expect, the difficulty here is that the child must adapt and learn two or more languages or dialects, the one used at home and the one used at school. The child is expected to become bilingual or bidialectical. This can be especially difficult if the child is bilingual, yet not proficient in the standard register of *either* language, which is sometimes the case.

Some argue that these adaptive demands result in a cognitive advantage; others contend that the schools are placing undue stress on children with language differences (Barry, 1983). As is the case with so many controversies, there is justification for both views—it depends upon the individual child. The task confronting teachers is a difficult one because, as Salinger (1988) describes,

> *Teachers in English dominant classes must find ways to teach proficient speakers and children of limited English proficiency. For all children, they must preserve self-concepts, preserve academic self-esteem and teach basic skills in content areas. Modeling, scaffolding, expansion, and peer teaching all contribute to children's success, as do meaningful social interactions requiring the use of the target language. (p. 60)*

The basic philosophy that should undergird instruction for linguistically different children is that language is for communication, not an object. It is more important for children to *use* language than to analyze its letters, phonemes, or grammatical structure.

Designing a Talk Environment

A classroom that supports children's speech should give them opportunities for five different kinds of talk:

Informing—talk used to explain, describe, report, or give instructions

Inquiring—talk used to seek information and ask

Conjoining—talk used to maintain and enhance social relationships

Moving into action—talk used to plan, control, or persuade

Enjoyment—talk used for the recreation and pleasure of self and others (Klein, 1979).

Characteristics of Positive Talk Environments

A **positive talk environment** has these attributes:

1. Adults use words to show affection for children and sincere interest in them.
2. Adults send congruent verbal and nonverbal messages.
3. Adults extend invitations to children to interact with them.
4. Adults listen attentively to what children have to say.
5. Adults use children's interests as a basis for conversation.
6. Adults speak courteously to children.
7. Adults plan or take advantage of spontaneous opportunities to talk with each child informally.
8. Adults avoid making judgmental comments about children either to them or within their hearing (Kostelnik, Stein, and Whiren, 1988).

Example: Ms. Jamie's Classroom

Ms. Jamie, a day-care provider, creates a positive talk environment in her class through her discussion-leader techniques. Notice that she has taught the children how to participate in a discussion, that the children feel their contributions are valued, and that Ms. Jamie uses open-ended questions to encourage participation.

Ms. Jamie: *"What is a hospital?"*

Missy: "A place where you go when your head cracks open."

Adam: "Like when you get sick and get an ear infection."

Jared: "A place where they got to make sure your heart is beating."

Aaron: "A place where you get stitches or a cast."

Ms. Jamie: *"What is a cast?"*

Missy: "It is something that keeps you dry and safe so it can heal."

Matt: "To keep your arm healthy."

Ms. Jamie: *"How would you get to the hospital?"*

Avanti: "Drive in a Corvette or bicycle."

Kellen: "You could drive there and get a popsicle while you wait."

Ms. Jamie: *"Who would you see there?"*

Missy: "Doctors, nurses, an x-ray person, babies, and parents."

Ms. Jamie: *"What would they do there?"*

Sammy: "Give you x-rays and shots that really hurt."

Avanti: "Take your blood pressure."

Matt: "I have an idea. You could ride in a wheelchair."

Ms. Jamie: *"How would you feel before you went?"*

Kellen: "Sad, mad, and happy."

Avanti: "Nervous!"

Matt: "Terrible!"

Ms. Jamie: *"How would you feel after you were there?"*

Avanti: "Fine, happy, much more better."

After reading this example of dialogue in Ms. Jamie's classroom, it is easy to imagine what a positive talk environment it must be. Notice that children are encouraged to talk about what *they* noticed, what made an impression on *them*, rather than guessing what is in the teacher's mind.

Developing Children's Speaking Abilities

Not only the opportunities for talk but also the *types* of talk that occur in classrooms are important. Too often, conversations between teachers and children are heavily centered on "petty management"—giving instructions, talking about cleaning up, washing hands, getting meals, and so forth. In Bruner's (1977) observational research, only twenty percent of all the verbal interactions in preschool classrooms were sustained conversations and two-thirds of those were with peers. Informal talk can build children's speaking skills as well as more formal speech activities. Children should be taught how to talk quietly as they work individually or in groups, and to differentiate between the loudness levels that are acceptable outdoors, when addressing the entire class, and when talking to a classmate seated near by.

   In planning speech activities, teachers should be guided by the principle that "the child can understand more than he or she can say, and [should] seek, above all, to communicate . . . There is no set of rules of how to talk to a child that can even approach what you consciously know. If you concentrate on communicating everything else will follow" (Brown 1977, p. 5). One specific approach that teachers can use to build children's competence as speakers is to demonstrate the connection between spoken and written language.

From Speech to Print: The Language Experience Approach

It was an exceptionally warm week in September. The windows had been opened, and several wasps had been hovering around the twelve-foot-high ceiling of the first-grade classroom. The teacher had told the children to ignore the wasps unless they came close. As she was sharing a book with the class, one of the wasps landed right on Saundra's ponytail. The teacher swatted the wasp with the book and stepped on it as soon as it dropped to the floor. The children cheered and they decided to write a story together using the language-experience approach. As the children contributed each part of the story, the teacher wrote their names and words on chart paper as follows:

Seth: Unless the wasps came near us, we didn't pay any attention to them.

Alicia: But on Friday, one of them did! We were listening to a story after lunch when a wasp landed right on Saundra's ponytail.

Saundra: I was so scared I was afraid to move.

Todd: Ms. R. squished it before it could sting us. She was really brave.

Teacher: Any ideas for a title?

Jackie: "Remember that story we heard, *Arthur's Teacher Trouble* (Brown, 1975)? Let's call our story *Wasp Trouble.*

Bryan: "Yes, and let's tell the principal or janitor to kill them."

The teacher incorporates these comments and the class reads the story aloud. Several children decide to illustrate the story and it is put on the bulletin board. Children read the story over and over again. Saundra makes her own illustrated version and takes it home to read. The theme of being rescued is popular so the teacher extends the idea by reading *Sheila Rae, the Brave* (Henkes, 1987), *Heckedy Peg* (Wood, 1987) and *The Rescue of Aunt Pansy* (Ernst, 1987). Then, because every child has a personal experience with rescue, sixth-grade volunteers drop by throughout the week and type children's stories on the word processor. The children illustrate their stories and the stories are compiled into a book called *Amazing Rescues*. The book is so popular that a dittoed copy is made for every child to take home. The original is laminated and kept in the classroom's library. In this way, speech has been used as the basis for developing literacy with print.

Using Drama to Enhance Children's Speaking

The word "drama" usually creates images of theater, a stage, props, costumes, and scenery. But that is formal, scripted drama, which is an art form, usually performed by professionals for the purpose of entertaining the audience. Informal, spontaneous drama has a very different purpose. It is intended to contribute to the growth of the participants rather than the observers (Combs, 1988). Drama expert Nellie McCaslin (1985) makes this useful distinction: "Theatre is something you look at. Drama is something you do" (p. 34). When using drama in the classroom, you need to "Remember, you're not selling tickets, you're teaching children" (Bodel, 1987, p. 79). **Creative dramatics** "includes all forms of improvised drama—drama created by children themselves and played with spontaneous action and dialogue and action. Pantomimes, creative work in puppet and shadow plays, creative plays based on literature or incidents from the social studies—each is a part of creative drama" (Burns, Broman and Wantling, 1966, p. 126).

Benefits of Spontaneous Drama

There are many reasons why spontaneous drama is appropriate for developing children's speaking skills:

> It adapts to the child's level of proficiency with speech. Children may perform only the physical gestures or make use of very limited vocabulary, yet still participate.
>
> It is relevant to learners because it builds upon prior knowledge and experience (McCaslin, 1987).
>
> It begins with physical response, moves to symbolism and finally, to abstraction, thus making the abstraction of language more concrete (San Jose, 1989).
>
> It promotes social uses of language: cooperation, problem solving, leadership, and sharing with classmates; identification with, empathy and insight about story characters (Smith, 1986).
>
> It invites expressive and imaginative uses of language (Nelson, 1989; Verriour, 1984).

Seven Types of Drama

There are at least seven types of creative dramatics activities that are appropriate for young children:

1. Re-enactment of Imaginary Scenes and Everyday Events

Drama in early childhood should draw upon the child's nonverbal and verbal enactment abilities. *Enactment* refers to the putting of body, mind, and emotions together in order to express and interpret an idea (Sebesta, 1989). Even the very young child knows how to use enactment. A toddler may pretend to do something she is not permitted to do, such as turn the buttons on the stereo, and look to her parent for a display of mock anger. During teacher-initiated enactment, children are invited to respond to various events they have observed or imagined. For example, a teacher might ask children to pretend they are snowmen on a warm sunny day (McCaslin, 1987). After children have mastered some simple pantomime-type activities such as those in *Pretend You're a Cat* (Marzollo, 1990), they are ready to move on to somewhat more involved imagination-stretchers.

One teacher used the following creative drama activity as part of a unit on pets. It also served as an introduction to two picture books, *The Last Puppy* (Asch, 1980) and *A Bag Full of Pups* (Gackenbach, 1981):

> *Let's pretend . . . let's pretend about puppies. Close your eyes and think about a basket full of cute and cuddly puppies. There's one that is very playful and one that is sleepy. Open your eyes. Let's see how you would pet the puppies. Remember, they're very small. Okay, let's look at the playful one. Show how you would pick her up . . . be careful, she's really squirming around! Now she's trying to lick your face. Put her on your lap and let's look*

at the sleepy one. He's a little bit bigger and isn't quite awake yet. Let's pick him up. Oh, he looks like he wants to go back to sleep. Let's see how you will hold him. Which puppy will you choose? Why?

2. Role-Playing Solutions

"Imagine that it's a freezing cold day," the teacher says, "and you are going to have a cup of hot chocolate. It's sitting on the table right in front of you. Watch out! It's *very* hot and the mug is *very* full with marshmallows bobbing around on top. Let's see how you would taste it." In this example, children are presented with a problem. If you were observing the class, you would see many different responses: some are pretending to use a spoon, some are blowing on the cup, and some are trying to sip it without picking up the mug.

3. Presenting a Puppet Show

Most adults who had the experience of using puppets in school remember a scripted drama. Often the play was the last selection in a basal reader and when it was performed, it was obvious that children were too busy fumbling with their books, trying to read their lines, and keeping their place to pay much attention to the puppet. That, of course, is a great advantage of spontaneous drama. The children can concentrate on operating their puppets and can speak to the audience instead of being dependent upon a script. By using very familiar stories or predictable books, children can easily put on a puppet play with an improvised script. The puppets themselves need not be elaborate. Figure 5.1 illustrates several types of simple puppets.

There are four reasons for using puppets in the classroom:

1. *Puppets improve communication skills.* Children will often talk to or through a puppet when they feel uncomfortable talking as themselves or talking to another person.
2. *Puppets speak a universal language.* Even when children with hearing impairments and limited English proficiency watch a puppet play, they usually can infer the meaning of the performance.
3. *Puppets encourage cooperation.* "Taking on" another persona and coordinating its behavior with that of others during a puppet play teaches children to work together.
4. *Puppets help to integrate curriculum.* All of the subject areas can be explored through puppetry. Children who performed puppet plays based on the books *Mr. Grigg's Work* (Rylant, 1989); *The Dove's Letter* (Baker, 1988); *A Letter to Amy* (Keats, 1968); and *A Letter to Santa Claus* (Impey, 1989) not only acquire literacy skills, they also find out more about the postal system, the purposes of letters, and the results of correspondence.

4. Dramatizing a Portion of a Story

Books that are suitable for dramatization are: (1) understandable and meaningful to students; (2) lend themselves to simple, dramatic improvisation; and (3) are used

RECYCLABLES

FOOD CONTAINERS

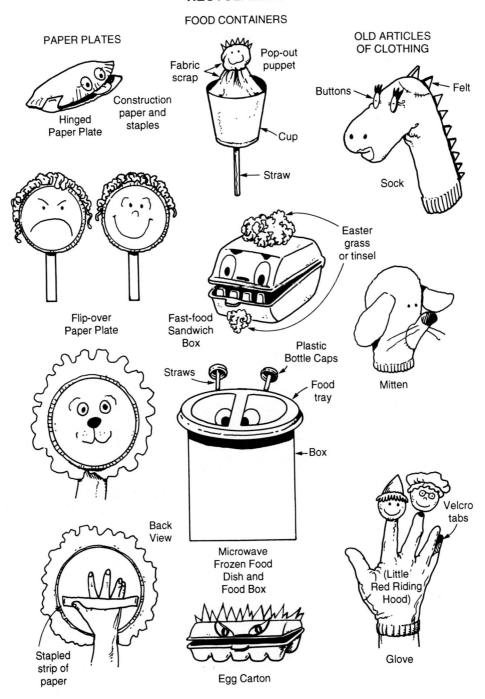

PAPER PLATES

Fabric scrap

Pop-out puppet

OLD ARTICLES OF CLOTHING

Hinged Paper Plate

Construction paper and staples

Cup

Straw

Buttons

Felt

Sock

Flip-over Paper Plate

Easter grass or tinsel

Fast-food Sandwich Box

Mitten

Straws

Plastic Bottle Caps

Food tray

Box

Back View

Microwave Frozen Food Dish and Food Box

Velcro tabs

(Little Red Riding Hood)

Stapled strip of paper

Egg Carton

Glove

FIGURE 5.1 Simple Puppets

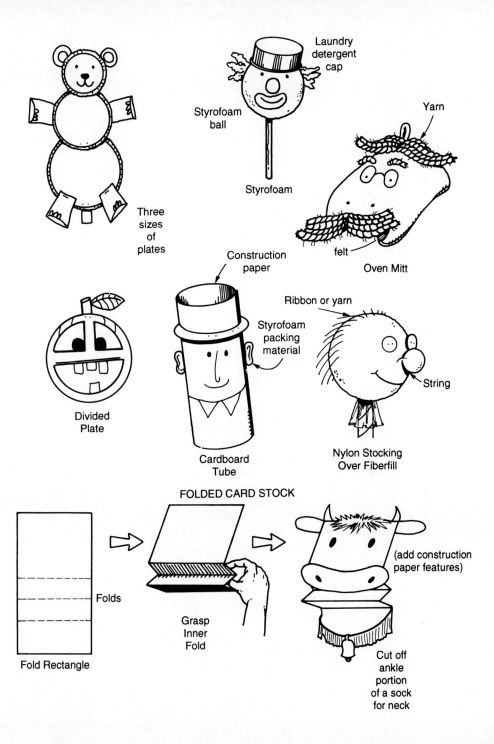

Three sizes of plates

Laundry detergent cap

Styrofoam ball

Styrofoam

Yarn

felt

Oven Mitt

Construction paper

Ribbon or yarn

Styrofoam packing material

String

Divided Plate

Cardboard Tube

Nylon Stocking Over Fiberfill

FOLDED CARD STOCK

Folds

Fold Rectangle

Grasp Inner Fold

(add construction paper features)

Cut off ankle portion of a sock for neck

flexibly by the teacher so that every child can participate (e.g., developing several skits from one story, creating new parts) (Bodel, 1987). One teacher involved children in enacting Little Red Riding Hood by providing simple props—a red hood for Little Red, a nightcap for Granny, paper ears, a scarf tail for the wolf, and a hunting cap for the woodsman. The script was invented by the children as they went along, based upon their general knowledge of the world and their specific knowledge of the story. Part of what makes spontaneous drama so entertaining is the combination of the two. I once observed a child playing the role of Papa Bear in a dramatization of The Three Bears. He was seated at a table set with small, medium, and large plastic bowls and spoons. When the teacher asked, "What does Papa Bear say?" the child said in a deep, gruff voice, "Woman, bring me my coffee!" Surprises like these are far more interesting than listening to an adult standing in the wings and using a stage whisper to remind children of the script they have forgotten due to stage fright.

Picture books with a simple plot are also appropriate for spontaneous drama. Some excellent choices are:

> *The Snowy Day* (Keats, 1971)
> *What Do You Say, Dear?* (Joslin, 1958)
> *The Grouchy Ladybug* (Carle, 1977)
> *Have You Seen My Duckling?* (Tafuri, 1986)
> *Frederick's Fables* (Lionni, 1985)
> *Too Much Noise* (McGovern, 1967)
> *One Fine Day* (Hogrogian, 1971)

The entire book needn't be dramatized in order for spontaneous drama to occur. Children may also choose to enact just one favorite scene from books such as:

> *The Talking Eggs* (San Souci, 1989)
> *Bea and Mr. Jones* (Schwartz, 1982)
> *The Story of Jumping Mouse* (Steptoe, 1984)
> *Chita's Christmas Tree* (Howard, 1989)
> *Song and Dance Man* (Ackerman, 1989)

5. Narrated Theater

Another way to use drama in the early childhood classroom is through an adaptation of a technique used with older children called readers' theater. In readers' theater, small groups of children perform a work of literature by reading it aloud. The actions in the story may be imagined by the audience, or they may be performed by another group of children (Bromley, 1988). Because most young children are not yet reading independently, early childhood educators can adapt this technique to become narrated theater, where an adult or child narrator reads most of the text of a book and the children perform the actions and say the key phrases that are repeated throughout the story. *Hattie and the Fox* (Fox, 1987) is a good choice for this type of drama. The text of the stories used in narrated theater may also be printed on large chart paper or accompanied by a big book version. This enables children to become more familiar with the story and gradually take over the narrator's role.

Ada Dawson Stephens, Professor Emeritus at the University of Toledo was fond of using *Caps for Sale* (Slobodinka, 1940) in narrated theater. She supplied several brightly colored caps and a large table as props. She read most of the text of the book as narrator. In the story, a peddler walks around town crying "Caps! Caps for sale! Fifty cents a cap!" On his head he wears a stack of caps, topped by his own black and white checked cap. Business is slow, so he decides to take a nap under the tree. In this narrated theater version, the table becomes a tree and a group of children sit on the table, playing the role of the mischievous monkeys. When the peddler falls asleep, the monkeys climb down and steal every cap, except the peddler's own black and white checked one. The peddler sees what has happened and he alternately yells, stamps his foot, and shakes his fist, saying each time, "You monkeys, you. Give me back my caps." But every time the monkeys just say, "Tss tss." Finally, the peddler gets so angry that he throws down his own cap and the monkeys (being mimics that they are!) throw down all of the other caps as well. Then the peddler puts his caps back on and resumes calling, "Caps! Caps for sale! Fifty cents a cap!"

Some other suggestions for narrated theater are:

The Cat Who Loved to Sing (Hogrogian, 1988)
Rabbit Makes a Monkey of Lion (Aardema, 1990)
Where the Wild Things Are (Sendak, 1963)
Best Friends (Kellogg, 1986)
A Chair for My Mother (Williams, 1982)
One Tough Turkey (Kroll, 1982)

6. Choral Speaking and Story Songs

After nearly all of the children can recite a poem, tell a story, or sing a song from memory, this can become the basis for drama. Children may enact the story themselves or they may use different types of visual aids such as simple puppets, a story scroll, a flannel board, cue cards or an illustrated chart. Some good selections for choral speaking are *This Is the House That Jack Built*, modern tales with a similar cumulative format such as *Drummer Hoff* (Emberley, 1967), or *The Napping House* (Wood, 1984). Repetitive rhymes like *Jesse Bear, What Will You Wear?* (Carlstrom, 1986) or short rhymes with strong rhythms like *Barn Dance!* (Martin and Archambault, 1986) are also good choices. Songs that might be sung and dramatized in person or with puppets are:

Mary Wore Her Red Dress and Henry Wore His Green Sneakers (Peek, 1985)
The Fox Went Out on a Chilly Night (Spier, 1961)
On Top of Spaghetti (Glazer, 1982)

Six Little Ducks (Conover, 1976)
Follow the Drinking Gourd (Winter, 1988)

7. Scripted Drama

Generally speaking, an introduction to traditional scripted drama is more appropriate for children in the upper elementary grades. Children who write an original story and want to perform it themselves or with puppets, however, should certainly be encouraged to do so. Scripted drama is appropriate for young children if the following questions can be answered in the affirmative:

- Is the script suited to the children's reading abilities?
- Is the idea of a play enthusiastically pursued by children rather than an adult imposition?
- Does the performance of the play take place in a familiar, supportive environment (such as a classroom) rather than in an unfamiliar, pressured environment (on stage before parents, teachers, and children)?
- Is the story one that the children have selected or an original story, rather than an "assignment" from an adult?

If the scripted drama is child-centered and child-developed and the criteria can be met, then it is suited to young children (Brown, 1985). Sometimes the book itself can supply a basic script. A group of third-graders used the letters from *The Jolly Postman and Other People's Letters* (Ahlberg and Ahlberg, 1986) in a scripted play. This book contains actual correspondence to or from a fairy tale or nursery-rhyme character. Several pages of the book are fashioned into envelopes with a letter, card, or invitation inside. The second-graders removed these bits of correspondence from the book as the basic script. Some examples of the book titles that lend themselves to scripted drama from children in the primary grades are the following:

Space Case (Marshall, 1980)
Swamp Monsters (Christian, 1983)
Leo the Late Bloomer (Kraus, 1971)
A Weekend With Wendell (Henkes, 1986)
The Biggest Pumpkin Ever (Kroll, 1984)
Sylvester and the Magic Pebble (Steig, 1969)

Conclusion

If we as teachers build upon all of the oral language learning that has already taken place in the young child's home, children will learn to speak more competently and confidently. By appreciating the rich diversity in the language of students and emphasizing functional language activities, teachers make a significant contribution to the child's expressive language abilities.

Summary

Young children's speech is generally categorized as noncommunicative (monologue, repetition, dual or collective monologue) or communicative (adapted information; criticism; commands, threats, and requests; questions). Because young children are becoming users of language, they frequently have speech immaturities—difficulty with pronunciation, word meaning, irregular forms, and the social appropriateness of language. If children's speech difficulties are more serious, as in speech delays or disorders, they should be referred to a specialist for evaluation. Many young children come to school with language differences such as limited English proficiency, dialectical differences, bilingual or multilingual abilities, and/or gifted and talented with language. In every case, it is important for teachers to master the use of semantically contingent speech and to build positive talk environments. Creative dramatics, choral speaking, and the Language Experience Approach are an essential part of the positive talk environment and an important way of fostering communicative competence in all children.

Focus On: Choral Speaking

If children are to hear, use, and appreciate the beauty of language they need opportunities to speak beautiful words. By using their speaking voices as instruments, children can recite poetry, stories, and chants in a number of different ways.

Fingerplays are one of the first kinds of **choral speaking** used with young children. In a fingerplay, children use their hands to make gestures that accompany the poem.

Action rhymes usually involve the whole body in enacting or interpreting a short poem or chant.

Echo poems are another simple form of choral speaking. In an echo poem, the children simply repeat after the leader. A fine example is Lorraine Bayes' Tickle Tune Typhoon 1983 recorded version of "Bear Hunt" in which the rhythm and intonation of each line are repeated by the listeners.

Going on a Bear Hunt
(Echo each line through entire story and slap thighs)
I'm not afraid!
It's a beautiful day
The sun is shining
The birds are singing
The bees are buzzing
What's that?
Tall grass
(Sweeping arm motions making swishing sounds)
Going on a bear hunt
I'm not afraid

What's that?
It's a tall tree
(Arm motions climbing up, then back down)
Going on a bear hunt
I'm not afraid
What's that?
Oh it's mud
Better put on your boots
(March through the mud making sloshing mud noises)
Going on a bear hunt
I'm not afraid
What's that?
It's a river
We're going to have to swim
(Swim across the river)
Going on a bear hunt
I'm not afraid
What's that?
Oh it's a dark cave
(Put fingers and hands in binocular circles around eyes)
I can't see anything
I can feel something
I can hear something
We better take out our flashlights
(Take out flashlight and flick it on)
Oh it's a bear . . . RUN
(Very dramatically and loud)

Repeat the sequence in reverse quickly and dramatically slapping thighs and doing all the actions for each verse. Figure 5.2 contains "cue cards" to accompany the "Bear Hunt" echo poem.

Line-a-child is another strategy for choral speaking. This approach works very well with cumulative poems such as *The Rose in My Garden* (Lobel, 1984) or *Do You Want to See Something?* (Merriam, 1965). If the children design pictures or masks or costumes to accompany the poem, each child can step forward and speak his or her line.

Unison adds more and more children's voices until the poem becomes louder and more forceful. Or, it can move from loud to soft. Two poems that are suitable as unison selections are the big-book version of *Noisy Nora* (Wells, 1973) and *Shoes* (Winthrop, 1986).

Refrains are a type of choral speaking in which the leader speaks most of the poem or chant and the group is responsible for the part that is repeated. This repetition can occur at the beginning, as with Mary Ann Hoberman's (1986) chant:

Yellow butter purple jelly red jam black bread
Spread it thick
Say it quick
Yellow butter purple jelly red jam black bread

FIGURE 5.2   Visual Aids for Going on a Bear Hunt

Now repeat it
While you eat it
Yellow butter purple jelly red jam black bread
Don't talk
With your mouth full! (p. 67)

or the refrain can conclude each page, as in *Koala Lou* (Fox, 1989) where the mother tells her child: "Koala Lou, I love you."

In the Field: Conducting Semantically Contingent Conversations with Children

In **semantically contingent speech**, adults are responsive to the child's words (Snow, 1983). In this In the Field assignment, you will be using the four basic types of semantically contingent speech in a conversation with a young child. As described previously in this chapter, encouraging extended conversations with young children requires four basic strategies:

1. *Expansions*—in which the adult *elaborates upon what the child has to say.*
2. *Semantic extensions*—in which the adult goes beyond extending a topic and *adds new information.*

3. *Clarifying questions*—These are the questions that *request more information from the child*. In this type of question, adults are really interested in what the child has to say, believe that he or she has more to say, and probably do not know the answer themselves. Ideally, more of teacher's "questions should relate to topics that children know something about—preferably, even more than the teacher does" (Hendrick 1986, p. 254).

4. *Answers to the child's questions*—in which teachers lead children to discover answers for themselves rather than telling them the answers.

Conversing with a young child is an important skill for educators and depends upon two abilities. The first ability is identification with the child. The second ability involves following and supporting the child as she moves back and forth between reflection (inner thoughts) and projection (speaking about thoughts) (Tough, 1977). To test your skills in conversing with a child, do the following:

1. Arrange to conduct an extended conversation with a young child. Ideally, it should be a child who knows you and feels comfortable conversing with you. If this is not possible, ask a teacher to recommend a confident, talkative child to be your partner in an informal conversation.

2. Bring a tape recorder and cassette tape. Make certain that all the equipment is in working order. Collect some pictures of things that are likely to interest a child.

3. Begin by introducing yourself. Tell the child that you want to talk with him or her about favorite things. Allow the child to select whatever picture he or she likes and begin the conversation.

4. During the course of the conversation, make every one of your utterances semantically contingent (related to what the child has just said).

5. Use all four of the research-based strategies to enhance children's speech: expansions, semantic extensions, clarifying questions, and answers to the child's questions.

6. List the strategies in item 5 above and transcribe excerpts from the tape that illustrate how you used each one.

7. Be prepared to share your example of each language strategy in class.

References

Barry, J. E. (1983). Politics, bilingual education, and the curriculum. *Educational Leadership*, *40*(8), 56–60.

Black, J. (1979). Formal and informal means of assessing the communicative competence of kindergarten children. *Research in the Teaching of English, 13*, 49–68.

Bodel, M. (1987). Taking the trauma and tedium out of class plays. *Learning '89, 16*, 76–79.

Bromley, K. D. (1988). *Exploring connections: Language arts*. Boston: Allyn and Bacon.

Bromley, K., and Jalongo, M. R. (1984). Song picture books and the language disabled child. *Teaching Exceptional Children*, 16, 115–119.

Brown, R. (1977). "Introduction." In C. Snow and C. Ferguson (Eds.). *Talking to children: From input to acquisition*. Cambridge, MA: Cambridge University Press.

Bruner, J. (1977). *Under five in Britain* (Vol. I.). Ypsilanti, MI: High Scope Press.

Burns, P. C., Broman A. L., and Wantling, A. L. (1966). *The language arts in childhood education*. Chicago, IL: Rand McNally.

Cicourel, A. V. (1972). Cross-modal communication: The representational context of socio-linguistic information processing. In R. Shuy (Ed.). *Monograph Series in Language and Linguistics* (pp. 187–272). Twenty-third round table. Washington: Georgetown University Press.

Combs, C. E. (1988). Theatre and drama in education: A laboratory for actual, virtual or vicarious experience *Youth Theatre Journal, 2*(3), 9–10.

Fields, M., and Lee, D. (1987). *Let's begin reading right*. Columbus, OH: Merrill.

Gardner, H. (1980). *Artful scribbles: The significance of children's drawings*. New York: Basic Books.

Genishi, C. (1988). Young children's oral language development. Urbana, IL: ERIC Clearinghouse on Elementary and Early Childhood Education.

Heath, S. B., and McLaughlin, W. (1987). A child resource policy: Moving beyond dependence in school and family. *Phi Delta Kappan, 68*(8), 576–580.

Hendrick, J. (1986). *Total learning: Curriculum for the young child* (2nd ed.). Columbus, OH: Merrill.

Hennings, D. G. (1986). *Communication in action: Teaching the language arts*. Boston: Houghton Mifflin.

Holdaway, D. (1979). *The foundations of literacy*. Sydney, Australia: Ashton/Scholastic.

Klein, M. (1979). Designing a talk environment for the classroom. *Language Arts, 56*, 647–651.

Kostelnik, M. J., Stein, L. C., and Whiren, A. P. (1988). Children's self esteem: The verbal environment. *Childhood Education, 65*(1), 29–32.

Lovel, K. (1968). Some recent studies in cognitive language development. *Merrill Palmer Quarterly, 14*, 123–138.

McCaslin, N. (1987). Creative drama in the classroom. *Teaching K-8, 17*, 39–41.

McCaslin, N. (1985). Quoted in Theatre of happy accidents. *Early Years/K-3, 15*(7), 34.

Menyuk, P. (1988). *Language development: Knowledge and use*. Glenview, IL: Scott, Foresman.

Nelson, O. (1989). Storytelling: Language expression for meaning making. *The Reading Teacher, 42*(6), 386–390.

Piaget, J. (1959). *The language and thought of the child*. (M. Gabain and R. Gabain, trans.). London: Routledge & Kegan Paul. (Original work published in 1926.)

Salinger, T. (1988). *Language arts and literacy for young children*. Columbus, OH: Merrill.

San Jose, C. (1989). Classroom drama: Learning from the inside out. In S. Hoffman and L. L. Lamme (Eds.). *Learning from the inside out: The expressive arts*. (pp. 67–76). Wheaton, MD: Association for Childhood Education International.

Scollon, R., and Scollon, B.K.S. (1981). *Narrative, literacy and face in interethnic communication*. Norwood, NJ: Ablex.

Sebesta, S. (1989). The story is about you. In S. Hoffman and L. L. Lamme (Eds.). *Learning from the inside out: The expressive arts* (pp. 22–28). Wheaton, MD: Association for Childhood Education International.

Smith, G. (1974). Listening to the language of children. *Young Children, 29*, 135–140.

Stewig, J. W. (1983). *Exploring language arts in the elementary classroom*. New York: Holt, Rinehart and Winston.

Stone, L. G., and Church, J. (1984). *Childhood and adolescence*. New York, NY: Random House.

Tough, J. (1977). Children and programmes: How shall we educate the young child? In A. Davies (Ed.), *Language and learning in early childhood* (pp. 20–88). London: Heinemann.

Verriour, P. (1984). The reflective power of drama. *Language Arts, 61*(2), 125–130.

Children's Books

Aardema, V. (1990). *Rabbit makes a monkey out of lion*. New York: Dial.

Ackerman, K. (1989). *Song and dance man*. New York: Knopf.

Ahlberg, J., and Ahlberg, J. (1986). *The jolly postman or other people's letters*. Boston: Little, Brown.

Asch, F. (1980). *The last puppy*. Englewood Cliffs, NJ: Prentice-Hall.

Baker, K. (1988). *The dove's letter*. San Diego, CA: Harcourt Brace.

Brown, M. (1975). *Arthur's teacher trouble*. New York: Scholastic (big book).

Carlstrom, (1986). *Jesse Bear, what will you wear?* New York: Macmillan.

Carle, E. (1977). *The grouchy ladybug*. New York: Scholastic.

Christian, M. B. (1983). *Swamp monsters*. New York: Dial.

Conover, C. (1976). *Six little ducks*. New York: Crowell.

Ernst, L. (1987). *The rescue of Aunt Pansy*. New York: Viking.

Emberley, E. (1967). *Drummer Hoff*. Englewood Cliffs, NJ: Prentice-Hall.

Fox, M. (1989). *Koala Lou*. San Diego: Harcourt Brace Jovanovich.

Fox, M. (1987). *Hattie and the Fox*. New York: Bradbury.

Gackenbach, D. (1981). *A bag full of pups*. New York: Clarion.

Glazer, T. (1982). *On top of spaghetti*. New York: Doubleday.

Henkes, K. (1987). *Sheila Rae, the brave*. New York: Greenwillow.

Henkes, K. (1986). *A weekend with Wendell*. New York: Greenwillow.

Hoberman, M. A. (1986). "Yellow butter purple jelly red jam black bread." In J. Prelutsky (Ed.). *Read-aloud rhymes for the very young*. New York: Knopf.

Hogrogian, N. (1971). *One fine day*. New York: Macmillan.

Howard, E. T. (1989). *Chita's Christmas tree*. New York: Bradbury.

Impey, R. (1989). *A letter to Santa Claus*. New York: Delacorte.

Joslin, S. (1958). *What do you say, dear?* New York: Scholastic.

Keats, E. J. (1971). *The snowy day*. New York: Scholastic.

Keats, E. J. (1968). *A letter to Amy*. New York: Harper & Row.

Kellogg, S. (1986). *Best friends*. New York: Dial.

Kraus, (1971). *Leo the late bloomer*. New York: Crowell.

Kroll, S. (1984). *The biggest pumpkin ever*. New York: Holiday House.

Kroll, S. (1982). *One tough turkey*. New York: Holiday House.

Lionni, L. (1985). *Frederick's fables: A Lionni treasury of favorite stories*. New York: Random House.

Lobel, A. (1984). *The rose in my garden*. New York: Greenwillow.

Martin, B., and Archambault, J. (1986). *Barn dance!*. New York: Holt.

Marzollo, J. (1990). *Pretend you're a cat*. New York: Dial.

McGovern, A. (1967). *Too much noise*. New York: Scholastic.

Merriam, E. (1965). *Do you want to see something?*: New York: Scholastic.

Peek, M. (1985). *Mary wore her red dress and Henry wore his green sneakers*.

Rylant, C. (1989). *Mr. Grigg's work*. New York: Franklin Watts.

San Souci, R. D. (1989). *The talking eggs*. New York: Dial.

Schwartz, A. (1982). *Bea and Mr. Jones*. New York: Puffin.

Sendak, M. (1963). *Where the wild things are*. New York: Harper.

Slobodkina, E. (1940). *Caps for sale*. Reading, MA: Addison-Wesley.

Spier, P. (1961). *The fox went out on a chilly night*. New York: Doubleday.

Steig, W. (1969). *Sylvester and the magic pebble*. New York: Windmill.

Steptoe, J. (1984). *The story of jumping mouse*. New York: Lothrop, Lee & Shepard.

Tafuri, N. (1986). *Have you seen my duckling?* New York: Penguin.

Wells, R. (1973). *Noisy Nora*. New York: Dial.
Williams, L. (1986). *The little old lady who was not afraid of anything*. New York: Crowell.
Williams, V. (1982). *A chair for my mother*. New York: Greenwillow.
Winter, J. (1988). *Follow the drinking gourd*. New York: Knopf.
Winthrop, E. (1986). *Shoes*. New York: Harper & Row.
Wood, A. (1987). *Heckedy Peg*. San Diego: Harcourt Brace Jovanovich.
Wood, A. (1984). *The napping house*. New York: Harcourt Brace Jovanovich.

Children's Records and Tapes

Bayes, L. (1986). "Bear Hunt." Tickle Tune Typhoon, P.O. Box 15153, Seattle, WA, 98115.

PART THREE

Literature-Based Language Learning

PART THREE EXAMINES THE powerful influence of personal narratives, the oral tradition of storytelling, and the type of published literature best suited to the young child, the picture book. Chapter 6, "Narratives and Storytelling," discusses the development of the child's storytelling abilities and suggests strategies that teachers can use to develop children's concept of story and show teachers how to become effective storytellers themselves. Chapter 7, "Picture Books and the Literature-Based Curriculum," describes how picture books can become a valuable resource for early childhood educators in child-centered language arts programs.

Photo: Margaret Stanek

6

Narratives and Storytelling

OUTLINE

Key Concepts and Terms
Introduction

I. Types of Narratives
    A. Recounts
    B. Accounts
    C. Event Casts
    D. Stories

II. Development of the Child's Narrative Abilities
    A. Setting
    B. Characterization
    C. Plot and Theme
    D. Style

III. Why Tell Stories to Children?

IV. Teachers as Storytellers
    A. Who Can Become a Storyteller?
    B. Getting Started

V. Selecting Stories to Tell
    A. Story Elements
    B. Story Language
    C. Story Appeal

VI. How to Tell a Story

VII. Ways of Presenting Stories
  A. Traditional Storytelling
  B. Storytelling With Props
    1. Overhead projector
    2. Apron stories
    3. Storytelling with real objects
    4. Draw and tell, fold and cut
    5. Participatory telling
    6. Storytelling in costume
    7. Poster and flannel-board cutouts
    8. Storytelling with toys
    9. Three-dimensional puppets
  C. An Integrated Approach to Story Sharing
  D. Extension Activities
    1. Discussion
    2. Sensory experiences with things in stories
    3. Role playing and enactment
    4. Retelling
    5. Dramatic play
    6. Reconstructing through pictures
  E. Creative Dramatics Based on Personal Narratives

Conclusion
Summary
Focus On: Group Stories
In the Field: Observing Children's Narrative Abilities

Our lives are made of stories. From our earliest years we construct stories about our real and imaginary experiences and share these stories with other people. Such stories allow us to explore our lives, to try out alternative possible ways of acting and being in the woprld, and indeed to help shape our future actions . . . Humankind is not so much the language-using animal as it is the storytelling animal
                                        —FRANCES E. KAZEMEK (1985)

KEY CONCEPTS AND TERMS

narrative
recounts
accounts
event casts
stories
folktales

event-structured material
oral tradition
storytelling
narrative abilities
wordless picture books

All around the world, in hundreds of different languages, children speak these words: "Tell me a story." Why are children so enthralled by stories? Perhaps it is because

> *stories think for themselves, once we know them. They not only attract and light up everything relevant in our own experience . . . They are little factories of understanding. New revelations of meaning open out of their images and patterns continually, stirred into reach by our own growth and changing circumstances. (Hughes, 1988, pp. 34–35)*

We use stories to reflect upon, organize, and communicate human experience:

> *The collective strength of a people lies in the cultural memory embedded forever in their stories. Participating in those stories, either as teller or audience, is a fundamentally human activity that gives pleasure to both. At the same time, stories are a deep well from which people—young and old alike—have drawn strength, renewal, and inspiration. From stories we learn what makes us human. (Moir, 1989, p. 86)*

Types of Narratives

Researchers who study the stories created by human beings use the word **narrative** to describe our ability to produce and comprehend event-structured material. Heath and Branscombe (1986) have identified four basic categories of narratives: recounts, accounts, event casts, and stories.

Recounts

Recounts are *retellings*, either self-initiated or in response to questioning. A recount could be a real life experience, such as a child retelling a well-known family story. Recounts can be imaginary too, like second-grader Lisa's written retelling of *Snow White and Rose Red*, reproduced here just as she wrote it:

> *One day when Snow white and Rose red and their mother were siting in the living room, there was a knock on the door. When they opened the door a big brown bear rushed in. He told them he was cold and hungry and would not hurt them. for many winters they took him in and cared for him. In the summer, the bear did not come. Snow white and Rose red were lonely, one time when they were shopping for their mother And a mean dwarf jumped out of the bushes and grabbed them. then they heard a bears growl. A big brown bear was running toward them. the bear pushed the dwarf So that he fell and hit his head on a rock and was killed Then the bear called to Them Hello Snow white and Rose Red. It was their friend from witer then his fur fell off and there was a hand some young man in his place.*

Figure 6.1 is the drawing Lisa made to accompany her retelling.

FIGURE 6.1   Lisa's Drawing to Accompany Her Retelling of Snow White and Rose Red.

Accounts

Accounts differ from recounts in that they *provide new information or new interpretations of information* that may already be known to the teller and the listener. The account can be initiated by the teller or by another party. Justin gave this account of his heart surgery:

> *I had a pink robe and a bed with three yanks (an adjustable bed). I was hooked up to an I.V. One day a nurse came in and said, "Justin, we're going to take your picture." It got put in the newspaper. Mommy bought me a new tractor. I was real sick and nauseated. I had the flu with a bad fever. I ate lots of popsicles. I wasn't scared—just sick! There were 25 doctors. I was there three days. I saw a guy with a broken leg in a wheelchair. They took my blood. They had a big needle and stuck it in my arm (he demonstrates). My dad was there and it didn't hurt a bit.*

The picture Justin drew to accompany the account is in Figure 6.2.

Event Casts

Event casts differ from recounts and accounts in their play-by-play description. Event casts are *running commentaries* about events in the attention of teller and listener. The event cast may be simultaneous with events or it may precede them. Nathan, age 6, creates an event cast which is simultaneous with his experience of the wordless picture book, *The Apple and the Moth* (Mari and Mari, 1970). His teacher, Ms. Brunetta, takes dictation as follows:

FIGURE 6.2   Justin's Picture Drawn to Accompany His Account of His Hospital Stay.

. . . On the branch, it is starting to make its cocoon.

It is fall now. The leaves are starting to turn brown. The cocoon is done now.

Now it is winter. The leaves are falling off. The cocoon is still there.

Now it is summer. The buds are starting to grow on the trees. The caterpillar is breaking its way out of the cocoon.

After it is out of its cocoon, it starts to spread its wings.

Now it is flying away.

It's flying over the sky.

It's flying over to the apple tree with blossoms on it.

There it is laying an egg on one of its blossoms . . .

Stories

Stories are *fictional narratives in which an inanimate being moves through a series of events with goal-directed behavior.* In a story, two elements are introduced: nonliterality and change. Nonliterality means that the story is more than a factual report of a real life event. Imagination and creativity are essential elements in a story.

The second element, change, is equally important. If no changes take place as a character pursues the goal, then it is not a story. A "story is something happening to someone you have been led to care about . . . whatever its subject matter, every story is about change" (Shulevitz, 1985, p. 7, 47). Story skills include: knowing how to begin a story, explaining the setting, describing characters, identifying theme, sequencing events, explaining reactions, and concluding the story (Feagans, 1982). Here is a story by Jillian, a third-grader:

FREDDY THE BALLOON

There was once a hot air balloon named Freddy. Freddy lived in Hawaii, but no one liked Freddy and his friends because he had nothing to weight him down. Everyone was scared to use him. One day the mayor said, "These balloons have to go!" Freddy cried, "I want to be used, not thrown away!" But it didn't help. He was sent to New York, split up from his friends and gone forever.

Ten years later, he was found by a wise man. "We can make use of this thing," he said. "All we need are some bags of sand."

Freddy was so excited he jumped. He went up, up, up. The only person who ever saw him after that was his friend Jack, while he was flying.

It is said that he landed on the moon, and if you look close, you can see him smiling at night.

It is also said that when anyone tries to touch or harm a balloon, Freddy zaps them back in time, never to return.

Figure 6.3 is the picture Jillian drew to accompany her story.

Development of the Child's Narrative Abilities

If we look at how children come to understand stories, there is a definite developmental sequence. By relating this process to the five traditional literary elements— setting, characters, plot, theme, and style—we can gain insight into the child's concept of story.

Setting

The setting for children's narratives tends to begin at home and gradually move farther and farther away (Applebee, 1978). Toddlers' and three-year-olds' narratives are usually about home and family; four to six-year-olds' narratives are often about institutions less familiar than home (such as school, the hospital, the zoo) or an indefinite place (such as the forest, outer space, or jungle), and seven to eight-year-olds' narratives often take place in a definite, distant locale such as Africa or Saturn. As children mature in their storytelling, their settings are less like a scenery backdrop and more integral to the story, such as first-grader Mitchell's story about a rainstorm, a rainbow and a leprechaun illustrates:

FIGURE 6.3 Jillian's Picture to Accompany Her *Freddy the Balloon* Story.

CHESTER AND THE LEPRECHAUN
by Mitchell

One day after a big rain in Connecticut, Chester was hopping alone. Then, all of a sudden, he saw a rainbow. He figured he would hop over and see if anybody was there. All he found was a big, black pot. On the pot he saw a little man dressed in green, with a hat that had a three leaf clover on it. He remembered what Tucker had told him about a leprechaun before he had left.

Characterization

The *characters* in children's narratives begin as agents, one-dimensional figures who perform a particular action, rather than characters with a personality, motives, and intentions. A typical toddler's or three-year-old's narrative contains one agent and one action that achieves some practical end, such as Nicholas's narrative about his cat:

I have a Cat name Sammy Cat 'cause I like it. My dad wanted me to name Sammy Cat "Top Cat," but I want Sammy name better. Mummy likes mine name better for Sammy too.

As children gain experience with various types of narratives, their characters are described in greater detail but those details are usually descriptions of physical traits that have little bearing on the plot. The characters in a typical preschooler's stories become very action-oriented and spirited; they sometimes seem to be involved in a never-ending series of adventures (Gardner, 1982).

Gradually, the characters in children's stories begin to evidence change during the course of the narrative. At first, those changes are often rather superficial, like six-year-old Courtney's duck character:

> *Once upon a time there was a little boy and the little boy had a little duck. The duck's name was Quacker and the boy's name was Tommy. Every morning and night, Tommy fed his little duck. And one morning the duck has babies . . . has three babies, two boys and one girl. The boy's name was Mike and one of the girls' names was Cindy. The other girl's name was Bethany. The end.*

By the time that children are in second or third grade, they begin to invent characters who are more individual, characters who grow and change meaningfully during the course of the story.

Plot and Theme

Children's storytelling moves in two basic directions simultaneously, chaining and centering (Applebee, 1978). *Chaining* refers to the linkage of events to one another in some type of sequence. *Centering* refers to the theme, focus, problem, etc., which unifies those events. Many two- and three-year-olds begin to create "heaps," collections of whatever enters their minds with little linkage from one sentence to another. Fours tend to combine events based on similarity. At first, the connecting linking is fairly superficial; a child might begin by talking about a toy bear and then suddenly switch to a lion, for instance. Later, the connections have more of an "and then . . ." sequence; the chaining of events is more apparent than the centering. Children sometimes recount an event but tell it out of sequence, or their stories may be quite long but simply stop without any feeling of concluding or "wrapping it up." Here is Sarah, age four, telling about her puppy:

> *I got a new puppy, Mommy—Daddy got me a new puppy. We all got to name him and, uhm, his name is Rusty. Mommy gets all mad when he pees on the new carpet. But I . . . but I play wif him and I throw him his ball and he chews on my shoes.*

Style

With ample opportunity to enjoy stories, the child's use of literary style may emerge quite early. By the age of five, most children with experience listening to stories use these elements of literary style:

They give a title to their story.

They began using formal opening ("Long ago and far away . . .") and closing ("The End")

They use the past tense of the verb to describe story events.

They lower their voices when telling the story so that listeners will have to pay closer attention.

When first-grader PJ shared his original story about a gorilla with his classmates and family, he used all of these literary elements (Figure 6.4).

```
                       THE GORILLA
                  THAT I MET AT THE ZOO




                           BY


                     P.  J.  MURRILL












              Lansdowne Publishing Co.
                  6400 Prett Court
              Charlotte, N.  C.   23226
                  (704) 366-3923
```

FIGURE 6.4

```
Copyright Date: 1988
Publisher:  Mrs. Sue Walthall
            Mrs. Laura Buckner
Lansdowne School Press
Charlotte, N. C.
```

FIGURE 6.4   *Continued*

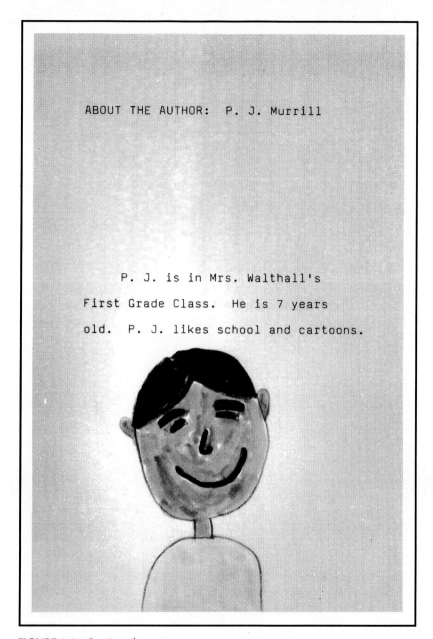

ABOUT THE AUTHOR: P. J. Murrill

P. J. is in Mrs. Walthall's
First Grade Class. He is 7 years
old. P. J. likes school and cartoons.

FIGURE 6.4   *Continued*

FIGURE 6.4 *Continued*

FIGURE 6.4 *Continued*

And then the gorilla broke the
cage and got out.

- 3 -

FIGURE 6.4 *Continued*

And then he killed the zoo keeper.

- 4 -

FIGURE 6.4   *Continued*

And then he got back in the cage
and ate bananas.

- 5 -

FIGURE 6.4   *Continued*

Then he threw the banana peel on
the floor and then he slipped and
died.

- 6 -

FIGURE 6.4   *Continued*

```
This Book Is Dedicated To Mom
and Dad
```

FIGURE 6.4 *Continued*

Why Tell Stories to Children?

Margaret Spencer's (1976) observational research with children who were learning to read suggests that there is a definite connection between stories heard by children and stories told by children. In fact, this relationship was so strong that it led Meek (1982) to conclude that children "absorb" story structures. Listening to stories, then, is entertainment in the original sense of the word. Although the word "entertain" is commonly used as a synonym for lighthearted fun, the word "entertain" literally means to completely absorb us for a time, to become part of us.

Sharing stories with children is an essential part of their growth in literacy because stories:

increase children's knowledge and understanding of other races and beliefs

teach children more about narrative structures—beginnings, sequencing, endings, etc.

introduce children to a wider range of story-sharing experiences

stimulate children's imaginations

expand vocabulary and provide children with good models of usage, enunciation, and pronunciation

suggest models for the child's own stories, both oral and written

encourage children to listen, concentrate, and follow event-structured material

challenge assumptions and introduce new ideas in a nonthreatening way

develop children's thinking skills; problem-solving strategies, cause-effect, compare/contrast, etc.

nurture and encourage a sense of humor

increase children's appreciation of literature

reinforce cultural values (Roe, 1988; Scott, 1985; Smith and Park, 1977).

Teachers as Storytellers

Sharing a story with someone is a warm, personal act. As Ramon Ross (1980) writes:

There is a humanism inherent in sharing language, sharing stories, dancing and singing in the old ways. These are kindly approaches to learning about yourself and those around you . . . there needs to be, I think, a strong and vital strain of tenderness, love and slippery feeling stuff in our lives. And that's where storytelling comes in. (p. 5)

Who Can Become a Storyteller?

The people who tell stories are memorable to children and adults. "Ms. L.," a retired first-grade teacher and avid storyteller, is warmly referred to as the "story lady" by children and greatly admired by college students and colleagues. She is particularly fond of the narrative poem, *I Met a Man* (Ciardi, 1961) which she relates to young children in a participatory way. Ms. L. has created a huge fabric bag that she uses to swallow up passersby, just like the sack in the story. The listeners participate by reciting the talking sack's words in a mysterious-sounding voice: "Put in another one, just like the other one." The sack continues to engulf up a few giggling child volunteers until the story concludes with their release. This particular story was requested often by her first-graders and storytelling was an important part of Ms. L.'s curriculum.

Whenever teachers consider becoming storytellers, they usually think about the professional storyteller who can spellbind a diverse audience ranging from preschoolers to senior citizens. "How could *I* ever hope to be that good?" they ask, comparing themselves to professionals like Jackie Torrence or The Folktellers. As a result, educators' initial reaction to the idea that they should tell, rather than read, some stories is frequently met with resistance. The first step in convincing yourself is to remember that, just as when sharing music with children, the goal is *enjoyment*, not competing with the nation's leading performers.

Getting Started

The primary responsibility of an adult who shares a story with the child "is to create a memorable experience" (Barton, 1986, p. 7). Keeping this advice in mind, learning to tell a story to young children is not such a difficult task. Actually, you probably already know several stories well enough to tell rather than read them. Sometimes those stories are the traditional ones that you have heard many times, stories such as Goldilocks and the Three Bears, Little Red Riding Hood, and The Three Little Pigs. These traditional tales, called **folktales**, are a good starting point for the beginning storyteller. A *folktale* is a story that has been passed from one generation to the next for many years. Most folktales are part of the **oral tradition**: they were originally told rather than read. Also part of this oral tradition are folk songs which tell a story song such as "Six Little Ducks" or "Fiddle-i-fee." You may also know some narrative poems by heart or recall some favorite books from your childhood that you can tell rather than read with a little practice.

Recordings of storytellers can be very helpful in learning a story too. You can listen to audiotapes while traveling or to records as you straighten up your classroom after school. Watching videotapes of storytellers in action, attending a storyteller's live performance, participating in a storytelling workshop, or asking the local librarian to tell stories to your class are all good ways to get started with **storytelling**. The bibliography at the end of this chapter suggests print and nonprint resources for the beginning storyteller.

Selecting Stories to Tell

When selecting a story to tell, teachers should consider four basic features. Good stories to share with young children

1. represent the best quality that literature has to offer.
2. match the interest and conceptual level of the audience.
3. have a compact, action-filled plot.
4. capture the children's interest immediately.
5. build to a satisfying conclusion.

Some excellent story collections that meet these criteria are: *Grandfather Tales* (Chase, 1948); *Best Loved Folktales of the World* (Cole, 1982); *A Story, a Story* (Haley, 1970); *Stories From the Big Chair* (Wallace-Brodeur, 1989); *Twice Upon a Time* (Sierra and Kaminski, 1989); *How Many Spots Does a Leopard Have?* (Lester, 1990); and *Turtle Knows Your Name* (Bryan, 1989).

Story Elements

Brewer (1984) has identified three universal story elements that we should look for in the stories we tell:

Surprise—the author deliberately withholds information, often revealing the listener's or reader's expectations

Suspense—the author adds information to prolong the wait before the question in the reader's or listener's mind is answered

Curiosity—the author provides just enough information to let the reader know that something is missing

Surprise, suspense, and curiosity are found in varying degrees in all of the familiar folktales and children's classic books. Take, for example, the story of Chicken Little. It begins with the surprise of the main character getting hit on the head, it creates suspense as Chicken Little stops to speak to several other birds, and it builds curiosity because the listener wonders whether the fowl will manage to escape from the wily fox. Some other traditional stories for young children with these elements include: *Bony Legs* (Cole, 1983); *The Three Sillies* (Galdone, 1981), *The Gunniwolf* (Harper, 1967), *The Mitten* (Brett, 1989) and *A Penny a Look* (Zemach, 1971).

Story Language

Good stories for the telling also use rhythm and repetition to the best possible effect: "But it was too cold . . . but it was too hot . . . And it was just right." Without writing, we tend to think in terms of sound groupings rather than in individual words (Lord, 1964, p. 25). Those sound groupings can help us to remember the story sequence. We remember, for example, that the Little Red Hen gets a "Not I" from each animal when she asks, "Who will help me plant the wheat?", "Who will help me grind the flour?", and "Who will help me bake my bread?" But when she asks for help eating the finished product, every animal replies, "I will!"

Story Appeal

The teacher should select a story that he or she enjoys and wants to share in this personal way with students. Enthusiasm is a key element in successful storytelling because it is enthusiasm that will sustain you through the effort it takes to learn the story.

How to Tell a Story

There are several things to consider as you prepare to tell a story:

1. Know the story and practice it until there is no chance of forgetting it.
2. Tell the story simply, directly, and sincerely, using your voice and body to maximum effect.
3. Trust the medium—words—and the rich heritage of the oral tradition.
4. Pace your telling by changing the tempo when necessary and using pauses effectively.
5. Establish rapport with your listeners to make the story come alive for them (Tooze, 1959).

Ways of Presenting Stories

Basically, there are two ways of telling stories. The traditional way is to use only voice and gesture to share a story. The second basic way of telling a story is to accompany it with various types of props such as flannel-board figures, puppets, and so forth.

Traditional Storytelling

For centuries, telling stories has been the basic way of keeping them alive. In traditional storytelling, the teller uses nothing but verbal and nonverbal communication skills and nothing comes between the teller and the listener (Baker and Greene, 1987). Although traditional storytelling emphasizes its origins in oral language, beginning storytellers in our print-oriented society often begin with a published or recorded version of the stories they tell.

Folktales are often recommended to the beginning storyteller because they are already familiar and their form has been perfected. "They are closely knit, have few digressions, move logically through the development of their plots, and come to a satisfying conclusion. They are easy to prepare because they move rapidly, are full of action, humor, and color" (Viguers, 1974, p. 2).

Storytelling with Props

In storytelling with props, real or representative objects are used to introduce a character, underscore a key concept, build suspense, or surprise the listeners. A videotape by Caroline Feller Bauer (1986) contains excellent examples of traditional and modern storytelling with props. She uses line drawings on the chalkboard to tell *Monkey Face* (Asch, 1977) and a stuffed toy dog to recite *Mother Doesn't Want a Dog* from Judith Viorst's (1982) collection of poems *If I Were in Charge of the World and Other Worries*. Additional examples of storytelling with props are described below.

Overhead Projector

As story characters in Ruth Hurlmann's (1977) *The Proud White Cat* are introduced, a paper silhouette or scrap of fabric is projected onto the screen. In this story, an arrogant cat believes that no one is worthy to be his wife so he decides to get Mrs. Vixen's advice. The clever fox takes the cat through this sequence: the moon is the finest lady but the sun is stronger; it makes the moon pale. But the sun can't shine through the mist, the mist is stronger. The wind is stronger than the mist because it can blow it away. Each time a stronger force is identified, the cat agrees to marry it. But Mrs. Vixen continues by saying that the tree is stronger than the wind since it cannot be blown down. The fire is strong enough to devour the tree but the rain puts out the fire. The house stands through the rain, but the mice that live beneath undermine the walls and since Kay Cat is even stronger than the mice, she is just the wife for a proud white cat! This tale can be told on the overhead projector by using a piece of nylon stocking for the mist, strips of open weave polyester for the wind, and a bit of seeded voile for the rain.

Apron Stories

By creating an apron with pockets, teachers can introduce story characters as they enter the story. Most adults are familiar with the counting song that begins: There were ten in the bed and the little one said, "Roll over!" This story song can be shared with children using paper or fabric puppets as props. The characters from Merle Peek's (1981) illustrated picture-book version can be used to create the ten characters in the story and an apron with ten pockets can serve as a "headboard" for the bed. At the beginning, each character is positioned inside a pocket, then removed when "they all roll over and one falls out." (See Figure 6.5.)

Storytelling With Real Objects

A single item can be used to introduce a story, such as a bone inside a pocketbook to tell William Steig's (1976) *The Amazing Bone*, a handful of beans to tell "Jack and the Beanstalk," a pair of goggles to tell *Goggles!* (Keats, 1969), a pencil and book bag to tell *The Good Luck Pencil* (Stanley, 1986), or a patchwork quilt to tell *The Quilt Story* (Johnston and de Paola, 1985).

FIGURE 6.5 Ten in the Bed.

A collection of real objects can be used to tell Catherine Stock's (1985) story of *Sophie's Bucket*, a story about her day at the beach. Sophie gets two packages at the beginning of the story—a swimsuit and a plastic bucket and shovel. While she is at the beach, she plays in the sand, looks at the seaweed, finds a starfish, watches a pink crab, and saves some seawater in a jar. Each of these objects can be introduced at the appropriate time as the story is shared with young children.

Draw and Tell, Fold and Cut

Some stories, such as Paul Zelinsky's (1981) *The Maid, the Mouse, and the Odd-Shaped House* can be drawn as the story is told. Other stories are illustrated by the teller's paper cutouts of simple objects, such as a jack-o-lantern used to tell a Halloween story (Hart, 1987).

Participatory Telling

Children can participate in storytelling, both through speaking the words and through enactment. *The Fat Cat* (Kent, 1972) is a Danish folktale in which a cat devours everyone he meets on the road until a woodcutter's ax helps them to escape. One interesting way of telling the story is to make a cardboard face for the cat and attach it to a paint stirrer or ruler. Then the stick is pulled through a hole cut in the center of an old sheet and a child stands underneath. As the teacher tells the story, other children who play the characters crawl underneath the sheet and the Fat Cat expands rapidly. When the Woodsman intervenes, the other characters emerge in reverse order until the cat is reduced to his original size. As a grand finale, the children can wrap a strip of sheet around the Fat Cat's "incision."

Some stories have been converted into chants that can be recited by the teacher and gradually learned by the children, like "The Jazzy Three Bears" (Fink, 1984).

Storytelling in Costume

In Arnold Lobel's (1980) book of *Fables*, the story of "The Bear and the Crow" is about a vain and foolish bear who tries to impress others with his finery. On the way into town, the bear meets a crow who tells him that his attire is completely out of fashion. Librarian Paige Price tells the fable to children by dressing herself in the latest style, just as the crow recommends: with a frying pan on her head, paper bags on her feet, and a bedsheet wrapped around her middle. When the bear arrives in town, he is the object of ridicule, and as he runs home, he meets the crow again:

> *"Crow, you did not tell me the truth!" cried the bear. "I told you many things," said the Crow, as he flew out of the tree, "but never once did I tell you that I was telling the truth!" (p. 16)*

Even though the message of fables can be too abstract for young children, the fact that Ms. Price makes it concrete through her ridiculous attire enables even pre-schoolers to understand the moral of the story: "When the need is strong, there are those who will believe anything."

Poster and Flannel-Board Cutouts

A teacher at a church-affiliated preschool created laminated cardboard figures to accompany the song picture book *One Wide River to Cross* (Emberley, 1966). By writing the numerals 1 to 10 on each story character, she could use the story-song for practice in counting and numeral identification.

The focus of *Jennie's Hat* (Keats, 1966) is her creation of a hat that can be built at the flannel board with pieces of brightly colored felt by the storyteller. Some other good choices for the flannel board are Charles Shaw's (1947) classic, *It Looked Like Spilt Milk*; the folktale, *The Three Billy Goats Gruff*; *Little Red Riding Hood* (use Dick Bruna's [1966] version for the patterns).

Storytelling With Toys

A kindergarten teacher shared *Crictor* (Ungerer, 1958), the story of a pet boa constrictor, with a crocheted toy snake as a prop. In the story, the Crictor owner is a teacher and when he visits the classroom, he becomes a lively visual aid by forming different letters of the alphabet and numerals with his body. Of course, when the teacher shared the story, her knitted boa could be used to do the same thing.

The classic story of *The Mitten*, recently redone in Jan Brett's (1989) beautiful illustrations, is another good story to tell with toys. The basic story line is found in many cultures. It is the theme that there is not always room for one more. The story begins when a mitten is left in the forest and a series of different animals crawl inside to get warm. Eventually, the mitten bursts at the seams and all the animals go back into the forest. To tell the story with toys, cut out a giant mitten from fabric and tack the edges together with a temporary adhesive, like a glue stick. Then, collect small stuffed toys to represent each forest animal and squeeze them inside until the mitten comes apart at the story's conclusion.

Shirley Hughes' (1981) *David and Dog* is another good story to tell, using toys as props. A well-worn toy "Dog" can be used to represent the one that David loses at the school fair. A new toy dog can be used to represent the one that his older sister wins and then trades to get Dog back for David.

Three-Dimensional Puppets

Two student teachers created a caterpillar puppet that metamorphoses just as it does in Eric Carle's (1969) *The Very Hungry Caterpillar*. At the beginning of the story, they created a large leaf backdrop and wiggled the little finger of an old glove through the center to represent the caterpillar crawling on the leaf. They switched to a finger of the glove as the caterpillar grew and the fully grown caterpillar was fashioned from the hand and wrist portion of the glove. Polyester fiberfill was used for a cocoon. For the book's final scene they made a butterfly from nylon stockings stretched over two metal hangers and decorated it with brightly colored fabric scraps. As the "cocoon" wriggled and dropped off the stage, the butterfly first appeared with the hanger wires bent. Then they were fully expanded and the butterfly appeared to flutter out from underneath the stage.

An old workglove and pompom or felt characters that attach to each finger of the glove with velcro can be used to tell a story with a simple sequence such as *There*

Was an Old Lady Who Swallowed a Fly, The Three Little Pigs, Goldilocks and the Three Bears, The House That Jack Built, Chicken Little, and *The Gingerbread Man.*

Leo Lionni's (1960) *Inch by Inch* can be told by using a finger from an old glove to represent the inch worm and making posters of each of the things he measures during the story. An excellent resource in the use of every type of puppet is Hunt and Renfro's (1982) *Puppetry in Early Childhood Education.*

An Integrated Approach to Story Sharing

Melissa Renck, a children's librarian, planned a preschool story hour with a camping theme that included storytelling, story reading, singing, and watching a film. First, she rolled up brown construction paper into log shapes and decorated them with orange and yellow crepe paper streamer "flames." When the children arrived, they were seated in a circle around the "campfire." The librarian started the session by assessing children's prior knowledge with questions like:

What is camping?

Have any of you ever been camping?

What are some of the things you do when you camp out?

Next, she read the book *Bailey Goes Camping* (Henkes, 1985). Bailey is the littlest bunny in the family and his older brother and sister get to go camping while he has to stay home. With the help of his parents, Bailey gets to go on a simulated camping trip. He has hotdogs for lunch; goes (teddy) bear hunting; lives in a tent (a blanket over a clothesline); goes swimming and fishing (in the bathtub); tells ghost stories (to his parents); and toasts marshmallows (on the stove). After the story, the children sang "The Bear Went Over the Mountain." Then the librarian read *Sophie's Knapsack* (Stock, 1988) while unpacking a real knapsack filled with the items from the story. Next, they did the echo chant, "Going on a Ghost Hunt," an adaptation of "Going on a Bear Hunt." After the librarian told them a ghost story *Thump, Thump, Thump!* (Rockwell, 1981), the children were anxious to participate in telling stories around the campfire. Sean told his own version of *A Dark, Dark Tale* (Brown, 1981) while Yolanda shared an embellished version of Mercer Mayer's (1976) *There's a Nightmare in My Closet.* Three-year-old Frank said "I have one!" and told this one-sentence "scary story," complete with a quavering voice and menacing gestures: "Once there was monster and he would scratch little children." The session concluded with the film *Mickey's Trailer* (1981) and the children sharing the animal crackers that were in the knapsack.

Extension Activities

When a professional storyteller performs, the story ends, and it is up to the audience to reflect upon what they have heard or discuss it with others. But when storytelling takes place in an early-childhood classroom, it needs to be followed by response activities:

> *Just telling story after story was not enough. Much of the experience of listening is lost if story is poured upon story with no chance for reflection. The youngsters needed time to process what they had heard. However, direct questioning is not always the best approach. A question-and-answer discussion can quash the sense of wonder and impose conformity in each listener's reaction. (Reed, 1987, p. 38)*

Some activities recommended to follow up a story are discussed below.

Discussion

After hearing a story, each child should be given the opportunity to comment and to react to one another's comments. As Meek (1982) points out, "left to comment on their own, without the stimulus of a question, children often choose to talk about quite other aspects of a tale than those that preoccupy their elders" (p. 289). When teachers allow children to take the lead and follow the children's agenda for the story, the results are far more satisfying. Literature discussion groups can give children the opportunity to respond to the story elements (plot, theme, characterization, setting, style), to relate the book to books by the same authors, by other authors or student authors, to relate the book to their life experiences (personal, others, social issues) or to evaluate (like or dislike, prove a point, clarify an idea) (Pierce, 1990).

Sensory Experiences With Things in Stories

After hearing a story, children can smell, taste, hear, see, and touch what was portrayed in the story. A group of five-year-olds, for example, made fried bananas after hearing the Philippine folktale *Un Cuento de Cocodrillo/A Crocodile's Tale* (Aruego, 1972) about a monkey who gets a ride across the river to some banana trees by outsmarting him. Some third-graders had a similar sensory experience with *Stone Soup* (Brown, 1947). This folktale tells about a group of hungry soldiers who come to a town and tell the inhabitants that they have a magic stone that can create a huge kettle of soup. They place the stone in some water and then keep asking the curious onlookers to contribute just a little of various ingredients to the pot, until finally, like magic, there is soup enough for everyone.

Role Playing and Enactment

Children need not enact the entire story. They can choose a single behavior, enact a single scene or interview children who are "in character" (Sebesta, 1989). Ms. Heasley told the story of The Ugly Duckling to a small group of first-graders. Then she interviewed them:

Teacher: "Mother duck, are you worried about your baby duckling?"

Maria: "I felt mad, but I wasn't worried."

Teacher: "Ugly duckling, how did *you* feel after you turned into the beautiful swan?"

Urie: "I wanted to go back to the barnyard and show everyone that I turned out to be very pretty."

Teacher: "After you became a swan, how did the others treat you?"

Kirstie: "They treated me with respect, and they said they were sorry."

Of course, character enactment is not the only type of dramatization possible. A group of preschoolers in Mr. Tanaka's class created their own *Color Dance* in response to Ann Jonas' (1989) concept book by using sheer, colored scarves that could be combined to form new hues.

Retelling

After Ms. Hennings tells *The Elves and the Shoemaker* to a small group of children, she distributes plastic spoons, permanent markers, and small squares of fabric. The children make puppets on the spot by drawing a face on the back of the spoon, pulling the spoon handle through a small slit in the fabric, and gathering the material around the base of the spoon with tape. Then the children tell their own version of the story, inventing dialogue as they go.

Dramatic Play

Pam Conrad's (1989) *The Tub People* is an imaginative picture book about the adventures of the pudgy, miniature, plastic figures that are often used as tub toys by children. The perspective drawings in the book really sparked the imagination of Mr. Aswar, a preschool teacher, and he invented some of his own adventures for the tub people to share with the children. When he equipped the water play area with similar toys, the children created original narratives about the toys. Mr. Aswar used the children's dramatic play as the basis for a writing project. The children dictated stories, dramatized them for the other children and, as a grand finale, they made a videotape called "The Adventures of the Cherry Lane Nursery School Tub People," which was shared with the children's parents at their First Annual Film Festival.

Reconstructing Through Pictures

Drawing is another way of responding to stories. Because the child has not seen pictures to accompany the story, his or her imagination can run free (Reed, 1987). This particular activity can be adjusted to groups of children with widely divergent levels of ability by letting children draw, paint, cut out pictures from magazines, and/or write original stories inspired by the stories they have heard.

Creative Dramatics Based on Personal Narratives

After hearing a true account of someone's personal experience, children can invent spontaneous dialogue, replay the story with a different cast, create the original or a different setting, and evaluate their efforts. Ms. Buckwalter, a Head Start teacher told her students the story of Rosa Parks (Greenfield, 1973). Afterward, the children enacted the scene where Rose took a stand against racial prejudice and refused to give up her seat on the bus. For many excellent examples of preschool children dramatizing real historical events, read Vivian Paley's (1981) *Wally's Stories.*

Conclusion

Through the symbols in stories, children are able to answer these questions:

> What are people like?
>
> Why are they like that?
>
> What do they need?
>
> What makes them do what they do? (Lukens, 1986)

In fact, storytelling is so fundamental to human existence that common sense might even be conceptualized as "our storehouse of narrative structures" (Shafer, 1981). Narratives are basic in human life because: "The world we know is the world we make in words, and all we have after years of work and struggle is the story" (Rouse, 1978, p. 187).

When we develop children's narrative abilities, we give them an overarching concept that enables them to learn more efficiently and to enrich their lives. We tell them stories and teach them to be storytellers because, in the words of novelist Henry James, stories happen to people who know how to tell them.

Summary

Narrative abilities are those language skills that enable children to understand and use event-structured material. These narrative abilities are the principal way that children acquire knowledge of the traditional literary elements (setting, characterization, plot, theme, and style). When teachers share stories with children, it builds children's knowledge of story structures, ability to create original stories, and appreciation of stories. Some important resources available to teachers as they build children's narrative abilities are the oral tradition of folktales, the use of wordless picture books, and the use of group story-writing techniques.

Focus On: Group Stories

Usually when we picture an author in our mind's eye, we envision a writer in self-imposed solitude and isolation. Although this is the predominant way in which novelists function, it clearly is not the only way that text is generated. We can also envision several business associates writing a report, a team of comedy writers working on a script, or a faculty member and a graduate student collaborating on an article for publication. Despite the prevalence of co-authorship in our society at large, much of the writing that children do in school requires them to work alone and keep quiet. In recent years, these assumptions have been challenged (Bromley, 1989).

Composing text with someone else, however, changes the writing process. When one author writes in solitude, it is an expressive language art. When others participate in brainstorming, writing, revision, and editing, the process becomes receptive *and* expressive. Members of a writing team are learning, not only how to put ideas into words, but also how to relate interpersonally with a co-author. Additional advantages of co-authorship include:

Opportunities to capitalize upon each other's strengths and improve overall quality of the product

"Instant" audience and immediate feedback as ideas are generated

Practice in the skills of negotiation that will be useful throughout life

A chance to study and participate in another writer's writing process

Increased motivation that results from seeking peer approval of what has been written

Imagine, for example, an author-illustrator team creating a picture book together. Both children might compose and revise at the word processor, one might write while the other child illustrates, or one child might agree to write if her partner agrees to present it to the class. However the children define their roles, learning is taking place and it is far more exciting than staring at a blank piece of paper trying to get started.

A good way to orient children to writing with one or more others is to write a class book together. Thaler (1989) offers the following guidelines for collaboratively creating a picture story book:

1. Introduce the project by discussing favorite books. List topics on the board and vote on a topic for the book.
2. Create the story by selecting and naming a character (also by vote). Then ask questions such as: Where does he live? Does he live alone? Who are his friends? Who are his enemies? What does he do? What does he wish he could do? What are his problems and how does he solve them? Does he go anywhere? What does he need to take? How is he/she/it getting there?

3. Number the sentences sequentially and use the list to make a story. Revise as needed.

4. Distribute drawing and writing materials. Read each sentence aloud and have the students choose one or more they would like to print and/or illustrate. After drawing and writing is completed, ask children to write their names and sentence numbers on the page.

5. Assemble the picture book and read it together.

6. Vote on a title. Choose a student to illustrate the front cover, one to write an "about the author's page," a dedication page, and/or a back cover. An instant photo can be taken to go with the author's page. Bind the book. Insert a library pocket and checkout card.

7. Read the story together and share it with students. Take to other classes, donate books to the school's library, or start a classroom library.

In the Field: Observing Children's Narrative Abilities

This In the Field assignment is designed to give you insight about the young child's narrative abilities.

1. First, check several wordless books (picture books without any text) out of the library.

2. Next, obtain a copy of a young child's original story, either by interviewing the child and tape-recording your session or by obtaining one recent example of the child's original story from the teacher or parent.

3. Now use the wordless books that you gathered and ask the same child to browse through and select one to tell a story about. Record the child's words and transcribe them.

4. Compare the two stories in terms of

  length and complexity
  richness of vocabulary
  orientation (setting information)
  chaining (sequence)
  centering (theme/focus)
  uses of literary conventions (opening and ending)

How might *wordless picture books* be used to build children's storytelling abilities?

References

Applebee, A. (1978). *A child's concept of story: Ages two to seventeen*. Chicago, IL: University of Chicago Press.

Baker, A., and Greene, E. (1987). *Storytelling: Art and technique*. (2nd ed.). New York: Bowker.

Barton, B. (1986). *Tell me another*. Portsmouth, NH: Heinemann.

Brewer, W. F. (1984). The story schema: universal and culture-specific properties. In D. R. Olson, N. Torrance, and A. Hildyard (Eds.). *Literacy, language and learning: The nature and consequences of reading and writing* (pp. 167–194). London: Cambridge University Press.

Bromley, K. D. (1989). Buddy journals make the reading-writing connection. *The Reading Teacher, 43*(2), 122–129.

Chase, R. (1948). *Grandfather tales*. New York: Houghton Mifflin.

Cliatt, M.J.P., and Shaw, J. M. (1988). The storytime exchange: Ways to enhance it. *Childhood Education, 64*(5), 293–298.

Cole, J. (Ed.). (1982). *Best loved folktales of the world*. New York: Doubleday.

Feagans, L. (1982). The development and importance of narratives for school adaptation. In L. Feagans and D. C. Farran (Eds.) *The language of children reared in poverty* (pp. 95–116). New York: Academic Press.

Gardner, H. (1982, March). The making of a storyteller. *Psychology Today*, 49–50, 53, 61–63.

Haley, G. (1970). *A story, a story*. New York: Atheneum.

Hart, M. (1987). *Fold-and-cut stories and fingerplays*. Belmont, CA: Fearon.

Heath, S. B., and Branscombe, A. (1986). The book as narrative prop in language acquisition. In B. B. Schieffelin and P. Gilmore (Eds.). *The acquisition of literacy: Ethnographic perspectives* (pp. 16–34). Norwood, NJ: Ablex.

Hughes, T. (1988). Myth and education. In K. Egan and D. Nadaner (Eds.). *Imagination and Education* (pp. 30–44). New York: Teachers College Press.

Hunt, T., and Renfro, N. (1982). *Puppetry in early childhood education*. Austin, TX: Nancy Renfro Studios.

Lord, A. B. (1964). *The singer of tales*. Cambridge, MA: Harvard University Press.

Lukens, R. (1986). *A critical handbook of children's literature* (3rd ed.). Glenview, IL: Scott, Foresman.

Meek, M. (1982). What counts as evidence in theories of children's literature? *Theory Into Practice, 21*(4), 284–292.

Moir, H. (1989). I've got a story to tell! In S. Hoffman and L. L. Lamme (Eds.) *Learning from the inside out: The expressive arts* (pp. 86–93). Wheaton, MD: Association for Childhood Education International.

Paley, V. (1981). *Wally's stories*. Cambridge, MA: Harvard University Press.

Pierce, K. M. (1990). Initiating literature discussion groups: Teaching like learners. In K. G. Short and K. M. Pierce (Eds.) *Talking about books: Creating literate communities* (pp. 177–198). Portsmouth, NH: Heinemann.

Reed, B. (1987). Storytelling: What it can teach. *School Library Journal, 34*(2), 35–39.

Roe, B. D. (1988). Extending learning and knowledge through storytelling. *Houghton Mifflin Educators' Forum*, fall, 10, 15.

Rouse, J. (1978). *The completed gesture: myth, character and education*. New Jersey: Skyline Books.

Scott, R. (1985). *Storytelling: A guide to the art*. New South Wales, AU: Primary English Teaching Association. (ERIC Document Reproduction Service No. ED 263 552).

Sebesta, S. (1989). The story is about you. In S. Hoffman and L. L. Lamme (Eds.). *Learning from the inside out: The expressive arts* (pp. 22–28). Wheaton, MD: Association for Childhood Education International.

Shafer, R. (1981). Narration in the psychoanalytic dialogue. In W. T. J. Mitchell (Ed.). *On narrative*. Chicago: University of Chicago.

Shulevitz, U. (1985). *Writing with pictures*. New York: Watson-Guptill.

Sierra, J., and Kaminski, R. (1989). *Twice upon a time: Stories to tell, retell, act out, and write about*. Bronx, NY: Wilson.

Spencer, M. (1976). Stories are for telling. *English in Education, 10*(1), 16–23.

Thaler, M. (1989). Creating a class book. *Learning, 4*, 84.

Tooze, R. (1959). *Storytelling*. Englewood Cliffs, NJ: Prentice-Hall.

Viguers, R. H. (1974). *Storytelling and the teacher*. Washington, DC: National Education Association.

Children's Books

Aruego, J. (1972). *Un cuento de cocodrillo/A crocodile's tale*. New York: Scholastic.
Asch, F. (1977). *Monkey face*. New York: Parents' Magazine Press.
Brett, J. (1989). *The mitten*. New York: Putnam.
Brown, R. A. (1981). *A dark, dark tale*. New York: Dial.
Brown, M. (1947). *Stone soup*. New York: Scribner's.
Bruna, D. (1966). *Dick Bruna's Little Red Riding Hood*. Chicago, IL: Follett.
Bryan, A. (1989). *Turtle knows your name*. New York: Atheneum.
Carle, E. (1969). *The very hungry caterpillar*. Cleveland, OH: Collins-World.
Ciardi, J. (1961). *I met a man*. Boston: Houghton Mifflin.
Cole, J. (1983). *Bony legs*. New York: Four Winds.
Conrad, P. (1989). *The tub people*. New York: Harper & Row.
Emberley, B. (1966). *One wide river to cross*. Englewood Cliffs, NJ: Prentice-Hall.
Galdone, P. (reteller). (1981) *The three sillies*. New York: Clarion.
Greenfield, E. (1973). *Rosa Parks*. New York: Crowell.
Harper, W. (1967). *The gunniwolf*. New York: Dutton.
Henkes, K. (1986). *Bailey goes camping*. New York: Greenwillow.
Hughes, S. (1981). *David and dog*. New York: Lothrop.
Hurlman, R. (1977). *The proud white cat*. New York: Morrow.
Johnston, T., and de Paola, T. (1985). *The quilt story*. New York: Putnam.
Jonas, A. (1989). *Color dance*. New York: Greenwillow.
Keats, E. J. (1969). *Goggles!* New York: Macmillan.
Keats, E. J. (1966). *Jennie's hat*. New York: Harper & Row.
Kent, J. (1972). *The fat cat*. New York: Scholastic.
Lester, J. (1990). *How many spots does a leopard have? and other tales*. New York: Scholastic.
Lionni, L. (1960). *Inch by inch*. New York: Aston-Honor.
Lobel, A. (1980). "The Bear and the Crow" In *Fables*. New York: Harper & Row.
Mari, E., and Mari, E. (1970). *The apple and the moth*. New York: Pantheon.
Mayer, M. (1976). *There's a nightmare in my closet*. New York: Dial.
Rockwell, A. (1981). *Thump, thump, thump!* New York: Dutton.
Shaw, C. (1947). *It looked like spilt milk*. New York: Harper & Row.
Stanley, D. (1986). *The good luck pencil*. New York: Macmillan.
Steig, W. (1976). *The amazing bone*. New York: Farrar, Straus & Giroux.
Stock, C. (1988). *Sophie's knapsack*. New York: Lothrop Lee & Shepard.
Stock, C. (1985). *Sophie's Bucket*. New York: Lothrop, Lee & Shepard.
Ungerer, T. (1958). *Crictor*. New York: Harper & Row.
Viorst, J. (1982). Mother doesn't want a dog. In *If I Were in Charge of the World and Other Worries*. New York: Atheneum.
Wallace-Brodeur, R. (1989). *Stories from the big chair*. New York: Macmillan/McElderry.
Zelinsky, P. (1981). *The maid, the mouse, and the odd-shaped house*. New York: Dodd.
Zemach, H. (1971). *A penny a look*. New York: Farrar, Straus & Giroux.

Nonprint Media

Bauer, C. F. (1986). *Storytelling*. New York: Wilson. (Videotape)

Fink, C. (1984). "The Jazzy Three Bears" *Grandma Slid Down the Mountain*. Takoma Park, MD: Kids' Records.

Mickey's Trailer. (1981). Burbank, CA: Walt Disney Educational Media. (Film)

Photo: © 1990 Frank Siteman

7

Picture Books and the Literature-Based Curriculum

OUTLINE

Children's literature is undeniably the first literary experience, where the reader's expectations of what literature is are laid down. Books in childhood initiate children into literature; they inaugurate certain kinds of literary competencies . . . They offer a view of what it is to be literate.   —MARGARET MEEK (1982)

KEY CONCEPTS AND TERMS

literature	presenting literature
picture books	literature-based curriculum
benefits of literature	book discussion groups
book selection criteria	extension activities
genre	

Suppose that someone described a marvelous new gift for children with these attributes:

- inexpensive and durable
- does not require direct electrical current or batteries
- will capture a child's attention and sustain interest over an extended period of time
- has a positive effect on the child's ability to listen, speak, read, and write

That gift is literature.

What Is Literature?

Literature may be defined as "the imaginative shaping of life and thought into the forms and structure of language" (Huck, Hepler, and Hickman, 1989, p. 4). As we saw in Chapter 6, stories originated with the oral tradition: in the beginning, they were told and listened to rather than written and read. Thus, "Despite the implications of its name, literature does not seem to have been the invention of literate people" (Peabody, 1975, p. 1).

Literature in early childhood education is a general term that includes stories, songs, rhymes, and nonfiction. Figure 7.1 contains an overview of literature for the very young child using these four classifications and the four primary means of sharing literature: through the spoken word, through the written word, through pictorial images, and through enactment.

Benefits of Literature

Children's literature is the ideal learning medium for the young child because it educates the intellect as well as the imagination. Literature is *the* major way for children to become literate (Cazden, 1972) and a major way of stimulating creativity. The **benefits of literature** will include the following:

Begins with enjoyment—Quality literature teaches children to associate pleasure with literacy events. It uses language in surprising and satisfying ways.

Provides a language "scaffold"—A book holds a sample of language constant so that children can return to it again and again, building more meaning with each encounter (Bruner, 1984).

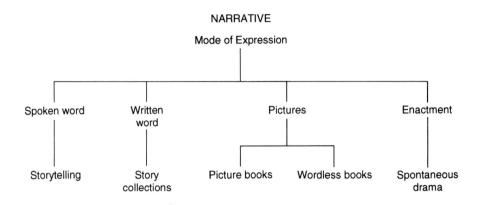

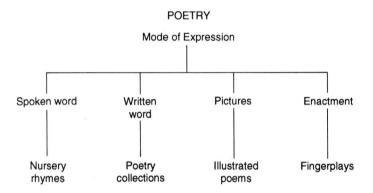

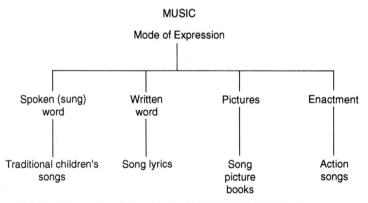

FIGURE 7.1 *Major Categories of Literature in Early Childhood Education.*

Extends experience—Literature simultaneously affirms what the child already knows and extends beyond what is immediately known (White, 1984).

Provides models—When adults share a book with a child, they provide a role model of the literate adult in action, a model that the child can emulate.

Increases vocabulary, comprehension, and thinking skills—Picture books introduce new words in meaningful contexts, supply children with pictorial clues, and give them the opportunity to ask questions and explore answers.

Develops insight—Insight, looking into the heart of the matter, is something that literature is supremely well suited for. One of the great puzzles of childhood is understanding why people do what they do. By sharing a book, children get to glimpse the inner workings of characters' minds and thereby gain a perspective on personal feelings and motives.

Stimulates imagination—Literature activates "hopeful dreaming" (Carlson, 1974) and creates new worlds. If we look at some of the children's classics, we can see how the worlds being created invite them in: the circus train of *The Little Engine that Could* (Piper, 1945); or the little schoolgirl from France, *Madeline* (Bemelmans, 1939).

Immerses children in another culture or subculture's folklore, such as *The Talking Eggs: A folktale from the American South* (San Souci, 1989) or *How the Guinea Hen Got Her Spots* (Knutson, 1990), an East African tale.

Builds self-image and transmits social values—Literature shows children what it means to be human and function as a member of a richly diverse social group (Jalongo, 1991). Books foster multicultural education when they: 1) communicate the universality of human emotions, such as *My Friends* (Gomi, 1990); 2) model prosocial behavior, such as *Chita's Christmas Tree* (Howard, 1990); 3) give children pride in their ethnic heritage, such as *Rabbit Makes a Monkey of Lion* (Aardema, 1990); 3) introduce children to contemporary families both alike and different from their own, such as *How My Parents Learned to Eat* (Friedman, 1984); 4) reveal to children how it feels to be different, such as *I Hate English!* (Levine, 1990); 5) enable children to participate in another social era, such as Aliki's (1989) *The King's Day: Louis the XIV of France*; and 6) show a wide range of human characteristics and aspirations, as in *Laura Charlotte* (Galbraith, 1990).

How to Use Literature

If you picture a successful story-sharing session in your mind's eye, it would no doubt include children gathered around, enthralled by the book. The realization of this ideal is not a happy accident, it is the outgrowth of careful planning. Actually there are several issues here:

Issues of quality: Which books are better than others? Why?

Book selection issues: Which books are best suited to which child or group of children?

Categories of books: Which types of books are generally appropriate for the very young?

Presentation issues: How should books be shared with young children?

Quality in Picture Books

Good **picture books** are more than "cute." As James Hymes (1981), once said, think of cute as a one-word insult that means something is childish rather than childlike. Children's book author Joan Aiken (1982) offers this description of a good book for young children:

> Good books for children are never perfunctory, dull, meaningless or trivial; they do not contain a hidden sales message, do not moralize or preach, and do not speak condescendingly to children. (p. 31).

But even in a small library, there are hundreds of picture books to choose from. How do you begin? One way is to consult a reference guide. Books such as Trelease's (1989) *New Read-Aloud Handbook*, Kimmel and Segal's (1983) *For Reading Out Loud!* Lima and Lima's (1989) *A to Zoo: Subject Access to Children's Picture Books*, and Gillespie and Naden's (1990) *Best books for children* are excellent guides to quality literature.

Additional **selection guidelines** are described in Figure 7.2.

When evaluating the illustrations in children's books, adults should look for illustrations that are "understandable, evoke emotional identification and intense emotional response, that allow room for the exercise of the reader's own imagination, that provide the reader with a new, wholesome and vital way of looking at the world and life" (Ciancolo, 1984, p. 847). The five basic elements of art are line, color, texture, shape, and arrangement. In a picture book, each of these elements should be used in a way that complements the story. An artist may use delicate sketch marks or bold black outlines; soft chalk pastels or bright fluorescent colors; a smooth, lustrous texture or texture that looks rough and almost three-dimensional; shapes that are distinct or shapes that are subtle and impressionistic; and confine pictures to a portion of one page or span two pages with one picture.

Book Selection Criteria

One of the challenges in literature is "matching" a book to the child or group of children who will be the audience. You might begin by looking for a recommended age group printed directly on the book by the publisher. You can also use resource people—librarians, faculty, and experienced teachers. Refer to periodicals that

General evaluation questions:

1. Does the book compare favorably with other picture books of its type?
2. Has the picture book received the endorsements of professionals?
3. Are the literary elements of plot, theme, character, style, and setting used effectively?
4. Do the pictures complement the story?
5. Is the story free from ethnic, racial, or sex-role stereotypes?
6. Is the picture book developmentally appropriate for the child?
7. Do preschoolers respond enthusiastically to the book?
8. Is the topic (and the book's treatment of it) suitable for the young child?
9. Does the picture book appeal to the parent or teacher?

Additional evaluation questions for illustrations:

1. Are the illustrations and text synchronized?
2. Does the mood conveyed by the artwork (humorous/serious, rollicking/quiet) complement that of the story?
3. Are the illustrative details consistent with the text?
4. Could a child get a sense of the basic concepts or story sequence by looking at the pictures?
5. Are the illustrations or photographs esthetically pleasing?
6. Is the printing (clarity, form, line, color) of good quality?
7. Can children view and re-view the illustrations, each time getting more from them?
8. Are the illustrative style and complexity suited to the age level of the intended audience?

FIGURE 7.2   Evaluation Questions for Picture Books in Early Childhood Education
Sources: Huck, Hepler, and Hickman, 1987, and Jalongo, 1988.

review children's books like *Young Children, Childhood Education, The Reading Teacher*, and *Booklist*. Appendix D of this book, "Storytime Selections," contains an extensive list of books particularly well suited for group story sharing with preschool and primary grades children.

Eventually, you will gain confidence in your own professional judgment, just like Chris, a student teacher, who is at the library looking for a copy of *The Three Little Pigs*. She locates four different versions. The first follows the old folktale closely; the wolf eats two of the little pigs and the third pig avenges his brothers (Zemach, 1988). The second is also a tale about coming of age, but this time it is a fox who is outsmarted by big sister Hamlet in an Appalachian version of the story. Hamlet is the only one of the three who remembers the three things her Mama told her:

> One: *Watch out for that mean, tricky old drooly-mouth fox.*
> Two: *Build myself a safe, strong house out of rocks.*
> Three: *Come home and visit my dear, sweet mama every Sunday.*

The third version, by James Marshall (1989) includes witty dialogue like:

"I know," said the Little pig.
"I'll buy your straw and build a house."
"That's not a good idea," said the Man.
"Mind your own business, thank you," said the little pig.

Finally, she reads Scieszka's (1989) *The True Story of the Three Little Pigs! by A. Wolf* which is a completely different tale told from the wolf's perspective. He rationalizes the destruction of the first house by saying that after he sneezed:

That whole darn straw house fell down. And right in the middle of the pile of straw was the first little pig—dead as a doornail. He had been home the whole time. It seemed like a shame to leave a perfectly good ham dinner there in the straw so I ate it up. Think of it as a cheeseburger just lying there."

Based upon her knowledge of child development and of picture books, Chris decides that the first version is best suited for preschoolers because it is a simple, straightforward, and familiar story. She chooses the Marshall version for kindergarten or first grade because the children know the story well enough to appreciate the humor. She decides that the Appalachian version would be perfect for storytelling and makes plans to learn the story so that she can use it with a mixed-age group of children she has volunteered to work with at the community center. Finally, she decides that the satire of the fourth version is best suited to older children and checks out the book for her roommate who is student teaching in third grade. Chris is using **book selection criteria**.

Types of Picture Books

An equally important aspect of book selection is to become aware of the different types of picture books. In a true picture book, both the words and the illustrations are read (Shulevitz, 1989).

Picture Books in the Traditional Style

Children's books in the traditional style are basically of two types: those that truly are traditional (like the folktales described in Chapter 6) and those that are modern nursery rhymes, folktales, and fairy tales told in the traditional style.

In a local community, three teachers are using children's literature in the traditional style at the beginning of the school year. As we visit each classroom, we can see how these teachers have incorporated literature into their curriculum.

Nursery Rhymes   Mrs. Fetters is a retired teacher who has volunteered to work with infants and toddlers at a day-care center. She cuddles them, rocks them, and sings lullabies to them. She also uses *nursery rhymes*, the short, traditional nonsense verse that adults recite to children. Mrs. Fetters knows that the babies are listening carefully beause they stop whatever they are doing and really concentrate on her words. In fact, Mrs. Fetters would tell you that Cruz's favorite is the soothing bedtime rhyme *Wynken, Blynken and Nod* (Field, 1982), while Rose prefers *Three*

Blind Mice (Ivimey, 1991). She has found collections of the traditional nursery rhymes like *Tail Feathers from Mother Goose* (Opie and Opie, 1988) to be an invaluable resource, but she also uses contemporary authors and illustrators who write new nursery rhymes in traditional styles. Her favorite published source for nursery rhymes of this type is *Tickle Toe Rhymes* (Knight, 1989).

Folk Tales   Mr. Hanson teaches first grade and today is "Gingerbread Day." *The Gingerbread Boy* (Galdone, 1975) is a story with a long history and many variants. In fact, Mr. Hanson's grandfather remembers that on his first day of school, they heard a story called "The Pancake" in which the main character rolled away from all the hungry pursuers—except the wily fox (Power, 1934). In that one-room schoolhouse in rural Colorado two generations ago, the children made "pancakes" out of paper, but a gust of wind blew grandfather's across the prairie, something that upset him *and* made the possibility of a personified pancake seem real. *The Gingerbread Boy* has been passed down through the generations by word of mouth but also in picture-book form. During Mr. Hanson's unit on *The Gingerbread Boy*, the children made fresh ground ginger, made gingerbread following a rebus recipe, and decorated their gingerbread people with icing and raisins. Back in the classroom while they waited for the gingerbread to bake, they listened to Rowena Bennett's (1988) poem:

> The gingerbread man gave a gingery shout
> "Quick! Open the oven and let me out!"
> He stood straight up in his baking pan.
> He jumped to the floor and away he ran
> "Catch me," he called, "if you can, can, can." (p. 50)

Afterward, the children enacted the story using paper-plate masks. When the children returned to the school cafeteria to take their gingerbread out of the oven, they were introduced to the cook who told them that it must have run away. They met the janitor in the hallway and asked him if he had seen their gingerbread. He said he had seen trays of gingerbread while waxing the floor and suggested that they report the incident to the principal. The children went to the office and met the school secretary who then introduced them to the principal. He greeted them and said that he had spotted gingerbread moving down the hallway and advised them to check back in their classroom. After the children returned from meeting school personnel and touring the building, they found their gingerbread creations and milk waiting for them at their seats.

Fairy Tales   Fairy tales are high-fantasy stories that have been passed down through several generations. Fairy tales contain many familiar themes, including ordeals that must be endured in pursuit of a goal and a triumphant return home (Campbell, 1949), ferocious and deceitful beasts, magical objects, the fulfillment of wishes, beauty disguised as ugliness, and good triumphing over evil (Bettelheim, 1976).

Mr. Johnson, a junior-high-school English teacher, and Ms. Gemmellaro, a second-grade teacher, are collaborating on a fairy-tales project in their urban school district. The project began with the second-graders hearing many different fairy tales. Some were familiar favorites that originated with the Brothers Grimm ("Beauty and the Beast") and Hans Christian Andersen ("The Nightingale"). Some were fairy tales from other lands (such as Carol Carrick's (1990) *Aladdin and the Wonderful Lamp*), and some were modern fairy tales (such as Berenzy's (1989) *A Frog Prince*). Of all the fairy tales they heard, the second-graders liked *Mufaro's Beautiful Daughters* (Steptoe, 1987) the best. Mr. Johnson's challenge to his junior-high students was to make that fairy tale come alive for the second-graders, which they did with great relish. They created African costumes, lush jungle scenery, and developed a script from the book.

Other Types of Picture Books

Books for Infants and Toddlers   Because infants and toddlers are being introduced to books for the first time, their books usually have the most minimal text; often the words are more like labels or captions for the pictures. Plot in books for babies, when it exists at all, is often a single event within the child's daily experience such as getting dressed (Wantanabe, 1980-1982) or taking a bath (Hughes 1985). Often these author/illustrators create a series of three or four simple books especially for infants and toddlers (Burningham, 1976).

The typical toddler is just learning how to manage a book so books that are especially durable are appropriate. These books are often referred to as *board books* because they have pages made of cardboard that are easier for the child to grasp. Some author/illustrators of good board books in a series are Jan Omerod (1985), Helen Oxenbury (1981), and Rosemary Wells (1979, 1985).

Participation Books   Participation books involve the child in some sort of direct physical interaction with the book. Some of these books have textured surfaces for the child to feel, such as *Pat the Bunny* (Kundhardt, 1962), or flaps that lift up, like Eric Hill's (1980) series about Spot the dog.

Concept Books   Concept books teach one basic idea, for example, colors, shapes, letters, numbers, opposites, and so forth. Children's book editor Ellen Roberts (1984) says that concept books are almost like a commercial for an idea. Three books by Ehlert (1989, 1989, 1990) are good examples of concept books: *Eating the Alphabet*: *Fruits and Vegetables from A to Z*, *Color Zoo*, and *Fish Eyes*: *A Book You Can Count On*. For older children, there are more challenging concept books such as Bruce McMillan's (1989) photographic essay on comparisons, *Super Super Superwords*.

Information Books   Roberts (1984) refers to the *information books* as a child's version of an article in *National Geographic*. Information books are nonfiction explanations about the world and how things live or function. Aliki is author and illustrator with many information books to her credit, including *Corn Is Maize*: *The Gift of the Indians* (1976) and *Digging Up Dinosaurs* (1981).

Picture Story Books   These books are somewhat more dependent upon words; it would be possible to understand the story without the pictures, but the pictures definitely contribute to an understanding of the story. *Hot-air Henry* (Calhoun, 1981), the adventures of a Siamese cat who decides to go hot-air ballooning on his own after watching his family enjoy it so much, is a good example of a picture story book.

Illustrated Story Books   When the text of a book is longer, can be understood without the illustrations, and the pictures are few and far between, the book is an *illustrated story book*. The typical illustrated story book is usually intended for somewhat older readers or for reading aloud. A good example of an illustrated story book is E. B. White's (1953) *Charlotte's Web* with sketches by Garth Williams.

Books Especially for Emergent Readers

The style and format of some picture books make them especially helpful to emergent readers or children who have just begun to read independently. Let's look at how Ms. Movesian, a first-grade teacher, uses these books in her reading program.

Predictable Books   Just as their name implies, predictable books are structured to support children in their educated guesses about what the text says next. Devices such as rhythm, rhyme, repetition, and familiar sequences (such as days of the week, numbers, etc.) encourage the child to participate and build the young reader's confidence. A special favorite of the students is *Bringing the Rain to Kapiti Plain* (Aardema, 1981). It is a cumulative story, one that repeats words and phrases from the previous verse, and it uses rhythm and rhyme to great effect.

Big Books   Big books are simply oversized versions of picture books for children. The pages are large (often 24' × 36') so that children can see both the text and the illustrations, even in a group setting. Many big books are also predictable books that enable emergent readers to practice reading skills. The favorite big book in Ms. Movesian's class is *Who Said Red?* (Serfozo, 1988), a big book that Ms. Movesian made herself, using drawings and cutout magazine pictures. (See Appendix E for additional suggestions on creating your own big books). The teacher uses a pointer to identify each word to the children as they read the big book in unison. She also gives them practice reading the book independently, with a partner or in groups. Ms. Movesian also sends small paperback copies of the book home with the children so that they can show their parents the progress they've made.

Easy Readers   Easy readers are controlled vocabulary books designed to build the beginning reader's confidence. Although few of these books in the past would also qualify as good literature, some of the contemporary easy readers are creative, entertaining, and appropriate for many purposes, in addition to initial reading practice. Nancy Shaw's (1986) *Sheep in a Jeep*, for instance, is the hilarious, rhyming misadventure of foolish rams.

Wordless books   Some picture books, called *wordless books*, are completely or practically textless so that comprehending the story is entirely dependent upon the illustrations. These books are especially useful for beginning readers because they provide a sequential set of illustrations for which the child can tell, dictate, or write an original story. See Appendix F for a bibliography of wordless books.

Poetry and Lyrics

Those picture books that place special emphasis on the lyrical quality of language—rhythm, rhyme, cadence—are poems and songs.

Poetry and Stories Told in Verse   Some poetry picture books are a single poem that is illustrated like Ruth Heller's (1981) *Chickens Aren't the Only Ones*. Other poems, called narrative poems, tell a story like *Nicholas Cricket* Maxner, 1989), a fantasy story about an insect performer at a miniature nightclub.

Song Picture Books   Song picture books are illustrated versions of songs. Ms. Lemeiux is using Glen Rounds' (1989) boldly illustrated version of *Old MacDonald Had a Farm* with her kindergarten class. Because the children already know the song, they are able to read it in unison right away. "I want the children to begin reading to one another and to their parents immediately," Ms. Lemeiux says, "and these song picture books are an ideal way of convincing children that they can read and enjoy it, too."

Poetry and Song Collections   In addition to the individual poems and songs, there are also illustrated collections of poetry and music such as *The Diane Goode Book of American Folk Tales and Songs* (Durrell, 1989) and *Joyful Noise: Poems for Two Voices* (Fleischman, 1989). Refer to Appendix C. for a listing of illustrated poetry collections.

Presenting Literature Effectively

Before reading any book to a child or children, the teacher should be thoroughly familiar with it and be able to read it skillfully. After that initial preparation, **presenting literature** effectively is dependent upon four adult roles (Cochran-Smith, 1984):

1. *Informer/mediator*—The adult "negotiates the meaning" of a story with a child by making brief comments that show the child how the book is related to his experience ("Look, she has a little brother just like you.") or brings her experience to bear upon the story ("Remember when we went to the zoo?")
2. *Co-respondent*—In this role, the adult shares personal reactions and invites responses from the child (Roser and Martinez, 1985). ("Hmm. That dog Ralph certainly seems interested in Benny's birthday cake (Rice, 1981). (I wonder what will happen next?")
3. *Monitor*—Young children often need to hear a story several times before they understand it. In the role of monitor, adults recap the child's understanding of a story and provide additional information as needed. ("It looks like the good witch knows some magic too.")
4. *Director*—When adults assume leadership by introducing a story, pacing the story, and announcing the conclusion, they are functioning as directors.

There are two basic ways of using these roles to share a picture book with children: individually and in a group.

Presenting Literature to an Individual Child

When a teacher is responsible for an entire class, it is easy to overlook the option of sharing stories one-to-one, yet this is often the best way to invite the child with limited book experience into the world of literature. More opportunities for individual story sharing can be accomplished in many ways, such as finding volunteer readers among parents or grandparents, high school or college volunteers, and cross-age tutors from the elementary school or peers.

Presenting Literature to a Group

It is fall and the children are intrigued by the squirrels who scamper through the large oak trees in the play yard. At circle time, Ms. Dee discusses the squirrels with the children "I wish they'd let us catch 'em," says Chuckie. "I want to touch one," says Earlene wistfully, "but they run away when you get close, just like the birds." Ms. Dee says, "I know how much you like the squirrels, so today I've brought some things that will let us look at squirrels very closely. First, here is a book with photographs in it. My favorite is this one; it shows the babies all snuggled up in their nest." (The children examine the pictures carefully.) "I also brought a squirrel, but this one is not alive. It died and someone took its skin and stuffed it, like a stuffed toy. I borrowed this squirrel from my science teacher at college. Have any of you seen animals that used to be alive?" Sean says, "My dad has a buck's head. My Mom won't let him hang it in the living room, so he put it in the cellar." Colleen adds, "Wolves . . . I saw them at the museum." Ms. Dee continues, "Here it is. You can touch it if you want to." The children stroke the squirrel's body, tentatively at first, then with more confidence. "How'd they do its eyes?" Nancy asks. "They're made out of glass." "I like the tail," says Chaka. Ms. Dee continues: "Now, look at the cover of this book. Here is another animal that is related to the squirrel. How is this chipmunk like a squirrel? How is it different?" The children answer, then Ms. Dee remarks, "If you were as small as a chipmunk or a squirrel, you could do all kinds of things that you can't do now. This book *Chipmunk's Song* was written by Joanne Ryder." (1987) "It is about a child who gets to play with the chipmunk." The children listen to the story and discuss it, then Ms. Dee introduces the concept of hibernation through the book *Do Not Disturb* (Packlam, 1989).

Children with Low Book Interest

These presentation techniques make the assumption that children are interested in stories and usually they are. But what about children with low book interest, children who appear to be disinterested in books? Based upon their observational research, Raines and Isbell (1989) recommend the following measures:

1. Identify low book interest children, determine their ways of interacting with books and other materials, and adapt the environment to meet the child's needs. Sometimes books with unique formats such as moving parts were preferred by low book interest children. One child referred to a lift-the-flap book as a "book with doors," while another was intrigued by a cardboard wheel showing the different maturational stages of animals (Shapiro, 1979).
2. Provide more opportunities for children to share books with an adult mediator. If children are lacking in lap-reading experience, they need to acquire it. If children do not gravitate toward books on their own, they need an adult to lead the way. Students who appear disinterested in books may need scheduled time in a well-designed library corner so that they can select books in a supportive, unhurried environment.
3. Emphasize connections between books, book characters, and children. Familiarity with a book frequently determines how children will respond. Children "connect" with books that speak to them, both cognitively and emotionally. Often, a child will search (in the words of one third-grade boy) for a "book about somebody like me." The best authors enable children to identify with characters even though the specifics of their lives may be very different, such as *Darkness and the Butterfly*, the story of an African child conquering her fear of the dark (Grifalconi, 1987).

The Literature-Based Curriculum

Ms. Eisen is a second-grade teacher at a university laboratory school. If you talked with her about her program, you would know that she is committed to young children and values children's literature. Today's story is *The Wolf's Chicken Stew* (Kasza, 1987). In this tale, a perpetually hungry wolf finds a chicken for supper but decides to fatten her up first. He leaves food on her porch every night—first, 100 pancakes; then 100 doughnuts; and finally a 100-pound cake. But when he goes to claim his prize, he is greeted by 100 thankful chicks (Figure 7.3). After all these accolades and a dinner prepared by Mrs. Chicken, he gives up on the idea of chicken stew. As the wolf walks home, he thinks, "Aw shucks, maybe tomorrow I'll bake the little critters a hundred scrumptious cookies."

Designing a Literature-Based Unit

Ms. Eisen introduces *The Wolf's Chicken Stew* with a question: "Did you ever change your mind about something?" The children cite several examples, then she says, "Well, this story is about a hungry wolf who changes his mind; in fact, you might say that he has 'a change of heart.'" After the story, Ms. Eisen leads a **book discussion group** based on these open-ended questions (Knipping and Andre, 1988):

5. Glue each child's picture at the top of his chart tablet page.

Something to think about—
Reread the chart tablet stories whenever you are in the library corner reading with children. As they become more comfortable storytellers, the length and complexity of their stories will increase. The young preschoolers can tell you captions to go with their drawings or dictate sentences for the three sets of wordless pages in GRANDFATHER TWILIGHT.

STORY STRETCHER

For Mathematics And Manipulatives Center: Stringing Pretend Pearls

What the children will learn—
To create a pattern with the beads

Materials you will need—
Beads of varying sizes, shoelaces or yarn

What to do—
1. Discuss how Grandfather Twilight took a pearl from an endless string of pearls.

2. Ask the children how we might create a long string of beads like Grandfather's Twilight's pearls.

3. Give each child some beads. Have him create a pattern with the beads, completely filling his string.

4. Tie the strings together end to end and see how long they are. Decide if these are enough strings of pearls or whether the group wants to make it even longer.

Something to think about—
To count the number of days in the month string thirty or thirty-one beads on a string. Each day during circle time, a child can take a bead from the string and place it in a treasure chest like Grandfather Twilight's. The children can then count the beads on the string to see how many days are left in the month, or they can count the beads in the chest to know how many days have passed in the month.

STORY STRETCHER

For Music And Movement: Pass The Pearl

What the children will learn—
To follow the rules of a game

Materials you will need—
Quiet, restful music, record player or cassette player, playdough pearl

What to do—
1. Have the children sit in a circle.

2. Darken the room and pretend it is nearly twilight time.

3. Explain the rules of the game in a hushed tone.

4. Play the music at a low volume. Have the children place their hands behind their backs and close their eyes. You be Grandfather Twilight and put the pearl in someone's hands. Stop the music and call on someone to guess who has the pearl. It doen't matter if the child is right or wrong. After the child guesses, the one with the pearl says, "I'm Grandfather Twilight." The child who is Grandfather Twilight now goes around the circle while the music is playing and drops the pearl in someone's hand. Grandfather Twilight keeps pretending to drop the pearl until the music stops. You stop the music and call on someone to guess. The new Grandfather Twilight then begins the process all over again.

Something to think about—
After the children have played the Grandfather Twilight game, have them play the game with a golden bead for Grandmother Sunrise based on their stories in the library corner.

STORY STRETCHER

For Science And Nature Center: Oysters And Pearls

What the children will learn—
To recognize oyster shells and know pearls come from oysters

Materials you will need—
Oyster shells, children's reference book on food from the sea, Costume jewelry pearl, magnifying glasses

What to do—
1. Discuss oysters, where they live and how they are caught from the ocean. Show the oyster shells. Use live oysters if possible.

2. Tell how the pearl is created from a tiny grain of sand.

3. Hide a costume jewelry pearl inside or under an oyster shell.

4. Have the children find the pearl and then examine the inside and outside of the oyster shell. Use the magnifying glasses and look at the inside of the shell. Compare their descriptions of the inside of the shell to how a pearl looks.

Something to think about—
Children who live near the seacoast may be familiar with a variety of shellfish; however youngsters from other areas of the country may know little about them. Whenever possible, create a display of many kinds of shells, or living shellfish, and extend the real display with pictures and reference books.

(Adapted from Korey Powell's classroom.)

FIGURE 7.4 *Continued*

NIGHT IN THE COUNTRY

By Cynthia Rylant

Illustrated by Mary Szilagyi

"There is no night so dark, so black as night in the country," and with this opening line the mood is set for the night observer to see and hear. The sights and sounds of the night carry the visitor through the countryside. In addition to Cynthia Rylant's sensitive wording, Mary Szilagyi's dark, but not scary, illustrations make the listener and viewer want to linger in the scene and enjoy the almost silence and the almost stillness of a country night. The drawings look like layered crayons with just enough of the darkness scrapped away to expose an animal or a scene from the night.

Circle Time Presentation

Talk with the children about their experiences visiting or living on a farm. Have the children try to recall what night was like in the countryside. Read NIGHT IN THE COUNTRY. Discuss the night sounds they would like to hear if they were living on a farm.

S T O R Y   S T R E T C H E R

For Art: Crayon Etching

What the children will learn—
To etch a design in multiple layers of colors

Materials you will need—
Crayons, paper, plastic knives

What to do—
1. Show the children Mary Szilagyi's illustration of NIGHT IN THE COUNTRY. Discuss the way she used colors on top of colors. See if they can find any places where it looks like the crayons are scraped away. Look at the lines on the tree and the raccoon.

2. Have the children completely cover their papers with different colors of crayon. To speed the process along, have them place the crayons sideways and color using the entire length of the crayon. Encourage them to use many different colors.

3. Then using black or another dark color, deep purple or blue, color over the entire first layer of crayons.

4. Take the plastic knife and demonstrate how to use it to etch out a pattern in the crayons. When a line is scraped, it exposes the colors underneath.

5. Leave the book in the art area for continued inspiration of crayon etchings.

Something to think about—
Younger preschoolers can create a similar effect using fingerpaints and multiple colors. Their fingers create the etching. Avoid using too many colors or the paints turn muddy.

S T O R Y   S T R E T C H E R

For Cooking And Snack Time: Country Apples

What the children will learn—
The names and tastes of different kinds of apples

Materials you will need—
Golden delicious apples, red delicious apples, green cooking apples, knives, cutting boards, baskets

What to do—
1. If possible, let the children help you shop for the apples. If not, bring the apples to the classroom in a grocery bag. Let interested children help you wash the apples.

2. Have other children arrange a variety of apples in a basket for each snack table.

3. During snack, cut slices from the kind of apple the child says he likes best. Then ask him to try at least one other kind and to tell you how it tastes.

4. Remember to use descriptive words as sweet, tart, tangy.

Something to think about—
You can extend the apple tasting snack by polling the children and deciding which apple is the class favorite. You also can do a simple mathematical graph by having the child select a strip of construction paper the same color as the type of apple he likes. Each child then glues the strips onto a poster and the class can compare visually or count and decide what their

FIGURE 7.4 *Continued*

favorite flavor of apple is. This graph is both a pre-number and a numerical graph.

(Adapted from an activity in Penny Clem's classroom.)

For Listening Station: A Quiet Retreat

What the children will learn—
To appreciate a quiet story

Materials you will need—
Tape recorder, cassette tape

What to do—
1. At a quiet interlude in the activity in the library corner, ask children to tell you how different books make them feel.

2. Show the children NIGHT IN THE COUNTRY and ask them to tell you how they felt after you read the book at circle time.

3. Discuss how the illustrations make them feel that it is night without being scared. Elicit their understanding that it is a peaceful and relaxing book that someone can enjoy alone.

4. Read NIGHT IN THE COUNTRY to the group of children in the center, and record it as you read.

5. After the reading, tell the children that anytime they want a quiet and peaceful book to help them relax, they can come and get the tape and listen along while looking at the pictures of the book.

Something to think about—
In full-day programs where young children are active all day, it is important to design activities which alternate between being quite active and those that are relaxing. Also, it is imperative that we show individual children ways to relax on their own.

For Sand Table: Country Geography

What the children will learn—
To shape the sand and dirt to simulate the countryside

Materials you will need—
Sand table, shovels, small watering can, small blocks, twigs, grasses, playdough, small plastic animals, small toy truck, tractor

What to do—
1. Refer to NIGHT IN THE COUNTRY and the way it seemed you were looking over hills and valleys to see the countryside at night.

2. Suggest that the children form and shape the sand to look like hills, valleys and fields in the country. Show them how to sprinkle water from the watering can to get just enough moisture to shape the sand.

3. On their own, children will think of building houses and barns. Then someone will think of the plastic farm animals.

4. If they do not think of how to make the trees and fields, provide the playdough, twigs and grasses, and let them improvise.

Something to think about—
Depending upon their experiences in the country, older preschoolers may remember to plow the fields and create the rows. Younger preschoolers will enjoy driving the tractor and the truck and rearranging the sand more than they will enjoy creating scenes.

For Science And Nature Center: Animal Babies

What the children will learn—
To associate the names of animals and their young

Materials you will need—
Pictures of baby animals and their mothers

What to do—
1. Show the pictures of the baby animals and their young found in NIGHT IN THE COUNTRY. There are raccoons, rabbits and cows with their young.

2. Collect pictures of other farm and wild animals and tell the names for each one. Go beyond the usual baby cow is a calf, dog is a puppy, cat is a kitten. Include unusual ones as a baby goose is a gosling. Baby foxes and wolves are also called pups.

Something to think about—
Many of the books for young children humanize animals as the main characters. In science and nature study, it is important to separate the real and the imaginary. Include in your displays for the science and nature center only pictures and illustrations of real animals. For instance, do not place a copy of the RUNAWAY BUNNY in a display of mother animals and their young, even though the story is about a mother rabbit and her son. Avoid combining the humanized animal stories and real animal information. Check with a reference librarian at the school or a community library for many excellent sources about real animals and their young.

(Adapted from Darlene Cobb's classroom.)

FIGURE 7.4 *Continued*

REFERENCES

Arnold, Tedd. (1987). **NO JUMPING ON THE BED!** New York: Dial Books for Young Readers.

Berger, Barbara. (1984). **GRANDFATHER TWILIGHT**. New York: Philomel Books.

Brown, Margaret Wise. (1947). **GOODNIGHT MOON**. New York: Harper and Row, Publishers.

Mayer, Mercer. (1987). **THERE'S AN ALLIGATOR UNDER MY BED**. New York: Dial Books for Young Readers.

Rylant, Cynthia. (1986). Illustrated by Mary Szilagyi. **NIGHT IN THE COUNTRY.** New York: Bradbury Press.

Additional References for Naptime/Bedtime

Bourgeosis, Paulette. (1986). Illustrated by Brenda Clark. **FRANKLIN IN THE DARK**. New York: Scholastic, Inc. *A little turtle is afraid to go inside his shell and sleep until his friends help him conquer his fear.*

Freedman, Sally. (1986). Illustrated by Robin Oz. **DEVIN'S NEW BED**. Niles, IL: Albert Whitman and Company. *Devin is reluctant to give up his crib and accept his new grown-up bed, until he discovers how much fun the new bed can be.*

Koide, Tan. (1983). Illustrated by Yasuko Koide. **MAY WE SLEEP HERE TONIGHT?** New York: Atheneum Press. *Many animals become lost in a dense fog and as each finds the log cabin, they ask, "May we sleep here tonight?" Finally, the bear owner returns to tell them he has been out looking for anyone who might be lost in the fog and that everyone may sleep here tonight.*

Rice, Eve. (1980). **GOODNIGHT, GOODNIGHT**. New York: Greenwillow Books. *Goodnight comes to all the people in the town and to the little cat as well.*

Stoddard, Sandol. (1985). Illustrated by Lynn Munsinger. **BEDTIME FOR BEAR**. Boston: Houghton Mifflin Company. *Small bear uses every excuse to avoid going to bed much to the exasperation of Big bear.*

FIGURE 7.4 *Continued*

of going to the library." Clearly, Sarah has positive responses to literature. Some classroom indicators of positive responses to literature are the following:

Children create art, music, drama, dance, writing, etc., in response to literature.

Children relish the opportunity to read and listen to favorite stories.

Children identify with story characters, use story themes in their play, and story language in their conversations.

Children return on their own to the books that have been shared; they ask adults to "read it again."

Children seek other books similar to their favorites; they begin to recognize particular authors and artists.

Children discuss their favorite books enthusiastically; they make recommendations to peers and adults. Burke, 1986 (p. 250).

Figure 7.5 contains three children's artistic responses to their favorite books; *Corduroy*, *The Story About Ping*, and *The Little Rabbit Who Wanted Red Wings*.

Conclusion: Benefits of Literature for the Teacher

Jo Beth, a student teacher, went to the university library to locate a big book so that she could use it with her second-grade reading group. As she sat reading a 17′ × 22′ version of *Bunches and Bunches of Bunnies* (Matthews, 1978), passers-by teased her about her reading level, her reading interests, and her eyesight. As Jo Beth left the library, she noticed people looking at her rather curiously. Children's literature expert Nicholas Tucker (1982) talks about Jo Beth's dilemma when he observes that most adults feel rather foolish when they are seen reading in the children's section of the library, and feel embarrassed to have an armful of books, none of which is more than three quarters of an inch thick. Fortunately, these feelings are dispelled as soon as teachers begin to discover the many ways that children's literature benefits them as educators. Picture books can help early childhood educators to

Function as Model Readers and Writers   Children learn more from deeds than from words. Linda Lamme (1988) contends that teachers lose credibility as role models of literacy if they are not readers and writers themselves.

FIGURE 7.5   Three First-Graders Respond to Their Favorite Books.

FIGURE 7.5   *Continued*

> *Would a parent let a child take piano lessons from a teacher who did not play the piano? Teachers need to learn how to love to read and write before they can help children become avid readers and writers. A good way for teachers to become readers is to read large quantities of children's literature. Some of the best books being published today are children's books. (p. 124)*

Gain Curricular Inspiration   When excellent teachers are in the midst of lesson or unit planning, one of the first things they do is turn to children's books. Sue says, "We have to write a lesson on economics for my early-childhood curriculum class. I couldn't think of anything until I remembered that book you showed us about the father losing his job, *Tight Times*." (Hazen, 1979). Pete says, "I volunteered to read books at the readathon. I decided to use a humorous big book so I used the opaque projector to make *Three by the Sea*." (Marshall, 1981) "It was a big hit!"

Remain Current   Whereas the textbooks in your classroom may be outdated or the materials on your shelves may not have kept pace with social trends, recently published picture books can be borrowed from the library to make teaching and learning resources more current. Ariel, a college sophomore, was planning a unit to develop multicultural concepts. She found that Native Americans were virtually absent in most of the published curriculum materials, and, if they were portrayed at all, it was in a stereotypic way. Then, with the help of an annotated bibliography, she found *The Legend of the Blue Bonnet* (de Paola, 1983); *The Gift of the Sacred Dog* (Goble, 1980); *Knots on a Counting Rope* (Martin and Archambault, 1987); and *Annie and the Old One* (Miles, 1971) at the library, and her unit was a great success.

I Lic his wins
And I Lik his the
well

FIGURE 7.5 *Continued*

Provide Developmentally Appropriate Explanations Ms. Langdon kept a classroom chart with seven different pockets. Each pocket had a drawing of a face on it: one for very sad, a little sad, very happy, pleased, surprised, confused, and just okay. Every day, each child would place a card with his or her name in the pocket that best represented his or her feelings. At first, nearly all the children placed their names in the "happy file." Gradually, they became more candid. Ms. Langdon would review the contents of the pockets each morning. On one particular day, Jaimie's name card was in the "very sad" pocket because his "cat got runned over by a car this morning and now he's dead." This is obviously a very sensitive issue, one that demands careful handling and developmentally appropriate answers to the children's questions. Once again, literature can be a resource for teachers as they strive to deftly deal with children's crises. Books such as *The Dead Bird* (Brown, 1958), *The Tenth Good Thing About Barney* (Viorst, 1971), and *I'll Always Love You* (Wilhelm, 1985), all deal with the loss of a beloved pet. In addition, these books respect the child's need to grieve and model appropriate coping strategies for the child (Jalongo 1986; Jalongo, 1988). The teacher decided that she would console Jaimie and wait until he had a new cat to use one of these books with the group.

Satisfy Our Need for Beauty   Two Christmas stories, *The Polar Express* (Van Allsburg, 1985) and *Max's Christmas* (Wells, 1986) illustrate how different books can be stylistically, yet still satisfy our aesthetic sensibilities. The first uses oil paintings to reawaken our belief in the Santa Claus myth: the second uses primary colors and cartoon-style drawings to tell the comic story of a rabbit-child who tries to stay awake and meet Santa Claus face-to-face. Even though these two books are dramatically different from an artistic standpoint, both satisfy our need for beauty.

As schools become inundated by the blurry bluish purple of ditto pages or the black line drawings of workbooks, we crave color, excitement, and beauty in both language and art from published materials. Picture books are a rich resource for both teachers and children. Outstanding language arts teachers instill a love of literature in young children by sharing their enthusiasm for picture books and emphasizing enjoyment.

Summary

Literature is the imaginative transformation of experience and ideas into language. Literature for young children includes rhymes, songs, and stories. The cornerstone of modern children's literature is the picture book, a blend of pictorial art and the language arts. There are many thousands of picture books and many different genres within the classification of picture book. The teacher's role in promoting picture books includes being knowledgable about children's literature, selecting books carefully, presenting books effectively, building a literature-based curriculum, designing extension activities, and assessing children's literary responses.

Focus On: Understanding Picture Books

Group Activity One: Reviewing Picture Books

These small group activities are designed to give you an opportunity to immerse yourself in quality picture books and to develop sound professional judgment about literature for young children.

   1. Write your name on an index card.
   2. Walk around the room and browse through the picture books. Then write down the titles and authors of your three favorites on the card.
   3. Select one of your favorites and do the following:

- read the text.
- look at the harmony between the words and the illustrations.
- locate a favorite passage and picture.
- note any special features of the book: dedications, borders, endpapers, and so forth.

4. Next you will report on your book to group members of a small group (4 to 5 students). Select a recorder to take notes and summarize the discussion. The questions listed below should help to focus your presentation and discussion (Elleman, 1986):

> What is the illustrator attempting to do?
>
> Why is a certain effect used? Is it successful?
>
> Are the illustrations or photographs aesthetically pleasing and of good quality?
>
> Are story and picture well integrated?
>
> Is there flow from page to page?
>
> Has the artist considered the constraints of format?
>
> Has the child been kept in mind? What age child?
>
> Could a young child get a sense of the basic concepts of story sequence by looking at the pictures?
>
> What about balance, harmony, mood, composition, line, and color?

Allow time for each group member to comment on the book and discuss your reactions. Be prepared to report to the total group the highlights of your small group discussion. Did any of you choose the same books as favorites? Were your reasons for choosing it the same or different?

Group Activity Two: Why Are Some Books Better Than Others?
Same Stories/Different Versions

These guidelines were developed by Janet Brown McCracken to evaluate print and nonprint media submitted for review in the journal *Young Children*:

What Is a Good Book or Recording for Young Children?

Quality books and recordings for young children

- reflect an understanding of how children grow and develop, and how development can be enhanced and enriched.
- respect children's and adults' good taste.
- are appropriate for children in the age range of birth through eight.
- are free of stereotypes.

- accurately portray reality and history.
- demonstrate attention to detail—illustrations match the text, and words on the song sheets match the music, for example.
- contain elements of good literature—plot, depth of character, creative use of language, and timelessness of story.
- are aesthetically appealing.
- deal with human emotions sensitively and offer constructive methods for coping with difficulties.
- do not use humor at the expense of others.
- do not "talk down" to children.
- are good quality productions.

Within your group you have award-winning versions of several popular children's stories and versions of the same stories that are widely available but not particularly noteworthy. Compare the two versions by making lists of the *differences* between them. Write a short statement that explains why the award-winning book might be evaluated more favorably.

Group Activity Three: Humor in Children's Literature

The books that children refer to as "funny" are among their favorites. Every year, the International Reading Association sponsors a major research project and publishes "Children's Choices" in the October issue of *The Reading Teacher*. Generally speaking, there are more humorous books in the list of best books selected by children than there are in lists of best children's books compiled by adults. How does the child's sense of humor develop?

Do the following in your group:

1. Choose someone to take notes for your group.
2. Think about each of the following age groups and what sort of humor might be generally appealing: infants/toddlers, preschool, and primary grades.
3. Compare your ideas with the following chart.

The Development of Humor

Infant/Toddler
Sensory stimulation; direct physical participation

Early Childhood/Primary Grades
All of the above plus clowning, slapstick, nonsense expressions, and chants
Middle Childhood
All of the above plus riddles, word play and conventional jokes

Source: Jalongo, M. R. (1985). Children's literature: There's some sense to its humor. *Childhood Education, 62,* 109–114.

4. Examine the humorous books for children gathered by the members of your group. Which would you share with children in each of the four groups on the chart? Why?

Group Activity Four: Crisis-Oriented Books for Young Children

Often the books that we select for children suggest ways of handling powerful emotions or coping with difficult situations. In addition to the general picture book selection guidelines, crisis-oriented books warrant additional criteria, including the following:

1. Can children identify with the plot, setting, dialogue, and characters?
2. Does the book use correct terminology, psychologically sound explanations, and portray events accurately? Does the book have professional endorsements?
3. Are the origins of emotional reactions revealed and respected?
4. Does the book reflect an appreciation of individual differences?
5. Are good coping strategies modeled for the child?
6. Does the book present crises in an optimistic, surmountable fashion?

Group Activity Five: Selecting Books for the Very Young (Infancy to Three Years Old)

In her classic case study *Cushla and Her Books*, Dorothy Butler (1975) discusses four basic qualities of books for the very young (infancy to three years old):

1. appropriateness of subject matter or theme
2. use of words that have precision and yet explore the resources of language, deftly and eloquently setting the scene and moving action along
3. plots that proceed in a straight line (with no tangents)
4. stories that build to a satisfying conclusion

According to Butler, each book should have "form, unity, color, climax."

INSTRUCTIONS:

Locate one example of a quality book for the very young child and bring it to class. Using the rating scale, assess each of the infant-toddler books supplied by group members. First, rate each book independently of other group members. Then, after everyone has rated each selection, compare and contrast your rankings. If you rated a book differently from some or most group members, give a rationale for doing so. Do you think that Butler's criteria are useful for assessing literature for the very young?

Evaluating Books for the Very Young

Scale: 5 = Excellent 4 = Good 3 = Average 2 = Fair 1 = Poor			
	Book 1	*Book 2*	*Book 3*
Book Title:			

Criteria:

1. Appropriateness of theme or subject matter

2. Skillful use of language

3. Simple plot

4. Satisfying conclusion

5. Quality of illustrations

Source: Butler, D. (1975). *Cushla and her books.* Boston, MA: The Horn Book

Group Activity Six: Sharing Literature with Young Children

What should children's literature *do* for children? Jot down your ideas, then compare and contrast them with those of the other group members.

Now consider these uses for picture books identified by John Stewig (1980).

Goals of the Literature Program

Picture books should

- provide enjoyment for both child and adult.
- stimulate the child's imagination.
- help children understand themselves and realize that they are not alone.
- enable children to meet others unlike themselves.
- give children an opportunity to explore and use language in many ways.
- allow children to explore other times and places.
- provide children with information.
- give children a vehicle for escaping from their daily routines.

Which of the following statements by teachers are reflective of a commitment to children's literature? Why?

1. "I will dismiss you by rows to go and get your coats while I read the story."
2. "Please sit where you can see the pictures."
3. "Because we got our new guinea pig today, I have a special book for you all about guinea pigs."
4. "I will put this story on the bookshelf so that you can look at it whenever you like."

5. "Dana, you said this was your favorite book. Why do you choose it as your favorite?"

6. "I agree, Nikki. Rumplestiltskin *does* have pretty pictures. Here's another book illustrated by Paul Zelinsky that you might like."

7. "If you look very carefully at these pictures in *The Three Bears*, you can see little pictures all around the edges of each page. Have you ever seen any other books with borders like this one?"

8. "How is this story like some other books we've read?"

9. "Juanita, if you can't behave you can go sit at a table by yourself and look at a book."

10. "Now that we all know *The Three Billy Goats Gruff*, let's act out the story. Any ideas on what we could use for the bridge?"

11. "What was the dog's name in the story? Carla? Children, Carla doesn't know the answer. Who can help her?"

12. "Yes, Leona, these pictures in *The Grouchy Ladybug do* look like the ones in *Brown Bear, Brown Bear*. How could we find out if the artist is the same?"

13. "Children, Brian scribbled all over this book with a crayon and ruined it. Who can tell him the rules about borrowing books?"

14. "Look, there is a dedication in the front of this book. Some of you may want to dedicate *your* next book to a special person."

15. Let's read this part together and really make our voices sound gruff, like the wolf. 'Little pig, little pig, let me come in.' Now let's try to sound like a piglet: 'Not by the hair of my chinny chin chin.'"

16. "Today the sixth-graders have a very special puppet play made especially for you. Maybe we can go to their classroom and show them how we tell *The Little Red Hen* story."

17. "Please don't interrupt. I only have five minutes to finish this story."

18. "This time when we read *Teddy Bear, Teddy Bear*, let's pretend to do all the things he does."

In the Field: Books Children Love

A graduate student brought Jarrod, her six-year-old son, to my office to borrow some books. Mixed in among the many quality books was an awful book that came free with the purchase of a sugar-laden breakfast cereal. (I used it in children's literature class as an example of everything a children's book should *not* be). Imagine this mother's embarrassment when Jarrod spied a cartoon character from Saturday morning cereal commercials on the cover and asked to borrow it! As a testimonial to Jarrod's good taste, this book was not one that he asked to hear again, nor did he respond to it with a picture (Figure 7.6) as he did for *Frog and Toad Together* (Lobel, 1972). Yet, as Jarrod's reaction illustrates, familiarity often influences children's book choices. The central issue of literary response is: How do children come to love a particular book?

FIGURE 7.6   Jarrod's Drawing of Arnold Lobel's Story Characters, Frog and Toad.

The following options will enable you to explore this question with a parent, a child and/or a children's librarian.

Option One

You will need to locate a parent and a young child who share books frequently and who have some of the child's favorite books available in the home.

Questions for Parent

Can you name any stories, books, songs, or poems that are (or were) your child's favorites?

Why do you think this particular piece of literature was so appealing to your child at that particular time?

Do you recall any of the discussion that took place surrounding a favorite book of your child or any specific comments that your child made about it?

Has your child ever liked a book that you disliked? (If yes) What book was it? Why did you dislike it?

For the Child

Tell the child that you would like to read some books to him or her. Ask him to select several favorites. After reading each one, ask the child what he likes about the book and jot down verbatim notes of comments the child made while sharing the book.

Option 2

Conduct the same interview with the parent in Option 1 above, but instead of meeting with the child once, ask the parent to tape several sessions in which the same book is read. Transcribe the essential parts of the dialogue during each of the sessions and then label and organize them chronologically. How did the child's comments change over time? Was there any evidence that the child had built upon previous conversations about the book?

Option 3

Interview a children's librarian with the following questions:

What picture books are checked out most often by parents and children?

In your opinion, are the most popular titles representative of the best that children's literature has to offer? Why or why not?

What are some of your personal favorites to use at story times with young children?

Have you ever received any complaints about a controversial picture book? Which ones?

References

Aiken, J. (1982). *The way to write for children.* New York: St. Martin's.

Bettelheim, B. (1976). *The uses of enchantment: The meaning and importance of fairy tales.* New York: Knopf.

Bruner, J. (1984). Language, mind and reading. In H. Groelman, A. Oberg, and F. Smith (Eds.). *Awakening to literacy.* Exeter, NH: Heinemann.

Burke, E. M. (1986) *Early childhood literature: For love of child and book.* Boston, MA: Allyn & Bacon.

Butler, D. (1975). *Cushla and her books.* Boston: The Horn Book.

Campbell, J. (1949). *The hero with a thousand faces.* Princeton, NJ: Princeton University.

Carlson, R. K. (1974). A baker's dozen of personal values of children's literature. Vienna, Austria: World Reading Congress, August 10. (ERIC Document Reproduction Service No. ED 097 628).

Cazden, C. (1972). *Child language and education.* New York: Harper & Row.

Children's books in print. (1989). New York: Bowker.

Ciancolo, P. (1984). Illustrations in picture books. In Z. Sutherland and M. C. Livingston (Eds.), *The Scott Foresman anthology of children's literature* (pp. 846–878). Glenview, IL: Scott Foresman.

Cochran-Smith, M. (1984). *The making of a reader*. Norwood, NJ: Ablex.

Elleman, B. (1986). Picture book art: Evaluation. *Booklist, 82*(20), 1548.

Gillespie, J. T., and Naden, C. J. (1990). *Best books for children: Preschool through middle grades* (4th ed.). New York: Bowker.

Huck, C.; Hepler, S.; and Hickman, J. (1989). *Children's literature in the elementary school*. New York: Holt Rinehart and Winston.

Hymes, J. (1981). *Teaching the child under six*. (3rd ed.). Columbus, OH: Merrill.

Jalongo, M. R. (in press). Children's play: A resource for multicultural education. In E. B. Vold (Ed.). *Multicultural education in early childhood*. Washington, DC: National Education Association.

Jalongo, M. R. (1988). *Young children and picture books: Literature from infancy to six*. Washington, DC: National Association for the Education of Young Children.

Jalongo, M. R. (1986). Using crisis-oriented literature with young children. In J. B. McCracken (Ed.). *Reducing stress in young children's lives* (pp., 41–46). Washington, DC: National Association for the Education of Young Children.

Jalongo, M. R. (1985). Children's literature: There's some sense to its humor. *Childhood Education, 62*, 109–114.

Kimmel, M. M., and Segal, E. (1983). *For reading out loud!* New York: Delacorte.

Knipping, N., and Andre, M. (1988). First graders' response to a literature-based literacy strategy. In B. F. Nelms (Ed.). *Literature in the classroom: Readers, texts and contexts*. Urbana, IL: National Council of Teachers of English.

Lamme, L. (1988). Reflections on raising literate children. In G. F. Roberson and M. A. Johnson (Eds.). *Leaders in education: Their views on controversial issues* (pp. 122–125). Lanham, MD: University Press of America.

Lima, C. W., and Lima, J. A. (1989). *A to Zoo: Subject access to children's picture books* (3rd ed.). New York: Bowker.

Morrow, L. M. (1988). Young children's response to one-to-one story readings in school settings. *Reading Research Quarterly, 23*, 89–107.

Morrow, L. M. (1982). Relationships between literature programs, library corner designs and children's use of literature. *Journal of Educational Research, 78*, 339–344.

Peabody, B. (1975). *The winged word*. Albany, NY: State University of New York.

Power, E. (1934) "The Pancake" In *Bag o' tales*. New York: Dover (revised edition, 1969).

Raines, S. C., and Canady, R. (1989). *Story s-t-r-e-t-c-h-e-r-s*. Mt. Rainier, MD: Gryphon House.

Raines, S. C., and Isbell, R. T. (1989). A description of the book interest behaviors of four-year-olds. Paper presented at the Research Forum, Annual Study Conference, Association for Childhood Education International, Indianapolis, IN, April 5–10.

Roberts, E. (1984). *The children's picture book*. Cincinnati, OH: Writer's Digest Books.

Rosenblatt, L. (1982). Literary transaction: Evocation and response. *Theory Into Practice, 21*(4), 268–277.

Roser, N., and Martinez, M. (1985). Roles adults play in preschoolers' response to literature. *Language Arts, 62*, 485–490.

Shulevitz, U. (1989). What is a picture book? *The Five Owls, 2*(4), 49–53.

Stewig, J. W. (1980). *Children and literature*. Boston, MA: Houghton Mifflin.

Teale, W. H. (1984). Reading to young children: Its significance for literacy development. In H. Goelman, Oberg and F. Smith (Eds.). *Awakening to literacy* (pp. 110–130). London: Heinemann.

Trelease, J. (1989). *The new read-aloud handbook*. New York: Penguin.

Tucker, N. (1982). *The child and the book: A psycholinguistical and literary exploration*. New York: Cambridge University Press.

White, D. (1984). *Books before five*. Portsmouth, NH: Heinemann. (originally published 1954).

Children's Books

Aardema, V. (1990). *Rabbit makes a monkey of lion*. New York: Dial.

Aardema, V. (1981). *Bringing the rain to Kapiti Plain*. New York: Dial.

Alexander, M. (1970). *Bobo's dream*. New York: Dial.

Aliki. (1989). *The king's day: Louis XIV of France*. New York: Crowell.

Aliki. (1981). *Digging up dinosaurs*. New York: Harper/Trophy.

Aliki. (1976). *Corn is maize: The gift of the Indians*. New York: Harper/Trophy.

Allard, H. (1977). *It's so nice to have a wolf around the house*. New York: Doubleday.

Bemelmans, L. (1939). *Madeline*. New York: Viking.

Bennett, R. (1988). "The gingerbread man" In B. S. de Regniers et al. (Eds.) *Sing a song of popcorn*. New York: Scholastic.

Berezny, A. (1989). *A frog prince*. New York: Holt.

Brown, M. W. (1958) *The dead bird*. Reading, MA: Addison-Wesley.

Burningham, J. (1976). *The blanket. The friend. The dog. The cupboard*. New York: Crowell.

Calhoun, M. (1981). *Hot-air Henry*. New York: Morrow.

Carrick, C. (1990). *Aladdin and the wonderful lamp*. New York: Scholastic.

de Paola, T. (1983). *The legend of the bluebonnet*. New York: Putnam.

Durrell, A. (1989) (compiler). *The Diane Goode book of American folk tales and songs*. New York: Dutton.

Ehlert, L. (1990). *Fish eyes: A book you can count on*. San Diego, CA: Harcourt Brace Jovanovich.

Ehlert, L. (1989). *Color zoo*. New York: Harper/Lippincott.

Ehlert, L. (1989). *Eating the alphabet: Fruits and vegetables from A to Z*. San Diego, CA: Harcourt Brace Jovanovich.

Field, E. (1982). *Wynken, blynken and nod*. New York: Dutton. (illustrated by Susan Jeffers)

Fleischman, P. (1989). *Joyful noise: Poems for two voices*. New York: Harper/Zolotow.

Friedman, I. R. (1984). *How my parents learned to eat*. Boston: Houghton Mifflin.

Galbraith, K. O. (1990). *Laura Charlotte*. New York: Putnam/Philomel.

Galdone, P. (1975). *The gingerbread boy*. New York: Scholastic.

Goble, P. (1980). *The gift of the sacred dog*. New York: Bradbury.

Gomi, T. (1990). *My friends.* New York: Chronicle.

Griego, M. (1980). *Tortillitas para mama*. New York: Holt, Rinehart and Winston.

Grifalconi, A. (1987). *Darkness and the butterfly*. Boston: Little, Brown.

Hazen, B. S. (1979). *Tight times*. New York: Penguin.

Heller, R. (1981). *Chickens aren't the only ones*. New York:

Hills, E. (1980). *Where's Spot?* New York: Putnam.

Hooks, W. H. (1989). *The three little pigs and the fox*. New York: Macmillan.

Howard, E. F. (1990). *Chita's Christmas tree*. New York: Bradbury.

Hughes, S. (1985). "Nursery Collection" *Bathwater's Hot. Noisy. When we went to the park*. New York: Lothrop.

Ivimey, J. W. (1991). *Three blind mice*. New York: Putnam. (Illustrated by Lorinda Cauley.)

Kasza, K. (1990). *When the elephant walks*. New York: Putnam.

Kasza, K. (1987). *The wolf's chicken stew*. New York: Putnam.

Kellogg, S. (1985). *Chicken little*. New York: Morrow.

Knight, J. (1989). *Tickle toe rhymes*. New York: Franklin Watts/Orchard.

Knutson, B. (1990). *How the guinea fowl got her spots*. New York: Carolrhoda.

Kundhardt, D. (1962). *Pat the bunny*. New York: Golden Books. (orig. pub. 1940)

Levine, E. (1990). *I hate English!* New York: Scholastic.

Lobel, A. (1972). *Frog and toad together*. New York: Holt, Rinehart and Winston.

Marshall, J. (1989). *The three little pigs*. New York: Dial.

Marshall, J. (1981). *Three by the sea*. New York: Dial.

Martin, B. and Archambault, J. (1987). *Knots on a counting rope*. New York: Holt.

Matthews, L. (1978). *Bunches and bunches of bunnies*. New York: Scholastic.

Maxner, J. (1989). *Nicholas cricket*. New York: Harper & Row.

McMillan, B. (1989). *Super super superwords*. New York: Lothrop, Lee & Shepard.

Miles, M. (1971). *Annie and the old one*. Boston: Little, Brown.

Omerod, J. (1985). "Baby Books" *Dad's back. Messy baby. Reading. Sleeping*. New York: Lothrop.

Opie, P., and Opie, I. (1988). *Tail feathers from Mother Goose*. Boston, MA: Little, Brown.

Oxenbury, H. (1981). "The Baby Board Books" *Dressing. Family. Friends. Playing. Working*. Boston: Simon and Schuster.

Packlam, M. (1989). *Do not disturb*. Boston: Little, Brown.

Piper, W. (1945). *The little engine that could*. New York: Platt and Munk. (originally published in 1930)

Preston, E. M. (1974). *Squawk to the moon, little goose*. New York: Penguin.

Rice, E. (1981). *Benny bakes a cake*. New York: Greenwillow.

Rounds, G. (1989). *Old MacDonald had a farm*. New York: Holiday.

Ryder, J. (1987). *Chipmunk's song*. New York: Dutton.

San Souci, R. (1989). *The talking eggs: A folktale from the American South*. New York: Dial.

Scieszka, J. (1989). *The true story of the 3 little pigs! by A. Wolf*. New York: Viking/Kestrel.

Serfozo, M. (1988). *Who said red?* New York: McElderry/Macmillan.

Shapiro, L. (1979). *Baby animals: A change picture book*. Los Angeles, CA: Franklin Watts.

Shaw, N. (1986). *Sheep in a jeep*. Boston, MA: Houghton Mifflin.

Spier, P. (1961). *The fox went out on a chilly night*. New York: Doubleday.

Steptoe, J. (1987). *Mufaro's beautiful daughters*. New York: Lothrop, Lee & Shepard.

Tejima. (1985). *Fox's dream*. New York: Philomel.

Van Allsburg, C. (1985). *The polar express*. Boston: Houghton Mifflin.

Viorst, J. (1971). *The tenth good thing about Barney*. New York: Atheneum.

Voight, E. (1980). *Peter and the wolf*. Boston: David Godine.

Wantanabe, S. (1980–1982). "I Can Do It All By Myself Series" *Get set, go* (1981). *I can ride it* (1982). *I'm king of the castle* (1982). *What a good lunch!* (1980). *Where's my daddy?* (1982). New York: Philomel.

Wells, R. (1986). *Max's Christmas*. New York: Dial.

Wells, R. (1985). "Very First Books": *Max's bath, Max's Bedtime, Max's Birthday, Max's Breakfast*, New York: Dial.

Wells, R. (1979). "Very First Books" *Max's First Word. Max's ride. Max's toys*. New York: Dial.

White, E. B. (1953). *Charlotte's web*. New York: Harper.

Wilhelm, H. (1985). *I'll always love you*. New York: Crown.

Zemach, M. (1988). *The three little pigs*. New York: Farrar Straus & Giroux.

Nonprint Media

Raffi (1985). "De Colores" *One light, one sun*. Hollywood, CA: A & M Records.

Van Ronk, D. (1990). *Peter and the wolf play jazz*. Waterbury, VT: Silo/Alcazar.

PART FOUR

The Young Child Learns to Use Language Symbols

ONE OF THE GREAT achievements of young children is learning to think symbolically, to use and interpret pictures and print. Chapter 8, "Drawing and Writing: Composing Processes," discusses the interrelationships between the child's pictorial and graphic symbol-making. It also suggests strategies that teachers can use to support emergent writers as they strive to communicate with others and strategies for working with beginning writers in composition, spelling, and handwriting. Chapter 9, "Emergent and Early Reading," deals with the process of learning to read, beginning with the infant's earliest experiences with literature and concluding with the young reader's growing independence. Controversies about reading instruction and the latest strategies for teaching reading are examined.

Photo: Anne Peterson

8

Drawing and Writing: Composing Processes

OUTLINE

Key Concepts and Terms

I. Relationships Between Drawing and Writing
    A. Skill Similarities
    B. Cognitive Similarities
    C. Expressive Arts
    D. Developmental Similarities
    E. Common Purposes

II. Developmental Stages in Drawing and Writing
    A. Prealphabetic Writing and Nonrepresentational Writing
       1. Random scribbling
       2. Controlled scribbling
       3. Naming of scribbling
    B. Representational Drawing and Alphabetic Writing
       1. Early representational drawing, mock letters, and letters
       2. Preschematic drawing and semi-conventional alphabetic writing
       3. Schematic drawing and conventional writing
    C. Children's Understanding About Writing and Spelling

III. Guidelines for Supporting Children's Composing Processes

There are no children with nothing to say; only children who have decided that it is not worth writing because no one will hear them through the barrier of incomplete skill. Children need to talk about what is real for them.
—ESTHER S. FINE (1987)

KEY CONCEPTS AND TERMS

composing processes
prealphabetic writing
nonrepresentational drawing
alphabetic writing
representational drawing
writing principles

manuscript
cursive
stages in spelling
invented spelling
dialogue journals

Three kindergarten children are playing restaurant in a sociodramatic play center that they helped to create. Their drawings of hamburgers, french fries, beverages, and sweets are on the wall. A sign that reads "McDonald's" is posted over the "doorway" of a refrigerator box. The children are using a small table for the counter and a cutout in the side of the box for the drive-through window. Casey is the window clerk, Josh is the manager; and Amanda is the cook.

Casey: "A bus is coming through! (Writes furiously on order pad) We need 30 burgers, 50 fries, 20 Big Macs, and 70 Cokes."

Josh: "Well, do it, but they'll have to wait."

Amanda: (Rolls her eyes and wipes her forehead) "I think I'm quitting, Josh."

Josh: "You can't quit! Just keep makin' those hamburgers."

By envisioning these three five-year-olds at play, we can see how they use one thing to represent another (Suhor, 1982). They are learning how to think symbolically and how to use pictorial and written symbols to represent their ideas. Through symbols, they are able to invent new worlds.

Relationships Between Drawing and Writing

Particularly for young children, drawing and writing go together: "Art is an essential part of young children's writing. Pictures tell stories as well as print" (Thorne, 1988, p. 13). Because the drawings of young children usually emphasize "the communication of thoughts rather than the production of pleasing visual images" (Hipple, 1985, p. 255), many experts look at both drawing and writing as **composing processes**. Jeremy, age four, is a good example. He had a funny dream about a monster last night. As he illustrates the dream (Figure 8.1), he discusses it with his teacher:

J: I had a dream about a monster.

T: Were you afraid?

J: No, cause we be'ed friends. We played cards.

T: Let's make a picture of the monster.

J: Okay. (while drawing) Here is the big fat monster's belly. This is his head. Here's his feet and his hair. There's his great, great big ears.

T: Where are you?

J: I'm right down here . . . by the table. We played cards here. See the cards? These is monster cards. You have man cards.

T: What else did you do?

J: We drank pop . . . in glasses.

T: Did you do anything else?

J: We setted on a rocking chair.

Jeremy can recreate his dream by drawing it and talking about it. His words can be written down first by an adult and eventually by Jeremy himself. Pictorial signs (pictures) and graphic signs (writing) share five important attributes.

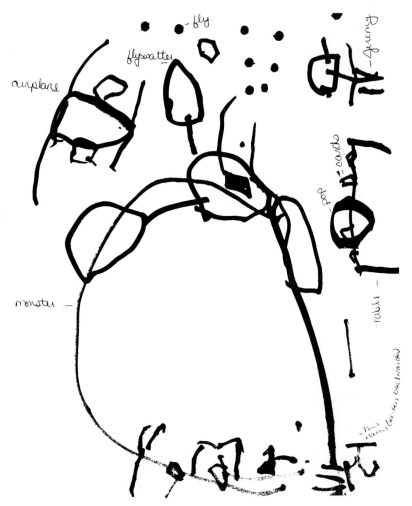

FIGURE 8.1   Jeremy's Dream.

Skill Similarities

Because drawing and writing both involve the fine motor skills of holding a writing implement and making marks on a paper, very young children do not differentiate between the two. Ask a two-year-old to draw and she scribbles; ask her to write and she scribbles. Even kindergartners may not yet differentiate between drawing and writing. Blazer (1986) interviewed 16 kindergarten children at the beginning of the school year. She found that there was "a definite lack of clarity" (p. 93) about the differences between drawing and writing. In fact, most of these five-year-olds based their ideas about "good" writing on what they knew about good drawing such as "staying in the lines" or "being neat." So both from the child's perspective and the perspective of research, drawing and writing share the same basic psycho-motor skills.

Victoria, age six, is excited about using a new box of crayons "with the points still on." For this special occasion, she decides to write and draw about her pet dog. Notice that she uses her skills in handling a crayon to communicate in both graphic and pictorial images:

Victoria: "This is Softy, he's my dog and he's a Pekingese. He's really fluffy and he gets so hot in the summer . . . you should see his coat . . . I'll draw a picture because I can't tell ya." (She scribbles furiously with a crayon all over the page, then prints the word "hot" on top). "His coat looks big, even bigger than that. Long, long, longer than *my* hair! I'll write my name. Here's my cursive 'C.' I like to draw Softy standing up because I give him a walking lesson every day." (See Figure 8.2.)

Whether Victoria is composing with pictures or with written language, she is striving to master the psychomotor skill of making marks on paper.

Cognitive Similarities

Even more fundamental than skill similarities between drawing and writing are the cognitive similarities:

> . . . *both are part of the symbolic function of the brain which makes possible the representation of an object, event, or conceptual scheme by means of a signifier or sign. There is a direct correspondence between the drawn symbol and the written symbol. Graphic images are part of a visual vocabulary which has intense personal meaning to the*

FIGURE 8.2   Victoria's Drawing of Softy, the Pekingese.

child. There is a symbiotic relationship among drawing, writing, reading, speaking and listening. (Platt, 1977, p. 262)

Beth, a four-year-old, is a good example of the think-draw-write connection. She decided to draw pictures of familiar objects, and make a corresponding list of the words for every item. Clay (1975) has referred to this behavior as "spontaneously taking inventory of knowledge." Figure 8.3 shows the pictures Beth drew, and the list she wrote, both based upon her knowledge and experience. It is clear that Beth sees both writing and drawing as ways of representing a concept.

Expressive Arts

A third relationship between writing and drawing is that each is an expressive art—a medium for communicating ideas and feelings to others. "Both drawing and language provide children with opportunities to reflect upon, organize and share experiences" (Dyson, 1988). Even very young children recognize the expressive

FIGURE 8.3   Beth Takes Spontaneous Inventory of Her Knowledge.

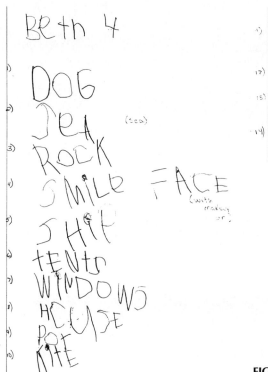

FIGURE 8.3   *Continued*

power of words and pictures. Alyssa, who has just had her third birthday, is asked by an interviewer if she can write and draw (Figure 8.4). Alyssa points to the "A" in the upper-left-hand corner and says, "There, that's Alyssa." Next, she draws a rectangular shape and puts several dots on it. She points to it and puts her fingers to her mouth saying "Yum! See, this is a banana." Finally, she scribbles on the page to show more writing. Alyssa's response, whether it is expressed through drawing or writing, is an authentic means of self-expression.

Developmental Similarities

The fourth and final way in which children's drawing and writing are related is that both are developmental. Both follow a basic, general pattern that is affected by the individual child's rate and style of development. In other words, both writing and drawing are dependent upon the child's level of understanding about the world. Fields (1988) categorizes the child's conceptual level as nonconventional and conventional. *Nonconventional* understandings about drawing and writing include experimenting with materials (such as the child who scribbles on the wall); refining forms (such as the child who controls the paint brush to make a particular design); and producing cultural symbols (such as the mandala, a stylized sun with rays emanating from it).

FIGURE 8.4   Three-year-old Alyssa Draws and Writes.

Conventional understandings result in forms that are recognizable to adults. If the child is using drawing conventionally, adults can tell what it represents and if the child is using print conventionally, adults can decipher it. Table 8.1 is an overview of the relationships among the child's level of understanding, drawing, and writing.

Common Purposes

The major purposes for teaching writing (Mosenthal, 1983) and their relationship to art are set forth below.

Practical—written and graphic symbols are a way to pass on cultural norms, a way to function in society.

Cognitive-development—both drawing and writing are used to promote intellectual growth and lifelong learning.

Emancipatory—art and literacy are ways of enhancing self-expression and promoting equal opportunity.

TABLE 8.1   Relationships Between Drawing and Writing

Child's Level of Understanding (Adapted from Fields, 1988)	*Stages in Writing* (Fields, 1988; Lamme, 1979)	*Stages in Drawing* (Brittain, 1979)
Nonconventional	*Prealphabetic Writing*	*Nonrepresentational Art*
Exploration of the medium	Non-linear scribbles	Random scribbling
Refining the form	Linear scribbles Repeated designs	Controlled scribbles
Awareness of the cultural relevance of the symbol	Letterlike forms	Naming of scribbles
Conventional	*Alphabetic Writing*	*Representational Art*
Beginning understanding of the conventions in drawing and writing	Random letters, letters or numbers in a string, letters or numbers clustered like words, early word-symbol relationships	Early representational attempts
Overgeneralization of rule hypothesis	Labels and lists, invented spelling, letters of inconsistent size/shape; moves to uniform size and shape, and upper and lower case letters used randomly, experiments with cursive writing	Preschematic drawing
Formal structure	Upper- and lower-case letters used correctly, standard spelling	Schematic drawing

Self-concept enhancement—both composing processes develop the child's sense of autonomy and self-worth.

Preschooler Samantha's invention of a personified pumpkin illustrates all of these purposes (Figure 8.3). As she draws and writes, she says: "I'm gonna draw a pumpkin . . . make his hair blue and kinda green. Gonna write his name . . . Sam. He needs a lot of feet because he has to go to a pumpkin meeting. He has to walk. He can walk on his head. Here's my name. My mom taught me how to write it."

Samantha has learned the *practical* value of drawing and writing; she uses both communication systems in ways that reflect the culture in which she lives. The *cognitive-developmental* value of drawing and writing are evident in her composing processes too. Samantha reasons that an object which is round and has feet on every surface could move very quickly. She also has some ideas about meetings; that they involve travel and require participation. Additionally, learning to draw and write has had an *emancipatory* influence on Samantha. If we observed her with the other four-year-olds in her nursery school, we would see how her drawing, writing, and the discussions surrounding them enable her to participate more fully in that social circle. Other children are intrigued by Samantha's drawing and writing; they ask her questions, comment on her efforts and sometimes ask her advice on especially challenging projects they have undertaken. When Kurt was trying to draw an explosion, for instance, he asked Samantha how to make it look "more fiery" and they

FIGURE 8.5   Samantha's Personified Pumpkin.

decided to mix orange, red, and yellow together. Finally, if we looked at the expression of pride on Samantha's face as she completes her drawing and writes her name all by herself, it would be clear that these newly acquired abilities in language and art have *enhanced her self-concept.*

Developmental Stages in Drawing and Writing

A general sequence for writing development (Lamme, 1985) and art development (Brittain, 1979) have been used to design the developmental sequence described below.

Prealphabetic Writing and Nonrepresentational Drawing

The initial stages in writing are called **prealphabetic**, meaning that no real letters are recognizable. The corollary to this stage in drawing is **nonrepresentational**, meaning that what the child draws does not look like the object. Even though a child's drawing or writing may not be *conventional* in form, children's efforts reveal much about their emerging concepts of communication through symbols.

Random Scribbling

The first scribbles of toddlers appear random and disordered; however, the scribbling is composed of definite lines made with simple movements. This is a first step for all children in developing their ability to control the marking tool and put marks only where they are wanted. At this stage the child does not differentiate between "drawing" and "writing" as such. Rather, the focus is on making marks on the paper. Chris, a seventeen-month-old, made the scribble in Figure 8.6.

Controlled Scribbling

Most three-year-olds have more control over the writing implement. As a result, they stay on the paper more and their scribbles acquire definite placement patterns. Later in this stage, scribbles become more linear. For examples of controlled scribbling, see Figure 8.7.

FIGURE 8.6   Examples of Random Scribbling.

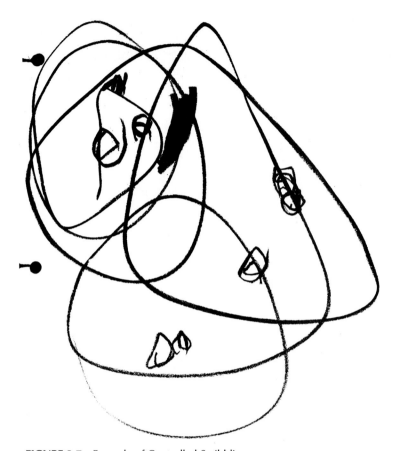

FIGURE 8.7   Example of Controlled Scribbling.

Naming of Scribbling

Four-year-olds often begin to attribute meaning to their scribbles. As evidence of their emerging knowledge of signs, children begin to name scribbles, squiggles, and designs. That meaning may be connected to words or to pictures. In both cases, the child sees the relationship between the marks on the paper and written words or real objects. Katie, a three-year-old, makes the scribbles in Figure 8.8. About the scribble in the upper lefthand corner, she says: "It says 'hello.' " About the second, she says, "It's a picture of Kirsty" (a dog).

As children work with the printed word, they start to hypothesize about how written language "works." Based upon observational studies of young children, Marie Clay (1975) has concluded that children at the prealphabetic stage of writing identify five **writing principles**. These principles about writing are highlighted in Figure 8.9.

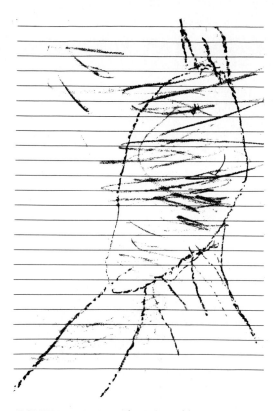

FIGURE 8.8   Katie, a Three-year-old, Writes
"Hello" and Draws a Picture of Kirsty, the Dog.

Representational Drawing and Alphabetic Writing

At this stage, both children's drawing and their writing are more conventional. Drawings begin to look like the objects being drawn and writing becomes more readable.

Early Representational Drawing, Mock Letters, and Letters

Usually, the drawings of four-year-olds begin to look more like whatever they represent. People or objects that have particular meaning for the child are placed randomly on the paper with no portrayal of space, and each figure is portrayed as a separate entity. Victor, a four-year-old boy, uses words to guide his drawing efforts and switches from a crayon to a pencil when he writes his name on the paper.

FIGURE 8.9 Principles About Writing (Clay, 1975)

The Recurring Principle

Children make the same marks over and over again because they recognize that there is a pattern to adult's writing. (See Figure 8.9A.)

The Generative Principal (Figure 8-9B)

Children realize that writing is not made up of only one mark repeated, but of different marks.

The Linear Principle

Children become sensitive to the horizontal aspect of writing. (See Figure 8.9C.)

The Flexibility Principle

Children begin to learn some letters, but they see unfamiliar letters and/or they see letters they know in an unfamiliar style. They need to determine how much a single letter can change stylistically and still be the same letter. Eventually they understand that some minor differences, (O and Q) change the letter, while some major features (a and A) do not. (See Figure 8.9D.)

The Sign Principle

Now the child recognizes that writing is intended to be read by others, not just the writer. They strive to master the conventions of print so that they can communicate more effectively. (See Figure 8.9E on page 214.)

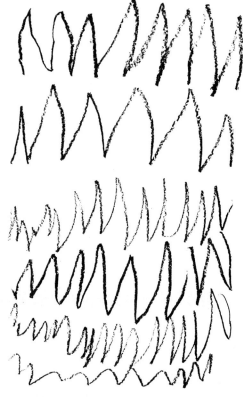

FIGURE 8.9A The Recurring Principle.

FIGURE 8.9B The Generative Principle.

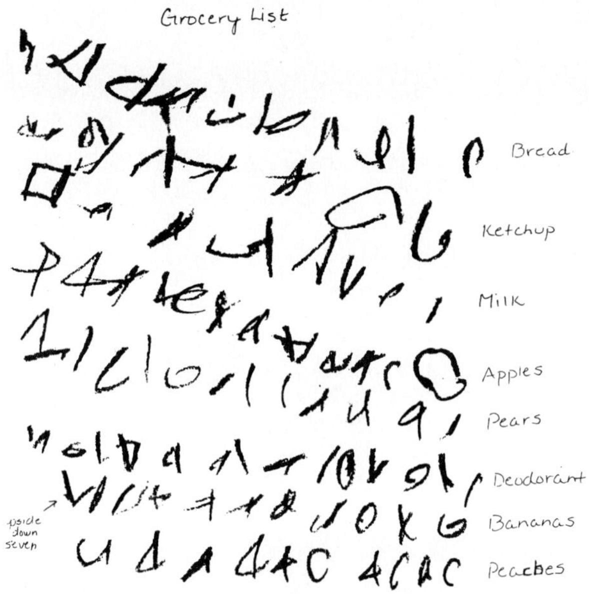

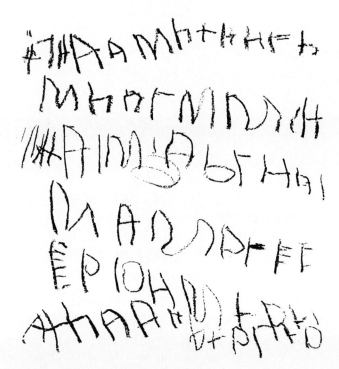

Grocery List

Bread

Ketchup

Milk

Apples

Pears

Deodorant

upside
down
seven

Bananas

Peaches

FIGURE 8.9C The Linear Principle.

FIGURE 8.9D The Flexibility Principle.

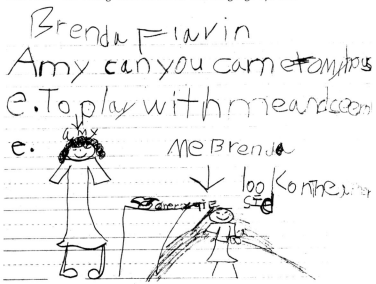

FIGURE 8.9E   The Sign Principle.

FIGURE 8.10   Four-year-old Victor's Drawing and Writing.

(Figure 8.10). "I'm making a horse. Horse, shoe, horse, shoe. That's how you make a tail—in and back out. I'm making a fox after this. This isn't a horse. Now it's a bird. I'll draw a horse down there where I put the dot. (He starts to draw the fox.) Yellow is my favorite color, my favorite color in the United States."

In writing, the child produces *mock letters*, repeated designs and shapes he calls "letters." Three-and-a-half-year-old Mandi uses early representational drawing and letter-like forms to print her name (Figures 8.11 and 8.11B).

Teacher: "Do you know how to draw? Show me how you draw."

Mandi: "Me can jaw (draw) . . . eyes, noss, mouse. I give her a pitty (pretty) necklace. She has lots and lots of hairs. She's a little, little girls. She is . . . can go to school."

Teacher: "Do you know how to write? Show me how you write."

Mandi: "I know how to do all the days. Me sometimes wites the biggest letters. Mommy taughts me tos. I been witing since I was one. I can wite like Mommy. She said I do weal good. I can wite . . . I can wite the best than anyone. "D" is the biggest witer (letter). And make some dots. I have a dot (referring to the dot over the i in her name) . . . Mandi. Done!"

Children may begin to write letters and numbers randomly, or arrange them in a string. Jenny, a three-year-old, wrote the string of letters and mock letters in Figure 8.12. In reference to her writing, she said, "It says Aunt Donna."

Elizabeth, age five, wrote the letters and numbers in a string in Figure 8.13.

FIGURE 8.11A   Three-and-a-half-year-old Mandi Draws "a Little Girl in a Pretty Necklace."

FIGURE 8.11B   Mandi Writes Her Name.

FIGURE 8.12 Three-year-old Jenny's Writing. "It Says Aunt Donna."

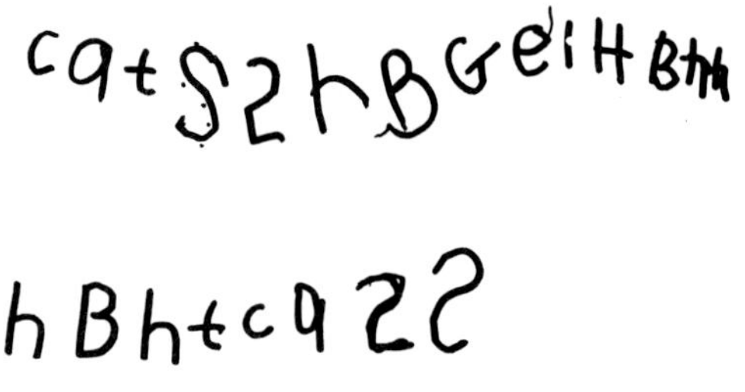

FIGURE 8.13 Five-year-old Elizabeth's Letters and Numbers.

FIGURE 8.14 Clustered Letters (and/or Numbers) of Inconsistent Size.

Preschematic Drawing and Semi-Conventional Alphabetic Writing

The majority of five-year-olds have gained the fine motor skills to organize drawings. Children experiment with drawings until they develop their own style of representing people. Many geometric shapes will begin to show up in pictures.

In writing, letters and numbers are often clustered like words, and letters of inconsistent size are common (Figure 8.14).

Schematic Drawing and Conventional Writing

As children enter the primary grades, they often produce detailed, precise drawings that reflect careful observation and planning. In writing, the child begins to make letters of uniform size, to reverse letters or numbers less, to experiment with cursive writing, and to use upper- and lower-case letters correctly. As David draws and writes, he adjusts his drawing and writing to the audience. The audience is his cousin, Leigh Ann, who is studying to be a teacher. David begins by displaying what he knows, assuming that this is what a teacher would like. He uses a combination of spoken and written words to imagine a situation that will entertain Leigh Ann. He predicts that she will react positively to his playfulness because they know each other well (Figure 8.15):

David (age 6½):   "I am going to make some shapes. I know how to spell circle. I know more shapes: diamond, stop sign, and ummmm, what else? (He looks around the room). Aha! Here is another shape (the oval-shaped knob on the stereo). All the shapes on the bottom are the same color because they are different shapes. (David sits and thinks, looking straight ahead with his chin resting on his hand.) I think I'll draw a tree. I'm good at trees. Here is the ground. Here is me; I have pants on. I'll put you beside me. You are bigger than me. I'll spell 'bigger' under you and 'little' under me. My hair is sticking up funny—it just got a little tangled in the tree. I was climbing the tree. Your hair got tangled too! I need a pen to write my words."

Children's Understandings About Writing and Spelling

As children enter the primary grades, their knowledge of composition, spelling, and handwriting become increasingly conventional because the child is building upon what he or she already knows about language and is continually expanding that repertoire of skills. Basically, learning to write involves four things:

1. An understanding of how writing and speech relate
2. The ability to form alphabet letters
3. An awareness of how form and style in writing vary depending on the situation
4. The intuitive ability to predict how readers might react to what the author has written (Schickendanz. 1986, p. 73).

FIGURE 8.15   Six-and-a-half-year-old David's Drawing and Writing.

But as we have seen, children do not learn to write conventionally by having someone tell them about writing. They learn to write by building their own knowledge about writing and spelling. Notice how these children gain more sophisticated understandings about writing with additional experience:

Jason (4½):   "It's marks on paper."

Desmond (5):   "Writing is putting down words and letters."

Camille (7):   "It's something we learn to do so we can write Grandma a thank-you note for the birthday gift. It's something the teacher gives us plus or minus on. And Dad writes Mom a note when he has to tell her something and she's not there."

Children gave these responses to the question, "Why do people write?"

Raquel (5):   "To work. My mom is a secretary and daddy has to read to drive—he has to read the signs."

Yukiko (6):   "So someone can write a letter instead of calling on the phone."

Neneh (7):   "To let people know things. You write so you can keep it."

Brian (8):   "So when they don't talk, they have something to say. People write to show their ideas."

Guidelines for Supporting Children's Composing Processes

More than two decades ago, James Britton (1970) conducted a study of writing instruction. He concluded that the vast majority of children's writing was purely for the purpose of proving to the teacher that the child had remembered bits of information previously presented by the teacher. In genuine written communication, a person writes a message that conveys new information (or at least conveys old information in new ways) to the reader. In Britton's view, real writing is not simply transcribing or copying, it is *communicating*. Because much of the writing that took place in schools did not have communication as its primary purpose, Britton (1970) argued that opportunities for authentic writing experiences were woefully inadequate.

Today, more schools have recognized the importance of "writing across the curriculum." This means that writing is not confined to an English class. Instead, it is used for different purposes across all subjects. A child might make observational notes on a plant or animal during science, create a greeting card with movable parts in art class, write an imaginary speeding ticket while playing outdoors with tricycles, or correspond with a classmate. In every case, the child has a good reason to write.

Whenever we work with young children who are learning to use the two major sign systems of drawing and writing, we must keep several things in mind (Dyson, 1988; Staton, 1982):

1. *Be aware of children's purposes*. Careful planning does not include planning the child's response. The teacher who distributes a packet of coloring-book pages for children to complete has not only set the task for the child, but has also determined the outcome. Everyone's paper is expected to look the same: neatly colored within the lines. The same holds true with writing. If we preselect the topic and format (such as asking children to copy a thank-you note from the chalkboard), then everyone's work looks the same and children's original ideas are negated. Allowing children to set the purpose for their composing processes helps them to appreciate the power of graphic and pictorial forms of communication.

2. *Provide opportunities for rehearsal and revision*. Giving children the time to discover a satisfying form is important. "Children need a predrawing or prepainting activity just as they need a chance for oral rehearsal of ideas before they write—a prewriting activity" (Sebesta, 1989, p. 24). Another advantage to using revision strategies is that they can function as invitations to more creative responses. One first-grade teacher shared *The Gingerbread Boy* with some first-graders and said, "I wonder what a real live gingerbread person would look like?" On the first draft, many children imitated the gingerbread people they had already seen in a bakery or in a book. But on the second revision, the teacher urged them to break those stereotypes and the results were amazing. There was a gingerbread boy with running shoes, a girl with glasses and two ponytails (just like the artist!), one with bib overalls and a piece of tissue in his pocket, even a gingerbread mother with a baby in her arms. These creations also led to imaginative stories about the characters because children were given a chance to rehearse and revise.

3. *Be sensitive in responding to children's efforts.* As teachers, we must resist the "right/wrong" mentality which prevents children from trying out their ideas. It matters little whether we use red pencil, green pen, or a grading stamp; the cumulative effect of negative messages about a child's drawing and writing can have far-reaching consequences. Too many people believe they cannot write and cannot draw because their efforts were criticized rather than supported. Instead, we must learn to encourage, in the literal sense of that word: "to give heart" and "embolden."

4. *Plan a varied curriculum.* Any teacher who is bored by the students' work is giving them boring work to do. If children are encouraged to experiment with drawing and writing, their work is a fascinating documentary of the themes, skills, and hypotheses that preoccupy them at that time. A classroom that values children's drawing and writing would find teachers and children using symbols together . . . making lists, creating posters, designing a mural, writing a story on a chart, creating an original song picture book, corresponding with others, and so forth. The audience for children's work should be varied too. Instead of children drawing and writing only for the teacher, children need opportunities to share their work with classmates, parents, children in other classes and grade levels, administrators or other school personnel, and visitors to the classroom, to name a few.

5. *Make activities concrete and functional.* Written language is more abstract than oral language because it is decontextualized, removed from the immediate situational context. Therefore, when children are first making the transition from oral language to written language, the writing should be tied to the child's experience. This makes writing less abstract and more concrete. Young children need to talk about their writing, draw pictures to accompany their writing and enact the stories they create.

Composing activities should be functional, meaning that they help children see that writing has a purpose beyond doing schoolwork. In order to appreciate the power of literacy, children must understand that drawing and writing are much more than copying.

6. *Provide opportunities for excellence.* Unlike an English workbook exercise done in solitude and corrected by the teacher, drawing and writing activities should provide feedback from a real, live audience to the writer and give writers opportunities to revise and revise again until they are satisfied with the outcome. Children should be encouraged to make their finished written products beautiful; for example, creating books with fabric covers or laminated pages and keeping them in the classroom library.

All of these guidelines share two assumptions: that children are "meaning makers," builders of their own knowledge about composing processes (Wells,

1986). Second, that meaning should be emphasized over correct form during the early years (Wells, 1990). We cannot assume that the child is a "tabula rasa" (a blank slate) where writing is concerned because, "we are not writing messages on a blank slate and we cannot—and do not want to—wipe the slate clean, even though it is incomplete and partially inaccurate" (Read, 1980, p. 148). Teachers who accept this philosophy treat pieces of writing as things to be nurtured rather than objects that need fixed (Bissex, 1981). In a classroom that supports children's writing, we would find children

- asking each other for help
- planning what they are creating
- rehearsing ideas
- questioning each other about their writing
- sharing their work with one another
- evaluating their work (Dailey, in press)

How does this "whole language" philosophy relate to instruction in handwriting and spelling?

Individualizing Handwriting and Spelling

What are your earliest recollections about learning to write? Did you

- trace over dotted lines and copy from the chalkboard?
- write in the air with your finger while watching the teacher?
- join the entire class in completing handwriting exercises?
- wait for the teacher to walk around and correct errors?
- use a large wooden pencil without an eraser?

You may be surprised to learn that none of these traditional handwriting instruction practices is supported by research.

Research on Handwriting

Handwriting research suggests the following:

- Children master handwriting better when they actually form letters than when they trace, copy, or write in the air (Peck, Askov, and Fairchild, 1980; Temple and Gillet, 1989).
- Although large group instruction is most common, it is not the most effective. Giving individualized feedback or working with small groups of children with similar writing needs is better for handwriting instruction than large group instruction (Koenke, 1986).

- Waiting for the teacher to correct mistakes is not the best practice, either. In handwriting, as with spelling and composition, we need to accept children's successive approximations of writing rather than point out every flaw. Actually, the teacher's energy would be better spent in speaking the procedure for letter formation while demonstrating printing or writing the letter. Children are also capable of correcting their own mistakes to some extent by comparing their letter formation with a model, such as the alphabet posted above the chalkboard in most classrooms.
- There is no support in the data either for the use of big pencils. Even young children prefer adult pencils and the oversized ones do not improve their writing (Peck, Askov, and Fairchild, 1980). By the time that children reach third grade, most children produce more letters more quickly and legibly when using ballpoint and felt tip pens (Askov and Peck, 1982).

Manuscript and Cursive Handwriting

In the United States formal handwriting instruction begins with manuscript (printing) in kindergarten and first grade. **Cursive** (handwriting) is typically introduced in second grade. Figure 8.16 contains sample alphabets in **manuscript** and cursive. The rationale for beginning with manuscript rather than cursive writing is as follows:

1. Printing requires two basic hand movements: straight lines and circles (or portions of circles).
2. Printing is more like the typing that children encounter when they are reading.
3. Manuscript is more legible than cursive writing, so adults can decipher the child's initial writing efforts more readily.

If you talk to some older people who are left-handed, you will find that it was once common practice to try and "break" children of this "bad habit." Today, we know that being left-handed is related to brain functioning and that it is useless, even detrimental, to force children to become right-handed.

Paper placement, the way that the paper is positioned on the child's desk, needs to be considered when teaching children to write. When the children are printing, the paper should be straight up and down because printing is straight, rather than slanted. If the children are doing cursive writing, however, the paper should be slanted in the direction opposite to the hand with which they write. This means that if you were looking over the shoulder of a right-handed child, her paper should be slanted to the left and if you are looking over the shoulder of a left-handed child, his paper should be slanted to the right.

Stages in Spelling Development

After children have gained many experiences interacting with print, they gradually begin to associate printed letters and words with talk. At first, the sound-symbol

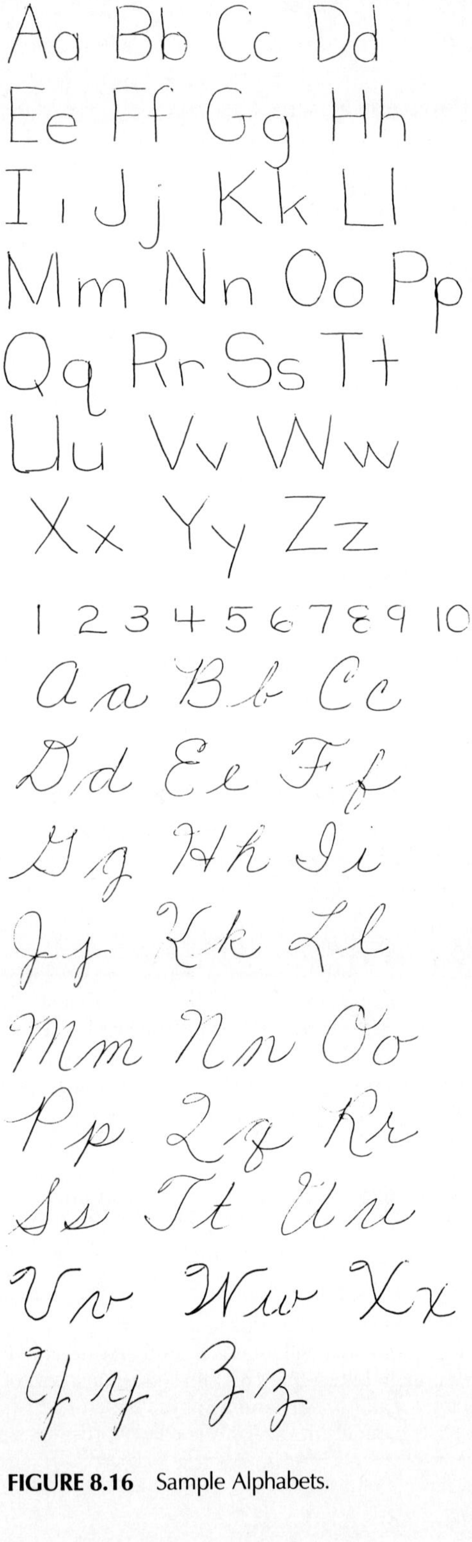

Aa Bb Cc Dd
Ee Ff Gg Hh
Ii Jj Kk Ll
Mm Nn Oo Pp
Qq Rr Ss Tt
Uu Vv Ww
Xx Yy Zz

1 2 3 4 5 6 7 8 9 10

Aa Bb Cc
Dd Ee Ff
Gg Hh Ii
Jj Kk Ll
Mm Nn Oo
Pp Qq Rr
Ss Tt Uu
Vv Ww Xx
Yy Zz

FIGURE 8.16 Sample Alphabets.

correspondence is absent, but eventually, the child connects sounds to letters and learns to spell even those words that are not phonetic. Table 8.2 is an overview of the stages young children go through in learning to spell.

Drawing and Writing Activities

Drawing and writing activities we plan for young children should be open-ended, providing many different responses rather than a single "correct" response. Classroom walls decorated with rows of nearly identical papers, neatly colored in the designated hues, accompanied by carefully copied proverbs or poems are (or should be) a thing of the past. These practices simply do not reflect current theory and research about how children construct their knowledge of pictorial and graphic symbols. Instead of being overwhelmed by the conformity when we see a display of children's work, we should be fascinated by the individuality. Some suggested activities that are designed to allow children that flexibility are described below.

Fingerpainting/Writing

Teachers sometimes think that materials such as fingerpaint or clay are strictly for art class, but these materials are excellent ways of supporting children's early writing and drawing efforts. Fingerpainting enables very young children to explore making marks on paper because it does not require managing a writing implement. It frees the child to be more fluid and flexible in the types of finger, hand, and arm movements made later during writing. For a different texture and feel, try a plastic dishpan partially filled with colored sand or cornmeal. Children can use the sand to make simple graphic symbols and change them at will.

TABLE 8.2   Stages in Spelling (Gentry, 1981)

Precommunicative—A child who is spelling precommunicatively usually does not know the entire alphabet, upper- and lower-case letters, or the left-to-right directionality of English. The child uses alphabet symbols but the letter-sound correspondence is absent. As a result, her spelling has the outward appearance of writing but does not function as writing (Temple, Nathan, and Burris, 1982). Even though it is impossible for an adult to read precommunicative or prephonemic writing, the child is usually able to translate what she has written.

Semiphonetic—At this stage, the child begins to associate sounds with letters, often using one letter to represent a syllable or word. Consonants predominate at this stage because they are the most clearly heard.

Phonetic—At this stage, the child tries to represent every sound heard with a letter.

Transitional—The child adds to her knowledge of phonology and even those words that differ from the correct spelling are easier for an adult to decipher.

Correct spelling or conventional spelling—By this time the child has acquired an extensive background in both reading and writing. Irregular spellings, silent letters, prefixes and suffixes are part of the child's repertoire of writing abilities. He or she has a greater understanding of the structure of words and acquires a mental picture (visual memory) by encountering correctly spelled words over and over again.

"Magic slates" can be created for use with kindergarten or primary-grades children by using heavyweight self-sealing sandwich bags and condiments. Just press the air out of the bag, put in a few tablespoons of ketchup or mustard, and glue the opening shut with waterproof glue. Be sure to tell the children that they should not use a sharp object to make their marks. The children can place the bag on a flat surface, smooth out the surface with the palms of their hands, and use their index fingers to make pictures or writing. To obliterate the marks they have made, all they need to do is smooth it out again. The "slates" have a cool, smooth, and interesting feel. They will keep for quite a while if they are refrigerated at night.

Creating Writing and Drawing Materials

As an alternative to drawing and writing with pencils or crayons, children can create different types of writing implements. For very young children who are just learning to make marks on paper, you can make multi- or single-color "crayon circles" out of recycled crayons by following this procedure:

> *Preheat oven to 300 degrees. Remove paper wrappers from pieces of broken crayons. Place the crayons in an old muffin tin, filling about half full.* TURN OFF *the oven and put the muffin tin inside. When cool, remove crayons from muffin tin and use to create multi-colored marks on paper.*

A writing implement that is especially useful when making large posters or signs is a discarded plastic deodorant bottle filled with a thin mixture of tempera paint. Just pry out the roller ball with a knife, fill several bottles with different colors of paint, and give them to the children to use when they want to create big, bold lines. This activity is also especially satisfying for the toddler or three-year-old who is just learning how to make marks on paper.

Second- or third-graders might enjoy experimenting with the special effects of double lines. All they need to do is to fasten two pencils together side by side with a rubber band and hold them so that both pencil tips touch the paper. This creates a double line that is particularly useful for creating lovely handwriting for home-made greeting cards, etc. There are also many different types of markers available with triple tips, zig-zag tips, or calligraphy tips that could be used by children who are already writing.

Words and Pictures in Different Formats

Vary the type of writing paper available to children by contacting a local print shop and using their scrap paper. Children can recycle computer paper and create huge letters, messages, murals, or comic strips. As they gain greater control over writing implements, they can create miniature books and stories using adding machine tape. The finished product can be coiled up inside a plastic yogurt container and pulled through a slit in the side to view the story one section at a time. Durable miniature books can also be created by putting each page inside a self-sealing plastic sandwich bag and stapling or sewing them together. Figure 8.17 contains some examples of writing and spelling activities.

As children begin to write more conventionally and draw representationally, they might try their hand at creating murals that are related to a subject of study. Large rolls of shelf paper can be positioned on two wooden dowel rods and pulled through a box with a "screen" cut out to share a story with a larger audience.

You can introduce the concept of a cartoon bubble that encapsulates the character's speech by making a paper cutout of a favorite cartoon character and posting a new and interesting message each day. Other conventions of cartoons, such as frames, could be introduced by using separate cards for each scene or by creating "comic strips" on adding-machine tape divided into "frames."

Using Picture Books as Models

Because picture books include both text and pictures, they often inspire children to create illustrated stories. Sometimes the influence is quite direct, with children using the same basic format as the story. The rhyming picture book *Where Have You Been?* (Brown, 1952) with verses such as:

> Little old fish, little old fish
> Where do you swim?
> "Wherever I wish," said the little old fish
> "That's where I swim."

This can lead to children's versions like this second-grader's:

> Little red car, little red car
> Where have you been?
> "I've been near and far"
> said the little red car.
> "That's where I've been."

In a kindergarten class, children heard *The Very Busy Spider* (Carle, 1984) that contains dialogue like:"'Moo moo!' said the cow. 'Want to eat some grass?' The spider didn't answer. She was very busy spinning her web." Five-year-old Michael invented and dictated the following episode, using the book as a model:

> The Very Busy Spider
>
> "Queep Queep," said the fox
> Want to come and bark at some dogs?
> But the spider didn't answer.
> She was too busy spinning her web.

STORY STORERS

MATERIALS

- Adding machine tape or long strips of paper
- Empty can with plastic lid (cottage cheese container, yogurt container, pretzel can, etc.)
- Markers or crayons
- Scissors
- Pencils

PROCEDURE

1. Write and draw a story on a piece of long thin paper

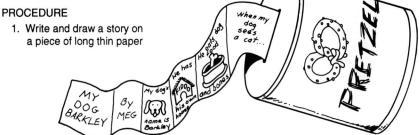

2. Cut a slot in the plastic lid.

3. Roll up the story and put it inside the can. Pull story through the lid to view.

ZIPLOCK BOOKS

MATERIALS

- 6 1/2 x 5 1/2 pieces of paper or 4 x 6 cards
- Sandwich size ziplock bags
- Stapler
- Markers or crayons
- Pencils

PROCEDURE

1. Draw and write a story on 6 1/2 x 5 1/2 pieces of paper.

2. Put each page of your story into a bag and seal each bag shut.

3. Sew or staple the bags together to make a book.

FIGURE 8.17 Drawing and Writing Activities for Primary-grades Children.

STITCH A NAME

MATERIALS

Scrap of burlap, pieces of yarn, large plastic needle, permanent marker

PROCEDURE

Print or write your name on a piece of burlap, thread the needle with yarn, and stitch around your name.

Make signs or pictures, too!

SPELLING BEANS

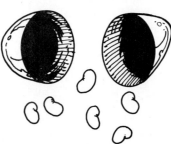

MATERIALS

Plastic pantyhose egg, dry lima beans, fine line permanent marker

PROCEDURE

Write vowels and consonants on dry limas with a permanent marker.

Put limas inside plastic egg, close tightly, and shake. Spill out beans and try to spell as many words as you can.

FIGURE 8.17 *Continued*

228

"Grr, grr," went the bobcat.
Want to growl at some foxes?
But the spider didn't answer.
She was too busy spinning her web.

And six-year-old Marlea wrote this version of Bill Martin Jr.'s (1967) *Brown bear, brown bear, what do you see?*

Brown horse, brown horse, what do you see?
I see a black cow looking at me.
Black cow, black cow, what did you see?
I see a red bird looking at me.
Red bird, red bird, what did you see?
I see a person looking at me.
Person, person, what did you see?
I see my mother looking at me.

Songs with distinctive patterns are good for this sort of activity too. In one first-grade class, the children had learned the cumulative song "Today Is Monday," which has a different food for each day of the week. The children had been studying the four food groups, so they created their own version of the song with favorite nutritious foods and made seven posters to accompany their song. Each day as they got ready to leave for the bus, the children would sing one child's version of the tune. The first verse to Jody's was:

Today is Monday, today is Monday
Monday, rizcakz (rice cakes)
All you hungry children, come and eat it up!

Designing an Abecedarius

Most of Ms. Stanecki's second-graders have learned the alphabet and the sounds generally associated with letters of the alphabet. They have looked at many different illustrators' versions of an abecedarius (an alphabet book) including *Anno's Alphabet* (Anno, 1974); *A Peaceable Kingdom* (Provensen and Provensen, 1978); *Alphabears* (Hague, 1984); and *Animal Alphabet* (Kitchen, 1984). Now she poses a challenge: create an alphabet book of their own, using the cursive writing they have learned. The variety in children's responses to this is amazing. One child uses yarn to stitch each letter. Another creates a type of robot for each letter of the alphabet. Some examples of simple alphabet books created by children are in Figure 8.18.

Interviews

Interviews are a good way to develop writing skills (Haley and Hobson, 1980). Children need to write to contact the interviewees, to formulate their questions, to summarize what they have learned, and to thank the interviewee afterward. At a

FIGURE 8.18   Alphabet Books Created by Children.

country school in a small town, a half-grown bear came into the schoolyard and rummaged through a few trash cans before it was shot with a tranquilizer gun by the game warden. The elementary-school children had seen the bear and were bursting with questions. They interviewed the game warden with questions like these:

> Does it hurt the bear when you shoot it to put it to sleep?
>
> How long before he wakes up again?
>
> What will happen to him now?
>
> Would he hurt you if he was awake?

As a grand finale to the interview, the children had the opportunity to look at the sedated bear sprawled out in the back of the game warden's station wagon. Afterward, some students wanted to find out more about bears and wrote reports,

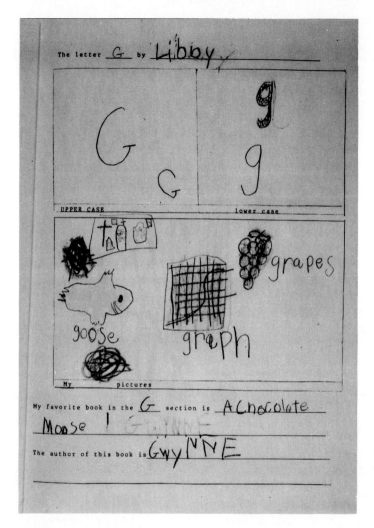

FIGURE 8.18   *Continued*

some wrote letters to relatives and enclosed the story and photographs that appeared in the newspaper, and some composed original stories or poems about bears in general or this bear specifically.

Dialogue Journals

Another highly motivating composition activity is the use of **dialogue journals**:

> *A dialogue journal is a bound composition book in which each student carries on a private conversation with the teacher for an extended period of time (school year,*

semester). Unlike much school-assigned writing, which is often only for the purposes of evaluation, dialogue journals are functional, interactive, *mostly about* self-generated topics, *and deeply embedded in the continuing life of the classroom. (Staton, 1987, p. 1)*

Hipple (1985) found that she could implement dialogue journal writing in her kindergarten classroom using the following procedure:

Staple together five pieces of paper (one page for Monday through Friday) and put them into each child's mailbox every Monday.

Devote 30 minutes per day to writing. Encourage children to talk quietly throughout this time period. Meet with several children each day and function as a listener: ("Tell me what you have written." "How's the writing going, Koji?") or take dictation if the child wishes. Notify two children a day in advance that they will be sharing their work. The other children practice giving positive feedback and posing open-ended questions (not just "What . . . ?" but "How . . . ?" and "Why . . . ?")

So the dialogue journal is *interactive*, meaning that not only the teacher but also the child's peers respond to what the child has written.

Conclusion

As this chapter has shown, drawing and writing are distinctive but related abilities in the young child. Those who initiate children into the world of graphic and pictorial symbols should remember that the child's experiences with drawing and writing will resonate throughout the child's life. Perhaps, as Herbert Read (1972) speculates, it is the first experience that remains with us always:

The echoes of my life which I find in my early childhood are too many to be dismissed as vain coincidences, but perhaps it is my conscious life which is the echo, the only real experience in life being those lived with virgin sensibility—so that we hear a tone only once, only see a color once, see, hear, touch, taste and smell everything but once, for the first time. All life is an echo of our first sensations. But it is more complicated than that, for the senses apprehend not only colors and tones and shapes, but also patterns and atmosphere, and our first discovery of these determines the larger patterns and subtler atmosphere of our subsequent experience. (p. 4)

Even if Read is overstating the significance of early development for later development, one thing is clear: teachers of young children play an important role in introducing children to the communicative power of pictures and words. If we make those early experiences challenging, stimulating, and satisfying, we will contribute greatly to the child's growth in the use of symbols.

Summary

Both drawing and writing are composing processes that the young child uses to communicate. The developmental sequence for drawing moves from nonrepresentational to representational; for writing, from prealphabetic to alphabetic. The young child's efforts to spell may be conceptualized as successive approximations in which he or she discovers various principles about writing and eventually begins to spell. At first, spelling cannot be read. Usually, the child is first taught to print (manuscript) and then moves into handwriting (cursive). Teachers can facilitate the child's process of building pictorial and written communication skills by using enabling strategies, such as encouraging children to experiment with different drawing and writing materials, create original books, transcribe interviews, and maintain a daily journal.

Focus On: Invented Spelling

In the past, children were often pushed to trace and copy words and most of their spelling efforts prior to conventional forms were ignored or corrected. But if we study children's spelling, we can see how children build their understandings about how to spell.

Even before children can independently produce letter forms through writing, they may type the letters, spell with blocks and magnetic letters or write with an index finger on a foggy window. These experiences, coupled with direct experience in trying to form alphabet letters, eventually enable children to write conventionally. But this does not happen because the child is doing "readiness activities." Rather, it occurs because the child has been directly applying his or her spelling strategies in functional writing activities within a community of writers.

See if you can read this list of words: stashun, ealafat, hiwy, opid, firplas. If you read station, elephant, highway, opened and fireplace, you were reading **invented spelling**. Quite simply, invented spelling is the child's best effort to spell a word based upon what he or she knows about language at the time (Bissex, 1980). That effort may be unconventional, but it still involves associating sound units with letters in a systematic way: rm (room), kol (coal), nabr (neighbor), razn (raisin), salr (cellar), and egl (eagle) (Richgels, 1987). Look at these messages that were typed on the computer by some kindergarten and first-grade children:

ILKSNFLR (I like sunflowers.)

IADWDRMLN (I ate watermelon.)

IWTBRZCRDR (I want to be a race-car driver.)

Now consider these issues:

1. Which would give a teacher more information about a child's knowledge of consonant letter sounds—independent writing or a worksheet in which the child matches a pictured object to the initial consonant in the corresponding word?
2. Teachers and parents worry that children will become poor spellers if they are "allowed" to use invented spelling. How would you explain to a parent that invented spelling promotes thoughtful analysis of words and encourages children to apply whatever they *do* know about words?
3. How should teachers respond when a child asks if something is spelled correctly? When a son asks his mother if POST OFISS is "right," she replies, "That's the way office sounds but it's not the way it looks." (Bissex, 1980). Discuss what you think the child's reaction might be to this approach. Compare/contrast it with the child's reaction to copying the teacher's writing from the board or having his own writing corrected.
4. Learning to spell is apparently a gradual process, not simply a good (or bad) habit. Children may spell the same word in many different ways as they acquire new information. When first-grader Rashid looked at some samples of his earlier writing, for instance, he said, "I wrote this before I knew about *-ing*." Does the "traditional" approach of "word list distributed on Monday, children memorize and are tested on Friday" treat spelling as a habit or as a developmental sequence?

In the Field: Children's Concepts About Drawing and Writing: An Interview

Conduct the following interview with a child between the ages of 2½ and 6½. You will need crayons and five sheets of plain white (unlined) paper.

PAGE ONE

"Do you know how to draw? Here are some crayons and a piece of paper. Show me how you draw." (Give the child the materials and record any comments he or she makes while drawing.)

PAGE TWO

"Do you know how to write? Write as many things as you can. Show me how to write." (If the child says he or she does not know how to write, say, "Well, pretend that you can write." Record the child's comments while he or she writes.)

PAGE THREE

"You have seen grown-ups writing before—in fact, you see me writing here today. Pretend that you can write like a grown-up. Pretend that you are writing a letter to someone." (Give the child paper and crayons. Record any comments her or she makes.)

PAGE FOUR

"Read what you wrote." (If the child refuses, direct him or her: *"Pretend to read to me."* Record the child's words.)

PAGE FIVE

"Do you know how to write your name? Write it on this piece of paper for me." (After the child finishes) *"Show me how to read your name."* (Take notes on the sounds and gestures, such as pointing, the child makes during this process.)

Label every page with the child's first name only and age. Type the child's comments and your interpretations for each of the five tasks on a separate sheet. Use the information in the developmental chart from this chapter to analyze the child's response. What evidence do you see of the characteristics of a particular writing stage? Support each of your statements with specific examples from the child's work. Make a cover sheet that contains the following information:

_____   _____
(child's first name)   (child's age)

_____
(your name)
                                            _____
                                              (date)

In Class

You will be assigned to a small group that represents the widest possible diversity in the ages of children interviewed.

Go through each page of the interview one by one and allow every group member to share the sample they collected. The instructor has the stages in drawing and writing posted around the room. When your group finishes, tape the samples you collected in the proper category. Then take a moment to go more slowly around the room (as if you were in an art gallery!) and appreciate the children's work.

References

Askov, E. N., and Peck, M. (1982). Handwriting. In H. E. Mitzel, J. H. Best and W. Rabinowitz (Eds.) *Encyclopedia of educational research*. New York: The Free Press.

Bissex, G. (1981). Growing writers in classrooms. *Language Arts*, *58*(7), 785–791.

Bissex, G. (1980). *Gyns at wrk: A child learns to read and write*. Cambridge, MA: Harvard University.

Blazer, B. (1986). "I want to talk to you about writing": five-year-old children speak. In B. B. Schieffelin and P. Gilmore (Eds.). *The acquisition of literacy: Ethnographic perspectives* (pp. 75–109). Norwood, NJ: Ablex.

Brittain, W. (1979). *Creativity, art and the young child*. New York: Macmillan.

Britton, J. (1970). *Language and learning*. Harmondsworth, England: Penguin.

Calkins, L. M. (1986). *The art of teaching writing*. Portsmouth, NH: Heinemann.

Clay, M. (1975). *What did I write?* Exeter, NH: Heinemann.

Dailey, K. in press. Writing in kindergarten: Helping parents to understand the process (manuscript accepted for publication, *Childhood Education*).

Dyson, A. H. (1988). *Multiple worlds of child writers*. New York: Teachers College Press.

Fields, M. (1988). Talking and writing: Explaining the whole language approach to parents. *The Reading Teacher, 41*(9), 898–903.

Fine, E. S. (1987). Marbles lost, marbles found. *Language Arts, 64*(5), 474.

Gentry, J. R. (1981). Learning to spell developmentally. *The Reading Teacher, 34*(4), 378–381.

Graves, D. H. (1984). *Balance the basics: Let them write*. Exeter, NH: Heinemann.

Graves, D. H. (1983). *Writing: Teachers and children at work*. Portsmouth, NH: Heinemann.

Hipple, M. (1985). Journal writing in kindergarten. *Language Arts, 62*(3), 255–261.

Koenke, K. (1986). Handwriting instruction: What do we know? *The Reading Teacher, 40*(2), 214–226.

Lamme, L. (1985). *Growing up reading*. Washington, DC: Acropolis.

Mosenthal, P. (1983). Defining good and poor reading—the problem of artificial lamp posts. *The Reading Teacher, 39*(8), 858–861.

Peck, M.; Askov, E. N.; and Fairchild, S. H. (1980). Another decade of research in handwriting: Progress and prospect in the 1970's. *Journal of Educational Research, 73*, 283–298.

Platt, P. (1977). Grapho-linguistics: Children's drawings in relation to reading and writing skills. *The Reading Teacher, 31*, 262–268.

Read, C. (1980). What children know about language: Three examples. *Language Arts, 57*, 144–148.

Read, H. (1972). (Quoted in J. S. Kells.) The roots of aesthetic experience. *Art Education, 24*, 4–7.

Richgels, D. J. (1987). Experimental reading with invented spelling (ERIS): A preschool and kindergarten method. *The Reading Teacher, 40*(6), 522–529.

Schickendanz, J. A. (1986). *More than the ABC's: The early stages of reading and writing*. Washington, DC: National Association for the Education of Young Children.

Sebesta, S. (1989). The story is about you. In S. Hoffman and L. Lamme (Eds.). *Learning from the inside out: The expressive arts* (pp. 22–28). Wheaton, MD: Association for Childhood Education International.

Suhor, C. (1982). Semiotics. Urbana, IL: ERIC Clearinghouse on Reading and Communication Skills.

Staton, J. (1987). Dialogue journals. Urbana, IL: ERIC Clearinghouse on Reading and Communication Skills.

Staton, J. (1982). Analysis of dialogue journal writing as a communicative event. Volume I, Report to National Institute for Education (grant no. G-08-0122).

Temple, C. A., and Gillet, G. W. (1989). *Language arts: Learning processes and teaching practice*. Boston: Little, Brown.

Temple, C. A.; Nathan, R. G.; and Burris, N. A. (1982). *The beginnings of writing*. Boston: Allyn & Bacon.

Thorne, J. (1988). Becoming a kindergarten of readers? *Young Children, 43*(6), 10–16.

Wells, G. (1990). Creating the conditions to encourage literate thinking. *Educational Leadership, 47*, 13–17.

Wells, G. (1986). *The meaning makers: Children learning language and using language to learn*. Portsmouth, NH: Heinemann.

Children's Books

Anno, M. (1974). *Anno's alphabet*. New York: Harper & Row.

Brown, M. W. (1952). *Where have you been?* New York: Scholastic.

Carle, E. (1989). *The very busy spider*. New York: Philomel/Putnam.

Hague, K. (1984). *Alphabears*. New York: Holt, Rinehart and Winston.

Kitchen, B. (1984). *Animal alphabet*. New York: Dial.

Martin, B. (1967). *Brown bear, brown bear, what do you see?* New York: Holt, Rinehart and Winston.

Provensen, A., and Provensen, M. (1978). *A peaceable kingdom: The Shaker abecedarius*. New York: Viking.

Photo: © 1990 Frank Siteman

9

Emergent and Early Reading

OUTLINE

Key Concepts and Terms
Introduction

The more elements of good parenting, good teaching, and good schooling
children experience, the greater the likelihood that they will achieve their
potential as readers.   —BECOMING A NATION OF READERS (1985)

KEY CONCEPTS AND TERMS

emergent reading   schema theory
early reading   graphic organizers
empiricist, interactivist, rationalist   basal reading series
reading environment   shared book experience
guided imagery   predictable books

Brandon, age five, has the book *The Three Little Pigs* on his lap. As he turns the
pages, Brandon invents text to go with each picture. Notice how his personal
experience with the game of hide-and-seek affects his rendition of the wolf's words:
"Three little pigs were going away from their mom and one was lively, one was

happy, and one was smart. The pigs went away and two little pigs found a man and asked him for sticks to build a house and one asked for straw to build a house. The one was smart and he didn't want sticks or straw. He asked the man to give him bricks to build a house. The mean bad wolf said 'Come out, come out, wherever you are,' and 'If you don't come out, I'll huff and puff and blow your house down.' "

Brandon's behavior raises many issues about reading, including how it is defined, when it begins, how children learn to read, and the best ways to insure that they do.

What Is Reading?

When the average person thinks about reading, he usually thinks of *materials* such as books, papers, workbooks; *settings*, such as the classroom, the library, or a parent's lap; and *behaviors* such as decoding words, reading aloud in reading group, or reading independently. Although all of these things are undeniably associated with reading, they do not adequately define reading. Before looking at experts' definitions for reading, let's look at how some first-grade children explain reading.

Children's Views

Seven-year-old Brian says that reading is "something you do when you look at books. It's words with letters." Jennifer says, "It's another way of telling you something, but no sound." When these newly literate children were asked why people read, Joseph, another seven-year-old, said, "So they will know how to read when they get older. Big people read long letters and different papers. If they did not read then nobody would have any newspapers . . . and who would read me a story at night?" Darci said, "To learn . . . for information."

Experts' Definitions for Reading

Reading is "a process in which a person reconstructs a message graphically encoded by a writer" (Goodman, 1982, p. 75). **Emergent reading** is the use of reading-like behavior to interpret printed material (Anderson, Teale, and Estrada, 1980). Brandon is an *emergent reader* because his efforts to make sense out of print are successive, spontaneous approximations of efficient adult reading behavior (Holdaway, 1979). **Early reading** refers to the child's first decodings of print.

Dimensions of Reading Behavior

What abilities are associated with emergent and early reading? Children who achieve literacy with print manifest the following behaviors:

1. *Oral comprehension skills*—the ability to understand an oral message
2. *Sensitivity to environmental print*—the ability to interpret signs and labels
3. *Print awareness in connected discourse*—learning how a book is handled, knowing print-related terms such as "read"
4. *Metalinguistic awareness*—growth in the ability to reflect on language, to distance themselves from it and to treat it as an object (Dickinson and Snow, 1987; Torrance and Olson, 1985).

Thus, reading behavior is affected by: *the reader's purposes*, including values, attitudes, perspectives, and motivation; *the interactive systems within the reader*, including the perceptual system, the cognitive processing system, and the linguistic system; and *environmental influences*, including distractions, time, other task demands, and teacher expectations (Singer, 1984). Figure 9.1 is an overview of influences on reading.

A Developmental Sequence for Emergent and Early Reading

As young children learn to read, they typically go through several sequential stages. Many researchers (Doake 1986; Holdway 1979; Marsh, Freidman, Welch, and Desberg 1981; Snow and Ninio 1986; Sulzby 1985) have described the general

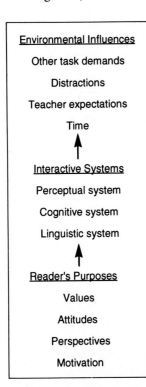

FIGURE 9.1   A Model of Learning to Read.

Source: Singer, H. (1981). Teaching the acquisition phase of reading development: An historical perspective. In O. J. L. Tzeng and H. Singer (Eds.). *Perceptions of print: Reading research in experimental psychology* (pp. 10–28). Hillsdale, NJ: Erlbaum.

sequence for the process of emergent and early reading. Throughout this overview, the assumption is that children have experienced books at home. If for some reason they have not, the sequence might be similar, but on a different timetable. You will also notice that the ages of the children in the examples do not follow a neat chronological order.

Level One: Understanding What a Book Is

At this stage, usually during late infancy and toddlerhood, children are differentiating between books and toys. They look at books briefly and stop when something interests them. Bright, clear, simple pictures of familiar objects are appealing to children at this stage. The following observation of Johnna's behavior illustrates how the typical toddler enjoys a book.

> *When I asked two-year-old Johnna to show me how Mommy reads, she moved her hand across the page of* Rock-a-Bye Baby *and pretended to read the words. She also made her voice go higher and lower, although no recognizable words came out. She used expressive jargon. When I asked her to show me how* Johnna *reads, she did the same thing. When I handed her a book, she took it and opened it up. At first, it was upside down, but when she saw a picture of the baby, she turned the book right side up. She seems to devote most of her time to those pages that depict action. Pages that just have an inanimate object (like an apple) on them are passed by. Like many other toddlers I have observed, Johnna does not move systematically through the book from front to back. She just opens to a page, looks at it, and then opens to another page, which could be any number of pages before or after the last picture.*

Because children are just starting to try and physically control the book, they need numerous opportunities to observe adults operating a book. They also need durable books that they can use themselves.

Level Two: How a Book Works

At approximately two-and-one-half to three years of age, the child begins to learn how a book "works." Such things as holding it right side up, turning the pages, and treating it differently from other possessions are some of the accomplishments of this stage (Snow and Ninio, 1986). Children's book use during this phase can best be described as "point-say-connect." They point to a pictured object and then (often in response to the parent's questions) say the object's name. Usually, after naming a pictured object, they relate the picture to their own experience. The following dialogue between Hua (thirty-three months old) and his mother illustrates this behavior:

Mother: "Who is this?" (pointing to a boy)

Hua: "Hua."

Mother: "Who is this?" (pointing to a girl and a dog)

Hua: "Renee!" (his sister) "Coco!" (the family dog) ... (Notices a picture of a bee) "Buzz-Buzzzz! Makes honey. Bee stings me, it hurts."

Older toddlers also enjoy stories with a simple plot such as *Ten, Nine, Eight* (Bang, 1983) or lyrical language, like the bedtime story *Where Does the Brown Bear Go?* (Weiss, 1990).

Level Three: Becoming a Listener and Participant

As children begin the preschool years, they learn more about the listener's role. They realize that the focal point of book-sharing sessions is the book. Like the previous stage, this stage is characterized by more talk about the book than the actual reading of the book's text. This adult-child dialogue often consists of commentary designed to help the child understand the story, the child's remarks relating the story to personal experience, and questions from the child to clarify concepts. Children often seek to hear the same story again and again and will repeat certain words or phrases if an adult encourages them.

By now, children have learned how to physically control books and can look at books independently. They may rehearse familiar favorites aloud, using the pictures as cues. Mandy, a thirty-nine-month-old, reads *Hand, Hand Fingers Thumb* (Perkins, 1969) by commenting on each picture and interspersing some of the words she remembers:

> Finger, finger, thumb
> One thumb drumming on a drum
> Hand, hand, drumming on a drum
> Dum di di,
> Dum, dum, dum ...
> Blow your nose
> Shake hands
> Bye bye

Level Four: Storying

Children who have shared books with caring adults now clearly associate pleasure with literature, have several favorites, and look for more good stories to add to their storehouse of familiar books. As a result, they strive to "gain independent access to books" (Doake, 1986). They can tell a story in a way that sounds more like book language. These retellings usually contain some actual words and phrases from the text. Here is Jessica, a forty-two-month-old reading her favorite book, Dr. Seuss's (1954) *Horton Hears a Who.* Notice how her emergent reading is more "book-like" than Mandy's or Hua's:

He was in the pool when he was in the jungle and it was a jungle and Horton heared a who. The speck was too little to see with hims eyes.

"I had a very, very trouble." He was going to jump in that pool, but the elephant said: "No, I gotta save my friend." So, he went running fast to save his friend and he knew where his friend was going. He was going in the pool so he got in the water and got the speck out. . .

Still, the focus is on meaning and context rather than the features of print (Marsh et al., 1981).

Level Five: Focus on Print, Meaning, and Story Knowledge

Now children realize that the text of a book is what makes it the same from one reading to the next. As a result, they are convinced that the print needs to be watched and matched somehow to the words on the page. They will often self-correct if a word does not fit their pointing or the context of the book. Amy, a three-year-old, is reading *A Pocket for Corduroy* (Freeman, 1976) with this self-correction evident:

> *On Saturday Lucy and her mother took their laundry to the laundromat. But the laundromat was the busiest place where washers and driers—"You stay here," said Lucy. "I'm going to help with the laundry." He waited. He waited and waited. Then her mother said, "Be sure you take everything out of your pockets, Lucy, so you will be—you don't want them to go—to go through the washer." "Pockets!?" said Corduroy. "I don't have a pocket!" He looked at all the towels and sheets. No! I mean washcloths . . . at a big heap of towels and washcloths."*

When Amy encountered an unfamiliar word, she substituted something that made sense: "towels and sheets" for "towels and washcloths." Amy draws upon her experience with laundry, her knowledge about this particular book, and her emerging concepts about print.

Level Six: Focus on Word Configuration and Sound-Symbol Correspondence

At this stage, children use the letters, words, and sounds they know and try to give a precise word-by-word reading of the book's text. Because children at this stage understand that adults' reading is an exact decoding of the text, they often refuse to "pretend read." Sometimes they focus so strongly on word appearance that the meaning and context are compromised in the process. They may, for example, substitute a familiar word for an unknown word even though it does not make sense in the story context. Vivian, a six-year-old, comes to the word "stripes" in a passage about tigers but she reads it as "stop." Behaviors like these occur because children are applying whatever word analysis skills they know at the time. They might know about initial, medial, and final consonants; know something about word configuration (length/shape); or know about looking for familiar letters and combinations of letters in the rest of the word (Willert and Kamii, 1985). In fact, their attention to print becomes so strong that they will sometimes produce nonwords, like second-grader Clara who read the "vanilla" flavor of pudding as "vanlah." Sulzby (1985) believes that this is a very important transition for the young reader. It often occurs in the midst of formal reading lessons during kindergarten or in the primary grades. If children are exposed to a barrage of letters, sounds, sight words, and rules at the wrong time, it may undermine their confidence and confuse them. As children work through this "awkward stage" in learning to read, the adult may mistakenly assume that they are regressing because they relied on memory and seemed more fluent before. Actually, children are "orchestrating" everything they know about reading and books (Doake, 1986).

Research suggests that children who make a successful transition from emergent to independent reading have learned to

believe in their own abilities

play with oral language (inventing rhymes, repeating phrases for the pleasure of it)

persist at the task of making sense out of print

enjoy literature in many different forms (stories, songs, rhymes)

choose reading activities freely

show self-correction in reading attempts

express an interest in writing (Waterland, 1985; Lass, 1982)

Level Seven: Putting It All Together

For some children, this stage occurs in first or second grade; for others much later, and, for illiterates, not at all. Here the child begins to coordinate all of the experience he has amassed in interacting with print. He uses sources of information available to a reader—phonics, syntax, semantics, and pragmatics—at the appropriate time. Usually, the child is functioning at higher levels of word analysis and practices what she knows without much prompting from adults. Children at this stage may be found spelling and practicing words over and over again until they become known and inventing and using a phonological system to sound out words (Willert and Kamii, 1985). The child has better self-correction and, with additional experience, is on the way to becoming an independent reader.

How Should Reading Be Taught?

One of the enduring debates throughout the child's journey from emergent to independent reading is What is the best way to facilitate the process? Some say

"Reading is a skill"; some say, "Reading is a psychosocial activity based on experiences with print," and still others say that "reading is a cognitive, hypothesis-testing process."

Philosophical/Theoretical Foundations

The three theoretical orientations to reading may be categorized into three orientations: **empiricist**, **rationalist**, and **interactivist** (Barbour, 1987). Table 9.1 is an overview of each of these theoretical perspectives. Actually, these outlooks on reading are similar to the theories about language acquisition discussed in Chapter 1.

Empiricist

Empiricists see reading as a set of skills to be mastered, much as behaviorists regard stimulus response as the foundation of language acquisition. Empiricists would teach children to break down reading into its component parts, then gradually add skills until reading behavior is complete. Empiricists see the teaching of reading as starting at the bottom and working its way up. They contend that children must be "ready" to read. Although the concept of reading readiness may seem like a recent development, it has been around since 1931 when Morphett and Washburn studied first-graders and recommended that initial reading instruction be postponed until age 6½. The current view of readiness no longer argues for delaying the onset of formal reading instruction, but it holds to the assumption that children must be amply prepared in basic skills before tackling the arduous task of learning to read.

TABLE 9.1   Three Theoretical Orientations to Reading Instruction.

Theoretical Orientation	Definition	Approach
EMPIRICIST	Reading is the process of attaching meaning to symbols	Begin with phonics or "bottom-up"
RATIONALIST	Reading is the process of obtaining information; it is dependent upon the setting, the child's general knowledge of the topic, and knowledge of text structure	Begin with whole language or "top-down"
INTERACTIVIST	Reading is transactual; readers simultaneously extract information about print as well as make hypotheses about the meaning of the text	Strategies that combine word analysis, sight-word recognition, and child's knowledge

Sources: Barbour, N. (1987). In C. Seefeldt (Ed.). *The early childhood curriculum: A review of current research* (pp. 107–140). New York: Teachers College Press.
Finn, P. (1985). *Helping children learn to read.* New York: Random House.

Rationalist

Rationalists in reading are theoretically similar to psychosocial language-acquisition theorists. They see the social dimension of reading as all important. Their approach to teaching reading is the exact opposite of the empiricists. Rationalists would begin with enjoyment of complete stories. Word analysis skills would be the outgrowth of extensive experience with books rather than the precursor of reading (as it is with the empiricists). Rationalists regard young children as emergent readers, meaning that they believe children bring a considerable body of useful knowledge about language to reading. It is by drawing upon this knowledge during sociolinguistic activity, the rationalist would argue, that children learn to read.

Interactivist

Interactivists have a constructivist perspective on the reading process. They see reading as a knowledge-building activity based upon hypothesis testing. The fluent adult reader, they argue, is the person who consistently has his or her hypotheses confirmed with the fewest number of guesses (Goodman, 1982). In terms of method, interactivists would also emphasize a "top down" rather than a "bottom up" strategy. Interactivists regard the child as the architect of his or her own reading abilities rather than a passive recipient of someone else's ready-made solutions.

In recent years, there has been a major shift in reading instruction in America. Two groups of theorists are advocating beginning with books, and the group that is staunchly supporting a "bottom-up" method is losing ground. This means that when you teach young children to read, you will probably use methods that are very different from those you experienced as a child.

Criticisms of Early Reading Programs

Perhaps the following simulation will help to explain why reading instruction in America has been the focus of so much criticism and controversy. Imagine that you are a student in this class.

Teacher: We have been learning the sprechenzeel. Today we will be practicing three new zingphats, ◎ and △. Tanya, what is this zingphat called? Right! It is a △. Let's look at some freeples that splark with △ (teacher points to these symbols on the chalkboard): △ ६ ५ ⌷   △ ∩ ☲ ◎

Can you think of some other freeples that splark with this zingphat avio? Ricardo? Yes. △ ⊂ ⌷ has the avio. Can you use your freeple in a funchpatter?

Confusing, isn't it? But if you guessed that sprechenzeel = alphabet, zingphat = letter, freeples = words, avio = sound, splark = begin, and funchpatter = sentence, then the lesson makes sense. It only makes sense, of course, because, as an experienced reader, you are familiar with all of these terms and their meanings. Unlike the young child, you have years of experience talking about these things.

This is one reason why formal, tightly structured ways of teaching reading to children are being challenged.

Pidgeon (1984) studied 120 classrooms of 4½ to 5½-year-olds over a three-year period and identified the following problems in initial reading instruction:

1. *Too many assumptions about children's prior knowledge*—There was insufficient preassessment of children's abilities and knowledge of the terminology being used. Even nontechnical words, such as "top," "down," and "middle" were cause for confusion in some students. The vocabulary associated with reading, "letter," "word," "consonant," "sentence," etc., was apparently a mystery to many students.
2. *Too great a learning load*—Many students were overwhelmed by all the work expected of them. When children did not understand what they were doing or why, attention often lapsed and children did not complete their assignments.
3. *Too heavy an emphasis in teaching children to read*—Instead of understanding why people read or knowing how to read, children were often expected to memorize. The amount of time actually spent reading (getting meaning from print) was insufficient.
4. *Too heavy an emphasis on the program*—Most teachers defined children's growth in reading by progress in the particular reading series being used.
5. *Too much reliance on sight and sound analysis of words*—Reading was taught from sight to sound. Pidgeon argued that it makes more sense to teach from known (listening) to unknown (reading). Even though some students learned to associate sounds with particular marks, they did not understand why.

General Features of Quality Reading Programs

The issue of early reading instruction has less to do with *when* and more to do with *how*. In other words, the chronological age of children is less important than the methodology. Any reading program for young children should

1. be developmentally appropriate, keeping in mind the learning styles of young children
2. focus upon broadening each child's experiential base
3. foster each child's desire to become literate
4. be structured (planned, organized, and monitored) but not formal (use reading and phonics programs, workbooks, dittos, and tests)
5. provide a print-rich environment including printed material and writing materials
6. emphasize language experiences that focus on meaning rather than skill development (Ellermeyer, 1988)

One way to address all of these programmatic recommendations is by reading aloud to and with children.

Sharing Literature: The Foundation of Reading

When an adult reads aloud to a child, it might seem like the adult is doing most of the work while the child is a passive recipient. Actually, nothing could be further from the truth. There are several different types of learning that take place when an adult shares a story with a child (Smith, 1989). Reading aloud has a positive influence on the child's

> reading competencies
>
> motivation to read, especially for children who are not yet reading independently or who are reluctant to read
>
> interests in and appreciation of literature
>
> speaking and listening skills
>
> understanding of narrative structure
>
> knowledge of different literary styles and writing abilities (Becher, 1985)

The full benefits of literature cannot be realized unless books are selected carefully and shared appropriately. The most important considerations (aside from the book itself) are how literature is shared and the characteristics of the reading environment.

Ways of Sharing Books

A mother and father who read regularly to their two-year-old daughter agreed to make a tape recording of several story sessions. But several weeks later, they decided that they just couldn't do it. "We tried," the mother said apologetically, "but when we played the tape back it was more talking than reading." Actually, discussions focused on the story are exactly what the young child needs. As Gordon Wells (1986) explains, discussion activates literature by meeting the developmental needs of the child listener.

> *At first they need a competent adult to mediate, as reader and writer between themselves and the text . . . The manner in which the adult—first parent and later teacher—fulfills this latter role is almost as important as the story itself. If stories are read simply as part of a daily routine, without being further discussed, they are likely to remain inert and without much impact on the rest of the child's experience. If they are used chiefly as the basis for display question sequences that focus on the meanings of particular words or on isolated items, such as the names of the characters or details of particular events, again they are unlikely to provide encouragement for the exploratory but controlled thinking that written language activates. (p. 253)*

Reading aloud to a child involves much more than "looking at a book." As Goodman says (1982) children "need a reason to read now," not because it will help them in high school, get them into college, or enable them to pursue a more satisfying career. Good stories shared by competent, caring adults give children an immediate and compelling reason to read: enjoyment. In order for children to become avid readers, they must associate books with pleasure.

Preparing the Reading Environment

Learning environments refer to not only the emotional climate of the setting but also to the physical planning and arrangement of the classroom. In general, **reading environments** have the following characteristics:

1. Availability and range of printed materials
2. Experiences with quality literature shared by competent, caring adults
3. Adults who model reading/writing behaviors
4. Opportunities to use print in meaningful ways
5. Opportunities to write as well as read (Teale, 1978)

Even something as simple as the way books are displayed in the classroom has an impact on the literary environment. Based upon observations of classroom libraries, the following guidelines are suggested (Morrow, 1982; Morrow and Weistein, 1982):

- *Make your library a focal area of the classroom* rather than a portion of a shelf that is indistinguishable from the rest of the classroom.
- *Partition the library from other areas* so that it is relatively free from distractions.
- *Display a variety of books* on open-faced shelves within easy reach of the children.
- *Make the area large* enough to accommodate four to five children at one time.
- *Visit the library yourself* and model the kinds of behavior you want to develop in children.
- *Make the area inviting* with literature-oriented displays and comfortable seating.

Reading aloud and planning the reading environment have been discussed first because they set the stage for reading. Next we will look at the strategies used by educators to teach young children how to read.

Connections Between Thinking and Reading

Basically, there is very little that is new where methods of teaching reading are concerned. Most approaches have been around for decades in one form or another (Singer, 1984). Even methods used in the new computer technology still depend on the old approaches—alphabetic, phonics, whole word, whole sentences, or whole stories (Fries, 1963). What *is* new, however, is our improved understanding of the reading-thinking connection. Working with emergent and novice readers demands particular attention to the things children have experienced and their ways of organizing those experiences.

Schema Theory

Schema is synonymous with prior knowledge. A person's schema is a representation of all their knowledge, including direct experience, vicarious experience, and training (Rummelhart, 1984). *Schemata* is that portion of the overall schema that is related to a particular situation.

The experiences of two children, Anna and Scott, illustrate why schema and schemata are so important in the process of learning to read. When five-year-old Anna hears the music that introduces the daily live drawing of the state lottery, she rushes into the living room, plops down right in front of the television screen, and says, "Two, Oooh, 4, 7." When it is over, she gets up and says, "I *love* that show," then resumes playing outdoors. For Anna, the lottery is like Sesame Street. She has no concept of gambling but she sees that adults are enthused about it and responds to it in her own way—as practice in the recognition of numerals. Without a schema for lottery, Anna may look forward to the program, but she does not understand how a game of chance operates.

Seven-year-old Scott, on the other hand, has a more sophisticated concept of how a lottery works because he was a winner. Figure 9.2 is the story he typed on the computer and the picture his friend Blair drew to go along with it. Scott's and Anna's very different concepts about the lottery illustrate how schemas affect learning. Three basic issues related to schema that have particular significance for reading instruction during the early childhood years are availability, selection, and maintenance (Vacca and Vacca, 1986).

Schema Availability

"One of the most neglected parts of reading instruction is the teacher's job of determining what children already know about a topic or their prior knowledge" (Durkin, 1984, p. 734). Unless readers have the necessary prior knowledge, they cannot "read between the lines" to make inferences or predictions. Nikki, age 5, is trying to read *The Gingerbread Man* (Schmidt, 1985). In the original text, the old woman says, "Now watch the oven, and when you can smell the gingerbread, call me. But do not open the oven door." Notice how this emergent reader calls upon her experience with baking to retell the story:

> *One day there was an old man and a little boy and an old woman. One day she said that she would make him a gingerbread man. And so, she made it. And she said, . . . Well, when this dings, when this timer dings, you* don't *open it—just call me." So she left. Then he* smelled *and he* smelled *it and so he opened it a little bit and saw it to see if it smelled like it* was. *So the gingerbread* ran out *and the little boy tried to catch him. He tried to close the door as fast as he could, but the gingerbread was* too *fast.*

I won a ticket to dinusr world
I won it because I had the same
nubrs on my ticket as the ticket
the man had. me and my mom
and dad and sisdr went on a jet
my sisdr said the cars look so
little. then we wor ther frist we
saw brotosois then we saw tardtl
then we saw stagasois then we saw
tri sau tops and then we saw it, tryanasres

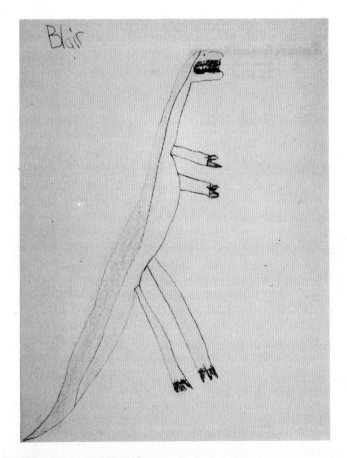

FIGURE 9.2 Scott's Lottery Story

In Nikki's retelling, the oven is equipped with a bell that tells the little boy when the food is ready, just like her oven at home. She incorporated an audible signal into her retelling because it is part of her schemata for baking cookies. If she had never seen an oven before, if her schemata for baking was to cook over an open flame, she would have retold the story differently.

This leads to the first precept in teaching children to read: when teachers share books with children, they must first assess the children's prior knowledge.

Schema Selection and Maintenance

We also know that learners need to devote just as much attention to maintaining old knowledge as they do to discovering new knowledge (Durkin, 1984). Children may have the prior knowledge and not realize it or they may have difficulty deciding when and how to call upon their prior learning. Teachers can help children to do all of these things by inviting them to make literature "come alive." A group of kindergartners from the Child Study Centre at the University of British Columbia are a good example of schema selection and maintenance in action. They had just heard several stories about the distant past including Aliki's (1983) *A Medieval Feast*. When the children decided to dramatize a banquet scene from the feast, they practiced schema selection and maintenance. They studied the book for details, they assembled the necessary props (crowns, goblets, flowing robes, and of course, food) and they dramatized the story events. Through these activities, the children selected and maintained their schema through three types of comprehension activities: connecting situations with events, linking actions to a series of happenings, and relating objects to a sequence of events (Rumelhart, 1984). This is the second basic precept where teaching reading is concerned: the key is to help children make logical connections—to find a common element between new ideas, the ongoing discussion, and the printed word (Mecca, 1989; Paley, 1981). In the next section, we will see how four teachers planned challenging reading activities based on their knowledge of schema theory.

Challenging Reading Activities

Reading activities should *challenge* children, meaning that they

capture the children's interest and attention

seem worthy of the time invested

present just enough information and support to keep children working through the process

reward them with meaning and the feeling of a job well done

have an enduring effect on learning

Mr. King: Guided Imagery

Mr. King has read several articles about using visualization techniques to improve listening and reading comprehension in listening and in reading (Rasinski, 1988; Mundell 1987). He does a few warm-up activities, such as inviting children to mentally create images of various jungle animals. They talk about what each child sees in his or her "mind's eye," and compare/contrast them, emphasizing that there are no right or wrong images. As a result, Mr. King is able to assess the children's prior knowledge. Next, he shows them the cover and the wordless picture book *Junglewalk* (Tafuri, 1988). On the first page, the boy has just finished reading a book and is switching off the light to go to sleep. Mr. King says, "I wonder what he was reading. Hmm. It says on the cover of his book *Jungles of the World*. Close your eyes for a minute and imagine what sorts of things he may have seen in the book he was reading." Before they look at the book, he asks the kindergartners to hypothesize about the story. All of these activities are a part of **guided imagery**. Then, after they look through the entire book together, the children compose a group story to go along with the pictures and read it aloud together. Later on, they create their own stories. Each child chooses a favorite story that they would read before bedtime and then draws, writes, and/or dictates a story about how that reading might become part of a fantastic dream. Mr. King is so delighted with the results that they have an "Author's Tea" during which each child is given an opportunity to read his or her book aloud.

Ms. DeCicco: Graphic Organizers

Children can learn to use tables, charts, and graphs to represent their schemata and relate it to reading. Ms. DeCicco uses a model that helps to develop children's understanding of information in a reading selection, to help them recognize that words can be used to explain something, how it functions and so forth. She uses the K–W–L strategy (Ogle, 1986):

> K: what we already *know* about this subject
>
> W: *what* we need to find out
>
> L: what we *learned* and still need to learn

Later that week, she introduces webbing (Bromley, 1991), the hierarchical concept map (Stice and Alvarez, 1987), and other types of **graphic organizers**. Figure 9.3 contains examples of two story charts based on picture books.

Mrs. Smith: Asking Good Questions

Mrs. Smith knows that questioning skills are important in the teaching of reading. This year, she has decided to improve her preschoolers' comprehension of stories by using the questioning strategies suggested by Raths and others (1986):

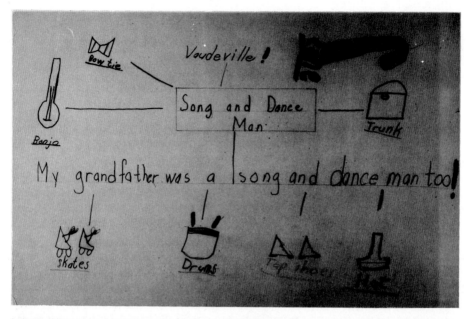

FIGURE 9.3　Story Maps of *Song and Dance Man* Created by Nikolas, age 7, and *Bringing the Rain to Kapiti Plain* by Joseph, age 8.

1. *Observing, gathering, and organizing data*—Children are encouraged to look carefully and describe what they see. They use observational data to support their ideas and try to organize what they have observed.

2. *Comparing and classifying*—Children look for similarities and differences and relate new information or ideas to what they already know. The teacher reminds children of previous learning that will assist them in solving the current problem.

3. *Summarizing and interpreting*—Children "recap" what they know so far and explain things from their point of view. In this way, the teacher gets a glimpse of the child's thinking process.

4. *Identifying assumptions and suggesting hypotheses*—Children are asked to articulate the assumptions they have made. They also function in a low-risk environment and feel comfortable making educated guesses.

5. *Imagining and creating*—Children are encouraged to use visualization and to create mental images that will help them solve the problem. Figure 9.4 contains some questions that can be used in leading a discussion with children. Using these questioning strategies has not only improved Ms. Smith's discussion-leader skills but also has improved the children's story comprehension.

Specific Instructional Strategies and Materials

There are several methods used today: basal reading series, the shared book experience, and the language experience approach.

Basal Reading Series

The **basal reading program** is far and away the most popular and widely used method of teaching reading. It is estimated that over ninety percent of American classrooms use the reading books, workbooks, and practice sheets that are produced by various publishers. In most elementary schools, the school or the district adopts a particular series and uses it from kindergarten through sixth grade. In concept, these "basal" materials are supposed to be *basic*—a sequential set of resource materials that the teacher draws upon to plan for effective reading instruction. In fact, most basal programs include so much material that if teachers follow them religiously, there will be little time for anything else. In some instances, the reading selections, the types of questions, the reading curriculum—even "what counts as reading" will be determined by the basal (Weaver, 1989, pp. 5-6). In the past, the great majority of these basal reading series placed a heavy emphasis on paper-and-pencil phonics and sight-word recognition activities. Because educators have demanded it, many publishers have changed their basal series to include more literature and less "drill on skill."

Classification
>   What is _____?
>   What kinds of _____s are there?
>   How did you decide?

Chronological
>   What happened first?
>   What happened next?
>   What did this lead to _____?

Cause-Effect
>   Why does _____ happen?
>   What were the effects of _____?
>   What is another way to _____?
>   What should we do to make _____ from _____?

Predicting
>   What do you think will happen if _____?
>   Now that _____, what will happen?

Comparison/Contrast
>   How are these things alike?
>   How are they different?
>   How did you decide?
>   How could you sort or arrange these things?

Connecting Actions With Events
>   What did you _____?
>   Can you do _____?
>   How did you do _____?
>   How could you _____?

Evaluation
>   What is good/bad about _____?
>   Which do you like _____?
>   Why did you like _____?

FIGURE 9.4 Questioning Strategies

Sources: Kamii, C., and DeVries, R. (1978). *Physical knowledge in preschool education: Implications of Piaget's theory*. Englewood Cliffs, NJ: Prentice-Hall.

Sigel, I. E., and Saunders, R. (1979). An inquiry into inquiry: Question asking as an instructional model. In L. Katz (Ed.), *Current topics in early childhood education*. (Vol. 2, pp. 169–193). Norwood, NJ: Ablex.

The Shared Book Experience

The **shared book experience** is often associated with a "whole-language" approach. It is a whole-language approach to initial reading instruction because:

1. *It begins with entire stories rather than moving from letters to words to sentences.* A whole-language approach uses a "top-down" strategy. The children begin reading stories immediately rather than doing exercises to help them decode words.

2. *It integrates all of the language arts.* In a classroom that reflects a whole-language philosophy, the language arts are not treated as separate subjects.

3. *It is developmentally appropriate.* In whole language, the child goes before the subject: we teach the child to read rather than teaching reading to the child.

4. *It is social and collaborative.* Whole language emphasizes human interaction. Whereas some other approaches to developing children's literacy skills would keep them working quietly and in isolation, a whole-language philosophy emphasizes communication.

How does this philosophy translate into teaching practice? The shared reading approach is emulative—it models what a reader does so that children can gain insight into the reading process. It accomplishes this by using oversized books, "big books" that are large enough for children to see each word as the teacher reads it. **Predictable books** are often used in the shared reading process. These books use rhyme, familiarity (folk songs and folktales), repetition (a catchy refrain), or familiar sequences (such as numbers, days of the week, etc.) to confirm a beginning reader's hypotheses about "what comes next" in the story. Predictable books should not be confused with the old preprimers that sounded like:

> *Oh look. See the cat. The cat can run. Look! Look! Look at the cat.*

Instead of this unnatural-sounding text, predictable books explore the richness of language (Bridge, Haley, and Winograd, 1983). The context, repetition, and colorful illustrations are used to support the child as he or she attempts to read along. A look at the story line of *One Cold, Wet Night* (Melser and Cowie, 1980), a predictable book from Australia, illustrates why this type of literature is recommended for beginning readers. The story begins:

> One cold, wet night,
> the farmer got into bed
> and went outside. Then . . .
> the horse jumped into the bed, and said,
> "I'm going to be warm tonight." (pp. 1–3)

The horse is followed by the cow, the sheep, the dog, and a giant weta (a huge insect), all of them reiterating the same words. Then the farmer returns and yells, "Get out of my bed!" Some of the highlights from some first-graders' versions of

One Cold, Wet Night are in Figure 9.5. Each animal runs out in turn with a "skiddle dee do," but the giant weta (a huge insect) remains. The story concludes with the farmer saying, "I'll sleep on the couch tonight." Several observational studies in classrooms have concluded that predictable books like this one are excellent material for reading instruction, particularly initial reading instruction (Bridge, Haley, and Winograd, 1983; Heald-Taylor, 1987; Rhodes, 1981).

The rationale for using the shared book experience is that

it builds on children's oral language

it builds children's self-concept as readers

it enables each child to participate at his or her own level

it increases children's recall of the story

it encourages attentiveness and interaction

it teaches skills within the context of whole language rather than in isolation (Combs, 1987)

FIGURE 9.5   First Graders' Versions of *One Cold, Wet Night.*

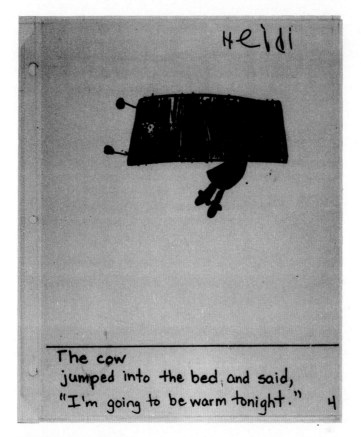

Heldi

The cow
jumped into the bed, and said,
"I'm going to be warm tonight." 4

FIGURE 9.5 *Continued*

The suggested procedure for presenting a big book is as follows (Butler, 1984; Strickland, 1988).

1. *Introduction*. Show children the cover of the book and read the title. Discuss any unfamiliar words in the title and ask children to make some hypotheses about the story. Assess and build upon children's prior knowledge.
2. *Read the story*. The teacher models the enthusiasm, intonation, and fluency of a literate adult. A big book and a pointer are used so that the children can see the text of the book as it is being read. This procedure shows children how speech is matched to print. The teacher should also wonder out loud, make comments and predictions, and draw conclusions so that children see how thinking is related to print.
3. *Invite reactions and participation*. Ask children to comment on their first experience with the book, then read it again. The teacher should pause during the reading to encourage children to read along, point to pictures to emphasize story events, interject brief comments that help to clarify the story, respond to children's comments with a nod or brief comment, and make brief

FIGURE 9.5 *Continued*

explanatory comments about the pictures or text that might be difficult for the children to understand (Cochran-Smith, 1984).

On a subsequent reading, children may be asked to read in unison, enact the behavior of story characters, look for particular sounds, words, endings, punctuation, or fill in words that have been covered by small flaps of paper.

4. *Independent practice.* Possible activities during this stage: one child or partners reading a small book; a small group rereading other books that they had read previously; reading another book with the same structure or theme; or teacher interviewing children about their story choices. If children are encouraged to point to the text as they read, the teacher can gain important information about children's progress by observing carefully.

5. *Extension.* These activities are natural outgrowths of the child's reading experience. Children may create their own versions of big books, make audio tapes of their reading to share with parents, dramatize a story with a small

group of peers, design a class big book, create pictures from the story and arrange them in sequence, write/illustrate original stories, design story charts, and relate the story to any of the other curriculum areas.

The Language Experience Approach

Another whole-language approach that is frequently used in conjunction with shared reading is the **Language Experience Approach** (LEA) that was discussed in Chapter 5. A Language Experience Approach begins with a concrete experience, results in a story, and uses that story as reading material. Bromley (1988) identifies these advantages to the LEA:

> *Experience stories use children's language and prior knowledge, build positive self awareness, depend on interactions among children, and involve them in the meaningful use of language in situations that are relevant to them. (p. 358)*

The shared experience that initiates a language-experience story varies. It might be a told or read story, a class, a party, a visitor, a newspaper article, a cooking experience, a science experiment, a film, a neighborhood field trip, or a musical or dramatic performance by other students. The story that results is written on a chart. Each sentence contributed to the story and the name of the child who contributed it is recorded. The LEA experience story chart is read by the group. In a subsequent reading, each sentence may be used by the child who contributed it. Some other reading activities centered on the LEA story are the following:

- Cut the story into sentence strips and reassemble it in sequence.
- Cover key words with flaps and reread, asking children to fill in the missing words.
- Make small versions of the story for each child.
- Convert the chart into an illustrated big book.
- Exchange charts with another class.
- Use brightly colored markers to highlight certain features (such as rhyming words or punctuation). (Coody and Nelson, 1982)

Through the LEA, the child's own language is used as the basis for reading instruction.

Conclusion

In all of these approaches to teaching reading, one thing should be uppermost in teachers' minds: to facilitate the child's reading process. It is not enough to teach children skills. Many children learn to decode words and acquire a lifelong distaste for reading as well. Our reading programs should, at the very least, convince children that learning to read is well worth the effort.

Summary

Young children's reading is conceptualized as a process that begins during infancy. Reading abilities are built on oral comprehension skills, sensitivity to environmental print, and metalinguistic awareness. Rather than waiting for children to be "ready" for formal reading instruction, current theory and research supports the concept of emergent reading, which is built upon enjoyment and extensive experience with literature. The three major theoretical orientations to reading instruction are empiricist, interactivist, and rationalist. Critical aspects of the teacher's role are preparing a reading environment, assessing children's prior knowledge (schema theory), providing challenging activities, and utilizing a wide array of teaching strategies that build upon and extend each child's reading abilities.

Focus On: Questions Parents Commonly Ask About Young Children's Reading Behavior

As a teacher, you will often be asked to give advice about children's reading. Here are five commonly asked questions and research-based answers. You may want to generate some additional questions parents are likely to ask and discuss appropriate responses, based on your reading thus far.

I've heard that it is important to read to your child. Why?

Children can develop the knowledge, skills, attitudes, and values of proficient readers by listening to literature. Numerous research studies have concluded that reading aloud to children increases their reading achievement scores, listening and speaking abilities, letter and symbol recognition, ability to use more complex sentences, ability to understand language, concept development, and positive attitudes toward reading (Becher, 1985).

When will my child begin to read?

Simmons and Brewer (1985) provide an excellent answer to this common question when they write:

> *Reading is a continuum that began when your child first started to use language, it will continue well into adult life. Even though our culture presently dictates that formal reading should begin early, much research tells us that an informal beginning eventually produces more skilled and willing readers. The most important component of the reading process is learning to love and appreciate books. Recognition of individual words follows—but must never precede—this step. Another vital ingredient in reading successfully is the reader's background of experience. One of the most important functions of the early childhood teacher is to build children's non-visual experiences so that meaning can be attached to print. Oral language development is the third major area of reading instruction*

for young children. Phonetically decoding words is of no value to children when the words have no meaning. (p. 177)

Why does my child ask me to read and then keep interrupting?

When children listen to a story, they are in on-the-job-training as readers. Reading is the process of deriving meaning from print and your child's questions show that he or she is actively constructing meaning. The best story-sharing sessions include playful discussions of the book. In fact, as much as 80 percent of the talk that takes place when a skillful adult reads a picture book to a child could be described as commentary about the pictures or text in response to the child's comments and questions.

Why does my child ask to hear the same book over and over again?

Picture books offer children a unique opportunity to hold language constant and study it, so to speak. "A picture book of real substance is enjoyed again and again. It is like visiting a favorite vacation spot. No matter how well you know it, going back is always a delight. It is a calm secure place with no real surprises, but a constant supply of good times nevertheless. All the memories are sweet, all the best views and secret places are recalled and anticipated, and the very familiarity is a comfort and a rest" (Picture Book Studio USA, 1985, p. 2).

My child already knows his letters and numbers. Doesn't this mean he is ready to read?

When children first recite the alphabet or sing the alphabet song, those sounds often have little meaning for them. If we listen carefully, we can even hear that children have memorized chunks of sound. The sequence l-m-n-o-p, for instance, is sung as if it were a word, "elemnopea," rather than individual letters. Behaviors like these should tell adults that the child needs more concrete experiences, not more memorization. Where reading is concerned, reading and discussing books together, making writing materials accessible, encouraging children to make marks on paper, providing creative play materials such as blocks, clay, sand, and water, all contribute to the child's ability to attribute meaning to these abstract symbols called letters and words. After all, interpreting symbols is what reading is all about.

In the Field: Children's Understandings About Reading

Arrange to interview a child between the ages of 5 to 8 who is just beginning to read, who is well established as a reader, or who is at any stage in between. Ask the child the following questions and write down child's responses.

1. What is reading?
2. What do you do when you read?

3. If someone did not know how to read, what would you tell her that she would need to learn?
4. What does a teacher do to help children to read?
5. Do parents help children learn how to read? If yes, how?

Bring the results of your interview to class and compare/tabulate the class's findings.

A previous study found that the vast majority of children saw reading as a school activity ("doing your workbook," "going to reading group") or decoding ("knowing your letters," "sounding out words") rather than deriving meaning from print (Johns and Ellis, 1976). Imagine if you thought that singing was "going to the music room" and "reading notes," or that football was "something you do in a field" and "looking at diagrams." Can anyone be expected to do something he or she can neither define nor understand?

References

Anderson, A. B., Teale, W. H., and Estrada, E. (1980). Low income children's preschool literacy experiences: Some naturalistic observations. *Quarterly Newsletter of the Laboratory of Comparative Human Cognition*, *2*, 59–65.

Anderson, R. C., Hiebert, E. H., Scott, J. A., and Wilkinson, I.A.G. (1985). *Becoming a nation of readers: The report of the Commission on Reading*. Washington, DC: United States Office of Education.

Barbour, N. (1987). Learning to read. In C. Seefeldt (Ed.) *The early childhood curriculum: A review of current resources* (pp. 107–140). New York: Teachers College Press.

Becher, R. M. (1985). Parent involvement and reading achievement: A review of research and implications for practice. *Childhood Education*, *62*(1), 44–50.

Bridge, C. A., Haley, D., and Winograd, P. N. (1983). Using predictable materials vs. pre-primers to teach beginning sight words. *The Reading Teacher*, *36*(9), 884–891.

Bromley, K. D. (1991). *Webbing with literature: Creating story maps with children's books*. Boston: Allyn & Bacon.

Bromley, K. D. (1988). *Language arts: Exploring connections*. Boston, MA: Allyn and Bacon.

Butler, A. (1984). *The story box in the classroom*. Auckland, NZ: Shortland (distributed by The Wright Group).

Cochran-Smith, M. (1984). *The making of a reader*. Norwood, NJ: Ablex.

Combs, M. (1987). Modeling the reading process with enlarged texts. *The Reading Teacher*, *40*, 422–426.

Coody, B., and Nelson, D. (1982). *Teaching elementary language arts: A literature approach*. Belmont, CA: Wadsworth.

Dickinson, D. K., and Snow, C. E. (1987). Inter-relationships among prereading and oral language skills in kindergartners from two social classes. *Early Childhood Research Quarterly*, *2*, 1–25.

Doake, D. (1986). Learning to read: It starts in the home. In D. R. Torrey and J. E. Kerber (Eds.) *Roles in literacy learning: A new perspective* (pp. 2–9). Newark, DE: International Reading Association.

Durkin, D. (1984). Is there a match between what elementary teachers do and what basal manuals recommend? *The Reading Teacher*, *37*, 734–744.

Ellermeyer, D. (1988). Kindergarten reading programs to grow on. *The Reading Teacher*, *41*(4), 402–404.

Fries, C. C. (1963). *Linguistics and reading*. New York: Holt, Rinehart and Winston.

Goodman, K. S. (1982). Comprehension-centered reading instruction. In F. Gollasch (Ed.), *Language and literacy: The selected writings of Kenneth S. Goodman* (pp. 75–86). London: Routledge and Kegan Paul.

Heald-Taylor, G. (1987). How to use predictable books for K-2 language arts. *The Reading Teacher, 40,* 656–661.

Holdaway, D. (1979). *The foundations of literacy.* Auckland, NZ: Heinemann.

Johns, J. L., and Ellis, D. W. (1976). Reading: Children tell it like it is. *Reading World, 16,* 115–128.

Lass, B. (1982). Portrait of my son as an early reader. *The Reading Teacher, 36,* 20–28.

Marsh, G., Freedman, M., Welch, V., and Desberg, P. (1981). A cognitive-developmental theory of language acquisition. In G. E. Mackinnon and T. G. Waller (Eds.), *Reading research: Advances in theory and practice.* New York: Academic Press.

Mecca, M. E. (1989). Philosophers in the classroom. *Childhood Education, 65*(4), 206–208.

Morphett, M. V., and Washburn, C. (1931). When should children begin to read? *The Elementary School Journal, 31,* 503.

Morrow, L. (1982). Relationships between literature programs, library corner designs and children's use of literature. *Journal of Educational Research, 78,* 339–344.

Morrow, L. M., and Weinstein, C. S. (1982). Increasing children's use of literature through program and physical design changes. *Elementary School Journal, 83,* 131–137.

Mundell, D. (1987). Mental imagery: Do you see what I say? Oklahoma City, OK: Oklahoma State Department of Education.

Ogle, D. (1986). K–W–L: A teaching model that develops active reading of expository text. *The Reading Teacher, 39*(6), 564–570.

Paley, V. (1981). *Wally's stories.* Cambridge, MA: Harvard.

Pidgeon, D. (1984). Theory and practice in learning to read. In J. Downing and R. Valtin (Eds.). *Language awareness and learning to read* (pp. 173–191). New York: Springer-Verlag.

Picture Book Studio U.S.A. (1985). *A note to grownups. Picture book studio journal I.* Natick, MA: Picture Book Studio.

Rasinski, T. (1988). Mental imagery improves comprehension. *The Reading Teacher, 41*(8), 867–868.

Raths, L. E., et al. (1986). *Teaching for thinking: Theory, strategies and activities for the classroom.* New York: Teachers College Press.

Rhodes, L. (1981). "I can read!" Predictable books as resources for reading and writing instruction. *The Reading Teacher, 34,* 511–518.

Rummelhart, D. (1984). Understanding understanding. In J. Flood (Ed.). In *Understanding reading comprehension.* Newark, DE: International Reading Association.

Simmons, B., and Brewer, J. (1984). When parents of kindergartners ask "Why?" *Childhood Education, 61*(3), 177–184.

Singer, H. (1984). Learning to read a skilled reading: Multiple systems interacting within and between readers and text. In J. Downing and R. Valtin (Eds.) *Language awareness and learning to read.* New York: Springer-Verlag.

Smith, C. B. (1989). Reading aloud: An experience for sharing. *The Reading Teacher, 42*(4), 320.

Snow, C., and Ninio, A. (1986). The contracts of literacy: What children learn from learning to read books. In W. Teale and E. Sulzby (Eds.), *Emergent literacy: Writing and reading* (pp. 116–138). Norwood, NJ: Ablex.

Stice, C. F., and Alvarez, M. C. (1987). Hierarchical concept mapping in the early grades. *Childhood Education, 64*(2), 86–96.

Strickland, D. (1988). Some tips for using big books. *The Reading Teacher, 41,* 966–968.

Sulzby, E. (1985). Children's emergent reading of favorite storybooks: A developmental study. *Reading Research Quarterly, 20,* 458–481.

Teale, W. H. (1978). Positive environments for learning to read: What studies of early readers tell us. *Language Arts, 55*(8), 922–932.

Torrance, N., and Olson D. R. (1985). Oral and literate competencies in the early school years. In D. R. Olson, N. Torrance, and A. Hildyard. *Literacy, language and learning: The nature and consequence of reading and writing.* London: Cambridge University.

Vacca, R. T., and Vacca, J. L. (1986). *Content area reading* (2nd ed.). Boston, MA: Little, Brown.

Waterland, L. (1985). *Read with me: An apprenticeship approach to reading.* Stroud, England: The Thimble Press.

Weaver, C. (1989). In C. Weaver and P. Groff *Two reactions to the report card on basal readers.* Bloomington, IN: ERIC Clearinghouse on Reading and Communication Skills.

Wells, G. (1986). *The meaning-makers: Children learning language and using language to learn.* Portsmouth, NH: Heinemann.

Willert, M. K., and Kamii, C. (1985). Reading in kindergarten: Direct vs. indirect teaching. *Young Children, 40*(4), 3–9.

Children's Books

Aliki. (1983). *A medieval feast.* New York: Crowell.

Bang, M. (1983). *Ten, nine, eight.* New York: Greenwillow.

Freeman, D. (1976). *A pocket for Corduroy.* New York: Viking.

Melser, J., and Cowie, J. (1980). *One cold, wet night.* Auckland, NZ: Shortland. (distributed by The Wright Group)

Perkins, A. (1969). *Hand, hand fingers thumb.* New York: Random House.

Schmidt, J. (1985). *The gingerbread man.* New York: Scholastic.

Seuss, Dr. (1954). *Horton hears a who.* New York: Random House.

Tafuri, N. (1988). *Jungle walk.* New York: Greenwillow.

Weiss, N. (1990). *Where does the brown bear go?* New York: Greenwillow.

Parents, Teachers, and the Child's Growth in Language

PART FIVE DEALS WITH an important responsibility of early childhood educators: communicating the results of our language arts teaching to others. Chapter 10, "Parents and Teachers: Partners in Promoting Children's Language Growth," highlights the many contributions that parents make to the child's language growth in the home environment and suggests strategies for building home-school relationships that foster the child's growth in literacy. Chapter 11, "Assessment Issues and Alternatives in the Language Arts," confronts the issue of how to assess child-centered language arts programs. Appropriate uses of formal and informal tests are discussed. The chapter profiles the efforts of several classroom teachers to implement more process-oriented types of emergent and early literacy assessment.

Photo: © 1990 Frank Siteman

_10

Parents and Teachers: Partners in Promoting Children's Language Growth

OUTLINE

Key Concepts and Terms
Introduction

Adults are at their best, their most civilized when tending to the nurture of children . . . . In saying what we wish a child to become, we are saying what we are.
          —NEIL POSTMAN (1982)

KEY CONCEPTS AND TERMS

parental roles
print-rich environment
parent involvement
bias and stereotypes

interaction styles
home-school continuity
conferencing

Of all the influences on children's language growth, parents are the most powerful. They not only affect the child through heredity but also through the type of language environment they provide in the home. Parents' attitudes toward education, aspirations for children, the language models they provide, the literacy materials they supply, and the activities they encourage—all make a substantial contribution to children's language development (Morrow, 1989; Silvern, 1989; White, 1982).

Parental Roles Prior to School

There are four roles that promote children's language development, roles that are initiated in the home and later reinforced by teachers. Four key **parental roles** are: observer; environment arranger; interactor; and motivator, stimulator, and encourager (Goodman and Goodman, 1979).

The Role of Observer

When parents function as observers, they monitor their children's progress, build on their strengths and help them to meet challenges. Georgie (short for Georgianna) is a twenty-nine-month-old who is making a tape recording of her language for a college student. Notice how her parents observe what Georgie does and respond to her needs:

Georgie: I baby. (singing) Mary had a little lamb.

Father: Go ahead.

Georgie: How you talk about on it? Huh?

Father: Say what you want to say. (Adults tell her to move closer to microphone)

Georgie: No. I don't want to . . . Hold it this way? Two hands . . . How Mummy talk? (pause) Hi, Mama. Hi, Mommy. What's my friends' names, huh?

Mother: Debbie, Dana, Kristy, Marty, Michelle, Tammy . . .

Father: (asking Georgie) Who else?

Georgie: And Glen.

Father: And?

Georgie: Who?

Father: How about who lives over here? (gestures next door)

Georgie: I don't know . . . Heidi.

Mother: What about her baby brother? What's his name?

Georgie: Baby brother.

Both of Georgie's parents supported her efforts and tried to make her feel at ease in using the recording equipment. Later, when they observed her obvious delight at hearing her own words played back on the tape, they honored Georgie's request to "do more."

Environment Arranger

Parents also contribute to the child's growth in literacy by creating **print-rich environments**. That richness need not come from costly materials, however. It can include books borrowed from the library, recycled paper, and simple writing implements. Nor does the literate home have to look like a model home. In her observational research, Taylor (1983) found that in the most literate homes, family members were practically tripping over books, papers, and writing implements because these items were in continuous use.

The Morrell family is a good example. They recently returned from a family reunion and camping trip just a few hours' drive from their urban home. Four-year-old Carl has been using the snapshots that were taken to identify family members and the activities they shared together. His mother suggests that they make a book about their vacation and, with a little glue and some pieces of cardboard salvaged from her hosiery packages, they assemble a durable booklet, complete with captions dictated by Carl. Before long, he can read the entire book aloud and does so regularly with both parents. By providing a print-rich environment, Carl's parents have supported his language development.

Interactor

When parents carry on extended conversations and listen thoughtfully to what their children have to say, they are functioning as interactors. The following conversation between David (nicknamed Boomer) illustrates the type of interaction that is fundamental to language growth. Boomer is three years and eight months old and he lives in the rural Appalachian mountains with his parents. Notice how skillfully his mother converses with Boomer while she is preparing dinner:

Boomer: I'm gonna be like Daddy when I grow up.

Mother: How will you be like Daddy?

Boomer: Simple, change fur (meaning that he will have body hair) and my hair will be black. My legs will be big and even my boots will be big.

Mother: What are you going to do when you're a Daddy?

Boomer: Fix things . . . and play with you when I'm a Dad.

Mother: What else?

Boomer: An' maybe take a glue gun an' fix stuff.

Mother: Are you going to have kids?

Boomer: Yeah.

Mother: Boys or girls?

Boomer: Oh, simply I'll play with Steve when I grow up.

Mother: You're going to play with Steve when you grow up like Dad?

Boomer: I hate Steve and I like Steve. (Steve is a neighbor who is two years older and has been calling Boomer a "pipsqueak.")

Mother: You hate Steve and you like Steve. Yeah, that's probably the way it is with a lot of friends, huh? What else are you going to do when you're a Daddy?

Boomer: Oh, when I grow up you're going to hang on my arm . . . and Mom when I go hunting, I'll have to be careful not to get bit by a bear.

Mother: Yes, you're right, bears do bite. Are you afraid of bears?

Boomer: No, not when I grow up. I'll kill it.

Mother: Kill it. And then what?

Boomer: I'll give it to you for a bear rug.

Mother: Oh, a bearskin rug. Oh, Boomer thank you! That would be *wonderful*.

This mother's support of her child's efforts to communicate lead to the third role, motivator, stimulator, and encourager.

Motivator, Stimulator, and Encourager

In this role, parents and teachers recognize children's functional language needs, stimulate children's interests, and encourage and respond to their efforts to communicate.

Marjorie, age three, is visiting her aunt and Peg, an elderly neighbor. The preschooler looks at the neighbor curiously, then hands her red Mickey Mouse sunglasses to her aunt and says, "Here, hold these." The aunt obliges by folding the glasses and placing them on her lap.

Marjorie: No, not *fold, hold*.

Aunt: But I am holding them.

Marjorie: No, I wanna hold them like Peg's.

Aunt: Oh, you mean you want them to hang around your neck, like Peg's?

Peg: Honey, they're on a chain. See? (she lifts the collar of her dress while Marjorie inspects)

Marjorie: I want one of those so I can hold my sunglasses.

Later, when they leave to go to a discount store, Peg takes Marjorie's aunt aside, gives her a few dollars and says, "Buy Marjorie the gaudiest chain you can find, and tell her it's a present from me." When you see what a motivator, stimulator, and encourager Peg is, it is easy to understand why her three children have matured into extraordinarily successful adults.

Parent Involvement in the Schools

When parents participate, cooperate, and collaborate with schools it is referred to as **parent involvement**. There are six basic categories of parent involvement in early childhood programs (Gordon, 1969; Day, 1983). These types of involvement and their implications for children's language learning are:

1. *Audience*—Parents listen to the children read, recite, and report. An example would be parents attending a puppet play the children have created.
2. *Classroom volunteer*—Parents working with individual or small groups. Parents might help children to "publish" their stories by typing each child's dictated story or helping children to assemble and bind their books.
3. *Teacher of own child*—Here the parent is contributing to the child's education at home. An example is the parents providing writing materials and assisting the child as requested when he or she wants to send a letter to a relative.
4. *Paraprofessional*—When parents are working with the teacher and the children to enhance the curriculum, they are functioning as paraprofessionals. Parents may be invited to share their hobbies or talents and be interviewed by the class. Parents may also reinforce a particular skill already taught by the teacher, such as listening to a child read a familiar story. At other times, parents might assist in the preparation of teaching materials, such as preparing a big book to be used in the shared-book experience.
5. *Decision-maker*—Parents who serve on committees or serve in an advisory capacity are functioning as decision-makers. Parent representatives on a school-policy review board are influencing school rules.
6. *Learner*—If parents try to increase their own learning and better help their child by attending PTA meetings, enrolling in classes, or participating in a Saturday workshop, then they are assuming the role of learner.

Building Parent–Teacher Partnerships

The language of parent involvement is the language of collaboration. We speak of parent–teacher partnerships, the parent–teacher bond, parents and teachers working together as a team, or the school–community interface. If educators ever hope to establish productive relationships between home and school, they will need to reassess their 1950s ideas about parent involvement where parents bake cookies, raise money, or chaperone field trips. Why? Because today's families are "more stressed, more isolated and often poorer than ever before" (Kagan, 1989, p. 109). We need to think in terms of *services for parents*, such as parent education, adult education, job training, employment referral, and emotional support and *services for children* such as health screening, child care, developmental screening, and home-based programs (Kagan, 1989). As a first step in providing resources to families, teachers need to examine their own biases and stereotypes.

Confronting Biases and Stereotypes

Whether we are supporting parents as they work with their children at home or whether parents are supporting the educational program, teachers need to confront their own biases and stereotypes—attitudes, values, and behaviors that jeopardize the parent-teacher partnership. The following excerpt from the *The Geranium on the Windowsill Just Died, But Teacher You Went Right On* by Albert Cullum (1971) is a poignant reminder of the way children and parents can feel about teachers and administrators:

> I want you to come to my house,
>   and yet I don't.
> You're so important,
> but our screen door has a hole in it.
> And my mother has no fancy cake to serve.
> I want you to come to my house, teacher,
>   and yet I don't.
> My brother chews with his mouth wide open,
> and sometimes my dad burps.
> I wish I could trust you enough, teacher,
> to invite you to my house

When teachers are judgmental or act superior, they build barriers between themselves and parents. As Phillips (1988) contends, "We must explore the stereotypes we have learned that are racist and ethnocentric, and develop strategies for changing what we believe about ourselves and others. Too many of us still unconsciously treat light-skinned children better than dark-skinned ones and the working mother better than the one on welfare" (p. 46).

Some teacher biases are more subtle than racial or ethnic stereotypes. The list of questions that follows is designed to help you identify those attitudes in yourself that undermine cooperation between the parents and language arts teachers of young children.

Do I fully appreciate all the language learning parents have fostered in their children?

Parents are the child's first teacher. By the time that teachers, even teachers of toddlers, begin to work with a child, the parents have already made a major contribution to the child's language development. In the vast majority of cases, the child has learned to talk and is capable of communicating in his first language by the time he enters preschool. It is easy for teachers to become so absorbed in the language arts curriculum that they overlook what parents have already done and are now doing to support the child's growth in literacy (Greenberg, 1989). It is fine to feel confident about our backgrounds as early childhood educators, but we must avoid smugness by remembering that parents are knowledgeable about their children and committed to their children in ways the school cannot be.

How do I honestly feel about children who come from families that do not emphasize literacy learning?

A teacher might remark, "Well, her parents have never read to her—she doesn't even own a book," as if that absolves the teacher of any responsibility for helping the child to break the cycle of illiteracy in her family. Parents who have limited educational opportunities themselves are often very dependent upon the school to help them get something better for their children.

Giving these parents a sense of their own power to effect change demands particularly perceptive and sensitive school personnel. If transportation, scheduling, or child care is a problem, the school can set up some informal car pools, use more flexible schedules, ask high school volunteers to babysit or encourage parents to bring their children along whenever possible. If the parents themselves have reading problems, we can call or send home an easy-to-read sheet that requires parents to check off (rather than write) responses.

How do I respond to parents with language differences?

When someone mentions that he or she is a language arts teacher, they often get a reaction like "Uh-oh, I better watch my grammar." Imagine how much stronger those feelings of inadequacy can be for parents who have limited English proficiency. Teachers are allowing language stereotypes to influence behavior when they grow impatient with parents whose language skill is less developed than their own and, conversely, when they feel intimidated by parents whose language skills are superior to their own. In both cases, the emphasis should be on communication rather than on the social or economic status of the speaker.

How do I react to parents who are outspoken, assertive, or even aggressive?

Parents sometimes use language in ways that make teachers feel unappreciated. If a parent says, "I attended that meeting about the new writing program, but it was a big waste of time," a teacher may want to defend the school against the criticism: "Well *I* think it was a great program." It is better to simply let the parent know you are listening and keep the tone positive. You might say, "Evidently the meeting didn't have much value for you. Do you have any suggestions on how we might make it more helpful?" When we talk with parents, even distraught or angry parents, we need to use the same tone and manner that we would use with a highly esteemed colleague. As teachers we need to learn how to be assertive instead of nonassertive or aggressive (Table 10.1).

Consider this common situation and how each of these three **interaction styles**—nonassertive, aggressive, and assertive—might handle it. Albie has a school adjustment problem that is evident in his prolonged bouts of crying each morning. The nonassertive teacher would complain bitterly to colleagues but tell the parent it is nothing to worry about. The aggressive teacher would resent the child and blame the parents. The assertive teacher would talk to the parent and the child and work together to solve the problem.

Deterrents to Parent Involvement

Even when we strive to work with parents and respect them, some parents may avoid communicating with school personnel. Why? There are many possible explanations.

A parent may have had unsuccessful learning experiences and feel ill at ease in a school setting.

TABLE 10.1   Interaction Styles

Nonassertive	Assertive	Aggressive
BEHAVIORS		
Quiet, passive, hesitant; strives to avoid conflict; does not react outwardly to situations	Direct, open, and appropriate to situation	May be disrespectful, inappropriate; often violates others' rights
INNER EMOTIONS		
Is often emotionally dishonest	Is emotionally honest	Is emotionally out of control
OUTCOMES		
Ineffective; rarely achieves goals	Effective; usually achieves goals	Ineffective; alienates others

Sources: Lloyd, S. R. (1985). Managing would be easy if . . . *Child Care Information Exchange, 43,* 5–8.

Single parents and working parents may have difficulty participating during regularly scheduled times.

Arranging for child care may be difficult and expensive.

A low-income parent may be ashamed of his or her clothing or be without transportation.

Parents who are not well educated may feel inadequate in a discussion with a teacher.

Parents may be experiencing some type of severe family stress themselves, such as separation or divorce, physical or emotional abuse. Fear of exposing these problems to others may make them reluctant to confer with their child's teacher.

A parent may be fearful of finding out that the child is failing academically or socially.

A parent may feel that his or her concerns, criticism, or complaints will be resented by school personnel and "taken out" on the child.

Greenberg (1989) suggests that closed, one-way communication from schools to parents may be partly to blame for a lack of parent participation. She points out that the "faint ditto" announcements of various school functions often do not get home at all or arrive home too late:

> *A notice may go unread because a parent cannot read, or be ignored because the parent sees it as announcing a meeting arranged by others on a topic of interest to others (or to nobody) in which the audience will be permitted to participate only by passive, silent attendance, or possibly asking a courteous, pertinent question (as defined by the organizers). Most recipients disregard such communication because the meeting mentioned will occur on alien turf, where they have felt uncomfortable, ill-dressed, stupid, and angry as children and later, as parents, or because they are wasting treasured time better spent*

> *at home with the child. Many parents attend one or two school meetings and decide never to go again. Many parents resent the stream of marching orders that flows from the school: send your trip money, sign up and assist and so on (Greenberg, 1989, p. 72)*

I once taught in a midwest rural school where many of the children were sharecroppers from the southern United States. After a rain, these children would arrive at school with their shoes encrusted with mud and as it dried, big clods of clay would fall off around the room. A few fastidious teachers complained bitterly about it—"How could parents send their children to school looking like that?" they would wonder aloud. But evidence of the children's cultural differences did not stop with physical things. Many of these children also had dialectical differences that grated on a few of the teachers' ears; sentences such as "We been workin' all morning" or "I ain't never seen sech a thin' " or "I'm afeared of makin' a *mis*take." Ironically, the same teachers who had very negative attitudes about these families and low expectations for the children were the first to complain if the parents did not attend parent–teacher conferences. When I went to visit the home of a child in my class who had been ill with pneumonia, I gained tremendous empathy for these families. I learned that only one parent in the group had any form of transportation, a dilapidated and unreliable truck; that their homes were without indoor plumbing, and that all around them was a virtual quagmire with sinking wooden boards to serve as the only "sidewalks." That "muck," as the whole neighborhood was called, was inescapable for an adult, much less a playful child. If every teacher had seen firsthand that these children got muddy while retrieving water to get clean, they surely would not have been so intolerant. If every teacher had talked to these parents face-to-face and seen how hopeful they were about a better quality of life for their children, they would have redoubled their efforts. But that is what prejudice *is*—*prejudging*, formulating strong opinions about people before we get to know them. The basic principle that should guide all of our parent-involvement efforts is that we can achieve more by working together than we can by working separately.

Parents, Teachers, and the Child's Language Growth

In order to maximize children's language growth, adults need to

1. create greater continuity between home and school
2. reduce the pressures on children
3. value children's growth in literacy

Home–School Continuity

When most people think about a learning environment they think about a classroom. Parent involvement literature generally assumes that the school is the site and source of information. Thus, parents come to the school to confer about children's progress (as in parent-teacher conferences), get information (such as attending a meeting about the school's new reading program), donate time (as in fund-raising), and help set policy (as in PTA meetings). Conversely, if they want to help their children learn at home, they use formal school-like tasks: practice sheets, flash cards, homework. Perhaps now, even more than before, educators need to challenge such assumptions about learning environments for the development of literacy. Instead, we need to refashion our schools to be more like our most literate homes (Lamme, 1988).

There are at least five reasons why good homes are good settings for learning (Tizard and Hughes, 1984):

1. There is an extensive range of activities within the home as well as various types of excursions from the home.
2. The parent and child share a common life that links past with present and present with future.
3. The interaction is usually one-to-one. Caregivers not only answer questions but also provide information and act as companions.
4. The daily experiences in the home have great personal significance for the child.
5. There is an intense loving, caring, sharing, and trusting relationship between the adult and child.

Many other researchers have reached similar conclusions about the need for greater **home–school continuity** (Silvern, 1988). In the words of James Hymes (1979), we need "not to go back to basics, but to go forward to fundamentals" (p. 16). Nothing is more fundamental, or more natural, than "homestyle" learning.

Reducing Literacy Pressures on Young Children

Adults who are not satisfied to allow a child to advance at his or her own rate and style of learning feel that these milestones—especially literacy milestones—must be forced to appear early, just as flowers are forced to bloom in time for a particular holiday. Adults usually pressure children for one or more of the following reasons:

1. because they are anxious about the highly competitive future children face
2. because a more mature child can help adults with their many responsibilities
3. because they want to fulfill their own needs for achievement through the child (Hills, 1987).

These pressures on children often lead to feelings of inadequacy and rejection for the child. Some specific ways in which language is used to put pressure on the child are the following:

The child might hear negative adult comments about his or her language skills ("He's in the lowest reading group," "I can't understand her at all.") and begin to doubt himself or herself, not only in language, but in general.

Feedback from school about the child's literacy learning could cause parents to question their child's abilities ("I thought he was doing fine, but the teacher says he can't spell," "Do you think we ought to have her tested?"). These negative messages can interfere with warmth and closeness in the family.

structured "busy work" can make the child frustrated in school ("Since you didn't get your work finished, you can stay inside and do it while the other children have recess.")

developmentally inappropriate expectations can make the child feel inadequate ("Now *everyone* in this kindergarten class ought to know all of the alphabet by now. Mica, what is this letter?")

Inappropriate testing practices can adversely affect the child's progress ("I'm sorry, Mrs. LaFontaine, but Nelson's reading readiness score on the entrance exam indicates that he is not ready for an academic preschool program like ours.")

Children begin to associate reading and writing with punishment ("Copy the poem from the board." "You have broken a school rule about throwing snowballs, so you will have to write 'I will not throw snowballs one hundred times.' ")

All of these high-pressure tactics inhibit children and those inhibitions stand in the way of children becoming more fully literate. Listening, speaking, and reading and writing—the path to all these abilities is marked by trial and error. If the child is afraid to take risks, his progress in literacy will surely be thwarted.

Good language learners begin with a function, a need to get something done with language, and move gradually toward the forms which reveal that function ... They experiment freely and try things unashamedly. (Shuy, 1981, p. 107)

Valuing the Child's Growth in Literacy

Allan, a first-grader, was very difficult to understand and was referred to the speech therapist. She found him to be a very unusual case because his language did not seem to fit into any of the typical categories. He understood others, so his receptive language was good, and he did not seem to have a language delay. His concept of conversation, was, if anything, advanced. The only problem was in his unusual pronunciation and articulation of words, which was unlike the speech immaturities commonly observed in young children. When Allan's guardians were called in, the mystery was solved. Allan was being raised by his two elderly grandparents. Both of them had severe dental problems and, as a result, moved their mouths as little as possible when speaking. Allan had learned to talk the same way. This first-grade boy's experience illustrates the influence of language models on young children. Allan was certainly capable of changing his speech to make himself better understood by people outside his family: he simply needed experience with other language models. Of course, differences in the language used at home and at school are not always as dramatic as Alan's, but the influence is there nonetheless.

Read these commonly mispronounced words. Which spelling sounds like your pronunciation?

poinsetta	pointsetta	poinsettia
preroggative	parrogative	prerogative

The correct spellings and pronunciations are on the right, but your ear for language might have indicated otherwise. Much the same thing happens with usage—the way we use language. Usage is tremendously affected by our language models. Basically, we rely on what "sounds right." As the novelist Joan Didion once said, "Grammar is an instrument I play by ear." That ear, of course, comes from our earliest introduction to language. It may be slightly modified or dramatically altered by later experience, but it remains with us always. This is why teachers are advised to accept and extend rather than criticize and correct children's language. Perhaps you have had the experience of asking a teacher, "Can I go get a drink now?" and heard the reply, "Of course you *can*; you need to ask if you *may*." Probably, if you are used to saying "can," this treatment only confused you, embarrassed you, and made you (if anything) more resolute about saying it "your way."

Valuing literacy does not mean humiliating children by making them feel that the school is "right" and their families are "wrong." It means that we are models of language ourselves and that we show children what language can do for them. The teacher who speaks about her admiration of the beautiful language in books and takes delight in children's work does more to influence children's language than the teacher who corrects their usage.

School-Home Activities

As we have seen, parent involvement for the 1990s has to be more than chaperoning a field trip or planning a class party. Some alternatives to these traditional types of parent involvement are described below.

Book Exchange

One of the least expensive and fastest ways to get books into children's homes is to organize a book exchange. By pooling resources in the community, books that are no longer at the child's reading or interest level can be exchanged for those that are. Some sources for books are: discards from the public library that are still usable, books that would otherwise be sold at the garage sale, books that just did not appeal to a particular child, and free books that teachers get from book clubs as dividends.

Birthday Packets

Ms. Spewock, a reading specialist, created birthday packets that she sends to the parents of every child in the district. The first packet is sent to the hospital shortly after the mother gives birth and the packets continue up through the primary grades. Parents of adopted children and children who are new to the district receive them too. Each packet contains child development information, suggested learning activities, recommended books available at the local library, and, beginning when the child is three, a birthday card for the child.

Original Story Tapes

Ms. Freeman, a first-grade remedial reading teacher, initiated a project to make children's homes more "print-rich." She used wordless picture books with her students. First she shared several wordless books with her students and they invented group stories to go along with the pictures. Then the children selected a favorite wordless book and wrote their own text to accompany the illustrations. Each child edited his or her own work and wrote the final copy on self-adhesive notes that could be placed inside the book without damaging it. Finally, each child made an audiotape of himself or herself reading the book. Ms. Freeman sent the books and the child's tape home, along with a letter explaining the project and asking the parents to invite their child to share what the child had done. Figure 10.2 contains some of the responses she received from parents. Instead of criticizing parents for not doing enough to support their children's growth in literacy, Ms. Freeman worked *with* parents to make the children's homes more literate environments.

Visiting Class Mascot

Ms. Malcolm's private nursery school had a panda as its emblem, so she sent home a stuffed toy panda and a "diary." The parent and the child kept a journal of the panda's adventures while he spent a week in the child's home. It was understood that these adventures could be real or imaginary and that the child was expected to participate in creating the journal entries. When the panda was returned to the classroom at the end of the week, it gave the teacher some insight about the families with whom she was working. It also encouraged parents and children to engage in literacy events throughout the week.

Information Board

Mr. Thornton, a teacher in an infant-toddler center, created an information center for parents. The bulletin board contained brochures gathered from physicians, nutritionists, counselors, psychologists, and various community-service organizations that he gathered at the "Health Fair" in the local shopping mall. A calendar of upcoming events in the classroom, school, and community was maintained as well as a daily "good news" item. Parents were asked to suggest other things that would be helpful and soon there was a "swap" section for toys, clothes, and baby furniture. As a result of the contacts made through the information center, parents initiated a babysitting cooperative and a carpooling service. One enterprising mother who lived close by the school even began a meal service where families could pick up a complete dinner by ordering and prepaying at least three days in advance.

Take-Home Activities

Instead of giving her second-graders homework, Ms. Usko gave them "home fun." The project began by sending home a list of "beautiful junk" to save at home. With

Comments:

Mary,
I thought it was nice. He was really thrilled about the tapes. We all got a laugh out of it. I think it was a neat idea.

Comments:

We loved reading and listening to Amanda's story. We thought she did very well at "guess" spelling several words. We hope she'll be bringing home another wonderful story soon.

Thanks
D. & G.

Comments:

We have listened to Jeremy's tape several times, he is very proud of it, so are we. the book was also nice. It's clear that you put some time in this project. It's really a nice idea. His spelling is really something else. As always thanks for your time.

FIGURE 10.1   Correspondence from Parents about the Stories and Tapes Children Made to Accompany Wordless Picture Books.

the help of junior high school students enrolled in a child development course and various teacher resource books, Ms. Usko was able to create fifty different "home fun" projects that the children could check out (see Figure 10.2). Each plastic bag contained all of the instructions for completing a project and children were free to borrow any materials that they did not already have at home from those collected by the class. The bag also contained a simple report form so that Ms. Usko could gather information on which projects were most successful and appreciated by the families.

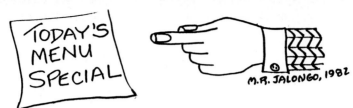

OBJECTIVE: TO PLAN BALANCED MEALS USING THE FOUR FOOD GROUPS, TO PRACTICE WRITING AND SPELLING SKILLS

MATERIALS: EVERY DAY EAT THE 1-2-3-4 WAY!
(AVAILABLE FROM LOCAL DAIRY COUNCIL)

PAPER, MARKERS

INSTRUCTIONS: IN ORDER FOR MEALS TO BE HEALTHFUL, THEY SHOULD CONTAIN FOODS FROM EACH OF THE FOUR FOOD GROUPS. USING THE ENCLOSED CHART AS A GUIDE, PLAN FIVE FAMILY DINNERS THAT ARE EXAMPLES OF WELL BALANCED MEALS. WRITE YOUR MENUS ON A CARD AND DISPLAY THEM SOMEWHERE SO THAT EVERYONE IN YOUR FAMILY WILL KNOW WHAT IS FOR DINNER ON THE EVENING THAT THE MEAL IS PREPARED AND SERVED.

OBJECTIVE: TO WRITE CLEAR INSTRUCTIONS

MATERIALS: BOOKS

CATALOG OF KITS - JEFFERY FEINMAN   NOTE CARDS

KITS FOR KIDS - NANCY BUTTERWORTH AND LAURA BROAD   SELF- SEALING PLASTIC BAG

INSTRUCTIONS: YOU HAVE TAKEN HOME AND COMPLETED MANY ACTIVITIES SO YOU SHOULD NOW BE ABLE TO DESIGN YOUR OWN TAKE HOME PACKET. YOUR IDEA SHOULD INCLUDE WRITTEN INSTRUCTIONS THAT ARE DIVIDED INTO THE FOLLOWING FOUR
SECTIONS: 1. TITLE

2. OBJECTIVE OR PURPOSE

3. MATERIALS (BE SURE TO LIST EVERYTHING THAT IS NEEDED!)

4. INSTRUCTIONS

LOOK AT THE KITS FOR KIDS BOOK TO GET IDEAS ON HOW KITS ARE PRESENTED AND DESIGNED. REMEMBER TO MAKE YOUR KIT INEXPENSIVE AND COMPLETE WITH ALL THE NECESSARY MATERIALS SO THAT EVERYONE CAN TRY IT. NOW LOOK AT THE CATALOG OF KITS BOOK. YOU ARE GOING TO ADVERTISE YOUR IDEA IN THE CLASS CATALOG OF KITS, SO DESIGN AN ADVERTISEMENT THAT WILL MAKE EVERYONE ANXIOUS TO USE YOUR IDEA AT HOME.

M.R. JALONGO, 1982

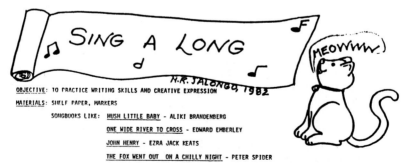

OBJECTIVE: TO PRACTICE WRITING SKILLS AND CREATIVE EXPRESSION

MATERIALS: SHELF PAPER, MARKERS

SONGBOOKS LIKE: HUSH LITTLE BABY - ALIKI BRANDENBERG

ONE WIDE RIVER TO CROSS - EDWARD EMBERLEY

JOHN HENRY - EZRA JACK KEATS

THE FOX WENT OUT ON A CHILLY NIGHT - PETER SPIER

INSTRUCTIONS: SELECT A SONG THAT THE CLASS USUALLY SINGS OR ONE THAT YOU WOULD LIKE TO TEACH THEM. THINK ABOUT SOME PICTURES THAT WOULD MAKE GOOD ILLUSTRATIONS THAT WOULD GO ALONG WITH THE SONG LYRICS. DESIGN AN ILLUSTRATED SONG CHART ON THE SHELF PAPER SO THAT IT CAN BE UNROLLED AS THE CLASS SINGS ALONG WITH THE WORDS. USE YOUR ILLUSTRATED SONG CHART TO LEAD THE CLASS IN SONGS DURING MUSIC TIME.

FIGURE 10.2   Examples of Take-home Activities.

Conclusion

In these activities or in any others you might initiate, remember that:

> *The real challenge for parents and teachers is building mutual trust and respect. Parents need to appreciate a teacher's ability to see the child in comparison to other students at the same grade level. Teachers need to value the parents' ability to round out their view of the child by contributing a perspective on home and family. By blending these two very different viewpoints, we can gain a clear picture of the child and make well-informed decisions that further a child's development. (Brown and Jalongo, 1986)*

Summary

In addition to being the child's first teacher, parents can function in many other roles related to the educational program. Both parent involvement in educational programs and school support for families are important. Particularly where young children are concerned, research supports making both environments "print-rich" and providing greater continuity between homes and schools. In order to work effectively with parents, teachers must confront their own **biases and stereotypes** and strive to maintain a multicultural perspective. In addition, teachers need to develop a positive **interaction style**, conduct productive parent-teacher conferences, conceptualize their relationship with parents as a partnership, and implement creative parent involvement strategies.

Focus On: Conferencing with Parents

Of all the types of interaction between parents and teachers, conferences are one of the most common and most valued by families and schools. These suggestions for improving your conferencing skills are quoted at length from an article that appeared in *PTA Today* (Brown and Jalongo, 1986):

> *Prepare students for parent-teacher conferences.* If students are uneasy about upcoming conferences, it is very likely that the parents are too. Teachers can put students at ease by communicating a friendly, eager attitude toward meeting parents so as to share students' successes.
>
> *Initiate contact with parents.* Parents tend to prefer direct personal contact with the teacher over other forms of home-school communication. Parent-teacher conferences continue to be rated by parents as one of the most effective ways to communicate. Teachers can also use written notes or telephone conversations to praise the child's academic achievements, social skills, behavior, or special talents and interests. When parents are reluctant to meet with teachers, it is even more important for teachers to assert a positive, caring attitude.
>
> *Invite parents to visit the school.* Parents can benefit from coming to school for reasons other than meeting with the teacher. Invitations to eat lunch with the children,

to attend a play or puppet show performed by the children, or to review a display of art work or projects can build rapport prior to conferences.

Create a welcoming environment. Before each conference the entire class can be involved in making the classroom an inviting place for parents to visit. Displaying children's work, designing bulletin boards and decorating the room not only generate enthusiasm among the students but also help make parents feel more comfortable.

Plan the seating arrangement. Teachers who sit at their desks with the parents sitting nearby create a physical barrier between themselves and parents. A parent in this situation may feel like a child in school again. The most successful conferences occur when the teacher and the parent are seated face to face on the same side of a table. This creates an open, warm atmosphere and a feeling of cooperative decision-making.

Prepare a general outline. Successful conferences are carefully planned. Before meeting with parents, teachers should develop a general outline for use during each conference. Five basic parts of every conference are an introductory conversation that establishes teacher-parent rapport; a discussion of positive attributes of the child; a presentation of the student's work arranged to highlight strengths and show progress; and a discussion of areas where parents and teachers can work together. Conferences should conclude on a positive and helpful note.

In the Field: Parent-Involvement Interview

This assignment is designed to help you gain insight into the relationship between home and school by looking at it from both the parents' and teacher's perspectives.

Teacher

How did your teacher education program prepare you to work with parents?

What expectations do you have for parent involvement in your early childhood program?

What special activities, educational programs, or services does your school provide for parents?

What strategies do you use to communicate with parents?

Describe some of the ways that parents typically become involved in their children's education.

What, if anything, do you find discouraging about efforts at parent involvement?

Describe your greatest success with parent-teacher cooperation.

Parent

How do you prefer to communicate with your child's teacher and the school?

Have you participated in any of the parent involvement activities at your school (such as conferences, PTA meetings, programs presented by the children, fund-raising activities)?

How do you usually prefer to be contacted by the school (written messages, telephone calls, or face-to-face conferences)? How would you prefer to be contacted when:

there is a formal meeting with a guest speaker

your child is having an academic problem? a social or personal problem?

your child is presenting stories, plays, poems, etc., that he or she has created?

What do you find discouraging about your efforts to work with your child's school?

What do you find satisfying about efforts to become involved with the school?

What suggestions do you have for improving home-school communication and cooperation?

References

Brown, L. J., and Jalongo, M. R. (1986). Make parent-teacher conferences better. *PTA Today*, *12*, 14–16.

Cullum, A. (1971). *The geranium on the windowsill just died but teacher you went right on*. New York: Harlin Quist.

Day, B. (1983). *Early childhood education*. New York: Macmillan.

Goodman, K. S., and Goodman, Y. M. (1979). Learning to read is natural. In L. B. Resnick and P. A. Weaver (Eds.) *Theory and practice of early reading* (pp. 137–155). New York: Erlbaum.

Gordon, I. J. (1969). Developing parent power. In E. Grotberg (Ed.) *Critical issues in research related to disadvantaged children*. Princeton, NJ: Educational Testing Service.

Greenberg, P. (1989). Parents as partners in young children's development and education: A new American fad? Why does it matter? *Young Children*, *44*(4), 61–75.

Hills, T. W. (1987). Hothousing young children: Implications for early childhood policy and practice. Urbana, IL: ERIC Clearinghouse on Elementary and Early Childhood Education [EDO-PS-87-4].

Hymes, J. (1979). Language in education: Forward to fundamentals. In O. K. Garnica and M. L. King (Eds.). *Language, children and society*. New York: Pergamon.

Kagan, S. L. (1989). Early care and education: Tackling the tough issues. *Phi Delta Kappan*, *70*(6), 433–439.

Lamme, L. (1988). Reflections on raising literate children. In G. F. Roberson and M. A. Johnson (Eds.). *Leaders in education: Their views on contemporary issues* (pp. 122–125). Lanham, MD: University Press of America.

Morrow, L. M. (1989). *Literacy development in the early years*. Englewood Cliffs, NJ: Prentice-Hall.

Phillips, C. B. (1988). Nurturing diversity for today's children and tomorrow's leaders. *Young Children*, *43*(2), 42–47.

Postman, N. (1982). *The disappearance of childhood*. New York: Dell.

Powell, D. R. (1989). *Families and early childhood programs*. Washington, DC: National Association for the Education of Young Children.

Shuy, R. (1981). A holistic view of language. *Research in the Teaching of English*, *15*, 101–111.

Silvern, S. (1989) (Ed.). *Advances in reading/language research: Volume 5, Literacy through family, community and social interactions*. Greenwich, CT: JAI.

Silvern, S. (1988). Continuity/discontinuity between home and early childhood education environments. *The Elementary School Journal*, *89*(2), 147–159.

Taylor, D. (1983). *Family literacy*. Portsmouth, NH: Heinemann.

Tizard, B., and Hughes, M. (1984). *Young children learning*. Cambridge, MA: Harvard University.

White, K. (1982). The relationship between socioeconomic status and academic achievement. *Psychological Bulletin*, *91*, 461–481.

Photo: © 1990 Frank Siteman

11

Assessment Issues and Alternatives in the Language Arts

OUTLINE

Key Concepts and Terms
Introduction

I.   What Is Assessment?

II. Purposes of Assessment

III. Assessment and Testing: How Do They Differ?
   A. Inappropriate Uses of Formal Tests
   B. Abuses of Standardized Tests

IV. Young Children as Test Takers: Proceed With Caution
   A. Inexperience
   B. Nonresponse
   C. Cultural Bias
   D. Artificiality
   E. Test Wiseness
   F. Test Construction

V.   Advantages of Standardized Tests
   A. Time and Money
   B. Credibility
   C. Anonymity
   D. Comparability

While inappropriate use of standardized testing can occur at all levels of the educational ladder, it would appear that the greatest potential for harm exists during the early childhood years. It is at this time that tests are often used to determine school success or failure which subsequently affects not only academic performance but also social and emotional development of young children.
            —JANET BLACK (1979), p. 49

KEY CONCEPTS AND TERMS

assessment	nonresponse
naturalistic observation	cultural bias
norm-referenced	artificiality
criterion-referenced	observations
standardized test	checklist and rating scales
reliability	teacher-designed evaluations
validity	

Three college students have just completed a final exam and, as they convene in the hallway afterward, the following conversation ensues:

> "That test was really hard, don't you think? I really studied, but tests always make me so nervous."

> "Well, I thought that the objective part of the exam covered the things that were discussed in class or in the textbook, but that essay question really gave me problems. I don't remember discussing that at all."

> "At least we didn't have to take the test the way that Sheila did. She had the flu, missed the test, and the professor made her come to her office and *asked* her the questions. I would find that really intimidating, wouldn't you?"

All of the points raised by these students are related to the topic of assessment.

What Is Assessment?

In general, **assessment** means to evaluate the level, importance, or worth of something. In the preceding example, some of the basic principles of assessment were identified in each student's comments. Namely, these are:

> Does the assessment accurately represent what a student has learned?

> Is there congruence between what is taught and tested?

> How does the response format (the way that the person is expected to display his or her competence) affect performance?

Obviously, issues like these are important considerations when conducting an assessment. Before looking at the *how* and *what* of assessment, let's examine the *why*.

Purposes of Assessment

Why is it important to evaluate children's growth in language? Basically, there are four general reasons for doing so:

- To determine the child's instructional level and plan language arts experiences at the correct level of difficulty
- To evaluate an individual child's progress in language and literacy during an educational experience
- To make decisions about grouping (reading groups), to make appropriate referrals to specialists (speech therapist), or to determine eligibility for special programs (gifted and talented)
- To justify a program's existence and the expenditure of funds

Assessment and Testing: How Do They Differ?

Assessment is a general term that is a synonym for evaluation. It includes many different techniques: **naturalistic** methods (such as a case study); moderately structured methods (such as an interview), and tightly structured approaches (such as a formal, published test). Table 11.1 contains an overview of various assessment techniques.

Many psychologists would define a *test* as simply "a sample of behavior." Increasingly in America, the results of one such sample—the standardized test—is used to make important decisions about the child, the individual teacher's competence, or the relative success of the school program. **Standardized tests** have clearly specified administration procedures, are commercially published/marketed, and are often group administered/quick scoring. Usually, they are **norm-referenced**, meaning that they enable one group to compare its performance with that of other groups. **Criterion-referenced** tests document the child's performance on a set of objectives (i.e., capitalizes first word in a sentence, uses punctuation at end of sentence). Despite these features and the research that goes into developing them, standardized tests are not the same thing as an assessment.

Assessment is a much more comprehensive type of evaluation than a test. When a single test score is used to make promotion/retention decisions, to reward or chastise teachers and administrators, to determine the allocation of resources to schools, and to change the curriculum or "teach to the test," it is a "high stakes test" (Meisels, 1989). The next section will highlight what happens when assessment and testing are confused, and standardized tests are used inappropriately.

TABLE 11.1 Language Assessment Overview

Formal (most structured)			*Informal* (least structured)
	Norm-Referenced	*Criterion-Referenced*	*Naturalistic*
Purpose	To rank or compare one child's performance with that of peers	To assess child's performance on specific objectives	To study an individual child's performance
Basic assumption	The whole is the sum of its parts	The whole can be analyzed aspectually	The whole is more than the sum of its parts
Focus	Attempts to measure products or outcomes	Attempts to create a profile of the child's competencies to be used in planning instruction	Attempts to investigate a language skill holistically
Data	Usually quantitative (raw scores, percentages, etc.)	Diagnostic/prescriptive	Usually qualitative
Examples	Readiness tests, achievement tests	Developmental profiles	Anecdotal records, case studies

Inappropriate Uses of Formal Tests

In 1988, the National Association for the Education of Young Children issued a Position Statement on Standardized Testing (Bredekamp and Shepard, 1989). Based upon these general standards, tests of children's language should

> have a beneficial outcome for children
>
> be used for the purposes for which they were intended
>
> be *valid*, meaning that they should measure what they claim to measure
>
> be *reliable*, meaning that scores on the test should be attributable to real differences in an individual's abilities rather than to errors in measurement
>
> be just one component of a comprehensive assessment program

Abuses of Standardized Tests

Why might NAEYC issue this cautionary statement? There are several reasons. In some instances, tests are being used to deny children access to programs or to retain them in programs without evidence that these strategies are beneficial to the child (Bredekamp and Shepard, 1987). Furthermore, the results of tests with young children are even less *reliable* than they are with older children and adults. **Reliability**, as it is used in reference to tests, is comparable to reliability in transportation— we expect it to perform rather consistently and be relatively free from mechanical error. **Validity** is another important property of test. If a test is valid, it means that it measures what it claims to measure. Using the validity criterion, a test that reputedly measures children's readiness for first grade ought to provide evidence that the vast majority of children who were categorized as "ready," "not ready," or some stage in between performed as predicted by the end of first grade.

Young Children as Test Takers: Proceed with Caution

Even when tests *are* well constructed and used appropriately, young children are difficult to test for six reasons.

Inexperience

Generally speaking, young children lack familiarity with testing procedures and often do not realize the importance of a test. In everyday experience, for example, people ask children questions because they do not know the answer "Where did you put your shoes?", "Is Daddy's car in the driveway?"). In a testing situation, just the reverse is true. Children are asked "display questions," questions to determine what they know when the adults already know the answer. One mother described how her daughter's misunderstanding of display questions affected the preschooler's test performance:

I took Terri, my five-year-old daughter, to school for kindergarten-readiness testing. On the way home, I said, "What were some of the questions they asked you?" Terri replied, "A teacher had pictures on the little cards and she held them up for me to see. Then she said 'What is this?' One was a picture of a bird." "And what did you say?" I asked. "I didn't say anything. I figured if that lady doesn't know it's a picture of a bird, I'm not telling her."

Because Terri did not appreciate how important it was to "play along," she may be judged "not ready" for kindergarten when she clearly is.

Another difficulty with young test-takers is their tendency to interpret questions literally. One of the items on a readiness test reads: "What does mother put through a needle when she sews?" Sarah, a four-year-old, looked puzzled, then said, "But my Mom doesn't sew. Well, she does sometimes, but only when something needs fixed." Children may not understand that the question pertains to them and an answer is expected, even if the situation is hypothetical.

Nonresponse

Many times young children do not respond to test items. This does not necessarily mean that they do not know the answer. There are many possible explanations. The child may not understand the procedure or may be fearful of making a mistake. It could also be that the child feels uncomfortable with the person administering the test. Consider the experience of Jennifer, a bright, talkative kindergartner. Her parents are informed that she is being recommended for speech therapy and they are taken aback. When they ask Jenny what happened at school, she says, "A weird man I never saw at school before took me out of my room and into a little closet. He had a hole cut in the back of his hair (the man was bald!), and he was wearing a Mickey Mouse watch. He asked me lots of questions, but he was a *stranger*, so I didn't answer." Because **nonresponse** is usually scored as an incorrect answer, children's abilities may be greatly underestimated by tests (Paget, 1983).

Cultural Bias

A child's social background may serve as an advantage or a disadvantage if the test is "loaded" in favor of a particular cultural group. Usually, cultural bias is discussed from the standpoint that the dominant social group (members of the white middle class) are *advantaged* in their abilities to answer the questions. It is not surprising that this often occurs, given the fact that the authors, publishers, and purchasers of tests tend to be from the white middle class.

Envision two groups of first-graders taking a reading-readiness test: The first is a school in urban New York, the second, a rural school in New Mexico. In one section of the test, they are instructed to look at three different pictures in each row and circle the one named by the teacher. One item calls for children to "Circle the moccasin." A parent from New York City might say, "So *this* is the basis for making a decision about my child's academic ability? He's never even *seen* a moccasin!"

Meanwhile, nearly every child in the Arizona school gets the item correct because Native Americans make, wear, and sell moccasins in their community. This is what cultural bias means—the test items are culturally "loaded" in favor of one group over another; the item is much more difficult for one social group than it is for another. Unlike the example just given, though, the people *dis*advantaged on tests are usually members of minority groups.

Artificiality

If a child can circle the picture that corresponds to a word spoken by the school psychologist, or if a child can supply the missing word in a simple analogy, this does not tell us whether he or she can initiate a conversation with an adult or negotiate a dispute over a toy with a peer. So formal tests tell us *something* about children's language but it is clearly not enough. Because language is a social instrument, it is important to assess it in natural settings rather than relying exclusively on the contrived situations required by standardized tests. Some of those natural situations include: when the child is absorbed in an activity and is speaking aloud to himself, when a child is playing alongside or interacting with peers, and when a child is in the home environment.

A young child's language behavior in different settings can be radically different. Fonda, a solemn, subdued first-grader, rarely spoke at school, yet her mother described the very opposite behavior at home. Upon further investigation, it was discovered that Fonda's cousin had really frightened her about going to first grade by telling her that "if you talk or you're bad, you'll go to the principal's office and he has this GREAT BIG paddle that REALLY HURTS." As a result, Fonda was afraid at school. When Fonda was mistreated by peers at school, she said and did nothing. By the time she arrived home, she was often angry, frustrated, bursting to talk, and aggressive toward her little brother. If Fonda had not been observed across several social settings, she might have been incorrectly labeled as "language delayed."

Test Wiseness

Suppose that you were going to travel to a distant city to compete in a marathon and you heard about one of your major competitors practicing on that exact course every day. It would seem like your competitor had the advantage, had an "edge." A similar situation is occurring with testing in our society. Because these small samples of behavior called tests are being used to make monumental decisions, children are being coached in how to take tests. If a child who fails a test is labeled with some dreadful euphemism such as "needs a year to grow" and denied access to the public school, it is easy to see why working parents who are paying for child care might seek a tutor to prepare their child for the readiness test. If the children's scores on a test are used to rate teachers, it is also easy to understand why some teachers might "teach to the test."

When parents and teachers succumb to making the child more knowledge-able about test taking, the goal of educating the whole child is compromised in the process. No thirty-minute quick-scoring test can adequately evaluate all the things that children have learned during an academic year. The things children memorize in preparation for the test might be forgotten quickly and be of little consequence both now and in the future. The issue here is not whether children can learn to be better test takers. Of course they can. The question is: What has been sacrificed in the process? Our answers depend on whether we see education as a brief compet-itive event (like a marathon) or whether we see education as preparation for lifelong learning.

Test Construction

Another feature of test construction that puts young children at a disadvantage is the relative length of a testing session for a child. As teenagers or adults, we will sit for hours taking an important test like the Scholastic Aptitude Test, the National Teachers' Examination, or the Graduate Record Examination. For young children, some time period of less than twenty-five minutes is about the maximum unless the test is broken into several sessions. Of course, the moment the test is spread out over more than one time or day, it becomes more difficult to administer because some children may be absent. How do test developers handle this problem? Usually, they keep tests very short. Tests are not noted for holding children's interest either, so this is another reason to reduce the total administration time.

But something else is compromised in the drive to keep tests brief. Suppose that someone gave you a choice of two exams, one that was 100 items, 1 point apiece and one that was 10 items, 10 points apiece. Most of us would probably choose the first test, operating on the assumption that there would be less likelihood of missing just one item and receiving a low score. The same principle applies in some of the tests for young children. Because there are so few total items, just a few either way can greatly affect the total score.

The *response format*—the different ways that children can answer test items— is really very limited. Because young children are unsophisticated as test takers, they usually respond to a group-administered, paper-and-pencil test by circling the correct answers; putting an X on an object, shape, or letter; or drawing a line connecting two things that belong together.

The methods used to record children's responses before they know shapes or letters or even pictured objects are equally flawed. Very young children are usually tested individually on motor-skill tasks such as building a stack of blocks. As you might guess, tests of physical skills are notoriously poor predictors of language test performance later on.

Treating the child's linguistic ability as a collection of right or wrong answers flies in the face of recent research on young children's language learning (Silvern, 1988). Children do not learn language by absorbing correct ready-made answers.

Instead, their path to language mastery is littered with unconventional, yet systematic "errors," and their "wrong" answers have much to tell us about children's language growth. Contemporary methods of standardized testing deal with products, not with processes.

Advantages of Standardized Tests

If tests for young children have so many drawbacks, then why do we continue to use them? There are at least four reasons:

Time and Money

Without a doubt, the large-group, paper-and-pencil test is faster to administer, easier to score, and less costly than testing each child individually. Educators rely on formal tests because they are the most expedient way to get some indication of the child's language abilities.

Credibility

Because tests are developed through research studies and statistical techniques, they are very official looking and technical. If the scores are high, tests give educators facts and figures that seem impressive, "hard" evidence that can be reported to various publics.

Anonymity

Teachers have a responsibility to reach all of their students. None of us wants to be the bearer of bad news, to tell a parent that a child is functioning at a low level, or may fail a grade, for instance. But with test scores to rely upon, we have an impartial "third party." Tests give us "cut-off scores" that are used to draw the line between those children who will be accepted or rejected by an educational program. When irate parents demand to know why their child was categorized in a particular way, school personnel can appeal to the anonymous test score instead of saying that it is their collective professional judgment.

Comparability

Because a standardized test is standard in its items, administration procedures, and scoring procedures, it enables one school to compare itself with others locally, regionally, and nationally. When the public in a technological society lacks confidence in an organization's ability to give an accurate, impartial, and truthful accounting of progress, they look to external regulatory mechanisms (such as standardized tests) for this information.

Having raised all these questions about tests, it might seem there is little to recommend them. But testing has a place in education just as knowing a person's temperature or blood pressure can assist a doctor in making a diagnosis. Appendix G contains a selective listing of several tests used in the assessment of young children's language abilities (Kent, 1990). All of these formal measures should be supplemented with information about the child's language in the home and community (often supplied by the parents), and through observations of the child at school during interactions with adults and peers, both in formal and informal settings. Remember: A test is a sample of one type of behavior. It takes many samples of many different behaviors in various contexts to qualify as an assessment.

Informal Measures of Language Growth

Basically, there are three categories of informal measures: **observations** (incidental or planned); **checklists and rating scales** (teacher-developed or commercially developed); and **teacher-designed evaluations** (written, oral, or other performance-based methods) (Wortham, 1990). How do good teachers use the results of informal measures to help children learn?

Observations

In a recent article, Selma Wasserman (1989) says that "one of the most valuable yet rarely acknowledged assessment tools in educational practice is the sustained, thoughtful day-to-day observation of student behavior by a competent, professional teacher" (p. 368).

Ms. Schultz Observes Kim

Kim is a newly immigrated child who recently enrolled in a first-grade class. Because Kim arrived at school with very minimal knowledge of English, Mrs. Schultz has asked her student teacher to assist her in collecting anecdotes about his behavior. An anecdote is a brief episode of behavior which includes the setting (time, day, place); the physical and social context (activity, the behavior of other children, teachers); and, most importantly, the observable behavior of a particular child (physical responses, words, facial expressions, etc.). Table 11.2 contains some of the anecdotal records made by the teacher and the student teacher. Based upon her observations, Mrs. Schultz develops the following plan:

Involve Kim's parents in the program and plan a conference or home visit.

Observe Kim in other settings (the playground, in music class, art class).

Assess Kim's language development.

Re-evaluate some of my own teaching practices.

Interview Kim directly to find out more about his home environment.

An interview is a planned, indirect, focused, "self-report" observation in which the child functions as an informant about himself or herself. Here is an excerpt from Mrs. Schultz's interview with Kim.

Q: "May I see the picture you drew of your family?"

A: "No, no, no. I drew other things. This is grass, a rainbow, a house, a boy, and a goat named Shelly."

Q: "Is this a picture of your house?"

A: "Maybe."

Q: "What do you like to do in your house?"

A: "I like to play. I love to play. I have ten eighty-five toys. Some are junky toys. My mom says I have too many toys. Too many toys. I watch TV all the time and movies."

Q: "What else do you and your mom do together at home?"

A: "Talk. I like to talk. My mom says, 'Kim talk too much.' She says, 'Go watch TV.' "

Q: "Anything else?"

A: Kim sang "Ten Little Indians."

Q: "Do you like that song?"

A: "I like to sing." (Kim sings "The Alphabet Song," then counts to 100 aloud).

Q: "What is your favorite class in kindergarten?"

A: "I like to play. Play is fun."

Q: "What would you like to be when you grow up?"

A: "I want to be Superman. He flies in the air and is strong." (Kim then imitated Superman.)

Figure 11.1 shows the drawing that Kim did during the interview.

Checklists and Rating Scales

Sharon Kagan (1989) identifies a recent trend in early childhood education toward assessment based on observation.

TABLE 11.2 Anecdotal Records and Interview Data

Activity: Reading	*Date:* October 10
Setting: Classroom	*Time:* 9:30 AM

During a reading-readiness activity, K. was the mailman. He put on the mailman's hat, picked up the mailbag, and started to deliver the cards to his classmates. The children were instructed to look at the picture on their cards, say the name of the picture to themselves, and sit quietly until all the mail was delivered. K. skipped Amber so the teacher asked him to give Amber a card. "I didn't want her to have one because she never knows the letters," K. replied. The teacher instructed K. to give Amber a card anyway.

Activity: Storytime	*Date:* October 15
Setting: School Library	*Time:* 1:15 PM

All the children were sitting on the floor listening to a story. K. raised his hand and yelled, "Oh yucky! Duane is putting pee pee on the floor." I told Dwayne to go into the bathroom to get wet paper towels and clean up the floor. K. said, "I'm glad I put *my* pee pee in the bathroom."

Activity: Recess	*Date:* October 18
Setting: Playground	*Time:* 3:00 PM

K. asked the student teacher to zip up his jacket. She said, "Let me see *you* try to zip your jacket." He replied, "No, no, no. I will do it myself. You are just like my mom."

Activity: Party	*Date:* October 28
Setting: Classroom	*Time:* 2:45 PM

The children were having popcorn at their Halloween party. The teacher spread a clean queen-size bedsheet on the floor and positioned the popcorn popper in the center without its lid. She cautioned the children not to touch the popcorn and to stay seated at the edge of the sheet so that they would not get burned. K. roared with laughter while the popcorn was popping. He said, "I never see food dancing." When I asked him if he had ever tasted popcorn before, he said, "Yes, at the movies and at home, but my mom always makes it in the microwave." This was evidently the first time he could actually see the popcorn popping.

Activity: Reading/Small Group	*Date:* November 1
Setting: Classroom	*Time:* 10:17 AM

The teacher told the children to get their pictures out that started with letter "Tt." She asked K. why he did not have any pictures and K. said his mother would not let him bring pictures. The teacher told K. to remember next time. A few minutes later, when Carlotta gave him some of her pictures, K. looked surprised and then smiled.

Activity: Phonics lesson	*Date:* December 1
Setting: Classroom/Total group	*Time:* 11:00 AM

The teacher asked K. who wrote all over his alphabet line. (Every child has one taped to his or her desk.) He studied the alphabet line for a few seconds and then said, "I did." The teacher asked him why. K. said, "Because you and Ms. M. (the student teacher) wasn't in school and so I didn't want to learn." (The teacher had taken a personal day and the student teacher was ill.)

TABLE 11.2 *Continued*

Activity: Before school   *Date:* December 4

Setting: Classroom   *Time:* 8:30 AM

K. said, "My father shoot eight fifty deer yesterday." The student teacher looked at him skeptically and asked if he was sure. He laughed and said, "Oh, I was telling you a joke. He really shoot one deer three times." Then he laughed and laughed.

Activity: Snack   *Date:* December 6

Setting: Classroom   *Time:* 10:45 AM

The teacher gave everyone a piece of cheese and a few minutes later, K. asked for another piece of cheese. Ms. O. explained that he could have a cracker but there was not enough cheese to give everyone a second piece. K. said, "My mother always gives me what I want because I did not have much food in Korea."

Activity: Art   *Date:* December 7

Setting: Art room   *Time:* 1:45 PM

The children were to bring a piece of aluminum foil to school. K. did not bring foil. He said his mom did not have any. The art teacher said, "Did you ask her?" K. then said, "It was too heavy to carry." A few minutes later, K. said he "just couldn't bring any."

Activity: Reading   *Date:* December 9

Setting: Classroom   *Time:* 9:22 AM

K. showed the student teacher his pictures for letter "Hh." He was smiling and looked proud. He told her he cut them out by himself. She opened the envelope and saw they were coupons from a newspaper. K. brought in twenty pictures but only two of them started with Hh. Evidently, K's mother did not know he brought the pictures in.

Activity: Lunch   *Date:* December 10

Setting: Cafeteria   *Time:* 12:22 PM

When the teacher went to the lunchroom for the children, the person on duty told her that K. had popped a potato chip bag and it startled everyone. K. admitted that he did it, but he was laughing and said it was funny. When the children arrived back at their classroom, Ms. S. took K. aside and asked K. if he was permitted to pop bags at home. He said, "My mom says do it outside because she does not like the noise." "Well," Ms. S. said, "we have the same rule here."

Activity: Before School   *Date:* December 15

Setting: Classroom   *Time:* 8:49 AM

On the student teacher's last day, K. brought in a large bag of potato chips and gave them to her. He said, "This is for your party. I will not pop the bag. I miss you when you leave."

> *Because of the potential to misdiagnose based upon a single test score, the questionable validity of many of the tests being used, and the difficulty in testing young children, some have cautioned against the use of tests and have called for improved teacher observation and for recording keeping that includes developmental logs and checklists. (p. 436)*

A *checklist or developmental log* can be used to chart children's progress in language. These checklists may be published in various sources or may be designed

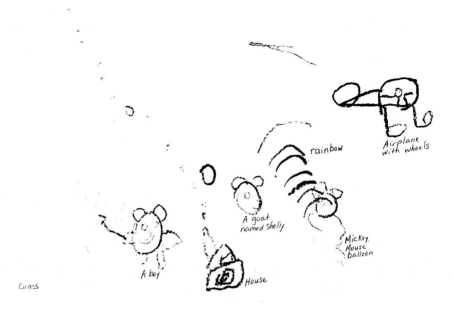

FIGURE 11.1   Kim's Drawing.

by the teacher. Table 11.3 is an example of a developmental log prepared by the National Institutes of Mental Health.

A **rating scale** differs from a checklist in that it evaluates not only the presence or absence of a behavior, but also indicates the amount or degree of that behavior (e.g., always, sometimes, rarely). Table 11.4 is Ms. Stratton's "Rating Scale for Writing" that she designed and uses at the beginning, middle, and end of her first-grade program as a way of documenting children's progress.

Teacher-Designed Evaluations

Basically, teachers use six criteria for assessing children's work (Potter, 1985):

1. *Correctness*—is used when a convergent answer is expected.
   Example of reinforcement: "Yes, the word 'cat' ends with a 't.' "
2. *Practical workability*—is a set of standards based on realistic, desired outcomes.
   Example of reinforcement: "Great! Your lift-the-flap book really works."
3. *Aesthetic*—are standards used if beauty is the criterion.
   Example of reinforcement: "The illustrations for your story have such beautiful colors!"
4. *Creativity*—standards are used when the product or process is evaluated on the basis of originality.

TABLE 11.3 Example of a Developmental Log

Average Age	Assessment Question	"Average" Behavior
3–6 months	What does the child do when you talk to him?	Awakens or quiets to the sound of mother's voice.
	Does the child react to voice even when he or she cannot see you?	Typically turns eyes and head in the direction of the source of sound.
7–10 months	When the child can't see what is happening, what does he or she do? When hearing familiar footsteps . . . the dog barking . . . the telephone ringing . . . candy paper rattling . . . someone's voice . . . or own name?	Turns head and shoulders toward familiar sounds, even when unable to see what is happening. Such sounds do not have to be loud to cause a response.
11–15 months	Can the child point to or find familiar objects or people when asked? Ex.: "Where is Jimmy?" "Find the ball."	Shows understanding of some words by appropriate behavior; for example, points to or looks at familiar objects or people, on request.
	Does the child respond differently to different sounds?	Jabbers in response to a human voice, is apt to cry when there is a sudden, loud noise, or may frown when scolded.
	Does the child enjoy listening to some sounds and imitating them?	Imitation indicates that child can hear the sounds and match them with his/her own sound production.
1½ years	Can the child point to parts of his or her body when asked? Ex.: "Show me your eyes."	Some children begin to identify parts of the body. Child should be able to show his nose or eyes.
	How many understandable words does the child use—words you are sure really mean something?	Child should be using a few single words. They are not complete or pronounced perfectly but are clearly meaningful.
2 years	Can the child follow simple verbal commands when you are careful not to help, such as looking at the object or pointing in the right direction? Ex.: "Pedro, get your hat and give it to Daddy." "Lisette, bring me your ball."	Should be able to follow a few simple commands without visual clues.
2½ years	Does the child know a few rhymes or songs? Does he or she enjoy hearing them?	Many children can say or sing short rhymes and enjoy listening to records or mother singing.
	What does the child do when the ice-cream man's bell rings out of his sight; when a car door or house door closes at a time when someone in the family usually comes home?	If a child has good hearing, and these are events that bring pleasure, he or she usually reacts to the sound by running to look or telling someone about what is heard.
3 years	Can the child show that he or she understands the meaning of some words besides the names of things? Ex.: "Make the car go." "Give me your ball." "Put the block in your pocket." "Find the big doll."	Should be able to understand and use some simple verbs, pronouns, prepositions, and adjectives, such as "go," "me," "in," and "big."
	Can the child find you when you call him from another room?	Should be able to locate source of the sound.
	Does the child sometimes use complete sentences?	Should be using complete sentences some of the time.

TABLE 11.3   *Continued*

Average Age	Assessment Question	"Average" Behavior
4 years	Can the child tell about events that have happened recently?	Should be able to give a connected account of some recent experiences.
	Can he or she carry out two directions, one after the other? Ex.: "Reggie, find Lawanda and tell her dinner's ready."	Should be able to carry out a sequence of two simple directions.
5 years	Do neighbors and others outside the family understand most of what the child says?	Speech should be intelligible, although some sounds may still be mispronounced.
	Can the child carry on a conversation with other children or familiar grown-ups?	Most children of this age can carry on a conversation if the vocabulary is within their experience.
	Does the child begin a sentence with "I" instead of "me," "he" instead of "him"?	Should use some pronouns correctly.
	Is the child's grammar almost as good as his parents'?	Most of the time, it should match the patterns of grammar used by the adults of his family and neighborhood.

Source: National Institutes of Health (1977). *Learning to talk: Speech, hearing and language problems in the preschool child.* Bethesda, MD: National Institutes of Health, pp. 22–24.

> *Example of reinforcement*: "I could imagine just what the planet would be like when I read your story."
>
> 5. *Speed*—is a standard used if the effort is evaluated in terms of the time variable.
>
> *Example of reinforcement*: "You really know how to print your name quickly."
>
> 6. *Model of product or process*—is used if a model or finished product prepared either by the teacher or a peer served as the standard for desired work.
>
> *Example of reinforcement*: "You've done a good job making your own book cover out of fabric like the one I showed you."

Four Teachers Using Informal Assessments

Mr. Orion: Using Play to Assess Oral Language

Mr. Orion knows oral language assessment should

> Occur in natural contexts.
>
> Emphasize function (how language is used to get things done) rather than form (correctness).
>
> Recognize that variability is the norm; what a child says on one particular occasion does not mean that this is characteristic of his or her language. The behavior could occur rarely, sometimes, or often.

TABLE 11.4   Rating Scale for Writing

	Usually	*Sometimes*	*Rarely*
1. Is aware of environmental print			
2. Expects meaning from print			
3. Freely chooses writing materials			
4. Differentiates between writing and drawing			
5. Dictates some stories to teacher			
6. Creates stories in response to wordless books			
7. Illustrates own stories appropriately			
8. Copies letters or words spontaneously			
9. Writes from left to right			
10. Writes from top to bottom			
11. Asks for correct spelling of words			
12. Associates letters with sounds			
13. Shares stories with others			
14. Enacts stories			
15. Revises stories based on input from peers			
16. Uses punctuation			
17. Uses capitalization			

Source: Morrow, L. M. (1989). *Literacy development in the early years*. Englewood Cliffs, NJ: Prentice Hall.

Recognize that oral language happens rapidly and has many different dimensions, so it needs to be tape recorded and studied at length. (Shuy and Staton, 1982)

Mr. Orion has also read that children's responses to peers were more complex than those given to adults (Mishler, 1976). During play, children used all seven of Halliday's (1975) functions of language while in a formal testing situation, they used only one, informative (Black, 1979). He decides to videotape the children's play. He analyzes the tape using ten types of language that young children use during socio-dramatic play (Garvey, 1984). These categories and some of his observations in his mixed-age preschool classroom are as follows:

1. *Definition of situation:* Two girls are playing with puppets and one says, "This is a talent show."
2. *Assignment of roles:* Two preschool girls resolve conflict over which roles they will play by creating new ones:

Lea: "I want to play Ghostbusters."

Marilee: "I do too."

Lea: "Well, pretend we're sisters."

Marilee: "Okay."

3. *Defining location:* A kindergarten boy slithers up to the teacher's desk on his belly. "Mr. Orion, I'm a python, and I'm really a mean snake. I am 12 feet long and this fat. (gestures with hands) Uh-oh—I have to go back to my hole 'cause some mean dogs are chasing me." (slithers back under the table).

4. *Specifying the action plan:* (while playing mommy and baby lion) "Let's growl, okay?"

5. *Assigning props:* "Remember that story, Snow White and the Seven Dwarfs? Well, I'm the mean old witch who goes around poisoning everyone. This is my poison apple."

6. *Correcting operating procedure and refining the script:*

   Anna: "You be the baby and I'll be the mommy."

   Shelley: "Can I have some candy?"

   Anna: "Okay, as much as you want."

   Shelley: "But, Anna, you are the mommy. You have to give me what's good for me."

   Anna: "I know. You can have a lot."

7. *Rejecting others' performance:* Tomas and Kent have built an airport with blocks and are all ready to begin landing aircraft. Throughout the building process, Kent keeps asking if he can fly into the airport and Tomas keeps telling him "not yet."

   Tomas: "Coming in for a landing!"

   Kent: "Can I come in now?"

   Tomas: "Yeah!"

   Kent: (he comes in for a crash landing and knocks down one corner of the airport)

   Tomas: "No! Not that kind!"

8. *Invoking rules relating to the real (versus the pretend):* Selma and Jenny are playing school, Selma is the music teacher, Jenny is the student.

   Selma: "I clap with sticks and you clap with your hands." (Jenny follows instructions) These sticks are magic and if I rub them over your hands, you'll clap faster."

   Jenny: "Teachers don't really have magic sticks . . . do they?"

9. *Termination of and/or transition from one organizing theme to another:* "I'm sick of playing school. Let's play Barbies."

10. *Commenting on the interpersonal climate in the group:* (The class has just finished a unit on friendships and the boys are using some of the techniques they learned through role play.)

    "Will you play with me?"

    "Sure! You're such a nice, nice guy."

"I like you too. (turns to another child) "You're really fun. Do you want to play?" (child nods yes) (talking to the teacher)

"We're all friends and we're playing."

Through his observations, Mr. Orion has gained a more thorough understanding of each child's language strengths. For example, he notices that his unit on friendship had a direct influence on the children's interaction. He targets additional areas of language and social development that would enhance the quality of the children's play: defining the situation and location, assigning roles, specifying the action plan, and refining the script. In a follow-up to his work with the class on friendship, Mr. Orion presents a lesson on cooperation and coaches children in these play behaviors through role-play.

Ms. Fayez: Assessing Responses to Literature

Ms. Fayez is curious about children's responses to literature. It seems that some children are less involved and enthusiastic. To investigate this hypothesis, she decides to use two informal means of assessment: a participation chart and a library use chart. She charts the children's participation during story time by asking her aide to tally their responses using the checklist in Table 11.5. Additionally, Ms. Fayez places a shoe box in each center of the classroom and asks the children to drop slips of paper with their names ("tickets") each time they visit that center. At the end of the week, she has some data about children's verbal responses to the stories she has shared and a tally of the participation patterns during storytime. Ms. Fayez discovers that Bruce, who seldom participates in story discussions, participated twice when the book was about dinosaurs. She had assumed that Sherlene, who always appears interested in the books and usually participates in the discussion, was frequenting the book center, when in fact she was not. An analysis of the types of comments and questions made during story-sharing indicates that there are few comments on the text, something that tends to occur more often in repeated read-alouds (Yaden, 1988). Based on these informal observations, Ms. Fayez decides on three courses of action to support children's responses to literature:

Locate some other books about dinosaurs.

Accompany Sherlene to the book center.

Return to some familiar, favorite books.

Mr. Ellis: Assessing Emergent Reading

Usually, when the assessment of young children's reading abilities is mentioned, the reading-readiness test comes to mind. The purpose of a reading-readiness test is quite simple: to predict who will succeed with formal reading instruction. Once again, there are less formal ways of obtaining similar information. Mr. Ellis, a

TABLE 11.5   Participation Chart for Story Discussion

Activity: Shared book experience			*Date:* September 10	
Observer: J. Hartmann			*Time:* 9:00–9:30 AM	

| | *Types of Comments/Questions* | | | |
Children's Names	About Pictures	About Text	Relates Book to Own Experience	Unrelated to Story
Alicia				
Brian				
Juan				
Kelly				
Lee				
Mei				
Paul				

kindergarten teacher, found two recent articles in *The Reading Teacher* that suggested ways of assessing emergent readers' understandings about the reading process (Agnew 1982; Weiss and Hagen, 1988). The first used the child's dictated story as a way of evaluating concepts about print and basic reading terminology ("letter," "word," "sentence," "top/bottom of page," "sound," etc.); the second was an interview in which the child was presented with printed materials (menu, newspaper, storybook) and asked how they would explain each to someone who knows nothing about reading and also give reasons why people read. By combining these informal measures with the results of a standardized reading-readiness test, Mr. Ellis has a more complete picture of each child's understandings about print. During their shared-book experiences with big books, he begins to introduce reading terminology in context so that children can begin to expand their concepts of print. He also begins a project with children on environmental print in which they create a bulletin board collage of the things that they know how to read or things that have meaning for their families. The collage contains a flyer containing coupons for a new restaurant, a newspaper article about an older sister's volleyball team, assembly instructions for a tricycle, and a wide variety of different food labels.

Ms. Dailey: Portfolio Assessment of Writing

Basically there are two approaches to evaluating children's writing. It can be assessed *directly* by evaluating a sample of written work, or, it can be assessed *indirectly* by asking children various questions about different aspects of writing, usually in a multiple-choice test format. The major criticism of the indirect approach is that knowing the rules of writing (such as capitalization and punctuation) does not reveal much about the writer. Simmons (1989) contends that, if anything, these tests reduce the total amount of time children spend writing:

> . . . *the statewide testing mania with its penchant for multiple-choice, machine-scored instruments has virtually mandated that large chunks of class time be spent prepping for the* big moment. *In such cram sessions, it is highly important that the students learn to read carefully and* not write *a word. (p. 70)*

To Ms. Dailey, the very terminology "language arts" suggests what some alternatives to assessing writing might be. If language is an expressive art like music, then why don't we assess it as such? When a dancer is evaluated, it is by a panel of judges who watch him perform. When an artist is evaluated, it is through a portfolio of her work. She carefully compiles each child's writing samples into a *portfolio* and evaluates the writing directly, using a set of *protocols* or criteria developed by the teachers in her district. She also assesses children's writing indirectly by conferencing with them and asking them questions about their writing process. Of course, she shares the portfolios and protocols with parents at conference time. Ms. Dailey has been using this "process approach" (Graves, 1983) ever since she attended a workshop on the subject several years ago. She believes, as May (1984) does, that "We can learn more from the stories children write about their progress as writers than any test can tell us" (p. 41).

Conclusion

The most important thing to remember about assessment is this: never make a major decision using one small bit of information. One test score may tell us something, but it doesn't tell us very much. Those who use the results of a test to label a child and, in so doing, diminish that child's opportunities are misusing the test and harming that child. Perhaps this sounds farfetched, but it happens to children every day. Consider, for example, the second-grade teacher who administers an end-of-unit reading test. The teacher decides, on the basis of that test score alone, to place certain children in a "low" reading group where they remain all year. As the year progresses, it becomes apparent that some children are more advanced than the other members of their group. But it would be too difficult for a child to catch up with the more advanced group and there aren't enough students at that level or enough instructional time for the teacher to form a fourth group. As a result of one test, these students are deprived of appropriate instruction.

Any conclusions about a child's language ability should include data about their language, not just on one occasion, but on numerous occasions, not just during a test, but also during normal conversation; not only at school, but also at home; not only in interactions with adults, but also in interactions with peers. It is only by looking for patterns within and across in these contexts that we can begin to glimpse the child's true language abilities.

Summary

Assessments of a young child's language growth may be informal (naturalistic observation, checklists, rating scales) or formal (norm-referenced and criterion-referenced tests). The task of assessing a complex process like language is a difficult one, something that is made even more difficult by the young child's lack of familiarity with testing situations and the paper-and-pencil format of most published tests. It is important for early childhood educators to be aware that tests are simply a sample of behavior. It is equally important for educators of young children to fight for more appropriate, comprehensive, valid, and reliable forms of assessment. The results of testing should be used to benefit children and maximize their potential rather than to label children and diminish opportunities for language growth.

Focus On: Explaining Assessment Issues to Parents

How would you handle these situations?

1. Your school district gives a readiness test to all children who are enrolled in kindergarten for the fall. Tyrone does well on the test with the exception of the section on identifying letters of the alphabet. "How can that be?" his mother demands to know. "He can sing the whole alphabet from A to Z."

2. Jan's parents tell you that the reason he is in public school is because he failed the entrance examination at the private school they had selected for him. They both confide that they are worried about getting him into the best college later on.

3. The parents of a second-grade girl who is having difficulty with reading tell you that they have purchased commercially available workbooks for her to use and that they make her practice every evening for an hour. The child was held back in first grade, and they feel that this will be the best way to help her pass the reading tests so that she won't be retained again.

4. After the Iowa Test of Basic Skills scores are compiled for the school district, the results indicate that the children's scores on the listening section of the test are lower than any other area. You are assigned to a curriculum committee that is supposed to investigate the problem. Where will you begin?

5. The principal asks your opinion of using a reading-readiness test score to determine which students will go on to first grade and which will be placed in transitional first grade. What will you say? Why? How will you support your position?

In The Field: Observing Children's Language in Various Contexts

This assignment looks at children's language behavior across three social contexts: with peers, with adults, and in formal language situations.

Do a "shadow" study of a kindergarten or primary-grades child. Follow his or her activities throughout the day. During your observations, record as many examples of children's speech as possible. Then categorize them using the following three classifications:

Interactions with Peers

Questions:

Answers:

Comments:

Interactions With Adults

Questions:

Answers:

Comments:

Assignments or Tests

Questions:

Answers:

Comments

In Class: Compare your findings with those of other class members. Which activities resulted in richer vocabulary, more complex sentences, and ease of expression? How might the failure to look at children's language across situations lead to erroneous assumptions about the child's language abilities?

Observing the Functions of Written Language

Arrange to observe in a first- or second-grade classroom. Look for examples of each of the six following language functions identified by Milz (1985):

1. *To establish ownership*
   labeling personal possessions
2. *To build relationships*
   writing messages such as letters or notes to others
3. *To remind*
   writing lists, notes, etc., for themselves and others
4. *To request*
   asking for assistance
5. *To record*
   documenting various kinds of information
6. *To create*
   using language to express imagination

Each entry should contain the date, the child's age and sex, the setting, and a description of the child's behavior. Here is an example:

October 15
R., a six-year-old girl, made a list of her family members' names on a large piece of unlined paper. They had been learning about one-to-one correspondence during a mathematics lesson earlier that day, so she also drew a picture of each person (and the family dog!) and then drew a line from each name to the corresponding picture. This is an example of using writing to *record*, to document information. Also, in a more subtle way, it is an example of establishing *ownership* because R. seems to be "labeling" her personal "possessions"—in this case, her family.

In Class: The six basic functions of children's language have been discussed in this chapter. Using the observations you have completed, write a one-sentence synopsis of your observation under the appropriate heading. If you observed a child making a list, for instance, you would write, "Child wrote a letter to her best friend" under the heading *To Build Relationships*. If any of your observations illustrate several categories, create another category called *Multiple Functions* and list the numbers of the six categories that relate to the observation. For example, "A child made a list of her toys" would be 1 (to establish ownership) and 5 (to record information). As the class discusses each category, be certain to give additional information about your observation.

References

Agnew, A. T. (1982). Using children's dictated stories to assess code consciousness. *The Reading Teacher, 35*, 450–454.

Black, J. (1979). Formal and informal means of assessing communicative competence of kindergarten children. *Research in the Teaching of English, 13*, 49–68.

Bredekamp, S., and Shepard, L. (1989). How best to protect children from inappropriate school expectations, procedures and policies. *Young Children, 44*(3), 14–24.

Garvey, C. (1984). *Children's talk*. Cambridge, MA: Harvard University Press.

Halliday, M.A.K. (1975). *Explorations in the functions of language*. London: Edward Arnold.

Kagan, S. (1989). Early care and education: Tackling the tough issues. *Phi Delta Kappan, 70*(6), 433–439.

Kent, C. (1991). A selective listing of language tests for young children (unpublished manuscript).

May, S. (1984). Story in its writeful place. In J. Miller (Ed.) *Eccentric propositions: Essays on literature and the curriculum* (pp. 27–41). London: Routledge and Kegan Paul.

Meisels, S. J. (1989). High stakes testing in kindergarten. *Educational Leadership, 46*(7), 16–22.

Mishler, E. G. (1976). Conversational competence among first graders. Paper presented at the conference on Language, Children and Society. Columbus, OH: Ohio State University.

National Association for the Education of Young Children (1988). Position statement on standardized testing. *Young Children, 43*, 42–47.

O'Donnell, H. (1984). *Large scale writing assessment*. Bloomington, IN: ERIC Clearinghouse on Reading and Communication Skills.

Paget, K. D. (1983). The individual examining situation. In K. D. Paget and B. A. Bracken (Eds.) *The psychoeducational assessment of preschool children* (pp. 51–61). New York: Grune & Stratton.

Potter, F. (1985). "Good job!" How we evaluate children's work. *Childhood Education, 61*, 203–206.

Shuy, R. W., and Staton, J. (1982). Assessing oral language ability in children. In L. Feagans and D. C. Farran (Eds.) *The language of children reared in poverty* (pp. 181–198). New York: Academic Press.

Silvern, S. (1988). Continuity/discontinuity between home and early childhood education environments. *The Elementary School Journal, 89*(2), 147–159.

Simmons, J. S. (1989). Thematic units: A context for journal writing. *English Journal, 78*(1), 70–72.

Spandel, V., and Stiggins, J. (1981). Direct measures of writing skill. Issues and applications (rev. ed.). Portland OR: Northwest Regional Educational Laboratory, Clearinghouse for Applied Performance Testing (ED 213 035).

Wasserman, S. (1989). Reflections on measuring thinking, while listening to Mozart's *Jupiter* symphony. *Phi Delta Kappan, 70*(5), 365–370.

Weiss, M. J., and Hagen, R. (1988). A key to literacy: Kindergartners' awareness of the functions of print. *The Reading Teacher, 41*(6), 574–578.

Wortham, S. C. (1990). *Tests and measurement in early childhood education*. Columbus, OH: Merrill.

Yaden, D. (1988). Understanding stories through repeated read-alouds: How many does it take? *The Reading Teacher, 41*(6), 556–560.

GLOSSARY

Accommodation   In Piagetian theory, the process of changing existing mental structures to integrate new experiences.

Acuity   (In reference to the senses of hearing and vision), the sharpness of auditory and visual reception.

Aliteracy   The behavior of people who have mastered the basic skills of reading but who are disinterested in reading or unwilling to read.

Articulation   The ability to pronounce and form spoken words in ways that are generally understood by listeners.

Assimilation   In Piagetian theory, the process of combining new experiences with existing mental structures.

Aural   Having to do with the sense of hearing.

Babbling   The consonant-vowel syllabic sounds typical of infants (e.g., "buh," "ma").

Behaviorism   In language acquisition, a theory that emphasizes the importance of imitation and reinforcement in shaping the child's language learning.

Bilingual   A person who is fluent in one language and has a reasonable degree of fluency in another.

Child-centered   Teaching practices that build upon what the child already knows, providing activities that are simultaneously challenging and developmentally appropriate.

Cognitive-developmental   In language acquisition, a theory developed by Jean Piaget that emphasizes the interaction between the child and the environment. Cognitive-developmental theory describes development as sequential stages that depend on the child's level of intellectual functioning.

Communication   The process of transmitting and receiving a nonverbal or verbal message through a particular medium and in a particular context.

Constructivism   The essential aspect of Piagetian theory that conceptualizes children as active constructors of learning rather than as passive recipients of adult knowledge.

Conventional   Forms of language that are standard and adult-like.

Cooing   An early prelinguistic stage of language in which the infant produces vowel sounds.

Criterian-referenced   A test that consists of a set of performance objectives and charts the child's mastery of each objective (criterion).

Critical listening skills   Higher-level listening abilities, such as comprehending a message, listening for a particular purpose, appreciative listening, active listening, or therapeutic listening.

Curriculum   An overall plan for the educational program in a school or classroom.

Cursive writing   Handwriting that is written in the flowing style of adult writing.

Developmentally appropriate practice (DAP)   An educational program that is based on knowledge of child growth and development; one that addresses the "whole child"—cognitive, physical, social, and emotional.

Dialect   A single language that is spoken in different ways by members of groups from different social classes, communities, or geographic regions.

Dialogue journal   A type of daily journal writing in which the teacher reads and responds in writing to the child's entries.

Emergent reading   A process orientation to reading that regards the child's earliest efforts as part of real reading rather than as "reading readiness."

Expressive jargon   A flow of gibberish that has the rhythms and intonation of speech, typical of children near the end of their first year of life.

Expressive language   Language that emanates from the sender; speaking and writing.

Genre   Major categories within literature.

Holophrases   The one-word utterances used to communicate complete ideas, which are typical of toddlers.

Home-school continuity   The contention that school environments for young children should more closely approximate the environments of our most literate homes.

Illiteracy   The inability to read and write at a level deemed minimally acceptable by the dominant culture.

Integration   (of language arts) Generally refers to teaching practices that unify listening, speaking, reading, and writing, rather than fragment them into specified time periods during the day.

Interaction styles   Ways of communicating with others (e.g., assertive, nonassertive, aggressive).

Intonation   The use of pitch (high-low), stress (emphasis) and juncture (pauses) to enhance the communicative power of spoken language.

Invented Spelling   The child's application of whatever he or she knows about language to the task of spelling a word (e.g., "Wunsapana" for "Once upon a . . .").

Language acquisition   The process that children go through in learning to talk and master oral language.

Language arts   The use of reading, writing, speaking and listening for communication, self-expression, and enrichment of life.

Language experience approach (LEA)   A strategy that begins with a concrete experience, moves into discussion, then to a group story (written so that everyone can see the words), and, finally, to reading the group's story aloud.

Linguistic   The verbal aspects of human communication.

Linguistically different children   Children who have different language experiences from those of the "average" child, such as being bilingual or multilingual, having dialectical differences, being gifted or talented with language, or having limited English proficiency.

Linguistics   The study of language.

Literacy with print   Writing and reading abilities.

Manuscript writing   Printing by hand; using straight lines and circles or portions of circles.

Maturationist   In language acquisition, a theory that emphasizes the role of biological readiness for various developmental milestones and regards language development as a gradual unfolding determined by the child's "inner clock."

Metalinguistic   Using language to think about language; for example, a person analyzing and discussing his reading interests.

Multicultural   An educational philosophy, curriculum, and school policies that affirm cultural diversity and the inherent worth of every child.

Narratives   Event-structured material including accounts, recounts, event casts, and stories.

Norm-referenced test   A formal test in which each child's performance is compared to that of another group of children's performance on the same test. That group sets the "norms," hence the name norm-referenced.

Oracy   Listening and speaking abilities; oral language.

Overregularization   The tendency of young children to apply rules of language consistently, even to irregular words (e.g., foots, goed).

Paralinguistic   Nonverbal means of communication.

Phonological awareness   Knowledge of the sound-symbol correspondences in language.

Phonology   The sound system of the language.

Picture book   A specific type of literature for young children that relies on pictures as well as on words to tell the story.

Pragmatics   The social appropriateness of language in different social contexts.

Preformationist   A theory that attributes language growth to a mechanism in the brain called the Language Acquisition Device; from this theoretical perspective, the young child's language learning is innate.

Prelinguistic   The period in the child's development before actual words or language are spoken by the child.

Private speech   Talking aloud to one's self, typical of preschoolers.

Process-oriented   A philosophy that emphasizes "learning how to learn" rather than memorizing fragments of information (content-oriented).

Psychosocial   A theory of language acquisition that emphasizes both the child's role as a "meaning maker" and the social contexts that influence language development.

Receptive language   Language that is transmitted to the receiver; listening and reading.

Schema theory   A theory about the way people integrate new information into existing information in order to make sense out of their world.

Semantics   The meaning aspect of language.

Spontaneous drama   Forms of enactment that are informal and improvisational rather than formal and scripted.

Syntax   The structure and rules governing language grammar.

Telegraphic speech   The two- or three-word sentences typical of young preschoolers that omit everything but the most essential words (e.g., "Doggie bark.").

Test   A sample of behavior used to measure some educational or psychological attribute of a person.

Visual literacy   The ability to identify, comprehend, and use visual images and symbols.

Whole language   A philosophy about the language arts curriculum that educates the whole child, builds on what the child already knows, provides a total curriculum, and casts teachers in the role of decision-makers.

___ APPENDIX A ___

Chapter-by-Chapter Self-Assessment

Instructions: Complete the preassessment column for each chapter before reading it. Complete the postassessment after reading the chapter and/or use it as a study guide.

| | *Preassessment* | | | *Postassessment* | | |
| | *(Date _____)* | | | *(Date _____)* | | |

Chapter 1: Language Acquisition

I can:

	Yes	Unsure	No	Yes	Unsure	No
1. define the terms communication and language	____	____	____	____	____	____
2. explain prelinguistic, paralinguistic, and linguistic speech	____	____	____	____	____	____
3. describe the general sequence for language acquisition, infancy through age eight	____	____	____	____	____	____

4. define phonology, syntax, semantics, and pragmatics	Yes ___	Unsure ___	No ___	Yes ___	Unsure ___	No ___
5. list and describe influences on young children's language	Yes ___	Unsure ___	No ___	Yes ___	Unsure ___	No ___
6. identify major theories of language acquisition and discuss strengths and weaknesses of each	Yes ___	Unsure ___	No ___	Yes ___	Unsure ___	No ___
7. list the seven functions of language and design activities to foster functional communication in the classroom	Yes ___	Unsure ___	No ___	Yes ___	Unsure ___	No ___

Chapter 2: Oracy and Literacy

I can:

8. define oracy and literacy	Yes ___	Unsure ___	No ___	Yes ___	Unsure ___	No ___
9. explain the literacy process and the role of literacy events	Yes ___	Unsure ___	No ___	Yes ___	Unsure ___	No ___
10. define and discuss different types of literacy (visual, oral, print)	Yes ___	Unsure ___	No ___	Yes ___	Unsure ___	No ___
11. list and describe positive influences on young children's language learning	Yes ___	Unsure ___	No ___	Yes ___	Unsure ___	No ___

Chapter 3: The Child-Centered Language Arts Classroom

I can:

		Yes	Unsure	No	Yes	Unsure	No
12.	define the terms curriculum, whole language, and developmentally appropriate practice	Yes ____	Unsure ____	No ____	Yes ____	Unsure ____	No ____
13.	model semantically contingent conversation with children	Yes ____	Unsure ____	No ____	Yes ____	Unsure ____	No ____
14.	compare/contrast content and process-oriented curriculum; teacher-directed and child-initiated activity	Yes ____	Unsure ____	No ____	Yes ____	Unsure ____	No ____
15.	analyze a teaching environment in terms of DAP	Yes ____	Unsure ____	No ____	Yes ____	Unsure ____	No ____
16.	design a child-centered language learning environment for young children	Yes ____	Unsure ____	No ____	Yes ____	Unsure ____	No ____
17.	plan, present, and evaluate a language arts activity for children	Yes ____	Unsure ____	No ____	Yes ____	Unsure ____	No ____
18.	compare and contrast a classroom that is content-oriented to one that is a developmentally appropriate curriculum	Yes ____	Unsure ____	No ____	Yes ____	Unsure ____	No ____

19. cite the five criteria for authentic learning experiences

Yes	Unsure	No	Yes	Unsure	No

20. identify basic principles of classroom management

Yes	Unsure	No	Yes	Unsure	No

Chapter 4: Listening

I can:

21. define hearing, listening, and auding

Yes	Unsure	No	Yes	Unsure	No

22. describe the general developmental sequence for listening

Yes	Unsure	No	Yes	Unsure	No

23. identify variables that affect listening behavior

Yes	Unsure	No	Yes	Unsure	No

24. plan active listening activities for children

Yes	Unsure	No	Yes	Unsure	No

25. explain three things that affect young listeners in a listening situation

Yes	Unsure	No	Yes	Unsure	No

26. discuss eight practical ways to improve communication skills with students

Yes	Unsure	No	Yes	Unsure	No

Chapter 5: Speaking

I can:

27. define oral language and explain why speaking is the basis for the other language arts	Yes ___	Unsure ___	No ___	Yes ___	Unsure ___	No ___
28. give a developmental overview of the sequence of children's speech development	Yes ___	Unsure ___	No ___	Yes ___	Unsure ___	No ___
29. identify unique features of children's speech	Yes ___	Unsure ___	No ___	Yes ___	Unsure ___	No ___
30. understand mild to moderate speech delays and disorders and criteria for referral	Yes ___	Unsure ___	No ___	Yes ___	Unsure ___	No ___
31. plan developmentally appropriate speaking activities for children	Yes ___	Unsure ___	No ___	Yes ___	Unsure ___	No ___
32. summarize the major types of noncommunicative and communicative speech	Yes ___	Unsure ___	No ___	Yes ___	Unsure ___	No ___
33. know how to develop a positive talk environment and build children's communicative competence	Yes ___	Unsure ___	No ___	Yes ___	Unsure ___	No ___
34. demonstrate the use of the language experience approach	Yes ___	Unsure ___	No ___	Yes ___	Unsure ___	No ___

	Yes	Unsure	No	Yes	Unsure	No
35. know how to use creative dramatics						
36. understand the teacher's role in helping children who are linguistically different						
37. implement ways of using choral speaking in the classroom						
38. understand and appreciate the diversity of children's language backgrounds						

Chapter 6: Narratives

I can:

	Yes	Unsure	No	Yes	Unsure	No
39. define the word narrative and describe four categories of narratives						
40. explain the developmental sequence for children's narrative abilities						
41. list and explain the five traditional literary elements						
42. identify and use effective storytelling techniques						

43. demonstrate ways of telling stories effectively, with and without props	Yes ___	Unsure ___	No ___	Yes ___	Unsure ___	No ___
44. explain and plan an integrated storytelling session	Yes ___	Unsure ___	No ___	Yes ___	Unsure ___	No ___
45. model various extension activities to accompany stories	Yes ___	Unsure ___	No ___	Yes ___	Unsure ___	No ___
46. guide children in creating group stories	Yes ___	Unsure ___	No ___	Yes ___	Unsure ___	No ___

Chapter 7: Literature

I can:

47. define literature	Yes ___	Unsure ___	No ___	Yes ___	Unsure ___	No ___
48. select quality books for young children	Yes ___	Unsure ___	No ___	Yes ___	Unsure ___	No ___
49. list and describe literary genre for young children	Yes ___	Unsure ___	No ___	Yes ___	Unsure ___	No ___
50. model appropriate ways of presenting literature to children	Yes ___	Unsure ___	No ___	Yes ___	Unsure ___	No ___
51. give a research-based rationale for using children's literature in the classroom	Yes ___	Unsure ___	No ___	Yes ___	Unsure ___	No ___

52. organize a literature-based language arts program	Yes ____	Unsure ____	No ____	Yes ____	Unsure ____	No ____
53. design a successful story-sharing session using appropriate literature	Yes ____	Unsure ____	No ____	Yes ____	Unsure ____	No ____
54. understand the role that books play in early literacy and explain it to others	Yes ____	Unsure ____	No ____	Yes ____	Unsure ____	No ____

Chapter 8: Drawing and Writing

I can:

55. explain how children's drawing and writing processes are related	Yes ____	Unsure ____	No ____	Yes ____	Unsure ____	No ____
56. explain the progression from nonrepresentational to representational drawing	Yes ____	Unsure ____	No ____	Yes ____	Unsure ____	No ____
57. explain the progression from prealphabetic to alphabetic writing	Yes ____	Unsure ____	No ____	Yes ____	Unsure ____	No ____
58. plan developmentally appropriate drawing and writing activities for young children	Yes ____	Unsure ____	No ____	Yes ____	Unsure ____	No ____
59. explain the developmental stages in children's spelling	Yes ____	Unsure ____	No ____	Yes ____	Unsure ____	No ____

60. summarize recent research on children's writing	Yes ___	Unsure ___	No ___	Yes ___	Unsure ___	No ___
61. identify the strategies that support the young child's ability to use the written word	Yes ___	Unsure ___	No ___	Yes ___	Unsure ___	No ___
62. understand children's composing processes and can design developmentally appropriate activities	Yes ___	Unsure ___	No ___	Yes ___	Unsure ___	No ___

Chapter 9: Reading

I can:

63. define the terms reading, emergent reading, and early reading	Yes ___	Unsure ___	No ___	Yes ___	Unsure ___	No ___
64. describe reading abilities and the stages in emergent reading	Yes ___	Unsure ___	No ___	Yes ___	Unsure ___	No ___
65. explain the theories and approaches to initial reading instruction	Yes ___	Unsure ___	No ___	Yes ___	Unsure ___	No ___
66. plan and evaluate reading activities for young children	Yes ___	Unsure ___	No ___	Yes ___	Unsure ___	No ___
67. summarize the characteristics of a quality reading program	Yes ___	Unsure ___	No ___	Yes ___	Unsure ___	No ___

	Yes	Unsure	No	Yes	Unsure	No
68. understand and implement the shared-book experience	____	____	____	____	____	____
69. define schema, understand schema theory, and discuss the importance of prior knowledge in the reading process	____	____	____	____	____	____
70. formulate questions that promote students' thinking skills	____	____	____	____	____	____
71. understand the use of graphic organizers in reading	____	____	____	____	____	____
72. can identify characteristics of a good response activity	____	____	____	____	____	____

Chapter 10: Teachers and Parents

I can:

	Yes	Unsure	No	Yes	Unsure	No
73. describe the crucial role that parents play in children's language development	____	____	____	____	____	____
74. understand the importance of home-school continuity	____	____	____	____	____	____
75. explain and use basic strategies for parent involvement	____	____	____	____	____	____

	Yes	Unsure	No	Yes	Unsure	No
76. understand how teacher biases can affect communication and interaction with parents	___	___	___	___	___	___
77. demonstrate interaction skills that build effective communication with parents	___	___	___	___	___	___
78. identify deterrents to parent involvement	___	___	___	___	___	___
79. recommend ways in which parents and teachers can work together to exert a positive influence on a child's language development	___	___	___	___	___	___
80. organize activities that support and involve parents	___	___	___	___	___	___
81. identify and practice good conferencing skills	___	___	___	___	___	___

Chapter 11: Assessment

I can:

	Yes	Unsure	No	Yes	Unsure	No
82. define assessment, and identify basic assessment issues	___	___	___	___	___	___
83. list and explain the purposes of assessment	___	___	___	___	___	___

84. understand the reasons why formal assessment of young children is so difficult	Yes ____	Unsure ____	No ____	Yes ____	Unsure ____	No ____
85. know how to use children's play as the basis for informal language assessment	Yes ____	Unsure ____	No ____	Yes ____	Unsure ____	No ____
86. summarize the advantages and disadvantages of formal and informal assessment	Yes ____	Unsure ____	No ____	Yes ____	Unsure ____	No ____

Early Childhood Language Arts Computer Resources

Criteria for Evaluating Software

When selecting computer software for young children, ". . . teachers need to see it as a child might, anticipate problems, estimate attention span, and evaluate attractiveness and value to children" (Sallinger, 1988, p. 274). In making these decisions, consider the following (Janello, 1984):

1. Examine the information about the software to determine if it is compatible with the hardware you have available. Some software requires a color monitor or a joy stick, for example. It is essential that the software be consistent with the goals of your language arts program and suited to the developmental level of your students. Some of the "story generator" software, for instance, will not accept children's invented spelling. As a result, it may be of limited value in your language arts program.

2. Note the organization and structure of the program, paying particular attention to ease of use. The programs should be "open-ended tools—programs that allow for a great deal of choice and control on the part of children" (Olson and Buckleitner, 1990, p. 43). Avoid software that is simply a high-tech workbook with one correct answer to every question.

3. Consider issues such as the following (Janello, 1984):

> Will young children understand the language of the program?
>
> Do the graphics and sound really add to the program?
>
> How does the program give feedback to the user?
>
> How does it deal with errors?
>
> What happens if the child has to stop in the middle of the program?

Does it keep track of the student's work?

Does the program have the potential to maintain children's interest over a period of time?

4. Preview the program at a store, the public library, or at a conference. Go through the program yourself, making deliberate errors, and see how the software handles these problems. If possible, try the software with children of different ability levels.

Recommended Software

Bank Street Writer. Scholastic, ages 5–8.

Color Me. Mindscape, 1986, ages 3–10.

Curious George in Outer Space. DLM Teaching Resources, 1988, ages 5–8.

Explore a Classic. William K. Bradford, 1989, ages 5 and up.

Explore a Story. D. C. Heath, 1988, ages 5–10.

KidSpeak. Apple/Macintosh.

KidsTime "Story Writer." Great Wave Software, 1987, ages 3–8.

Magic Slate. Sunburst, ages 5–8.

Muppet Slate Sunburst, 1988, ages 5–7.

The New Talking Stickybear Alphabet. Weekly Reader, 1989, ages 3–6.

Storytree. Scholastic, ages K–6.

SuperPrint. Scholastic, ages K–12.

Talking Text Writer. Scholastic, ages K–6.

Write to Read. International Business Machines (IBM), ages 5–8.

References and Resources

American Library Association (1988, December). Software's greatest hits. *Booklist*, December 1, p. 809.

Auten, A. (1984). How to find good computer software in English and language arts. ERIC Digest #400-83-0025 Urbana, IL: ERIC/Reading Communication Skills.

Balajthy, E. (1988). Can computers be used for whole language approaches to reading and language arts? ERIC Document Reproduction Service No. ED 300 766.

Buckleitner, W. (1988). *The 1988 survey of early childhood software*. Ypsilanti, MI: High/Scope.

Casella, V. (1988). Computers-in-the-curriculum workshop: It's never too soon to start kindergartners writing with computers. *Instructor*, *98*(3), 103.

Editors of *Classroom-Computer-Learning*. (1988). The 1989–90 Computer Learning Software Awards. *Classroom-Computer-Learning*, *10*(3), 14–15, 18, 21–23, 26–31, 34–35.

Field, C. E. (1987). Early learning software. *InCider*. *5*(9), 56–59.

International Reading Association Committee on Technology and Reading (1984). *Guidelines for Educators*. Newark, DE: International Reading Association.

Janello, P. (1984). *Software evaluation for the teacher of the English language arts*. Urbana, IL: ERIC Clearinghouse on Reading and Communication Skills.

Neill, S. B., and Neill, G. W. (1989). *Only the best: The discriminating software guide for preschool—grade 12*. Sacramento, CA: Education News Service.

Olson, K., and Buckleitner, W. (1990). Kids at the keyboard: Software to support development, discovery, and delight. *Child Care Information Exchange, 71*, 43–46.

Salinger, T. S. (1988). *Language arts and literacy for young children*. Columbus, OH: Merrill.

Sources for Software Reviews

Booklist

Childhood Education

Computers, Reading and Language Arts

Courseware Report Card

Teaching and Computers

APPENDIX C

Poetry Collections for Young Children

Adoff, A. (1988). *Greens*. New York: Lothrop.

Aldis, D. (1952). *All together*. New York: Putnam.

Behn, H. (1984). *Crickets and bullfrogs and whispers of thunder*. San Diego, CA: Harcourt Brace Jovanovich.

Bennett, J. (1981). *Tiny Tim*. New York: Delacorte.

Brown, M. (1987). *Play rhymes*. New York: Dutton.

Brown, M. (1985). *Hand rhymes*. New York: Dutton.

Ciardi, J. (1990). *Mummy took cooking lessons*. Boston: Houghton Mifflin, 1990.

Corrin, S., and Corrin, S. (1982). *Once upon a rhyme: 101 poems for young children*. Faber & Faber.

Delacre, L. (1990). *Arroz con leche: Popular songs and rhymes from Latin America*. New York: Macmillan.

Demi (1986). *Dragon kites and dragonflies*. San Diego, CA: Harcourt Brace Jovanovich.

deRegniers, B. S.; Moore, E.; White, M. M.; and Carr, J. (Eds.). (1988). *Sing a song of popcorn: Every child's book of poems*. New York: Scholastic.

Feelings, T., and Greenfield, E. (1981). *Daydreamers*. New York: Dial.

Fisher, A. (1986). *When it comes to bugs*. New York: Harper & Row.

Fisher, A. (1983). *Rabbits, rabbits*. New York: Harper & Row.

Fleischman, P. (1989). *Joyful noise: Poems for two voices*. New York: Harper/Zolotow.

Greenfield, E. (1988). *Under the Sunday tree*. New York: Harper & Row.

Greenfield, E. (1979). *Honey I love*. New York: Crowell.

Hayes, S. (1988). *Clap your hands: Finger rhymes*. New York: Lothrop, Lee & Shepard.

Hoberman, M. A. (1981). *Breakfast books & dreams: A day in verse*. New York: Frederick Warne.

Hopkins, L. B. (1988). *Side by side: Poems to read together*. New York: Simon & Schuster.

Hopkins, L. B. (1987). *Dinosaurs: Poems selected by Lee Bennett Hopkins*. San Diego, CA: Harcourt Brace Jovanovich.

Hopkins, L. B. (1986). *Best friends*. New York: Harper & Row.

Hopkins, L. B. (1984). *Surprises*. New York: Harper.

Hubbell, P. (1988). *The tigers brought pink lemonade*. New York: Atheneum.

Hughes, S. (1988). *Out and About*. New York: Lothrop, Lee & Shepard.

Knight, J. (1989) *Tickle-toe-rhymes*. New York: Franklin Watts/Orchard.

Larrick, N. (1988). *Cats are cats*. New York: Putnam/Philomel.

Larrick, N. (1983). *When the dark comes dancing: A bedtime poetry book*. New York: Putnam/Philomel.

Livingston, M. C. (1985). *Celebrations*. New York: Holiday House.

Livingston, M. C. (1984). *Sky songs*. New York: Holiday House.

Merriam, E. (1989). *You be good & I'll be night: Jump-on-the-bed poems*. New York: Morrow.

Merriam, E. (1985). *Blackberry ink*. New York: Atheneum.

Merriam, E. (1966). *There is no rhyme for silver*. New York: Atheneum.

Opie, P., and Opie, I. (1988). *Tail feathers from Mother Goose*. Boston, MA: Little, Brown.

Prelutsky, J. (1990). *Something big has been here*. New York: Greenwillow.

Prelutsky, J. (1988). *Tyrannosaurus was a beast*. New York: Greenwillow.

Prelutsky, J. (1986). *Read-aloud rhymes for the very young*. New York: Knopf.

Prelutsky, J. (1986). *Ride a purple pelican*. New York: Greenwillow.

Prelutsky, J. (1984). *The new kid on the block*. New York: Greenwillow.

Ryder, J. (1985). *Inside turtle's shell and other poems of the field*. New York: Macmillan.

Tripp, W. (1985). *Marguerite, go wash your feet*. Boston: Houghton Mifflin.

Watson, C. (1978). *Catch me and kiss me and say it again*. New York: Putnam/Philomel.

APPENDIX D
Storytime Selections*

Aardema, V. (1990). *Rabbit makes a monkey of lion*. New York: Dial.
Aardema, V. (1981). *Bringing the rain to kapiti plain*. New York: Dial.
Aardema, V. (1977). *Who's in rabbit's house?* New York: Dial.
Ackerman, K. (1989). *Song and dance man*. New York: Knopf.
Aesop (1987). Adapted by Janet Stevens. *The town mouse and the country mouse*. New York: Holiday House.
Ahlberg, J., and Ahlberg, A. (1990). *Bye bye baby: A sad story with a happy ending*. Boston, MA: Little, Brown.
Allen, P. (1983). *Who sank the boat?* New York: Coward McCann.
Aliki. (1987). *Welcome, little baby*. New York: Greenwillow.
Allard, H., and Marshall, J. (1977). *Miss Nelson is missing!* New York: Scholastic.
Ambercrombie, B. (1990). *Charlie Anderson*. New York: McElderry.
Anderson, P. (1987). *"Time for bed," the babysitter said*. Boston: Houghton Mifflin.
Arnosky, J. (1987). *Raccoons and ripe corn*. New York: Lothrop, Lee & Shepard.
Aruego, J., and Dewey, A. (1979). *We hide you seek*. New York: Greenwillow.
Aruego, J. (1972). *A crocodile's tale. Un cuento de cocodrilo*. New York: Scholastic.
Asch, F. (1986). *Goodbye house*. Englewood Cliffs, NJ: Prentice-Hall.
Aylesworth, J. (1987). *Two terrible frights*. New York: Atheneum.
Babbitt, N. (1990). *Nellie: A cat on her own*. New York: Farrar, Straus & Giroux.
Baer, F. (1990). *This is the way we go to school: A book about children around the world*. New York: Scholastic.
Baker, A. (1986). *Benjamin's portrait*. New York: Lothrop, Lee & Shepard.
Baker, K. (1988). *The dove's letter*. San Diego, CA: Harcourt Brace Jovanovich.
Bang, M. (1983). *Ten, nine, eight*. New York: Greenwillow.
Barton, B. (1986). *Airplanes/boats/trains/trucks*. New York: Crowell.
Berger, B. (1986). *When the sun rose*. New York: Philomel.
Blegvad, E. (1980). *The three little pigs*. New York: Atheneum.
Borstein, R. (1976). *Little gorilla*. New York: Seabury.
Brandenberg, F. (1989). *Aunt Nina, good night*. New York: Greenwillow.
Brandenburg, R. (1983). *Aunt Nina and her nephews and nieces*. New York: Greenwillow.
Breslow, S., and Blakemore, S. (1990). *I really want a dog*. New York: Dutton.
Brett, J. (1989). *Beauty and the beast*. New York: Clarion.
Brett, J. (1989). *The mitten*. New York: Putnam.
Brett, J. (1988). *Goldilocks and the three bears*. New York: Dodd, Mead.
Bridwell, N. (1972). *Clifford, the small red puppy*. New York: Scholastic.
Brinckloe, J. (1985). *Fireflies* New York: Macmillan.

---

*Compiled by Melissa Ann Renck, Children's Services Specialist, Toledo-Lucas County Libraries, and Mary Renck Jalongo.

Brown, M. (1983). *Arthur's Halloween*. Boston: Little Brown.

Brown, M. (1957). *The three billy goats gruff*. New York: Harcourt Brace Jovanovich.

Brown, M. (1947). *Stone soup*. New York: Scribners.

Brown, M. W. (1972). *The runaway bunny*. New York: Harper.

Brown, M. W. (1947). *Goodnight moon*. New York: Harper & Row.

Brown, R. (1981). *A dark, dark tale*. New York: Dial.

Browne, A. (1983). *Gorilla*. New York: Knopf.

Bunting, E. (1986). *The mother's day mice*. New York: Clarion.

Burningham, J. (1976). *Where's Julius?* New York: Crown.

Burton, M. R. (1989). *Tail toes eyes ears nose*. New York: Harper & Row.

Calhoun, M. (1981). *Hot-air Henry*. New York: Morrow.

Carle, E. (1990). *The very quiet cricket*. New York: Putnam.

Carle, E. (1977). *The grouchy ladybug*. New York: Scholastic.

Carle, E. (1969). *The very hungry caterpillar*. Cleveland, OH: Collins-World.

Carlson, N. (1987). *Bunnies and their sports*. New York: Viking.

Carlstrom, N. W. (1986). *Jesse bear, what will you wear?* New York: Macmillan.

Carrick, C. (1990). *Aladdin and the wonderful lamp*. New York: Scholastic.

Caseley, J. (1987). *Applie pie and onions*. New York: Greenwillow.

Cauley, L. B. (1986). *Puss in boots*. San Diego, CA: Harcourt Brace Jovanovich.

Cauley, L. B. (1981). *Goldilocks and the three bears*. New York: Putnam.

Causey, J. (1970). *QUACK! said the billy goat*. New York: Holt, Rinehart and Winston.

Charlip, R. (1987). *Handtalk birthday*. Bristol, FL: Four Winds.

Chorao, K. (1982). *Kate's snowman*. New York: Dutton.

Christian, M. B. (1983). *Swamp monsters*. New York: Dial.

Cohen, B. (1983). *Molly's pilgrim*. New York: Lothrop, Lee & Shepard.

Cole, J. (1983). *Bony-legs*. New York: Four Winds.

Coleridge, S. (1987). *January brings the snow*. New York: Dial.

Conrad, P. (1989). *The tub people*. New York: Harper.

Cook, B. (1956). *The little fish that got away*. New York: Scholastic.

Cooney, B. (1982). *Miss Rumphius*. New York: Viking.

Cox, D. (1985). *Bossyboots*. New York: Crown.

Craft, R. (1989). *The winter bear*. New York: Aladdin Books.

Crews, D. (1986). *Flying*. New York: Greenwillow.

Dabcovich, L. (1991). *Ducks fly*. New York: Dutton.

De Brunhoff, L. (1933). *The story of Babar*. New York: Scholastic.

DeHamel, J. (1985). *Hemi's pet*. Boston: Houghton Mifflin.

Delacre, L. (1990). *Las navidades*. New York: Macmillan.

Delacre, L. (198). *Arroz con leche: Popular songs and rhymes from Latin America*. New York: Macmillan.

Demi. (1980). *Liang's magic paintbrush*. New York: Holt, Rinehart and Winston.

de Paola, T. (1987). *An Early American Christmas*. New York: Holiday House.

de Paola, T. (1986). *Merry Christmas, Strega Nona*. San Diego, CA: Harcourt Brace Jovanovich.

de Paola, T. (1983). *The legend of the bluebonnet*. New York: Putnam.

de Paola, T. (1979). *Big Anthony and the magic ring*. San Diego, CA: Harcourt Brace Jovanovich.

de Paola, T. (1975). *Strega Nona*. Englewood Cliffs, NJ: Prentice-Hall.

de Regniers, B. S.; Moore, E.; White, M. M.; and Carr, J. (Eds.). (1988). *Sing a song of popcorn: Every child's book of poems*. New York: Scholastic.

de Regniers, B. S. (1978). *Waiting for mama*. New York: Clarion.

de Regniers, B. S. (1964). *May I bring a friend?* New York: Atheneum.

Diamond, D. (1980). *Swan lake*. New York: Holiday.

Domanska, J. (1973). *The little red hen*. New York: Macmillan.

Douglass, B. (1972). *Good as new*. New York: Lothrop, Lee & Shepard.

Dunrea, O. (1989). *Deep down underground*. New York: Macmillan.

Edwards, P. K. (1987). *Chester and Uncle Willoughby*. Boston: Little, Brown.

Ehlert, L. (1990). *Feathers for lunch*. New York: Harper/Lippincott.

Ehlert, L. (1987). *Growing vegetable soup*. San Diego, CA: Harcourt Brace Jovanovich.

Emberley, B. (1967). *Drummer Hoff*. Englewood Cliffs, NJ: Prentice-Hall.

Ernst, L. (1987). *The rescue of Aunt Pansy*. New York: Viking.

Everitt, B. (1990). *Frida the wonder cat*. San Diego, CA: Harcourt Brace Jovanovich.

Flack, M. (1931). *Angus and the cat*. New York: Doubleday.

Flournoy, V. (1985). *The patchwork quilt*. New York: Dial.

Fox, M. (1989). *Night noises*. San Diego, CA: Harcourt Brace Jovanovich.

Fox, M. (1987). *Hattie and the fox*. New York: Bradbury.

Fox, M. (1984). *Wilfrid Gordon MacDonald Partridge*. New York: Kane Miller.

Freeman, D. (1976). *A Pocket for Corduroy*. New York: Viking.

Freeman, D. (1968). *Corduroy*. New York: Viking.

Freeman, S. (1986). *Devin's new bed*. Niles, IL: Whitman.

Friedman, I. R. (1984). *How my parents learned to eat*. Boston: Houghton Mifflin.

Gackenbach, D. (1981). *A bag full of pups*. New York: Clarion.

Gackenbach, D. (1977). *Harry and the terrible whatzit*. Boston: Houghton Mifflin.

Gackenbach, D. (1974). *Claude the dog: A Christmas story*. New York: Scholastic.

Galbraith, K. O. (1990). *Laura Charlotte*. New York: Putnam/Philomel.

Galdone, P. (1975). *The gingerbread boy*. New York: Seabury.

Galdone, P. (1973). *The little red hen*. New York: Scholastic.

Galdone, P. (1973). *The three bears*. New York: Scholastic.

Galdone, P. (1968). *Henny Penny*. New York: Seabury.

Gantos, J. (1979). *Greedy greeny*. New York: Doubleday.

Garland, M. (1989). *My cousin Katie*. New York: Harper/Crowell.

Gauch, P. (1988). *Christmas Katerina and the time she quit the family*. New York: Putnam.

George, W. T. (1989). *Box turtle at long pond*. New York: Greenwillow.

Ginsburg, M. (1987). *Four brave sailors*. New York: Greenwillow.

Ginsburg, M. (1982). *Across the steam*. New York: Greenwillow.

Goble, P. (1980). *The gift of the sacred dog*. New York: Bradbury.

Goffstein, M. B. (1986). *Our snowman*. New York: Holt, Rinehart and Winston.

Golenbock, P. (1990). *Teammates*. San Diego: Harcourt Brace Jovanovich.

Gomi, T. (1979). *Coco can't wait*. New York: Puffin.

Goodspeed, P. (1982). *A rhinoceros wakes me up in the morning*. New York: Bradbury.

Greenfield, E. (1988). *Under the Sunday tree*. New York: Harper.

Greenfield, E. (1979). *Honey I love*. New York: Crowell.

Gretz, S. (1975). *It's your turn, Roger*. New York: Dial.

Grifalconi, A. (1987). *Darkness and the butterfly*. Boston, MA: Little, Brown.

Haas, I. (1979). *The Maggie B*. New York: Macmillan.

Hale, S. J. (1990). *Mary had a little lamb*. New York: Macmillan. Photo-illustrations by B. McMillan.

Hale, S. J. (1984). *Mary had a little lamb*. New York: Holiday. Illustrated by T. de Paola.

Hall, D. (1979). *Ox-cart man*. New York: Penguin/Viking.

Hawkins, C. (1988). *I know an old lady who swallowed a fly*. New York: Holt, Rinehart and Winston.

Hawkins, C., and Hawkins, J. (1983). *Boo! Who?* New York: Holt, Rinehart and Winston.

Hayes, S. (1986). *Happy Christmas, Gemma*. New York: Greenwillow.

Hazen, B. S. (1979). *Tight times*. New York: Penguin.

Heine, H. (1982). *Friends*. New York: Atheneum.

Helprin, M. (1989). *Swan lake*. New York: Houghton Mifflin.

Henkes, K. (1990). *Julius, the baby of the world*. New York: Greenwillow.

Henkes, K. (1987). *Sheila Rae, the brave*. New York: Greenwillow.

Henkes, K. (1986). *A weekend with Wendell*. New York: Greenwillow.

Henkes, K. (1985). *Bailey goes camping*. New York: Greenwillow.

Hennessy, B. G. (1989). *The missing tarts*. New York: Viking.

Hest, A. (1984). *The crack-of-dawn walkers*. New York: Macmillan.

Hill, E. (1980). *Where's Spot?* New York: Putnam.

Hines, A. G. (1986). *Daddy makes the best spaghetti*. New York: Clarion.

Hoban, T. (1987). *26 letters and 99 cents*. New York: Greenwillow.

Hoban, T. (1985). *A children's zoo*. New York: Morrow.

Hoban, T. (1978). *Is it red? is it yellow? is it blue?* New York: Random House.

Hoberman, M. A. (1981). *Breakfast books & dreams: A day in verse*. New York: Frederick Warne.

Hoberman, M. A. (1978). *A house is a house for me*. New York: Viking.

Hoffman, E.T.A. (1984). *The nutcracker*. New York: Crown. (originally published in 1820)

Hogrogian, N. (1988). *The cat who loved to sing*. New York: Knopf.

Hogrogian, N. (1971). *One fine day*. New York: Macmillan.

Hooks, W. H. (1989). *The three little pigs and the fox*. New York: Macmillan.

Hooper, M. (1985). *Seven eggs*. New York: Harper & Row.

Howard, E. T. (1989). *Chita's Christmas tree*. New York: Bradbury.

Howe, J. (1984). *The day the teacher went bananas*. New York: Dutton.

Howell, T. (1990). *The ugly duckling*. New York: Putnam.

Hughes, S. (1981). *David and dog*. New York: Lothrop.

Hurd, E. T. (1982). *I dance in my red pajamas*. New York: Harper.

Hurlman, R. (1977). *The proud white cat*. New York: Morrow.

Hutchins, P. (1986). *The doorbell rang*. New York: Greenwillow.

Hutchins, P. (1985). *The very worst monster*. New York: Greenwillow.

Hutchins, P. (1983). *You'll soon grow into them, Titch*. New York: Penguin/Puffin.

Hutchins, P. (1968). *Rosie's walk*. New York: Macmillan.

Hyman, T. S., reteller. (1983). *Little Red Riding Hood*. New York: Holiday House.

Jesche, S. (1987). *Lucky's choice*. New York: Scholastic.

Johnson, C. (1958). *Harold and the purple crayon*. New York: Harper & Row.

Johnston, T. (1985). *The quilt story*. New York: Putnam.

Jonas, A. (1989). *Color dance*. New York: Greenwillow.

Jonas, A. (1989). *The quilt*. New York: Greenwillow.

Jonas, A. (1986). *Where can it be?* New York: Greenwillow.

Jorgensen, G. (1989). *Crocodile beat*. New York: Bradbury.

Joslin, S. (1958). *What do you say, dear?* New York: Scholastic.

Kamen, G. (1989). *"Paddle," said the swan*. New York: Atheneum.

Kasza, K. (1990). *When the elephant walks*. New York: Putnam.

Kasza, K. (1987). *The wolf's chicken stew*. New York: Putnam.

Keats, E. J. (1975). *Louie*. New York: Greenwillow.

Keats, E. J. (1971). *Over in the meadow*. New York: Scholastic.

Keats, E. J. (1971). *The snowy day*. New York: Scholastic.

Keats, E. J. (1966). *Jenny's hat*. New York: Harper & Row.

Keats, E. J. (1964). *Whistle for Willie*. New York: Viking.

Keller, H. (1988). *Geraldine's big snow*. New York: Greenwillow.

Keller, H. (1986). *A bear for Christmas*. New York: Greenwillow.

Keller, H. (1984). *Geraldine's blanket*. New York: Greenwillow.

Kellogg, S. (1986). *Best friends*. New York: Dial.

Kellogg, S. (1979). *Pinkerton, behave!* New York: Dial.

Kellogg, S. (1976). *Much bigger than Martin*. New York: Dial.

Kent, J. (1985). *Joey runs away*. Englewood Cliffs, NJ: Prentice-Hall.

Kent, J. (1972). *The fat cat*. New York: Scholastic.

Kitamura, S. (1987). *When sheep cannot sleep: The counting book*. New York: Farrar, Straus & Giroux.

Knutson, B. (1990). *How the guinea fowl got her spots*. New York: Carolrhoda.

Koontz, R. (1988). *This old man*. New York: Putnam.

Kramer, A. (1987). *Numbers on parade*. New York: Lothrop, Lee & Shepard.

Kraus, R. (1987). *Come out and play, little mouse*. New York: Greenwillow.

Kraus, R. (1984). *The carrot seed*. New York: Scholastic.

Kraus, R. (1970). *Whose mouse are you?* New York: Scholastic.

Kitchen, B. (1984). *Animal alphabet*. New York: Dial.

Kroll, S. (1988). *Happy father's day*. New York: Holiday House.

Kroll, S. (1984). *The biggest pumpkin ever*. New York: Holiday House.

Kroll, S. (1982). *One tough turkey*. New York: Holiday House.

Kudrna, I. (1986). *To bathe a boa*. Minneapolis, MN: Carolrhoda.

Kundhardt, D. (1962). *Pat the bunny*. New York: Golden. originally published in 1940.

Lamorisse, A. (1956). *The red balloon*. New York: Doubleday.

Latimer, J. (1989). *Going the moose way home*. New York: Scribner/Macmillan.

Laurin, A. (1981). *Perfect crane*. New York: Harper & Row.

Leaf, M. (1936). *The story of Ferdinand*. New York: Viking.

Lester, J. (reteller) (1990). *How many spots does a leopard have?* New York: Scholastic.

Levine, E. (1990). *I hate English!* New York: Scholastic.

Levinson, R. (1985). *Watch the stars come out*. New York: Dutton.

Lindbergh, R. (1990). *The day the goose got loose*. New York: Dial.

Lindbergh, R. (1990). *Benjamin's barn*. New York: Dial.

Lionni, L. (1987). *Nicolas, where have you been?* New York: Knopf.

Lionni, L. (1985). *Frederick's fables: A Lionni treasury of favorite stories*. New York: Random House.

Littledale, F., reteller (1980). *Snow white and the seven dwarfs*. New York: Scholastic.

Lobel, A. (1984). *The rose in my garden*. New York: Greenwillow.

Lobel, A. (1980). *Fables*. New York: Harper & Row.

Lobel, A. (1970–1979). "Frog and Toad Series." *Days with Frog and Toad* (1979); *Frog and Toad all year* (1976); *Frog and Toad together* (1972); *Frog and toad are friends* (1970). New York: Harper & Row.

Lobel, A. (1964). *Giant John*. New York: Harper & Row.

Luenn, N. (1990). *Nessa's fish*. New York: Atheneum.

Lyon, G. E. (1990). *Come a tide*. New York: Watts.

MacDonald, S. (1986). *Alphabetics*. New York: Bradbury.

Machotka, M. (1990). *What do you do at a petting zoo?* New York: Morrow.

Maestro, B. (1990). *Snow day*. New York: Scholastic.

Maestro, B. (1975). *A wise monkey tale*. New York: Crown.

Mahy, M. (1987). *17 kings and 42 elephants*. New York: Dial.

Marshall, E. (1981). *Three by the sea*. New York: Dial.

Marshall, E. (1980). *Space case*. New York: Dial. York: Viking.

Marshall, J. (1989). *The three little pigs*. New York: Dial.

Marshall, J. (1988). *Goldilocks and the three bears*. New York: Dial.

Marshall, J. (1987). *Red Riding Hood*. New York: Dial.

Marshall, J. (1986). *Wings: A tale of two chickens*. New York: Dial.

Marshall, J. (1984). *The cut-ups*. New York: Penguin/Puffin.

Martin, B. (1967). *Brown bear, brown bear, What do you see?* New York: Holt, Rinehart and Winston.

Martin, B., and Archambault, J. (1989). *Chicka chicka boom boom*. New York: Simon and Schuster.

Martin, B., and Archambault, J. (1987). *Knots on a counting rope*. New York: Holt.

Martin, B., and Archambault, J. (1986). *Barn dance!* New York: Holt.

Marzollo, J. (1990). *Pretend you're a cat*. New York: Dial.

Matthews, D. (1989). *Polar bear cubs*. New York: Simon and Schuster.

Matthews, L. (1978). *Bunches and bunches of bunnies*. New York: Scholastic.

Maxner, J. (1989). *Nicholas cricket*. New York: Harper Row.

Mayer, M. (1987). *There's a nightmare under my bed*. New York: Dial.

Mayer, M. (1978). *Beauty and the beast*. New York: Four Winds.

Mayer, M. (1976). *There's a nightmare in my closet*. New York: Dial.

McCarthy, B. (1988). *Buffalo girls*. New York: Crown.

McCloskey, R. (1941). *Make way for ducklings*. New York: Viking.

McDermott, G. (1990). *Tim O'Toole and the wee folk*. New York: Viking.

McDonald, M. (1990). *Is this a house for a hermit crab?* New York: Watts/Orchard.

McGovern, A. (1967). *Too much noise*. New York: Scholastic.

McKissack, P. C. (1989). *Nettie Jo's friends*. New York: Knopf.

McKissack, P. C. (1988). *Mirandy and brother wind*. New York: Trumpet.

McMillan, B. (1989). *Super super superwords*. New York: Lothrop, Lee & Shepard.

McMillan, B. (1987). *Step by step*. New York: Lothrop, Lee & Shepard.

McPhail, D. (1984). *Fix-it*. New York: Dutton.

McPhail, D. (1980). *Pig pig grows up*. New York: Dutton.

Mendez, P. (1990). *The black snowman*. New York: Scholastic.

Merriam, E. (1987). *Halloween ABC*. New York: Macmillan.

Miller, E. (1964). *Mousekin's golden house*. Englewood Cliffs, NJ: Prentice-Hall.

Murphy, J. (1980). *Peace at last*. New York: Dial.

Musgrove, M. (1976). *Ashanti to zulu: African traditions*. New York: Dial.

Noble, T. H. (1989). *Jimmy's boa and the big splash birthday bash*. New York: Dial.

Noble, T. H. (1987). *Meanwhile, back at the ranch*. New York: Dial.

Noble, T. H. (1980). *The day Jimmy's boa ate the wash*. New York: Dial.

Nodset, J. L. (1963). *Who took the farmer's hat?* New York: Harper & Row.

Noll, S. (1990). *Watch where you go*. New York: Greenwillow.

Novak, M. (1987). *Claude and sun*. New York: Bradbury.

Oppenheim, J. (1986). *Have you seen birds?* New York: Scholastic.

Packlam, M. (1989). *Do not disturb*. Boston: Little, Brown.

Paterson, K. (1990). *The tale of the mandarin ducks*. New York: Dutton.

Patterson, F. (1987). *Koko's story*. New York: Scholastic.

Patterson, F. (1985). *Koko's kitten*. New York: Scholastic.

Paxton, T. (1990). *Belling the cat and other Aesop's fables*. New York: Morrow.

Paxton, T. (1990). *Englebert the elephant*. New York: Morrow.

Pearson, S. (1987). *Happy birthday, Grampie*. New York: Viking.

Pearson, T. C. (1983). *We wish you a Merry Christmas*. New York: Dial.

Peek, M. (1981). *Roll over!* New York: Clarion.

Perrault, C. (1990). *Puss in Boots*. New York: Farrar, Straus, and Giroux.

Petersham, M. (1950). *The circus baby*. New York: Macmillan.

Phillips, J. (1986). *My new boy*. New York: Random House.

Piper, W. (1945). *The little engine that could*. New York: Platt & Munk. (originally published in 1930)

Plath, S. (1976). *The bed book*. New York: Harper & Row.

Plume, I. (1980). *The Bremen town musicians*. New York: Harper.

Polacco, P. (1990). *Babushka's doll*. New York: Putnam.

Polacco, P. (1990). *Thunder cake*. New York: Putnam/Philomel.

Polushkin, M. (1978). *Mother, mother, I want another*. New York: Crown.

Pomerantz, C. (1989). *The chalk doll*. New York: Lippincott.

Prelutsky, J. (compiler). (1986). *Read-aloud rhymes for the very young*. New York: Knopf.

Prelutsky, J. (compiler). (1986). *Ride a purple pelican*. New York: Greenwillow.

Preston, E. M. (1974). *Squawk to the moon, little goose*. New York: Viking.

Raffi (1990). *Baby beluga*. New York: Crown.
Raffi (1990). *Wheels on the bus*. New York: Crown.
Raffi (1989). *Five little ducks*. New York: Crown.
Raffi (1989). *Tingalayo*. New York: Crown.
Raffi (1987). *Down by the bay*. New York: Crown.
Rayner, M. (1981). *Mrs. Pig's bulk buy*. New York: Atheneum.
Rice, E. (1981). *Benny bakes a cake*. New York: Greenwillow.
Rice, E. (1977). *Sam, who never forgets*. New York: Greenwillow.
Rice, E. (1975). *New blue shoes*. New York: Scholastic.
Richardson, J. (1986). *Clara's dancing feet*. New York: Putnam.
Robinson, D. (1981). *No elephants allowed*. Boston, MA: Houghton Mifflin.
Rosen, M. (1989). *We're going on a bear hunt*. New York: McElderry/Macmillan.
Rothman, J., and Palacios, A. (1979). *This can lick a lollipop: body riddles for kids/ Esto goza chupando un caramelo: Las partes del cuerpo en adivinanzas infantiles*. New York: Doubleday.
Russo, M. (1989). *Waiting for Hannah*. New York: Greenwillow.
Ryder, J. (1987). *Chipmunk's song*. New York: Dutton.
Rylant, C. (1989). *Mr. Grigg's work*. New York: Watts/Orchard.
Rylant, C. (1986). *Night in the country*. New York: Bradbury.
Rylant, C. (1985). *The relatives came*. New York: Bradbury.
San Souci, R. D. (1989). *The talking eggs: A folktale from the American South*. New York: Dial.
Schmidt, J. (1985). *The gingerbread man*. New York: Scholastic.
Schotler, R. (1989). *Captain Snap and the children of vinegar lane*. New York: Watts/Orchard.
Schwartz, A. (1987). *Oma and Bobo*. New York: Bradbury.
Schwartz, A. (1983). *Bea and Mr. Jones*. New York: Puffin.
Schwartz, A. (1983). *Begin at the beginning*. New York: Harper & Row.
Schwartz, H. (1989). *How I captured a dinosaur*. New York: Watts/Orchard.
Scieszka, J. (1989). *The true story of the 3 little pigs! by A. Wolf*. New York: Viking/Kestrel.
Scott, A. H. (1972). *On mother's lap*. New York: McGraw-Hill.
Sendak, M. (1963). *Where the wild things are*. New York: Harper.
Serfozo, M. (1989). *Who wants one?* New York: McElderry: Macmillan.
Serfozo, M. (1988). *Who said red?* New York: McElderry/Macmillan.
Seuss, Dr. (1990). *Oh, the places you'll go*. New York: Random House.
Seuss, Dr. (1957). *The cat in the hat*. New York: Random.
Seuss, Dr. (1954). *Horton hears a who*. New York: Random House.
Shaw, N. (1986). *Sheep in a jeep*. Boston: Houghton Mifflin.
Shaw, C. (1947). *It looked like split milk*. New York: Harper & Row.
Shott, S. (1990). *Baby's world: A first picture catalog*. New York: Dutton.
Siebert, D. (1990). *Train song*. New York: Crowell.
Siebert, D. (1989). *Heartland*. New York: Crowell.
Singer, M. (1989). *Turtle in July*. New York: Macmillan.
Slepian, J., and Seidler, A. (1990). *The hungry thing returns*. New York: Scholastic.
Slobodkina, E. (1947). *Caps for sale*. New York: Scott.
Snyder, D. (1988). *The boy of the three year nap*. Boston, MA: Houghton Mifflin.
Soya, K. (1987). *A house of leaves*. New York: Putnam.
Spier, P. (1988). *Fast-slow High-low*. New York: Doubleday.
Spier, P. (1982). *Peter Spier's rain*. New York: Doubleday.
Spier, P. (1961). *The fox went out on a chilly night*. New York: Doubleday.
Spohn, K. (1989). *Clementine's winter wardrobe*. New York: Watts/Orchard/Jackson.
Stanley, D. (1990). *Fortune*. New York: Morrow.
Stanley, D. (1986). *The good luck pencil*. New York: Macmillan.
Steig, W. (1969). *Sylvester and the magic pebble*. New York: Windmill.
Stevens, J. (1990). *How the manx cat lost its tail*. San Diego, CA: Harcourt Brace Jovanovich.

Stevens, J. (1987). *The three billy goats gruff*. San Diego: Harcourt Brace Jovanovich.

Stevens, J. (1986). *The three bears*. New York: Holiday.

Stevens, J. (1984). *The tortoise and the hare*. New York: Scholastic.

Stevenson, S. (1987). *Do I have to take Violet?* New York: Dodd Mead.

Stock, C. (1989). *Alexander's midnight snack: A little elephant's ABC*. New York: Clarion.

Stock, C. (1988). *Sophie's knapsack*. New York: Lothrop, Lee & Shepard.

Stock, C. (1985). *Sophie's bucket*. New York: Lothrop, Lee & Shepard.

Tafuri, N. (1988). *Junglewalk*. New York: Greenwillow.

Tafuri, N. (1987). *In a red house*. New York: Greenwillow.

Tafuri, N. (1983). *Have you seen my duckling?* New York: Greenwillow.

Tafuri, N. (1981). *Early morning in the barn*. New York: Greenwillow.

Tejima. (1988). *Fox's dream*. New York: Putnam/Philomel.

Testa, F. (1982). *If you take a pencil*. New York: Dial.

Thayer, J. (1958). *The puppy who wanted a boy*. New York: Morrow. (reissued with pictures by L. McCue, 1985)

Titherington, J. (1986). *Pumpkin, pumpkin*. New York: Greenwillow.

Turkle, B. (1981). *Do not open*. New York: Dutton.

Turkle, B. (1976). *Deep in the forest*. New York: Dutton.

Udry, J. M. (1961). *Let's be enemies*. New York: Harper & Row.

Ungerer, T. (1958). *Crictor*. New York: Harper & Row.

Van Allsburg, C. (1988). *Two bad ants*. Boston: Houghton Mifflin.

Van Allsburg, C. (1987). *The Z was zapped*. Boston: Houghton Mifflin.

Van Allsburg, C. (1985). *The Polar express*. Boston: Houghton Mifflin.

Van Allsburg, C. (1981). *Jumanji*. Boston: Houghton Mifflin.

Van Lann, N. (1987). *The big fat worm*. New York: Knopf.

Viorst, J. (1972). *Alexander and the terrible, horrible, no good very bad day*. New York: Atheneum.

Walsh, E. S. (1989). *Mouse paint*. San Diego, CA: Harcourt Brace Jovanovich.

Wantanabe, S. (1987). *I can take a bath!* New York: Putnam.

Watson, C. (1978). *Catch me and kiss me and say it again*. New York: Putnam/Philomel.

Watson, R. J. (1989). *Tom Thumb*. San Diego, CA: Harcourt Brace Jovanovich.

Wells, R. (1986). *Max's Christmas*. New York: Dial.

Wells, R. (1985). *Hazel's amazing mother*. New York: Dial.

Wells, R. (1981). *Timothy goes to school*. New York: Dial.

Wells, R. (1975). *Morris's disappearing bag: A Christmas story*. New York: Dial.

Wells, R. (1973). *Noisy Nora*. New York: Dial.

Westwood, J. (1985). *Going to squintum's*. New York: Dial.

Williams, L. (1986). *The little old lady who was not afraid of anything*. New York: Crowell.

Wild, M. (1990). *The very best of friends*. San Diego, CA: Harcourt, Brace Jovanovich.

Williams, K. L. (1991). *When Africa was home*. New York: Franklin Watts.

Williams, K. (1989). *Galimoto*. New York: Lothrop, Lee and Shepard.

Williams, S. (1990). *I went walking*. San Diego: Harcourt Brace Jovanovich.

Williams, V. B. (1990). *"More, more, more," said the baby*. New York: Greenwillow.

Williams, V. B. (1982). *A chair for my mother*. New York: Greenwillow.

Williams, V. B. (1981). *Three days on a river in a red canoe*. New York: Greenwillow.

Willis, J. (1987). *The monster bed*. New York: Lothrop, Lee & Shepard.

Winch, M. (1990). *Come by chance*. New York: Crown.

Winter, J. (1988). *Follow the drinking gourd*. New York: Knopf.

Winthrop, E. (1987). *Maggie and the monster*. New York: Holiday House.

Winthrop, E. (1986). *Shoes*. New York: Harper & Row.

Wood, A. (1987). *Heckedy Peg*. San Diego: Harcourt, Brace Jovanovich.

Wood, A. (1987). *King Bidgood's in the bathtub*. San Diego: Harcourt Brace Jovanovich.

Wood, A. (1984). *The napping house*. New York: Harcourt Brace Jovanovich.

Wood, D. (1984). *The little mouse, the red ripe strawberry, and the big hungry bear*. New York: Child's Play International.

Wolff, A. (1990). *Come with me*. New York: Dutton.

Xuqi, J. (1987). *The giant panda*. New York: Putnam.

Yolen, J. (1987). *Owl moon*. New York: Philomel/Putnam.

Yolen, J. (1987). *The sleeping beauty*. New York: Knopf.

Yorinks, A. (1986). *Hey, Al*. New York: Farrar, Straus & Giroux.

Zelinsky, P. (1990). *The wheels on the bus*. New York: Dutton.

Zelinsky, P. (1986). *Rumplestiltskin*. New York: Dutton.

Zelinsky, P. (1981). *The maid and the mouse and the odd shaped house*. New York: Dodd.

Zemach, M. (1976). *It could always be worse*. New York: Farrar, Straus & Giroux.

Ziefert, H. (1986). *All clean*. New York: Holt, Rinehart and Winston.

Ziefert, H. (1986). *Cock a doodle doo*. New York: Holt, Rinehart and Winston.

Zion, G. (1956). *Harry the dirty dog*. New York: Harper.

Zolotow, C. (1988). *Something is going to happen*. New York: Harper & Row.

APPENDIX E
Wordless Storybooks

Bonners, S. (1989). *Just in passing*. New York: Lothrop.

Briggs, R. (1978). *The snowman*. New York: Random House.

Carle, E. (1971). *Do you want to be my friend?* New York: Crowell-Collier.

Collington, P. (1987). *The angel and the soldier boy*. New York: Knopf.

Day, A. (1990). *Carl's Christmas*. New York: Farrar, Straus and Giroux.

de Paola, T. (1978). *Pancakes for breakfast*. New York: Harcourt Brace Jovanovich.

Goodall, J. S. (1989). *The story of a farm*. New York: Macmillan.

Goodall, J. S. (1977). *The surprise picnic*. New York: Atheneum.

Goodall, J. S. (1975). *Creepy castle*. New York: Atheneum.

Goodall, J. S. (1971). *Shrewbettina's birthday*. New York: Harcourt.

Hutchins, P. (1971). *Changes, changes*. New York: Macmillan.

Hutchins, P. (1968). *Rosie's walk*. New York: Macmillan.

Hogrogian, N. (1972). *Apples*. New York: Macmillan.

Keats, E. J. (1982). *Clementina's cactus*. New York: Viking.

Oxenbury, H. (1982). *Good night, good morning*. New York: Dial.

Mayer, M. (1977). *Oops*. New York: Dial.

Mayer, M. (1974). *Frog goes to dinner*. New York: Dial.

McCully, E. A. (1987). *School*. New York: Harper.

McCully, E. A. (1985). *First snow*. New York: Harper.

McCully, E. A. (1984). *Picnic*. New York: Harper.

Omerod, J. (1982). *Moonlight*. New York: Lothrop.

Omerod, J. (1981). *Sunshine*. New York: Lothrop.

Spier, P. (1982). *Rain*. New York: Doubleday.

Tafuri, N. (1988). *Junglewalk*. New York: Greenwillow.

Tafuri, N. (1987). *Do not disturb*. New York: Greenwillow.

Turkle, B. (1976). *Deep in the forest*. New York: Dutton.

APPENDIX F
Guidelines for Creating Big Books

1. *Selection*—Choose a predictable book—a picture book, story, song, or poem that has minimal text and uses devices such as rhythm, rhyme, and repetition to help students anticipate what happens next. Literature that is familiar to students, such as a folk tale, nursery rhyme, or a poem, may be used as well. Choose a piece of literature that you truly enjoy to sustain you through this project.

2. *Planning*—Plot out the page arrangement to determine the space allotted for pictures and words. Draw faint pencil lines or use lined chart paper to guide your printing. The style of your printing should match the manuscript style familiar to the children. If an existing small-sized picture book is being converted into a larger-size version, do not alter the text of the book in any way. Keeping the two texts identical enables children to practice reading the story individually at home or at school. During this planning phase, be sure to consider how you will fasten the book together. Heavy cord, staples, shower-curtain rings, notebook rings, spiral binding, and sewing are some of the alternatives. Allot space for these fasteners so that they do not cover or cut out the print or pictures.

3. *Illustrations*—Consider your talents and those of your students when planning this phase. You may enlist the help of older students in your school or school system, such as a group of sixth-graders or a high-school art class. It is not essential that the illustrations in your version of the book match those in the original. Primary-grades children who are drawing representationally might do the pictures in small groups or individually. Some other alternatives for creating the pictures are cutouts from magazines or copies of pictures from books of "clip art." Another way of drawing the pictures for nonartists is to use an opaque projector to trace simple drawings right from the book. Or, you can make a copy of each page, make a transparency, and project the pictures onto oaktag or heavy paper for tracing. Avoid using colored construction paper because it fades very quickly.

When the drawings are complete, they can be colored with crayons, markers, oil pastels, water colors, tempera paint, or given a hint of color with chalk or colored pencils. If the pictures of the book are large, simple shapes, you may want to use cutouts of colored oaktag for the main object, then use markers for the details.

Usually, some combination of different art materials works best. You can cover a large area much more quickly with paint and brush than with a marker, for instance. And, you can shade or intensify the color in water colors by allowing them to dry and shading in with oil pastels, markers, or colored pencils. Whatever technique is used, laminate each page or cover it with clear self-adhesive plastic when finished. There is far too much work invested in a teacher-made book to let it be ruined by the elements or the heavy use it is sure to receive. (*Note*: If a heat process is used to laminate, do *not* use crayons. They will melt and run.)

    4. *Assembly*—Arrange the pages sequentially and put your big book together. Follow the shared-book experience described in Chapter 9 when you use the book with your students. Encourage the children to choose a favorite story or an original story to create their own big book.

Some Sources for Published Big Books

It is also possible to purchase big books that are already made. Usually, these books have a cardstock cover and are approximately 17″ × 22″ and cost somewhere between $15 and $30. Blank big books that are already stapled together and ready for use are also available. The sources for these books are as follows:

    Resources for Creative Teaching
    P.O. Box 12399
    Department Y
    Salem, OR 97309-0399
    (503) 399-0040

    Scholastic Books
    P.O. Box 7502
    Jefferson City, MO 65102
    (313) 636-8890
    (They also have a good collection of big books in Spanish)

    The Wright Group
    10949 Technology Place
    San Diego, CA 92127
    (619) 487-8820

A Selective Listing of Language Tests for Young Children

Charmaine Kent, Compiler

Name of Test	For Grades/ Ages	Publisher
ABC Inventory to Determine Kindergarten and School Readiness	K–1 3½–6½	Research Concepts
Brigance Diagnostic Inventory of Early Development	0–7 yrs	Curriculum Associates
Burt Word Reading Test	6–12	New Zealand Council for Educational Resources
Fluharty Preschool Speech and Language Screening Test	2–6	DLM Teaching Resources
Kindergarten Language Screening Test	K	C. C. Publications
Linguistic Awareness in Reading Readiness	K–1	NFER—Nelson Publishing Co. (England)
Metropolitan Readiness Tests	K–1	The Psychological Corporation
Preschool Language Assessment Instrument	3–6	Grune and Stratton
PRI Reading Systems	K–9	CTB/McGraw-Hill
Psycholinguistic Rating Scale	K–8	Western Psychological Services

(Continued)

Name of Test	For Grades/ Ages	Publisher
Riley Preschool Developmental Screening Inventory, 1969	Pre K–K (3–5 yrs.)	Western Psychological Services
School Readiness Survey, K–1 1967; rev. 1975	K–1	Consulting Psychologists Press, Inc.
Screening Kit of Language Development	Preschool	University Park Press
Sand—The Concepts About Print Test Stones, and The Concepts About Print Test	Pre K–1	Heinemann Education Books
Stanford Achievement Test; Listening Comprehension Tests	1–9	The Psychological Corporation
Test for Auditory Comprehension of Language	3–10	DLM Teaching Resources
The Basic Concept Inventory	Pre K–1	Follet Publishing Co.
The Macmillan Diagnostic Reading Pack	5–9 yrs.	Macmillan Education
The Vane Kindergarten Test	4–6 yrs.	Clinical Psychology Publishing
Valett Developmental Survey of Basic Learning Abilities	Pre K–1 Ages 2–7	Consulting Psychologists Press

INDEX